HKU SPACE and Its Alumni
The First Fifty Years

Hong Kong University Press thanks Xu Bing for writing the Press's name in his Square Word Calligraphy for the covers of its books. For further information, see p. iv.

HKU SPACE and Its Alumni
The First Fifty Years

Lawrence M. W. Chiu and Peter Cunich

Hong Kong University Press
14/F Hing Wai Centre
7 Tin Wan Praya Road
Aberdeen
Hong Kong

ISBN 978-962-209-898-5

Secure On-line Ordering
http://www.hkupress.org

British Library Cataloguing-in-Publication Data
A catalogue record for this book is available from the British Library.

Printed and bound by Paramount Printing Co. Ltd., in Hong Kong, China

Hong Kong University Press is honoured that Xu Bing, whose art explores the complex themes of language across cultures, has written the Press's name in his Square Word Calligraphy. This signals our commitment to cross-cultural thinking and the distinctive nature of our English-language books published in China.

"At first glance, Square Word Calligraphy appears to be nothing more unusual than Chinese characters, but in fact it is a new way of rendering English words in the format of a square so they resemble Chinese characters. Chinese viewers expect to be able to read Square word Calligraphy but cannot. Western viewers, however are surprised to find they can read it. Delight erupts when meaning is unexpectedly revealed."

— Britta Erickson, *The Art of Xu Bing*

Contents

MESSAGE
Dr Victor Fung, Chairman of Council, The University of Hong Kong vii

FOREWORD
Professor Lap-chee Tsui, Vice-Chancellor, The University of Hong Kong viii

FOREWORD
Mr Linus Cheung, Chairman of Board of Directors, HKU SPACE ix

PREFACE
Professor Enoch Young, Director, HKU SPACE xi

ACKNOWLEDGEMENTS xv

ABBREVIATIONS xvii

INTRODUCTION 1

CHAPTER 1
External Studies at the University of Hong Kong, 1912–1957 7

CHAPTER 2
Establishing the Department of Extra-Mural Studies, 1945–1957 29

CHAPTER 3
Early Years in the Department of Extra-Mural Studies, 1957–1965 55

CHAPTER 4
From Retrenchment to Resurgence, 1965–1982 87

CHAPTER 5
The Cradle of Professional Studies in Hong Kong, 1964–1985 111

CHAPTER 6
From Department of Extra-Mural Studies to School of Professional and Continuing Education, 1985–1991 137

CHAPTER 7
The School of Professional and Continuing Education, 1992–2007 171

CHAPTER 8
The Community Colleges, 2000–2007 213

CONCLUSION 241

EPILOGUE 247
Dr Peter C. Y. Lee, President, HKU SPACE Alumni Association

APPENDICES 251

NOTES 279

BIBLIOGRAPHY 333

INDEX 341

Message

I am very happy to offer a congratulatory message to HKU SPACE on the occasion of its Golden Jubilee and the publication of this history. The University takes much pride in the achievements of the School and its predecessor, the Department of Extra-Mural Studies in the years since 1956. How Hong Kong has changed in that time! Yet the University and HKU SPACE have changed with the times and the School has done a fine job in fulfilling the University's role in the community.

Hong Kong's people are its only asset and, in the knowledge economy of the twenty-first century, the work of the School will become more important to Hong Kong's future as we strive to ensure that our skills and knowledge are at the cutting edge to provide our society with the human resources we need to thrive and prosper. I look forward to seeing the School continuing to do the community proud and fulfilling those commitments into the future.

Dr Victor Fung
Chairman of Council
The University of Hong Kong

Foreword

For half a century, HKU SPACE has led the way in the provision of extra-mural education for Hong Kong. Today, HKU SPACE continues to provide the territory with the lifelong learning opportunities that will enable its citizens to continually update their education and skills for a globalised knowledge-based economy.

In the provision of continuing education programmes for personal and professional advancement to people from all walks of life, HKU SPACE shares not only the University's philosophy of lifelong learning but also the HKU tradition of maintaining close ties with all levels of society.

This chronicle is a fitting tribute to all those who have contributed to the accomplishments of HKU SPACE. May it also mark the beginning of even further growth and success for the School.

Professor Lap-chee Tsui
Vice-Chancellor
The University of Hong Kong

Foreword

On behalf of the HKU SPACE Board of Directors I welcome the publication of this history of the first 50 years of the School's operation. In a sense it is a number of histories for, as we know, the University established the Department of Extra-Mural Studies in 1957, the School of Professional and Continuing Education in 1992 and, finally, incorporated HKU SPACE in 1999. These different organisational structures were designed to keep pace with the times and to reflect the necessary changes in order to deliver the University's mission in lifelong learning.

The original Extra-Mural Studies concept was borrowed from the UK and the subsequent iterations have also kept pace with the development of trends internationally. The School can now be said to be a leader in continuing education and lifelong learning, particularly as it is able to sustain its high quality and extensive operations in a self-financing environment. This represents many challenges for management and my fellow directors and I have enjoyed bringing to bear our collaborative experience — from the world of business, from the government and from the community — to advise and guide the School. We believe it should operate in an effective and ethical manner as is appropriate for an educational institution and to the high standards that our society can expect.

The School has worked hard to meet this challenge and the Board has set it a task of ensuring performance with integrity as the means through which it can deliver, on behalf of the University, relevant education programmes for our community. These have to be of high academic quality and also be supported by an efficient organisation that aims to provide high quality service to the learners. The School should also be a caring employer and a contributor to the human resource development needs of Hong Kong and China Mainland.

This history tells us how the operation has developed in the past half century and we hope it will continue to prosper in the next 50 years as it undertakes new challenges in Hong Kong, China and the region.

Mr Linus Cheung
Chairman of Board of Directors
HKU SPACE

Preface

My own association with the University of Hong Kong has been somewhat coterminous with the history of HKU SPACE. I joined the University as undergraduate student in 1958, only shortly after the Department of Extra-mural Studies had been formed and when it was entering its second year of operation. Gerald Moore was Director then and was succeeded by Ieuan Hughes before I graduated. Following my first degree in 1962 I went overseas for doctoral studies. This was also my first introduction to the teaching of adults as I taught adult education classes for the armed forces whilst at Bristol. I rejoined the University as a lecturer in 1968 and served for 20 years, thus I was familiar with the work of EMS in its phase of consolidation and development as a cradle of professional studies. This was more or less the period of Roger Williams as Director.

I rejoined as Director of the School in 1998 to succeed Lee Ngok. The School had expanded its overseas collaboration through the 1990s and was at a point where substantial re-organisation was necessary. The rest is my own history as Director in the last 10 years and this has also been a period of remarkable development.

Looking back on my career as an academic I can fairly say that much has changed but also that many values have remained constant. For that is one of the values of a University. The mission is to transmit the values of society whilst at the same time pushing forward the frontiers of knowledge and adapting to and leading change. The Department of Extra-Mural Studies was able to do this effectively in the wider community on behalf of the University from its inception and it is interesting to read the history of the challenges and tensions between the role of the Department and the mainstream academic departments of the University. Some of those challenges and tensions remain to this day but it has to be said that overall it has been creative tension and the synergy between the mainstream and what was the new frontier in 1956 has been fruitful. Indeed it may now be argued that the frontier has become the mainstream. It is generally recognised that all of us must be lifelong learners.

The University itself has recognised this in its role statement which has been endorsed by the University Grants Committee as the only tertiary institution in Hong Kong with lifelong learning as part of its mission. The University's own strategic plan eloquently describes the way the University would work with HKU SPACE in delivering this part of its commitment to society. I have therefore been privileged to see how the University can serve its community outside the ivory tower, bringing gown to town or whatever metaphor we may use for this wider sense of the University's role in society.

We in HKU SPACE are very conscious of our place in the University, and of the University, and this is something that is precious and that I hope will endure going forward. The first Director said when asked for comments on the first 10 years that

> the aim then was to create a movement in adult education which might match the energy and needs of the surrounding atmosphere.

I believe the work of HKU SPACE does do that and it also fulfills another of those early judgements.

> However, no such activities can ever rest on its achievements but must be always on the move, always looking for fresh opportunity and challenges in the society around it.

This I am sure will be a continuing legacy for HKU SPACE whatever future form it may take.

We have developed a wide range of liberal arts courses, continuing education courses, professional courses and award-bearing degree courses that serve the needs of second chance learners and of continuing and professional development. The more recent achievements in the Community College have enabled us to help meet government policy in extending post-secondary opportunities to a much wider proportion of the younger population.

When we look ahead, we recognise the need to serve more explicitly the needs of third age learners, those approaching or close to retirement who would yet want to remain active as learners. The working lifelong learner will need to reskill and retrain throughout a career as the pace of the technology and change accelerates. There is also the opportunity for first degrees and higher degrees that need to be extended more widely in the community and these I am sure the School will strive to meet to the best of its ability. In the next few years we have identified creative and performing arts and culture, online e-learning and the third age as priorities. We also need to understand better the appropriate policies for lifelong learning and will strengthen our research in these areas.

One of our values is partnership and this is an area that this history exemplifies well in that we have partnered with many institutions and bodies in Hong Kong and overseas throughout our 50 years of history. I am sure that this element will also continue in the future. Another of our values is accountability and our Board of Directors has reminded us this is a very important part of our relationship with the community — to be accountable to the whole community for what we do, to ensure that we deliver this to a high quality of provision and ethical standard. Our other values include service to learners, creativity and excellence in quality and all of these will sustain us in going forward beyond our golden jubilee to provide what we hope will be enduring commitment and contribution to Hong Kong society.

The Vice-Chancellor in a new institution elsewhere said recently that his dream was to make other dreams come true. HKU SPACE has very much been about delivering opportunities to learners to realise their aspirations and ambitions: the dream of higher qualifications, the dream of career change, the dream of courses that lead to self-fulfillment and the dream of career development. It has been a privilege for me to see these dreams being realised by HKU SPACE activities over the past 50 years and I hope that my successors will be committed to ensuring that these dreams will continue in the next 50 years.

Professor Enoch Young
Director
HKU SPACE

Acknowledgements

THE IDEA OF WRITING A JUBILEE HISTORY of HKU SPACE was the brainchild of Dr Peter C. Y. Lee who generously provided a grant for research in late 2005 and early 2006. Dr Lee has been supporting HKU SPACE from the time when he enrolled as a young medical graduate in some of the first courses offered by the Department of Extra-Mural Studies. He later became a co-opted member of the Committee on Extra-Mural Studies in 1976, a member of the Board for Continuing and Professional Education and Lifelong Learning in 2000, and was elected as inaugural President of the HKU SPACE Alumni Association in 2004. He has been a constant support for this project and the authors are very grateful for his unrelenting determination to bring the book to a successful conclusion. We are also grateful to the Department of History for providing space, salaries and miscellaneous expenses during the writing phase of the project. HKU SPACE has generously financed all publication expenses.

To say that this project has been completed in something of a rush would be an understatement. The authors would therefore like to thank all those who have assisted us in drawing the historical record together within such a short time. We are particularly grateful to Mrs Veronica Ho of the Records Section in the General Services unit of the Registry. She made our task much easier by searching far and wide for original documents and various long-forgotten University reports. Mrs Sheila Stimpson has been untiring in her interest in all things to do with the history of HKU, and Mr Henry Wai has been a continuing support of this and other projects. Ms Iris Chan and her staff in the Special Collections of the University Library were likewise of enormous assistance, as was Mr Edward Shen and his staff in the Faculty of Arts, and the staff of the Hong Kong Public Records Office. In the later stages of our work, the University Archivist Ms Stacy Gould assisted us in our ongoing search for data. We are particularly grateful to Mr Dan Quail of Los Angeles for allowing us to use his mother's student diary from 1929.

At HKU SPACE, Mr John Cribbin has been a constant source of information and advice and we would like to thank him for always making himself available to answer endless questions from his boundless personal experience with SPACE over a period of two decades. Dr Michael Luk very generously shared his own insights into the history of SPACE at a formative moment in the project and we have benefited from his overview. Other colleagues at HKU SPACE who gave valuable advice and assistance include Professor Enoch Young, Dr Dorothy Chan, Dr Peter Kennedy, Ms Diana Liu, Ms Helen Hung, Miss Reiko Lam, Ms Selin Poon and Miss Julia Wong. At the HKU SPACE Community College we would like to thank Professor K. F. Cheng, Ms Currie Tsang, Ms Irene Chan, Ms Lilian Fong and Miss Sophie Tsa. We are particularly grateful to Ms Iris Ng, formerly of the Department of History and now of the School of Humanities for her tireless efforts in helping to prepare the text. We are also grateful to Dr Colin Day and his staff at Hong Kong University Press for their expert advice on all matters to do with publishing.

We have relied on a large number of interviews to flesh out the story of HKU SPACE and we would therefore like to thank all those who agreed to be interviewed for this project. Their names are listed in the bibliography. We are especially grateful to Mrs Priscilla Tso Mark Yuen-yee and Mr T. C. Lai who were able to share their memories of the very earliest days of the Department of Extra-Mural Studies, and to Professor Lee Ngok whose term as Director proved to be such an important period of growth for professional and continuing education at HKU. We would also like to thank Professor Tony Sweeting who answered numerous questions over a long period of time regarding education policy in Hong Kong. We have been given much valuable feedback by those colleagues who have read various sections of the text and provided us with suggestions, and we would especially like to thank Professor Lee Ngok, Professor Enoch Young, Mr John Cribbin and Dr Peter C. Y. Lee. We are particularly grateful to an anonymous reader who made very helpful suggestions at an early stage in preparing the text for publication.

The authors would also like to acknowledge the very high degree of freedom which they have been given in writing this history of HKU SPACE. We have received the fullest help and assistance from both the University and HKU SPACE but we have been allowed to reach our own conclusions with complete independence. The views expressed in this volume are therefore ours alone and do not represent the official opinions or policy of HKU SPACE or the University. All inaccuracies and infelicities are, of course, ours.

21 May 2007

Abbreviations

Annual Report	*Annual Report* of the University of Hong Kong
ASAIHL	Association of South East Asian Institutes of Higher Learning
ASPBAE	Asia-South Pacific Bureau of Adult Education
BCPE&LL	Board for Continuing and Professional Education and Lifelong Learning (1999–2007)
BEMS	Board of Extra-Mural Studies (1957–67)
BSSPACE	Board of Studies of SPACE (1992–99)
Calendar	*The University of Hong Kong Calendar*
CCAB	HKU SPACE Community College Academic Board
CCAC	HKU SPACE Community College Advisory Council
CCC	HKU SPACE Community College Council
CCMC	HKU SPACE Community College Management Committee
CED	Centre for Executive Development
CEMS	Committee on Extra-Mural Studies (1967–91)
CIDP	Centre for International Degree Programmes
CO	Colonial Office
COE	Committee on Open Education
CPE	Continuing and Profession Education
CUHK	Chinese University of Hong Kong
DEMS	Department of Extra-Mural Studies (1957–91)
DGPC	Development and General Purposes Committee
Dispersal and Renewal	*Dispersal and Renewal: Hong Kong University during the War Years*, Clifford Matthews and Oswald Cheung (eds.), (Hong Kong: HKU Press, 1998)

DLU	Distance Learning Unit
EMS	Extra-Mural Studies
ESU	External Studies Unit
FCE[TI]	Federation of Continuing Education [in Tertiary Institutions]
GPC	General Purposes Committee
HKALE	Hong Kong A-Level Examination
HKCEE	Hong Kong Certificate of Education Examination
HKLA	Hong Kong Library Association
HKPRO	Hong Kong Public Records Office
HKU	University of Hong Kong
HKUA	University of Hong Kong Archives
HKUCM	Council Minutes
HKUCourt	Court Minutes
HKUFA	Faculty of Arts
HKUFCM	Finance Committee Minutes
HKUFM	Faculty of Medicine
HKUL	University Libraries
HKUR	University of Hong Kong Registry
HKUSM	Senate Minutes
HKUVC	Vice-Chancellor's Office
IUC	Inter-University Council for Higher Education in the Colonies
JCEMS	Joint Committee on Extra-Mural Studies (1967–70)
Keswick Report	*Report of the Committee of Higher Education* (Hong Kong, 1952)
OLI	Open Learning Institute
Ordinance	University of Hong Kong Ordinance (1911)
PLK	Po Leung Kuk
RO	Registrar's office files (now in University Archives)
SPACE	School of Professional and Continuing Education, HKU
SPACEBD	Board of Directors of HKU SPACE
SPACEMB	Management Board for HKU SPACE
Statutes	University of Hong Kong Statutes (1911)
TCM	Traditional Chinese Medicine
TLQPR	Teaching and Learning Quality Process Review
UGC	University Grants Committee
UPGC	University and Polytechnic Grants Committee

N.B. A letter 'M' at the end of an abbreviation signifies the official minutes and their appendices of the relevant committee or board.

Introduction

THE MISSION OF THE UNIVERSITY OF HONG KONG (HKU), like all great modern universities, has long been to promote and sustain international excellence through 'outstanding teaching and world-class research'. In recent years, however, these two core aims have been complemented by what has been dubbed a 'Third Mission' — the provision of opportunities for 'lifelong learning'. As one of the three basic goals of the University, 'lifelong learning' has been incorporated into the Council's strategic vision for the future. Two of the University's eight stated long-term goals encompass lifelong learning:

- To provide a comprehensive education, developing fully the intellectual and personal strengths of its students while developing and extending lifelong learning opportunities for the community; and
- To produce graduates of distinction committed to lifelong learning, integrity and professionalism, capable of being responsive leaders and communicators in their fields.[1]

This commitment to lifelong learning is manifested in many ways throughout the University, but the most obvious commitment to this goal is to be seen in the School of Professional and Continuing Education (HKU SPACE). HKU SPACE has been a successful component of the University over a long period, is currently the largest provider of continuing and professional education opportunities in Hong Kong, and has become one of the largest providers in the world. HKU SPACE celebrates its fiftieth anniversary in 2007 and the present volume marks that anniversary. It aims to provide a history of extra-mural, continuing and professional education at HKU which demonstrates clearly the University's sustained commitment to serving the Hong Kong community.

The formal provision of what used to be called 'extra-mural studies' began at the University of Hong Kong in 1957. However, the University has been providing opportunities for 'external' studies from its very first days. The number of students taking advantage of external studies fluctuated from year to year in the period up to and after World War II, but the University's early commitment to education outside the normal process of university matriculation perhaps helps to explain why extra-mural studies blossomed in the late 1950s. In the pre-War years a high value was placed on close relations between 'town' and 'gown', and many of HKU's early students (both undergraduates and non-matriculants alike) proved to have considerable leadership skills in their various fields. The move to provide 'external' studies on a more systematic basis than had been possible before the War was a recognition of the value of such studies for the community as a whole, and a response to the growing demand for such educational opportunities. Consequently, the Department of Extra-Mural Studies was able to find support from all areas of Hong Kong's varied business and professional community. There was little government policy or funding for post-secondary education in these years and much of the inspiration for extra-mural studies came from the United Kingdom which already had a long tradition of liberal higher adult education.

From small beginnings the Department grew quickly into a powerful institution in its own right, while at all times service to the wider Hong Kong community was a clear goal. Where the University was not able to provide educational opportunity, The Department of Extra-Mural Studies (renamed the School of Professional and Continuing Education in 1992, and HKU SPACE from 1999) stepped in and developed strong links with members of the community who would otherwise not have enjoyed such educational opportunities. It is not surprising, therefore, that the alumni of HKU SPACE and its predecessors have responded to such opportunities by making major contributions to Hong Kong's growth and development over the last fifty years. In this way, the early traditions of close partnership between 'town' and 'gown' continue, with HKU SPACE playing a very special role on behalf of the University.

While this study focuses primarily on the history of HKU SPACE, its wider aim is to integrate this story within the University's attempts to provide educational opportunities beyond the undergraduate population from its earliest years. It is therefore of interest to survey the 'pre-history' of the Department of Extra-Mural Studies in order to identify clearly the ways in which the early history of the University provided a positive environment for the eventual development of extra-mural studies in the late 1950s. Chapter 1 begins by examining the founding ideals of Lord Lugard and the supporters of his 'university project'. This is necessary in order to understand why it was that 'external studies' was initially thought of as inferior to the courses undertaken by matriculated students, even though both groups of students attended the same lectures. The early success of external studies as a source of student fee income ensured that the University would continue to provide opportunities for non-matriculated students throughout the first half of the twentieth century, but the reason for such provision gradually moved beyond the merely financial and would ultimately build a basis for the introduction of more formal structures of extra-mural studies in 1957. It has to be admitted, however, that the University's few efforts in extending its educational services beyond the confines of the campus before 1957 did not reflect the international trend for large-scale extension and extra-mural work in the first half of the twentieth century. Some of the reasons for this will be explored in the first chapter.

Chapter 2 deals with the process by which the Department of Extra-Mural Studies was established in the years between the publication of the wartime Asquith Report of 1945 and the formal decision by the Court of the University on 21 May 1957 to establish the Department. The Keswick Report of 1952 was of central importance in moving this process forward, but there were many reasons why HKU was slower than other universities in the British Empire to institute a dedicated department to provide extra-mural studies of a liberal and professional character. Chapter 3 moves the story forward in examining the earliest days of the Department's growth under the first two directors, Mr Gerald Moore (1956–60) and Mr Ieuan Hughes (1960–67). This was a period of financial and other difficulties which were not resolved for some years, and this phase of development was perhaps marked principally by the University's attempted marginalisation of extra-mural studies. Yet, during these early years the Department of Extra-Mural Studies very quickly established itself as one of the more dynamic areas of the University's overall development, and within only two years of establishment it had a larger student enrolment than the University proper.

Continuing difficulties with funding, staff retention and accommodation led to a period of retrenchment in the mid-1960s. New pressures from the University Grants Committee and competition from the Chinese University of Hong Kong created difficulties for the Department during this period, but there was also much consolidation and a number of advances, including the opening of an Extra-Mural Town Centre in 1967. These developments will be dealt with in Chapter 4. Until 1964 the Department of Extra-Mural Studies focused largely on 'liberal' courses, but from the mid-1960s a new focus was found in vocational and professional studies. The University had been founded in 1911 to provide professional training in medicine and engineering, and architecture was later added, but opportunities for professional training of any kind in Hong Kong remained limited until the 1960s. Chapter 5 therefore surveys the role of the Department of Extra-Mural Studies as what Michael Luk refers to as the 'cradle of professional studies' in Hong Kong. The twenty years covered by this chapter includes a wide range of developments which indicate a gradual change in priorities within the Department accompanied by a significant increase in size. Several of the new areas of extra-mural education, including legal and management studies, will be examined in detail.

Chapter 6 considers the key years of the late 1980s and early 1990s when, under the leadership of Professor Lee Ngok, the Department changed in both name and nature to become the institution that it is today. This was a time of rapid expansion in both student enrolments and the range of programmes provided to adult learners as an 'adult education market' developed in Hong Kong. The financial success of continuing and professional education set the scene for a reduction in government and University subventions during the 1990s, and the eventual financial independence of HKU SPACE from 2000. Chapter 7 considers more recent developments, including the acquisition of new learning centres across Hong Kong, the introduction of quality assurance mechanisms, and the expansion of HKU SPACE's activities into mainland China. Chapter 8 deals with a major new activity of SPACE, the two community colleges which have been established under its guidance to help extend the provision of post-secondary education in post-handover Hong Kong.

One of our problems in writing about the development of HKU SPACE and its predecessor over such a long period of time has been trying to identify exactly what sort of education it was that the institution was attempting to provide at various times. The terminology adopted in describing various types of adult post-secondary education over the last fifty years has changed dramatically.[2] Undergraduate education is the one constant against which this educational provision has been contrasted, and whenever we refer to 'undergraduate education' we understand this to mean the teaching of matriculated university students who, in the case of HKU at least, were normally full-time learners who had recently completed their secondary educational qualifications. In the pre-War period, all other students were referred to as 'external' students or simply 'externals', and this was a term that continued to be used until only recently when 'visiting' student became the norm. It should be noted, however, that in other jurisdictions, 'external' students are quite often defined as fully matriculated undergraduates who pursue their studies through distance or part-time learning modes. This has never been the case at HKU for reasons that will be discussed in Chapter 6.

In the early post-War years, the terms 'adult education' and 'extra-mural studies' were sometimes used interchangeably, but we have adopted a stricter usage. Whereas 'adult education' can refer to a very wide range of educational programmes (including all sorts of vocational and technical training) at different levels, from literature-for-interest classes to university-level degree programmes, the term 'extra-mural studies' has always been more limited in its application. Extra-mural courses are university-type courses which are taught to people who are literally *extra muros* (outside the walls) of the university. From the 1940s until fairly recently it was common for British universities to have 'departments of extra-mural studies' to describe the units which provided this form of education to 'non-students', and thus it was that the same nomenclature was adopted by HKU when the Department of Extra-Mural Studies was established in 1957. Such educational activity by universities was sometimes also referred to as 'extension' work, but in the British context this term was used at a much earlier period and had a more limited meaning. In Hong Kong the term 'extension work' was hardly ever used after the Second World War. Likewise, reference to 'tutorial classes', which is common in the British literature on adult education both before and after the War, is largely absent in the Hong Kong context.

Another term which sometimes appears in studies of adult education in Hong Kong is 'technical and further education'. While universities have in the past provided such educational opportunities elsewhere in the world, especially where polytechnic universities are common, in Hong Kong this has not been the case. The more common terminology, which HKU eventually adopted for its extra-mural activities in the early 1990s, is 'professional and continuing education'. This terminology covers a broad spectrum of adult educational programmes ranging from short courses for personal development and training for professional qualifications through to doctorate-level programmes which are difficult to distinguish from mainstream university programmes.[3] Indeed, around half of students currently engaged in 'continuing' education already hold an initial tertiary-level qualification, so the student body is very complex and learning expectations vary a great deal from one student to the next.

During the early 1980s the term 'open education' was used in Hong Kong to denote a variety of non-age specific manifestations of education ranging from basic literary to tertiary-level studies, and these learning opportunities were often linked to the distance mode of delivery.[4] A more recent addition to the lexicon of adult education is 'lifelong learning', a term which can be applied equally to the mission and teaching activities of both HKU SPACE and the University itself. Since its introduction into the Hong Kong higher education context in the late 1990s, it has been used by successive government administrations and educational policy bodies to force changes in the way that people think about adult education, a process which we are now encouraged to believe begins at the very earliest stages of formal education.[5] It has also been used as a major support for government policy initiatives to extend the provision of post-secondary educational opportunities to a larger proportion of the eligible age group in Hong Kong.

Both the University and HKU SPACE have used this new terminology of 'lifelong learning' rather creatively in 're-branding' themselves during recent 'vision and mission' exercises. This gives an impression of change and 'progress' in the educational philosophy behind the provision of adult education programmes by HKU. What strikes the non-specialist writers of the current study most forcibly, however, is the similarity between this new term and the sorts of views about adult education which were being expressed in the late 1950s when the Department of Extra-Mural Studies was established.[6] So while the mission of HKU SPACE can be interpreted as having changed significantly over the last fifty years, there is also a core vision which has remained largely unaltered and which perhaps helps to explain the obvious success of the institution. Part of this success is certainly due to an enduring commitment to serve the community at large, a value which was high on the University's agenda from its earliest days. HKU SPACE has also demonstrated an ability to respond in a timely fashion to new demands placed upon it by society, and this responsiveness no doubt enables it to claim an important place in the annals of education in modern Hong Kong.

Our aim in writing this book has been to provide a factually accurate and broadly comprehensive historical account of the first fifty years in the development of HKU SPACE. It is celebratory in nature because of the golden jubilee which it marks, but the authors have been given complete independence in arriving at their conclusions, and for this reason our findings are far from uncritical in places. While this book is aimed at a general audience which we believe will be primarily interested in the actual story of HKU SPACE, its teachers, and its alumni, we have nevertheless attempted to provide some analysis of the development of HKU SPACE as an educational institution, and the international and local contexts in which that development took place. We see our role more as providing signposts to future educational historians than as attempting to provide a definitive and academically critical study of HKU SPACE. Our main theme is therefore the ways in which HKU SPACE has attempted to provide opportunities for people in Hong Kong 'to feel the play of university influences upon them, and under the stimulus of those influences to unfetter imagination, to refine taste and judgement, and to deepen insight'.[7] This is therefore a story about people as well as the institution itself. While it has not been possible to include in this volume as many stories about HKU SPACE alumni as we would have wished, we nevertheless hope that the account which we give in the pages ahead will enable the hundreds of thousands of HKU SPACE alumni to place themselves and their educational experience in the context of the longer history of the University of Hong Kong and its School of Professional and Continuing Education.

CHAPTER ONE

External Studies at the University of Hong Kong, 1912–1957

THE UNIVERSITY OF HONG KONG'S Department of Extra-Mural Studies was not established until 1957 but, as this chapter will demonstrate, the University has provided opportunities for 'external' studies from its very first days. This chapter therefore concentrates on the 'pre-history' of the Department of Extra-Mural Studies. It seeks to identify clearly the ways in which the early history of the University eventually provided a positive environment for the development of extra-mural studies in the late 1950s. It is necessary first of all to examine the founding ideals of Lord Lugard and the supporters of his 'university project' in order to understand why it was that 'external studies' was initially thought of as inferior to the courses undertaken by matriculated students, even though both groups of students attended the same lectures. The early success and flexibility of external studies ensured that the University would continue to provide opportunities for non-matriculated students throughout the first half of the twentieth century and would build a basis for introducing the more formal structures of extra-mural studies in 1957. It also has to be admitted, however, that the University's few efforts in extending its educational services beyond the confines of the campus before 1957 did not reflect the international trend for large-scale extension and extra-mural work in the first half of the twentieth century. Some of the reasons for this will be explored in this chapter.

External Studies and the Purpose of the University

When the University of Hong Kong was established in 1911, the founders gave little thought to the provision of external or extra-mural studies. Like all universities in the British Empire at that time, HKU concentrated primarily on the education of its matriculated student body, those students who had successfully passed the entrance (or matriculation) examination and in so doing became full members of the University. Initially it seems that external students were not expected to form part of the student body.[1] Nor was there any mention of extra-mural work. Yet from the very beginning, non-matriculated students were present within the University and at times constituted quite a large proportion of the student body, particularly in the first few years. While the number of external students fluctuated greatly until the beginning of the Second World War, one of the defining features of university life at HKU in the first half of the twentieth century was the presence of a large number of non-matriculated 'external' students. Such 'externals' entered all three foundation faculties (Medicine, Arts and Engineering) but were probably most visible in the Faculty of Arts. From the beginning Arts had the largest number of external students, particularly in the commercial courses in economics and law. From its very beginnings, then, and despite the ambivalence of its founders regarding the provision of educational opportunities for non-matriculated students, the University of Hong Kong has had a tradition of external studies. The provision of courses for these external students was extended in 1957 with the foundation of a Department of Extra-Mural Studies to provide even more opportunities for cultural, professional, and continuing education in Hong Kong. Developments in the 1950s may therefore be seen as representing a culmination of efforts to provide educational opportunities for non-matriculated students rather than a beginning.

The University of Hong Kong's founding purpose was '... the promotion of Arts, Science and Learning, the provision of higher education, the conferring of degrees, the development and formation of the character of students of all races, nationalities and creeds, and the maintenance of good understanding with the neighbouring country of China'.[2] Although it was originally thought that the University would serve a large market for higher education in the vast new Chinese nation, it very quickly became apparent that the principal supply of students was likely to come from the tiny colony of Hong Kong itself — 'a mere speck on the map'. Lord Lugard and the other founders of the University were very clear in their understanding of the type of education which was to be offered by HKU: 'The problem before us in opening a University in Hong Kong is how to train character, and how to create moral ideals which shall have a vital and compelling force in the formation of character and the conduct of daily life, without introducing compulsory religious teaching.'[3] They proposed a fully residential university where 'carefully selected staff' could deeply influence 'the Spiritual and Emotional side of a young man's nature' on a daily basis.[4] Lugard had no intention of admitting women to his university for they were a distraction which young men could well do without in their formative years. The idea of a collegiate educational experience such as that offered by the older universities in Britain at the time presumed an undergraduate body of full-time matriculated students, and there is no mention of external or extra-mural studies in any of HKU's foundation documents. The notion of non-residential studies by non-matriculated students went against everything that Lugard had proposed for the new university. University studies were to be a privilege for a select few who passed a rigorous qualification procedure, just as it was in all universities at the time. External or part-time students were therefore not considered as being able to participate fully in the intensely formative residential life of the university, and so no mention of them was made at first.

This lack of interest in participation from the wider community is perhaps somewhat surprising for a university founded in 1911, the heyday of the 'civic university' on the other side of the world in Britain. Although Britain's higher adult education movement began in the Universities of Cambridge (1873) and Oxford (1878), it was the civic universities which had a strong commitment to 'extension' and 'extra-mural' work among workers and other adults who did not enjoy the luxury of aspiring to the sort of gentlemanly university education which Lugard and his peers knew from their days at Oxford and Cambridge. The movement for adult education had a long and generous history in the British Isles, stretching back to the late eighteenth century but gathering pace during the industrialised nineteenth century when mechanics' institutes, working men's clubs, and all manner of other educational institutions had arisen to cater for various forms of post-elementary adult education which instilled 'a new dignity' and a sense of independence among the working classes.[5]

The ancient universities of Cambridge and Oxford had taken the lead in developing 'extension work' in the 1870s, and in the last two decades of the nineteenth century these projects led to the founding of several new 'red brick' universities and the extension of London University's system of external degrees.[6] The London external degree had originally been intended for full-time undergraduates studying outside London (and even throughout the British Empire from 1850) but it was not until 1876 with the formation of the London Society for the Extension of University Teaching that university teaching reached a wider audience.[7] These developments also contributed to the founding of the Workers' Educational Association in 1903, leading to a massive extension of educational opportunities for adults throughout Britain in the first half of the twentieth century. From 1908 the system of university tutorial classes provided adults with an opportunity for serious study over longer periods in small classes.[8] These two-hour tutorial classes met weekly under university lecturers who often had to travel many miles to conduct their lessons, and normally involved a one-hour lecture which was preceded by a one-hour discussion of material introduced in the previous week's lecture. This method, introduced by R. H. Tawney in his 'Economic Class' in Rochdale, proved to be an extremely effective form of adult learning and gained immediate popularity. Between 1908 and 1920 the number of university tutorial classes offered in Britain grew from eight classes involving 237 students to 229 classes involving 5,528 students. Importantly, this development was led by the major universities.[9]

The crown colony of Hong Kong did not have the advanced industrial economy of its metropolitan patron, nor did it have a well-developed elementary education system like that established in Britain by the Education Act of 1870. In Hong Kong, numerous elementary schools existed by the end of the nineteenth century, many of them private Chinese schools but also a fair number of government schools. Efforts had been made to encourage the setting up of new schools through the grants schemes of 1873 and 1879, but the development of a secondary sector was very slow.[10] Education had a relatively low priority in government policy until 1909 when the first Director of Education was appointed, but it was not until 1913 that the Director's position within the colonial civil service reached that of a first-class cadet officer. When HKU was established in 1911, therefore, very few post-secondary students were qualified for entry to the University, and it was expected from the very beginning that a large proportion of the undergraduates would come from China and Malaya. It is hardly surprising, then, that non-vocational adult education was a relatively low priority for both the Hong Kong government and the University in the 1910s. This is not to say that no demand for adult or further education existed at the time. The Hong Kong College of Medicine for Chinese opened in 1887; numerous 'study groups' of a political nature sprang up in the colony after the founding of the Fu Jen Literary Society in 1892; 'evening continuation classes' in science, engineering, commerce and teacher training were introduced at Queen's College in 1906; and in the next year the Technical Institute was established to run similar 'continuation classes' in various technical subjects and for teacher training.[11] It should also be noted that a large number of students in secondary education in Hong Kong at the end of the first decade of the twentieth century were of an age that would be considered 'adult' today, so a clear distinction between secondary education and adult education is not easy to establish at the time when plans for the University of Hong Kong were being discussed. Strangely enough, in Hong Kong during the second half of the nineteenth century it was generally accepted that demand for schooling opportunities for Chinese students was driven by vocational considerations, but professional training was normally pursued overseas.[12]

The principal objective of Lugard's university plan was to extend the benefits of modern British technology and higher education to China through the young Chinese graduates who would be produced by HKU. Chinese undergraduates would come from the increasing number of secondary schools in Hong Kong, as well as from the Mainland and the elite schools in the Straits Settlements and Malaya. Sir Frederick Lugard was not an educationalist, however, and neither he nor his chief advisors in Hong Kong had extensive connections with educational circles in Britain. They were not therefore fully aware of the latest educational developments taking place at home with regard to extra-mural studies; even if they had been it is unlikely that they would have made much provision for adult education at HKU. In its first few years HKU struggled just to find enough suitably qualified applicants for undergraduate studies, so any 'market' which existed in 1912 for 'extension' activities must have been very small indeed. Once the University was established, however, it became clear that there was quite a significant demand for external studies of a particular type. The early records of the University are incomplete, but it appears that in its first few years of operation a number of boys from the local schools attempted to enrol at HKU but found it difficult to pass the Matriculation Examination. They therefore applied to continue their matriculation studies at the University as external students where they could enjoy the benefit of what was perceived as the superior teaching of university lecturers and the use of a well-stocked library. They therefore enrolled as non-residential students but took advantage of the other opportunities offered by undergraduate studies at HKU. In this sense the situation in the University's early years was analogous to the current associate degree programmes offered by the HKU SPACE Community College, providing a 'second chance' for students who failed at the first attempt to matriculate.

The first edition of the University *Calendar*, published at the start of the second academic year (1913–14), recognised this unexpected development, devoting a whole section to 'External Students':

> There are a few External Students who take advantage of the facilities offered by the University for advanced instruction in various subjects. Those students pay $25 per term for each subject. It is anticipated that in time the number of such students will be considerable, but at present the University Authorities are chiefly concerned with the residential side of the University's work, which must always be the more important of the two.

It is not clear exactly why it was anticipated 'that in time the number of such students will be considerable', but the emphasis of the University authorities on the residential undergraduate education of matriculated students as being always the more important of the two types of education offered at HKU is telling. The fees paid by external students for individual courses were certainly an important consideration for the University. These fees worked out to be exactly the same as those paid by matriculated students for whole programmes of study ($75 per annum) and by 1919 fee income from external students was a major component in the finances of the Faculty of Arts. In fact, without the presence of external students in the first five years of its existence, it is difficult to see how the Arts Faculty could have continued to function effectively (see Table 1.1).

It is not known how many external students were registered in the first two years of the University's existence, but by 1915 the Arts Faculty was admitting more externals than matriculated students. In the Faculty's first ten years, student

Table 1.1 New Students in the Faculty of Arts, 1912–1922

Year	Matriculants	Externals	Total
1912	18	–	18
1913	9	1	10
1914	10	8	18
1915	5	13	18
1916	11	7	18
1917	11	11	22
1918	29	19	48
1919	36	2	38
1920	27	1	28
1921	28	–	28
	184	64	248

(*Source:* Early Student Records of the Faculty of Arts, HKU)

numbers were very small, as was the case in the other two foundation faculties and a common feature of most new universities at the time. As can be seen in Table 1.1 however, more than a quarter of the students admitted were external students, although it should also be noted that a substantial number of these later matriculated and became full-time students of the University. Similar figures are not available for the other two foundation faculties, so it is impossible to determine whether external students were present in significant numbers elsewhere in the University at that time. Many of the external students in the Arts Faculty did not persevere with their studies, with most dropping out within the first year. This became a persistent feature of external studies at HKU until World War II. This problem was not, however, limited solely to external students. Matriculated students routinely left the University within a year or two of starting their courses and there does not seem to have been any shame attached to 'failing' examinations. In fact, it is difficult to ascertain any major differentiating features between external and matriculated students at the University in its earliest years. Both groups of students seem to have merged with each other in most academic activities. The major differences were that matriculated students were full members of the University who were able to take degrees at the end of their studies and resided in halls of residence, while external students did not enjoy all the rights and privileges of membership of the University, could not take degrees, and resided outside the campus. But even here the differences broke down because the two non-University-administered halls, St John's and Morrison, were allowed to take in external students as residents and such students enjoyed the full round of extra-curricular activities. In these cases, then, there was no discernible difference between matriculated and external students and many became firm friends and business partners after leaving the University.

External students re-sitting the matriculation examination seem to have fallen into two groups. There were those who pursued the full undergraduate course until the end of their first term when they re-sat the matriculation examination in order to become matriculated students and commence their proper university studies. Sometimes these students were given permission to count their first term of studies as external students towards their degree studies, and were probably treated from the beginning in the same way as 'normal' internal students. Other external students required more intensive preparation for the matriculation examination, however, and special classes had to be arranged to provide them with remedial teaching. At the beginning of 1919, for example, matriculation classes in mathematics, trigonometry, history, and geography were arranged for external students. The mathematics class met five times a week and students paid fees of $25 per term, with the teacher receiving an honorarium of $250 for each course.[13] It is not possible to gauge the demand for such courses, but it must have been considerable because the Faculty of Arts was facing severe funding shortages at the time and external students were seen as a means of raising revenue for the other work of the Faculty. In 1915–16, ten of the thirteen first-year externals were matriculation candidates, and in 1917–18 nine out of eleven, so it seems likely that they represented both an important source of revenue for the Faculty, and a potential pool of matriculated students.

The presence of large numbers of external students in the Faculty of Arts did, however, lead to some difficulties. In late 1919 the Registrar proposed formalising the previously informal policy of allowing non-matriculated students to count their first term of studies towards their degrees upon successful completion of the matriculation examination. This appears to have been in response to the unusually large number of applicants for such special consideration at the beginning of the 1919–20 academic year. The inclusion of an appropriate clause in the regulations seemed a pragmatic response to the aspirations of a large number of external students who wished to make the most of their first term of studies at HKU. However, the Faculty Board rejected the proposal on the grounds that 'it is not desirable that any change should be made in the regulations concerning the periods of study and residence required by the University'.[14] While the members of the Board did not spell out their objections to the Registrar's proposal, it seems likely that this decision was part of a more general tightening of standards within the Faculty of Arts. It seems that there were concerns that too lenient an approach to unqualified external students would be perceived as encouraging a diminution in the quality of Arts students. This concern was also expressed in other areas of the Faculty's academic programmes.

In its early years the Arts Faculty had, in fact, been a leader in the introduction of programmes which were of a more vocational nature than the traditional arts education common in universities. These programmes proved attractive to students and seem to have been favoured by many external students who later transferred to full-time studies. The degree and certificate courses in commerce and the degree course in teacher training were significant departures from the original intentions of the Bachelor of Arts degree and by 1920 both were proving popular. One significant attraction was that these programmes provided entry into professions for which there was a growing demand in Hong Kong, and jobs were relatively easy to find. Not surprisingly, enrolments increased and by 1920 the majority of students in the Arts Faculty were studying one of these two subjects. When a new Arts syllabus was approved in October 1920, the Teacher Training (Group 4) and Commercial Training (Group 5) streams were formally added to the more traditional fields of Letters and Philosophy (Group 1), Experimental Science (Group 2) and Social Sciences (Group 3). There remained, however, a concern among some academics that these areas were not sufficiently 'academic' to qualify as proper university programmes. This would become a familiar concern later in the twentieth century both in Hong Kong and elsewhere, resulting in very strict quality assurance mechanisms being imposed on external and extra-mural programmes. At HKU in 1921, the Arts Faculty Board thwarted an attempt by the Registrar to change the entry regulations in order to allow Edward Hotung, the son of wealthy entrepreneur Sir Robert Hotung, to enter the normal Group 5 degree programme on the basis of his having completed the Commercial Certificate earlier that year. Hotung was later admitted to the programme, but the Arts Faculty insisted that it should give 'special consideration of particular cases, as and when they may arise' in order to assure the quality of its student intake.[15] The position adopted by the Faculty Board appears to have been a matter of principle. Concerns about the quality of the student intake seem to have been largely based on the question of whether external students could be expected to transfer to the degree programme successfully without diluting the overall standard of the Arts curriculum. The early experiences of the Arts Faculty in dealing with this problem would lead to stricter policies regarding the admission of external students at HKU in the 1920s and subsequently.

External Studies at HKU in the 1920s and the 1930s

The position of external students at the University of Hong Kong changed drastically after the First World War. The demand for internal student places rose quickly and the Arts Faculty in particular no longer needed large numbers of external students to ensure its fee income. One gains the impression from the early records of the Arts Faculty that large numbers of external students were considered to be a 'necessary evil', tolerated only for as long as it took to attract adequate numbers of matriculated students to ensure the viability of the Faculty. The fortunes of the Arts Faculty began to improve from the beginning of 1922. Whereas there had been only twenty-seven internal students in the first year in October 1921, by January 1922 a total of fifty-five internal students had enrolled and no external students were accepted. Out of a total enrolment of 117 students in the Arts Faculty at that time, there was only one external student on the books, a second-year student.[16] By the beginning of 1923 there were 123 students in the Faculty, none of whom were external students.[17] This represented a remarkable change from only a few years earlier. The Arts Faculty and the University would never again have such a large proportion of external students, with matriculated student numbers increasing rapidly as the University's degrees became better recognised both locally and throughout East and Southeast Asia.

One important indication of the changing attitude to external students is that all mention of external studies disappeared completely from the *University Calendar* in 1922. It may well have been that this was a policy adopted by the Arts Faculty in response to earlier problems but no evidence of this has been found. The *University Calendar* is silent with regard to the presence of external students in the University until 1930 when a regulation applying to apprentices registered as external students in the Engineering Faculty was added, and in the next year fees for external students were mentioned again for the first time in nearly a decade.[18] Despite the lack of an obvious regulatory framework for external students between 1922 and 1930, non-matriculated students were again admitted to the Arts Faculty from 1923. In that year, the six new external students included four women, the first in the University's history. In the next seven years a total of forty-two externals were admitted, with equal numbers of men and women. The largest intake was in 1928 with six men and six women, five of whom (three men and two women) enrolled in the new subject group of Chinese Studies, introduced by the Faculty that year. In the period 1923–30, the most popular area for external students was the Letters and Philosophy group (14 students), followed by Commerce (6), Chinese and Science (5 each). During this period externals were predominantly local Chinese students, but others were drawn from different backgrounds, including British students such as James Smith (son of the Professor of Engineering), a number of Americans including the diarist Betty Draper, and even a Peruvian, Teresa Sanchez, in 1930. In 1928, two mature-aged Japanese were admitted to study as externals in the English Department and one was even allowed to reside in Lugard Hall for the year. Like most Chinese external students, however, these international visitors did not last long in their studies, usually leaving at the end of their first year.

Another attempt by the University to provide a different type of post-secondary education to Chinese students was the opening of the School of Chinese Studies, a scheme which was promoted by the Chancellor of the University, Sir Cecil Clementi. The new School aimed at drawing its students from the Government Vernacular Middle School, and its course was to lead to a diploma after four years of study, the same as for a regular degree.[19] Starting in 1929, seven non-matriculation students who had completed their course at the Vernacular Middle School began their 'advanced course' in Chinese and English at the University. Three more students joined in 1930, six in 1931 and one in 1932, but seven of these students had failed by the end of 1931, and the expense of having six teachers for only ten students made the continuation of this educational experiment untenable. The diploma course, having failed to fulfil the University's original expectations, was therefore abandoned in favour of a proper degree programme in Chinese from 1932.[20] Only two of the students in the School ultimately received their diplomas at the end of 1932, but both these and three others were able to matriculate in 1933 and all five eventually received their bachelor's degrees. One of these graduates was Fung Ping-wah, who enjoyed a long and successful career in business and followed his father's example in becoming a generous donor to the University.

Outside the Arts Faculty there were efforts made to attract apprentices to first-year courses in engineering because of declining numbers of matriculated students in the Engineering Faculty. In 1928 the Senate formally approved a scheme which allowed non-matriculated students to audit lectures in the Engineering Faculty.[21] Once again, however, the University tried to ensure the quality of these students by insisting that they pass entrance examinations in English and mathematics before they were admitted to lectures. These students could only proceed to second-year courses if they passed the matriculation examination at the end of their first year.[22] This regulation remained in the *Calendar* until the mid-1930s but it is not known how successful the policy was in attracting external students. Throughout the 1920s the Medical Faculty appears to have admitted no external students.

The 1930s saw a steep rise in student numbers at the University, so the few externals became an even smaller proportion of the student population. The Arts Faculty continued to be the place where externals were most likely to be found, and in some years there were surprisingly large numbers entering the Faculty. In 1931, twelve externals constituted 28 per cent of the new students, and in 1937–38 twenty externals represented a third of the total intake of sixty students. However, in 1939–40 there were only six new externals (13 per cent) and by 1941 the approach of war reduced the intake to a single external student. In the period 1931–41, ninety-six external students made up approximately 20 per cent of the student intake into the Faculty of Arts, a relatively high percentage. Not all of these students were retained, however, as Table 1.2 shows. Relatively few external students progressed beyond a single year of studies, and most seem to have dropped out after only one or two terms. The overall percentage of externals among the entire student population was never higher than 5.4 per cent, achieved in 1938.

The gender balance among external students fluctuated from one year to the next. Generally men outnumbered women throughout the 1930s, although 1935 and 1936 saw larger numbers of women externals. Between 1923 when women externals were first admitted and 1931, almost equal numbers of men and women

Table 1.2 External Students at HKU, 1930–1940

Year	Arts	Engineering	Medicine	Science	Total Externals at HKU	Total Students at HKU
1930	12	–	–	–	12	336
1931	10	2	1	–	13	346
1932	–	–	–	–	–	333
1933	4	1	–	–	5	366
1934	10	1	–	–	13	438
1935	15	–	–	–	15	404
1936	10	–	–	–	10	413
1937	13	2	2	–	17	441
1938	15	4	9	–	28	516
1939	–	–	–	–	8	503
1940	4	1	–	1	7	572

(*Source: University Reports*, 1930–1940)

were admitted to external studies courses in the Arts Faculty (29 men and 25 women). In the period 1932–41, however, a much higher percentage of men was admitted (48 men and 36 women). In the period before the Second World War, the Arts Faculty admitted 949 matriculated students (693 male and 256 female) and 202 external students (141 male and 61 female), with women forming a slightly higher percentage of external students (30 per cent) than matriculated students (27 per cent). External students constituted 18 per cent of the student population during this period. The age profile of external students is also of interest. In the period 1931–41, for which accurate age data is available, 60 per cent of external students were between sixteen and twenty-one years of age at the time of admission, while 39 per cent were over the age of twenty-one. The external student population was therefore relatively older on average than the main body of matriculated students. While they were perhaps less likely to remain at their studies than internals, external students were a very familiar component of the early student population within the Faculty of Arts right up to the outbreak of the War.[23]

There were some changes in the external student profile during the 1930s. In the 1920s commercial studies had not been particularly popular among externals but in the early 1930s it was the most popular subject, together with English language, both accounting for approximately 40 per cent of the intake. This change seems to have taken place quite rapidly and perhaps is explained with reference to the onset of the Great Depression. In 1928, eight externals were following courses in Letters and Philosophy and three were enrolled in Science, with none in Commerce, while in 1929 three were enrolled in Letters and Philosophy and two in Commerce. In

1930, however, seven out of the twelve externals were taking courses in commercial subjects, and in 1934 five of the seven new externals were studying Commerce. Economics continued to be a popular subject until the War, but it seems that the late 1930s saw a decline in the popularity of the commercial courses, a phenomenon which the 1937 Report attributed to a disjunction between the nature of Chinese business and the types of accounting methods being taught at HKU. It seems that the small-scale Chinese business enterprises had little need of Western accounting methods or economic theory. The Vice-Chancellor agreed with the findings of the committee and doubted whether the Department of Commerce could justify its continued existence. The University Development Committee also recommended that commercial courses be suspended in 1939, by which time there can have been few external students still taking these courses.[24]

While external students were a regular feature of the learning environment in the Arts Faculty, they were less common in the other faculties during the 1930s. It has already been noted that the Engineering Faculty attempted to attract external students to its first-year courses in the late-1920s, but the official enrolment figures do not suggest that this strategy attracted very many external students. There was, however, a small trickle of engineering externals throughout the 1930s. The Faculty of Medicine was the most impervious to externals, with very few admissions at any time in its early history. Medicine was the most sought-after programme of study at HKU but the nature of the medical profession did not allow for external studies. Doctors could only practise medicine after completing the full-time medical programme with all its clinical work. However, in 1938 nine unmatriculated students were allowed to enter the Faculty of Medicine to study pharmacy in the 'chemist and druggist course'.[25] This was an experiment which met with only limited success and was not repeated.

It is difficult to get much of a sense of what life was like for external students during these two decades, and the ways in which their experiences differed, if at all, from the lives of matriculated undergraduates. Although the only extant student diary from the period was written by an external student, she was hardly typical of her cohort. Betty Draper, an American high school graduate whose family had been living in Western China for some time, joined the Arts Faculty in the middle of 1928 and left immediately after her examinations in late 1929. Her academic credentials from Belmont High School in Los Angeles did not qualify her for matriculation so she enrolled as an external student, at first in English and French, but later adding Chemistry and Biology in 1929.[26] She joined the same classes as her undergraduate friends, with Sir William Hornell as her French teacher, Mr B. G. Birch as her English tutor, Professor Herklots lecturing in Biology, and Professor Byrne in Chemistry. Her diary is full of disparaging comments about her teachers, especially Mr Birch and Mr Hill, a junior Chemistry lecturer, but she praises the inspiring Professor Simpson, who directed her and her friends in two plays. She was good friends with the few female students of the University at the time, including Grace Hotung, Florence Wong, Parrin Ruttonjee, Hui Wai-haan, and Rose Perry, and she was elected president of the International Club.[27] Betty Draper frequented the University Union, played tennis on the University courts behind the Main Building, and studied in the Library. For all intents and purposes, she appears to have led the same sort of life as an undergraduate. While this may be true of the time she spent studying at the University, however, her life outside the campus was very different. She lived in a big house on the Peak, had a boyfriend in town whom she met at Lane and Crawford and the Hong Kong Hotel, and socialised with the likes of Stella Benson. She is therefore not typical of HKU's external students in the 1920s and 1930s, most of whom were Chinese, and we have no way of assessing what a 'typical' experience of being an external at HKU was like in these two decades.

It is equally difficult to trace the career trajectories of early external students or to evaluate whether their experience of higher education at HKU had any lasting impact on their lives. Betty Draper returned to the United States in late 1929 and became a student of Fine Arts at UCLA, but never did complete her undergraduate studies. Chan Sau Ung-loo (1935–38) was more successful, earning her BA from the University of Hawaii and an LLB from Yale. The scions of wealthy Hong Kong Chinese merchants such as Edward Hotung (1918–19), Fung Ping-wah (1929–32, B.A. 1933), Fung Ping-fan (1929–32), and William Eu (1938–39) all went into their family businesses and became prominent leaders in Hong Kong society. It is more difficult to trace the other externals after they left HKU, although we do know that James Middleton Smith (1924) became a businessman in Shanghai, so it is likely that other externals in the Commerce group also went into business.

By the end of the 1930s, external studies at the University of Hong Kong was typically an activity which took place in the Arts Faculty and involved students who usually stayed for no more than a year of study, sometimes as a preparation for matriculation, but in other cases simply out of interest or to fill in a year of otherwise free time. There was no real attempt to extend the University's teaching activities beyond the undergraduate population as had been the case in Britain during this period, and adult education remained almost completely undeveloped. The notion that the University might provide some opportunity for a liberal adult education or other forms of extension studies typical of what was happening in the British universities at the time never seems to have been seriously considered at HKU. Indeed, for most of the 1920s, even the opportunity to undertake external studies ceased to be mentioned in the *University Calendar*. That this was so should not be a cause for surprise. The University of Hong Kong was still establishing itself as an institution of higher education in the first half of the twentieth century and did not have the same level of confidence that typified its British sister institutions in this period. Several serious financial crises in the 1920s and 1930s meant that the

University lived very much 'from hand to mouth' and there was little enough revenue for the primary aim of teaching, let alone extension work among adults. It is also possible that there was very little demand for adult education in Hong Kong at that time, but even if there was, the elitist educational institution which HKU was rapidly becoming was probably not the place where such a demand would have been met with educational provision.

The University (1937) Report and the War

Despite the presence of quite large numbers of external students within HKU during its first thirty years of existence, the University paid very little attention to them and did very little to legislate for their studies. There seems to have been an implicit understanding that such students were free to take advantage of undergraduate courses if they paid the appropriate fees, but that the University's primary task of educating matriculated students must not be disrupted by their presence. For this reason, neither external studies nor any form of adult or continuing and professional education received very much attention at the policy level in any of the principal governing organs of HKU before 1938. The only mention of external students in Council meetings was with regard to setting fees, first in 1912 and later in 1930 when fees were increased from $75 to $100 per course per year in order to keep them in line with increases in fees for matriculated students.[28] In the Senate, external studies were discussed in 1928 when it was agreed that apprentices could be admitted to the Engineering Faculty and unmatriculated students into the new School of Chinese.[29] Moreover, the provision of higher educational opportunities to external students did not feature in any of the several reports submitted to the University or the government during this period. It was not until the University Development Committee report of 1939 that some form of continuing and professional education was envisaged. Unfortunately this development was arrested by the Japanese occupation of Hong Kong in late 1941. Despite some discussion during and immediately after the War, the issue did not resurface in any substantive form until the 1950s. This was in contrast to the situation in Britain where the 1919 Report of the Adult Education Committee had led to a massive increase in the provision of non-vocational adult education in the 1920s and 1930s. This development was accompanied and promoted by the establishment in the universities of extra-mural studies departments to co-ordinate the work of providing educational opportunities to non-matriculated students in the community.[30] Such developments in Britain appear to have had no impact on Hong Kong at all in the 1920s and 1930s.

By the end of the 1930s, however, HKU had reached a moment in its history when serious strategic planning was necessary in order to secure its future. Sir Andrew Caldecott, Governor of Hong Kong and Chancellor of the University, set up a small committee to enquire into the financial viability of the University and whether other changes might be desirable in the interests of the University's future utility and prestige.[31] The committee found that HKU's existing position was 'not satisfactory', that it had 'existed far too much from hand to mouth', and that expenses would have to be cut if the future of the institution were to be secured. The cost-cutting measures recommended by the committee included a more determined focusing of academic activities on teaching rather than overly-expensive research, a rigorous pruning of professors in the Arts and Engineering faculties, and maintaining the 10 per cent reduction in salaries imposed in the previous year.[32] Not surprisingly, the report made no recommendations about external or extra-mural studies as its focus was mainly financial and organisational rather than educational. It appears that external studies were not even considered as a potential source of additional revenue at this juncture, in contrast with earlier policies. The hornet's nest which the 1937 Report stirred up within the University led, however, to a wide-ranging discussion of the past performance and future mission of HKU. In February 1939, the new Governor, Sir Geoffry Northcote, set up a committee 'to consider and report upon what steps are necessary for the development of the University up to the standard at which it would be able to fulfil the high function for which it was founded'.[33] The University Development Committee met thirteen times between 14 March and 28 April and submitted its lengthy report on 10 May 1939. It was a landmark document for the University, guiding development for many years to come. It was also the first HKU report in which mention was made of adult and continuing professional education.

The man responsible for raising the issue of adult education was the new Vice-Chancellor, Mr Duncan Sloss. Soon after his arrival in Hong Kong he realised that in its first twenty-five years HKU had stressed 'what is sometimes regarded as the practical aspect of higher education' in all three of its original faculties. He agreed that providing an education for a livelihood was part of the function of a university but he also felt that 'No university can maintain its status or develop the right atmosphere if it does not make adequate provision for the disinterested pursuit of knowledge'. He was therefore an advocate of 'education for its own sake' and wanted to see the University focus more on 'pure culture'.[34] He was supported in this by many of the professors, and by none more so than Lancelot Forster, the professor of Education. Professor Forster believed that a 'technical and professional virus' had infected the Arts Faculty from its beginnings and had been a detriment to the development of truly liberal studies at HKU. He wanted a more 'philosophical' Arts programme without which he predicted that the University would continue to provide only 'an emasculated form of British higher education' which would render it powerless to exert any real influence on modern China.[35] These views seem to indicate a more purist approach to the education of undergraduates and the pursuit of postgraduate research, but both men also believed in the importance of extension work by the University.

Professor Forster had already been instrumental in setting up a night school to provide elementary education for the poor children of Sai Ying Pun in the early 1930s, and was very active in the more practical issues of teacher education in the colony through his contacts with the government's Department of Education.[36] This extension work did not, however, have any tangible impact on the policies of the University in the 1930s, nor did it open up any opportunities for adult education at HKU. He now joined the Vice-Chancellor in recommending that a range of extra-mural 'refresher' courses be offered to graduates of the University and other participants, especially professionals working in Hong Kong. These courses could be offered annually in medical and surgical subjects and admission to such courses 'should be given as widely as possible to medical practitioners in Hong Kong and the surrounding country'. An experiment in offering summer courses 'for men engaged in commerce' was suggested and Forster not surprisingly wanted to see established frequent refresher courses for teachers in Hong Kong and South China.[37] These suggestions for university extension work were contained in four separate paragraphs of the report and represented a strong statement regarding the sort of role in extra-mural education which it was felt the University should be pursuing within the Hong Kong community and the wider region.

These plans for the provision of wide-ranging adult education opportunities came to nothing. Such a failure to turn words into action can be attributed to the fact that HKU had more pressing needs to address immediately after the report's release in the summer of 1939. These related primarily to the establishment of the new Faculty of Science and a range of expensive building projects approved in the wake of the 1939 Report. However, there can be no doubt that the outbreak of war in Europe and the increasingly aggressive activities of the Japanese in China also diverted the attention of those in charge of University development. When the Japanese occupation in December 1941 brought the closure of the University and the internment of most of its expatriate teaching staff, all University development ceased and the campus was taken over by the enemy military authorities. During the first few months of internment, University staff members were too concerned with matters of survival to think too much about the future of the University, but by the middle of 1942, the Vice-Chancellor initiated preliminary discussions about the University's future within Stanley Civilian Internment Camp. Professor Forster was again very vocal in criticising the 'old pedestrian soulless existence' of HKU and proposed that the Arts Faculty should be at the centre of any development plans so as to produce 'the future statesmen and constructive political thinkers who will shape the destinies of China'.[38] As well as the generous provision of liberal arts subjects, he also wanted to see the establishment of an institute of education, one of the functions of which would be 'to organise extramural studies for adult education in the Colony' and provide educational conferences and vacation courses for teaching professionals. He felt strongly that 'the neglect of this work in the past has led to indifference and lack of sympathy on the part of the public with the University and its work'.[39] The extent to which this view was shared by other members of the University is difficult to judge, but it is certainly tempting to speculate that the lack of local support for HKU in the 1930s may have had something to do with the University's failure to establish any kind of extension activities. Doubtless the Vice-Chancellor was one of those who agreed with Forster, but there is no evidence that the more formal discussions about the University's future which took place in Stanley Camp in 1943 and 1944 developed the idea of extra-mural studies any further.

There was, nevertheless, some practical adult education work which the University undertook during the internment period. At both the Stanley civilian camp and at the Shamshuipo military camp, HKU staff and graduates gave informal lectures and short courses on a variety of cultural and vocational subjects.[40] While the bulk of the academic staff were at Stanley, Dr Norman Mackenzie found himself at Shamshuipo and was able to deliver lectures on the Romantic poets to appreciative fellow POWs, and Dr Solomon Bard even managed to form an orchestra in the camp.[41] These sessions no doubt helped the inmates cope with the monotonous life of internment by taking their minds off the problems of food and disease, if only for a short time. More importantly, however, the Senate at its meeting on 2 July 1943 heard a progress report about 'a proposed extension course' which had been suggested as an alternative to proper university courses during the remainder of the period of internment. A large informal committee had already met to discuss the syllabus of the programme on 25 May 1943. The academics present realised that the recent matriculation exam in the camp had produced very few students qualified for university study, and they must also have been acutely aware of the impossibility of mounting full degree programmes within the Stanley camp. While formal matriculation examinations were held in 1943, 1944 and 1945, the purpose of these was to provide candidates with credentials to pursue university studies once they were freed, rather than to qualify them for courses within the camp. The meeting of 25 May agreed, however, that something should be done about the further education of those who had already passed through the Stanley Internment Camp School and had attempted the matriculation exam, so an 'extension course' was arranged to begin in the middle of June.

Thus began HKU's first real attempt at extra-mural studies with teaching taking place in the garages outside the Stanley Prison walls. Courses were offered in English, Pure and Applied Mathematics, French, History, Geography, Theoretical Physics, and Economics, with up to twenty-one hours of lectures offered in the various subjects each week. Students were required to take at least two but not more than four courses, with class enrolments limited to ten, and the students were chosen on the basis of those who would profit most from the instruction given.[42] The programme was apparently a great success, with the Senate discussing in early 1944 the possibility of a Higher Certificate Examination for those who had followed the courses. At its meeting on 14 November 1944, the Senate decided not to hold an examination for the Higher Certificate students but noted 'it might be necessary merely to issue to the candidate a statement regarding the courses of study they had pursued, without specifying the standard reached'.[43] We do not know how many students passed through the HKU Higher Certificate internment programme, nor whether their lessons helped them in securing employment or further studies after the War. It seems likely, however, that this extension work was highly valued by teachers and students alike as it allowed a partial return to normal pre-War conditions, even though the context and mode of delivery were very different.

HKU's wartime experiment with educational extension work was quickly forgotten at the end of the War as the University began to look to the future. Several of the lecturers involved in teaching the Higher Certificate courses died in camp in the middle of 1944, and Professor Forster retired to England after release. Those who took on the task of reconstruction had little time for adult education when the first priority was to reopen the University for undergraduates. The Senate's Reconstruction Sub-Committee which met in mid-1943 had already proposed 'the reconstitution of the University only on the assumption that it may become by its scope, staffing and equipment an example of a British institution of higher education and research worthy of the respect of Chinese scholars and statesmen'; and in November 1944 Senate began to draw up a 'scheme of development' to take advantage of 'a unique opportunity to make a new start'.[44] That new start was delayed until 1948 by the decision-making committees of the Colonial Office in London, but in the meantime HKU was partially reopened in October 1946 with the organisation of first-year classes. A new schedule of student fees was approved which included external course fees of $125 per course per year, a 25 per cent increase on the previous fee structure set in 1930.[45] There was therefore an expectation that external students would return to the post-War university and contribute to HKU's finances in the same way they had until 1941.

After the War

It was recognised by the University Re-opening Committee that a large number of pre-War senior students would wish to continue their studies and evidently some complaints were received about the very partial reopening of the University. A notice was issued in January 1947 advising former students that 'it is virtually impossible to arrange for third or fourth year courses in September 1947. But to assist them the Interim Committee is prepared to admit them as second year students taking refresher courses next September, without charging tuition fees, and without requiring hostel residence in the case of students whose homes are in Hong Kong'.[46] Not all pre-War undergraduates wishing to renew their studies were able to take advantage of this arrangement, however, for many of them had to work for a living in the desperate economic conditions in the post-War colony. Some former students were particularly disgruntled, and when a summer course for social workers was organised in July 1947, one alumnus wrote anonymously to the Chancellor to complain. Students in his position had found it necessary to take on day-time work merely to survive and were not in a position to go back to full-time studies. Students like him were nevertheless prepared to attend evening classes 'should they be given the opportunity'. If it were possible for the University to hold evening classes in the summer for social workers, why was it not possible to extend this privilege to former students in the Arts and Science faculties to allow them to complete their degrees? The correspondent also made the point that 'There are evening classes and vacation classes held by the University of London in London, why cannot the University of Hong Kong hold evening classes in Hong Kong?'[47]

The Interim Committee took this complaint seriously, and at its joint meeting with the Provisional Powers Committee on 10 September 1947 approval in principle was given to a suggestion 'that the University should hold evening and vacation classes'. Unfortunately, further discussion of this proposal was left until the University was 'more adequately equipped and staffed', a situation that would not arise until later in the 1950s when other more formal influences came to bear on the matter of extra-mural studies.[48] The course for social workers which took place in the summer of 1947, the University's first such course in further education, was very successful but was not repeated. The promise of extra-mural studies at HKU which had been slowly taking shape since before the War was not therefore honoured in any real sense in the years of restoration in the late-1940s and early-1950s.

Elsewhere in the British Empire the situation was very different. While the University's Senate had been discussing the future of HKU in Stanley camp during 1943, the home government in London had established a Commission on Higher Education in the Colonies to plan for higher education in the Empire after the War. The provision of greater opportunities in higher education was seen by the members of this commission foremost as a means of improving the social and economic development of the colonies. This was not merely in fulfilment of Britain's 'moral obligations as trustees of the welfare of Colonial peoples, but is also designed to lead to the exercise of self-government by them. In the stage preparatory to self-government, universities have an important part to play; indeed they may be said to be indispensable'.[49] One focus of the commission's 1945 report (the Asquith Report) was the provision of extra-mural studies by colonial universities, and most of the recommendations contained in the report were eventually adopted by colonial governments throughout the Empire.[50] In the Far East, a special Commission on University Education in Malaya under the chairmanship of Sir Alexander Carr-Saunders made further recommendations to the home government regarding extra-mural studies which later influenced developments in Hong Kong, but the report on higher education in Hong Kong produced for the Colonial office in 1950 made no mention of extra-mural studies, perhaps reflecting the almost total lack of interest in such developments within the colony of Hong Kong. For this reason, therefore, together with the more pressing needs of reconstruction at HKU, no advances were made in the provision of extension or adult education until the mid-1950s (see next chapter).

The University of Hong Kong continued to provide opportunities for external students to take its undergraduate courses after the War and well into the 1960s, but there was never any serious attempt until the 1980s to extend the provision of external studies in the same way that institutions abroad such as the University of Queensland and the University of New England did in Australia during the early 1950s. In Britain, too, developments after the War were rapid, and by 1954 all major British universities had departments of extra-mural studies. These provided on average more than 150 extra-mural courses per year at each institution, with Birmingham and London universities providing more than 500 courses each, and Bristol more than 300.[51] In the same year a total of 7,448 adult education classes were held in Britain involving 147,782 students and 254 tutors at a cost to the British Government of £371,000.[52] Adult non-vocational education in Hong Kong did not develop at this rate until much later in the twentieth century. External studies at HKU remained a marginal activity and the visibility of external students rapidly declined as the number of matriculated undergraduates soared in the 1950s and 1960s. By 1962 the University was admitting only 27 external students among its 635 new students (a little more than 4 per cent of the intake) but, as in the pre-War years, these externals tended to be transient and most stayed for no more than one year of studies. As Table 1.3 demonstrates, even though the number of external students was healthier in 1962 than it had been in 1948, the percentage of externals in the overall student population was still only 2 per cent of the total.

Table 1.3 External Students at HKU, 1948–1963

Year	Arts	Engineering	Medicine	Science	Total Externals at HKU	Total Students at HKU
1948–49	7	2	–	2	11	518
1949–50	8	–	–	1	9	638
1950–51	17	–	–	2	19	871
1952–5	6	5	1	2	14	978
1959–60	16	1	1	–	18	1,268
1960–61	18	–	–	–	18	1,407
1961–62	22	1	–	1	24	1,600
1962–63	31	2	–	3	36	1,754

(*Source: HKU Vice-Chancellor's Reports*, 1948–1963)

Another element of continuity with the past was the dominance of the Faculty of Arts in the teaching of external students. But whereas the pre-War externals in Arts were generally attempting the same courses as the matriculated undergraduate students, after the 1940s increasingly large numbers of external students were enrolled in special language and education courses which were conducted by University staff, but were in other ways quite different from courses in the undergraduate curriculum. In 1963–64 there were 97 part-time external students admitted including 28 in the Language School and most others were studying for diplomas in education, but in the next year the number of new part-time students more than halved to 44.[53] There was, therefore, a gradual change in the nature of external studies offered by the University, but demand for these courses was sustained until the new Department of Extra-Mural Studies began to offer external degree courses in collaboration with overseas universities during the 1980s.

There also seems to have been some tightening of the regulations governing external students as the number of matriculated students increased. In the 1951–52 *Calendar* external students were still regulated by a fairly brief entry stating that any pupil with educational attainments which were 'sufficient' but who was not a matriculated student could be admitted as an external student, but such students would not be allowed to take the examinations of the University. The cost of external courses had by this time risen steeply to $250 per year with a maximum of $1,000 for a whole year (compared with a maximum of $1,050 for matriculated students).[54] In 1952–53 the fees remained the same, but Regulation G7 was much stricter than previously: 'An applicant whose educational standards in the English Language and in the subjects of his choice are considered adequate by the Head of Department concerned' could be enrolled, but such a student was still not permitted to take any examinations.[55] This was the first time that English language abilities had been mentioned with regard to external students, but inadequate English language ability had certainly been a concern in the pre-War years among undergraduates. Additionally, an external student was now forbidden to change his status to that of an undergraduate reading for a degree unless he had been registered as a matriculated student before his admission as an external.[56] Evidently some enterprising external students had managed to change their academic status by exploiting loopholes in the regulations, but the Senate was quick to reinforce the primacy of the matriculated student in the University's educational goals, something that was completely in keeping with a forty-year-old tradition at HKU. Such elitism would continue to infect the University until the 1970s.

Conclusion

In the pre-War and immediate post-War period the University of Hong Kong played a small role in the provision of adult and continuing education through external studies at the university level. It should be remembered that it was the only university in Hong Kong until the 1960s and therefore was the only institution which could have provided this form of adult education. There were clearly practical financial reasons for admitting external students at every stage of the University's development between 1912 and the 1960s, but we should not imagine that there was no underlying educational philosophy at work. As with Professor Lancelot Forster and Vice-Chancellor Duncan Sloss before the War, there continued to be committed advocates of extension and adult education within the professoriate at HKU after 1945, including the Vice-Chancellor, Sir Lindsay Ride, and the professor of Chinese, F. S. Drake. In retrospect, however, the performance of the University in adult and continuing education during this early period was rather dismal, despite a few instances of pioneering work in Stanley internment camp and immediately after the War. HKU's failure to provide adequate opportunities for adult education can be seen in many areas: a lack of professional training opportunities in business and legal studies; no refresher courses for teachers or medical graduates; and an almost total lack of interest in the provision of 'cultural' and liberal adult education studies for non-matriculated citizens of the colony. This failure was, perhaps, in the opinion of Lancelot Forster, one of the reasons why the Chinese population of Hong Kong had shown such indifference and so little sympathy for the University and its mission in the years before the War, even though it had achieved much in the realm of undergraduate education. This situation would gradually change after the re-establishment of the University in 1948, but it was not until 1957 that a Department of Extra-Mural Studies would finally complement the departments which worked to achieve the University's primary missions in teaching and research. Even then it would be many more years before extra-mural studies would become an accepted and important part of the University's mission.

What were the reasons for this neglect? No doubt the lack of interest from the Hong Kong government was a major factor. In Britain the Board of Education had played a central role in extending the provision of adult education from the 1920s and its Adult Education Regulations of 1924, 1931, and 1938 had done much to systematise and regulate the sector.[57] The British government had also provided a great deal of public funding for the expansion in provision of adult education in stark contrast to the notoriously tight-fisted attitude of the Hong Kong government in matters of higher education.[58] In Britain there had also been a number of vocal advocacy groups such as the Workers' Educational Association which took a lead in co-ordinating efforts. Probably more important, however, was the simple fact that Hong Kong in the first half of the twentieth century was struggling to establish an effective elementary and secondary education system and until that was in place there was little likelihood of any real demand for adult non-vocational education. All this would change in the 1950s as Hong Kong began to recover from the War.

CHAPTER TWO

Establishing the Department of Extra-Mural Studies, 1945–1957

THE UNIVERSITY OF HONG KONG provided relatively little opportunity for non-degree post-secondary education in the years immediately after the Second World War even though it continued to accept external students in varying numbers. The University focused its energies and finances on re-establishing itself and its undergraduate degree programmes after the devastation of four years of war and paid little heed to a growing demand for other types of post-secondary adult education. By the early 1950s, however, the demand within the local community for such educational opportunities had grown to such an extent that the University could no longer remain aloof any longer. Changes in British imperial educational policy during the 1940s and the localised recommendations of the Keswick Report in 1952 gave the University an opportunity to take the lead in providing high quality extra-mural education for a burgeoning market in the colony. It was not until 1957, however, that the Department of Extra-Mural Studies was finally established. This chapter aims to give an account of the issues influencing post-secondary education in Hong Kong immediately after the Second World War and the decision-making processes within the government and University which ultimately led to the establishment of the Department of Extra-Mural Studies on 21 May 1957.

Post-War Developments in Adult Higher Education in Hong Kong

The education system in Hong Kong was rehabilitated remarkably quickly after Britain resumed its administration of Hong Kong following the Japanese surrender in August 1945. Many primary and secondary schools which had operated before the Pacific War were reopened within months and the University of Hong Kong resumed classes in Arts, Engineering, Science and Medicine on 21 October 1946, barely six months after the creation of the HKU Provisional Powers Committee in late March 1946. It was not until early 1948, however, that the University was fully re-established with its formal governance structure of faculty boards, Senate, Council and Court.[1] These first few years of re-establishment were times of great hardship and uncertainty during which the University struggled to return to 'normal'. The most pressing needs were financial and it took several years to build the University back to the position it had enjoyed before the outbreak of war in 1941.

While the University faced the difficulties of rebuilding and eventual expansion, the wider education system in Hong Kong faced its own serious challenges. The colony experienced an astonishing rise in population in the late-1940s because of the post-war baby boom and an unprecedented influx of Chinese immigrants attempting to escape the civil war in China. The population increased from barely 600,000 in 1945 to approximately 2.4 million in 1955, with the largest growth taking place before 1950.[2] The government was at first reluctant to extend its educational services to these newcomers, who were often considered to be sojourners who would soon return to their homeland, but subsequent political and economic developments in the Mainland soon proved this perception to have been far too optimistic. High and persistent demand for various types of education among existing residents and new settlers put pressure on the whole education system and compelled the colonial government to consider the needs of both groups of inhabitants in Hong Kong.[3]

One of the most obvious deficiencies in the education system during the immediate post-War period was the lack of opportunities for school-leavers and adults to receive higher education. This was not the only problem, however, for the colonial administration did not have any definite plans to develop adult education at any level. A commission appointed by the Hong Kong government in 1950 commented that although Hong Kong needed 'a positive educational policy for adults', it was 'impracticable to embark upon much development of Further Education at present'.[4] The need for greater provision of adult education arose from the rapid expansion of Hong Kong after the War which in turn led to a pressing need for technical staff in many industries, such as medical services, education, social welfare and accountancy.[5] Workers were beginning to require more specialised technical training than secondary education could provide in order to gain entry into these and other professions. There were, however, very few channels through which school-leavers and adult learners could acquire the necessary knowledge and skills.

HKU did provide well-recognised degree programmes in medicine, engineering, science and arts subjects, but it could not satisfy the enormous and growing demands for various types of post-secondary education. First, it only admitted a small number of secondary-school graduates annually. In the year 1950–51, for example, there were 35,441 secondary students in Hong Kong but only 850 undergraduates at HKU.[6] Second, the University was expected to develop professionals with higher-level technical expertise, rather than technicians with lower-level skills. Third, the stringent English-language requirements for admission to the University also prevented most Chinese students from receiving higher and professional education locally. It was reported that for every three pupils who received secondary instruction in the medium of English, there were four who received it in the medium of Chinese. Of the 473 HKU undergraduates in 1952 who had studied in Hong Kong schools, only three came from Chinese middle schools.[7] Finally, the undergraduate courses offered by HKU were designed for school-leavers who wished to study on a full-time basis. Adult learners who were in full-time employment were not able to divert adequate time and energy to such programmes of study, nor did the University provide any organised extra-mural programme beyond the system of 'external studies' which had existed since before the War.

By the early-1950s the government operated a few post-secondary schools offering full-time or part-time courses for school-leavers and adult learners. Most of these courses were confined to vocational training and were organised on a modest scale. The Education Department, for instance, restored its pre-war provision of technical education quickly after the Japanese surrender. Its Evening Institute provided evening classes in language, commercial and technical subjects in order to 'assist those already engaged in industry by enabling the apprentice or young journeyman to learn the theory on which his practical work is based, with the idea that he will eventually qualify as a technician in his particular branch of industry'.[8] From 1947, the Hong Kong Technical College organised full-day and part-time evening courses in engineering, shipbuilding and wireless telegraphy.[9] Northcote Training College and two new teacher training colleges (Grantham Training College and the Rural Training College) trained qualified teachers at various levels through one- or two-year study programmes.[10] By the end of March 1952, it was estimated that 2,945 students were enrolled in all public post-secondary institutions, and 2,571 of them studied on a part-time basis.[11]

A major development in the government's provision of adult higher education in the immediate post-War period was the establishment of the Evening School of Higher Chinese Studies. In 1950, the Director of Education, Mr T. R. Rowell, appointed local community leaders to a committee to advise him on the problem posed by a large number of unplaced Chinese students.[12] The Advisory Committee suggested the establishment of a part-time school of Higher Chinese Studies.[13] The Keswick Report of 1952 gave a brief overview of the School which had been established in the previous year:

> This School was started by the Education Department in March 1951, in an attempt to meet the demand for post-secondary studies in the medium of Chinese, at least

> partially. It offers courses in General Arts, Commerce and Journalism, each course lasting three years and leading to a diploma to be issued by the Education Department. The hours of instruction are from 7 to 9 p.m. on five evenings a week, and the fees are $36 per month. The classes are held in the Tang Chi-ngong School of Chinese at the University. A staff of 21 lecturers, most of them previously lecturers and professors in universities in China, provides for the needs of 256 students, of whom 149 are in their second year . . . The majority of the students are clerks working in local firms, but some 40 come from universities in China. Enquires from places as far apart as Swatow and Saigon show how widespread the demand is for higher education at low cost, especially where there is a hope of obtaining a recognized diploma.[14]

The University was therefore providing a physical home for this important provider of post-secondary courses, helping to forge a connection between the provision of post-secondary and university-level education, but the number of students who could take advantage of these opportunities was small.

Private bodies also ran different types of post-secondary courses for adult learners. In March 1952, there were 2,141 students enrolled at private post-secondary colleges in Hong Kong, of whom 1,526 attended evening classes. The most important of these schools were the Chu Hoi Evening College, Chung Chi College, Canton Evening College, and Chung Ip Night School.[15] These private schools can be divided into four broad categories: (1) eight private institutions provided general academic courses in arts, science and commercial subjects to 527 students,[16] six of them offering evening courses which required one to four years of study;[17] (2) three institutions offered four-year full-time professional courses in theological studies to 146 students; (3) twenty-nine institutions provided commercial courses to 1,468 students, of whom about 70 per cent studied on a part-time basis; and (4) nine private post-secondary technical schools conducted courses in technical subjects for 609 students.[18] It is not clear to what extent these private schools were able to satisfy the demand for post-secondary courses which could not be met by government institutions.

While these private post-secondary schools attracted quite a large number of students, their academic standards and facilities were not very satisfactory. The Keswick Report of 1952 commented that 'none of the colleges grant degrees and none of them have equipment, premises or libraries of university standard, though some of the individual lecturers formerly held senior teaching posts in Chinese universities'.[19] Courses were not always taught by qualified teachers, and did not lead to well-recognised qualifications. The Keswick Report took accountancy courses as an example:

> Most of the courses, however, offer little more than simple book-keeping, and no local institution covers the syllabus for the final examination of any of the recognized professional bodies. Anyone who wishes to gain his final qualification locally must therefore depend for his instruction on one of the excellent

> correspondence courses in the United Kingdom. To complete the course successfully, however, demands not only the necessary ability, which includes a good knowledge of English, but also an uncommon perseverance and a strong resistance to the many social distractions of Hong Kong; we were not surprised, therefore, to learn that few succeed in qualifying.[20]

There was, therefore, an urgent need for Hong Kong to develop a diverse range of high-quality adult post-secondary courses to meet the growing demand for such programmes within the colony.

The Keswick Report (1952)

While Britain was still fighting against the Axis Powers and the future of its colonial empire remained unclear, the home government had already started to review higher education systems in its colonies and other overseas territories. The Commission on Higher Education in the Colonies was established in London in August 1943 under the auspices of the Colonial Office with the aim

> To consider the principles which should guide the promotion of higher education, learning and research and the development of universities in the Colonies; and to explore means whereby universities and other appropriate bodies in the United Kingdom may be able to co-operate with institutions of higher education in the Colonies in order to give effect to these principles.[21]

Chaired by Mr Justice Cyril Asquith, the Commission submitted its report to Parliament through the Secretary of State for the Colonies in June 1945. The Asquith Report sketched a blueprint for the development of higher education systems in the British Empire, and became the key document guiding overall education policy in the British colonies in the immediate post-War period.

Besides various overall recommendations on governance structure, finance, undergraduate studies, professional training, and research in colonial universities, the Asquith Commission paid particular attention to the function of universities as intellectual centres for colonial communities. The Report went to great lengths in discussing the necessity of establishing departments of extra-mural studies in each colonial university. The most important reason for extra-mural studies was intellectual:

> We have thought of the university so far as a centre of research and of the teaching of undergraduates. We hope that it will also take a leading part in the development of adult education in the region . . . Something should therefore be done for those who would have profited by university education, but have passed the age for it. Otherwise general progress and fresh educational advance will be gravely hindered

> by mass ignorance in the older generation. They too should be helped to lead their lives and do their work with more knowledge and intelligence.[22]

But extra-mural education also had an important social role to play in the colonies where higher education had the potential of creating great inequalities within the indigenous population:

> The fostering of extra-mural studies would in particular do much to guard against a danger, of which we are fully conscious, that the university graduates might become a separate community within a Colony, divorced from the concerns and aspirations of their fellow citizens. The development of a self-contained group of this kind is certainly no part of our purpose. The universities as we conceive them have on the contrary a vital contribution to make to the development of the community as a whole. We should therefore urge that from the earliest stage in their evolution, the university colleges should maintain direct contacts with those members of the population whose studies must necessarily be restricted to the leisure left from their other work.[23]

There were more pragmatic reasons for 'the special importance which we attach to extra-mural courses', however, and these were also outlined in detail in the Report:

> The university institutions must in the early years be few in number. The areas they serve will be extensive, and will stretch in many cases far beyond the boundaries of the Colony in which they are situated. The proportion of the Colonial populations which can come into direct contact with them must perforce be small. Local centres for extra-mural work will extend the influence of the university to the outlying parts of the region. We consider, therefore, that in every Colony served by a university, there should certainly be one centre for extra-mural studies, and that there should be similar centres wherever large urban or industrialised localities provide opportunity for part-time study.[24]

It was therefore recommended by the Asquith Commission that:

> . . . a strong and fully staffed department of extra-mural studies should be regarded as one of the normal features of a Colonial university. We hope too that opportunity may be given, through refresher courses and 'summer schools' to persons engaged in administrative work, teaching, the health services, agriculture and other activities, to refresh, extend and bring up-to-date their knowledge, and to think, learn and study anew.[25]

The Asquith Commission's recommendations, including those on extra-mural studies, were soon adopted throughout the British Empire. In the years that followed, various colonies published their own reports and proposals on reform of their higher education systems. Most of them proposed that some extra-mural work be carried out by local institutions of higher education. Commissions appointed by the Colonial

Office to review the higher education systems in the British West Indies and West Africa reported at the same time as Asquith and proposed that university colleges in these colonies should provide adult education and extra-mural activities to the local populations.[26] A similar recommendation was made in 1953 by the Commission on Higher Education for Africans in Central Africa, chaired by Sir Alexander Carr-Saunders, at the behest of the Central African Council.[27] The provision of extra-mural university courses in these colonies expanded in the following years. By 1951, a director of extra-mural studies and a staff tutor had been appointed in the West Indies. The teaching team appointed in the Gold Coast was even more impressive, consisting of a director, five full-time resident tutors, four full-time regional organisers, a central administrative staff, and a large number of part-time tutors responsible for teaching extra-mural courses.[28]

In the Far East, the Commission on University Education in Malaya was formed in 1946 under the chairmanship of Sir Alexander Carr-Saunders. Its Report (1948) provided a comprehensive discussion on the introduction of extra-mural studies in the new University of Malaya. The Malaya Commission reasserted the spirit of the Asquith Commission:

> If these contacts [between the University and the community] are not energetically sought and appropriately organized, there is a danger that the academic society may degenerate into an intellectual caste, tainted with the arrogance and snobbery that belong to caste systems.[29]

In particular, it explained the objective and content of extra-mural courses:

> To avoid confusion in the minds of readers who may not be fully conversant with university practice, it should be explained that the extra-mural courses of which we are speaking bear no resemblance to courses leading to an external degree . . . They are directed to persons who might have profited by university education but who never received it and have passed the usual age of it. They seek to give such persons a chance to feel the play of university influences upon them, and under the stimulus of those influences to unfetter imagination, to refine taste and judgment, and to deepen insight. Their main content will be the cultural values enshrined in science, art, and history; their main appeal will be to people who are already concerned to cultivate independent qualities of intelligence and temper, and who think that some experience of intellectual work at university standard might help them.[30]

The Malaya Commission recommended appointing a director of extra-mural studies and creating a University Extension Board in the new university. In 1950, a Council for Adult Education was established in Singapore to co-ordinate adult education in the colony.[31] While the Asquith Commission established a general policy of extra-mural work in colonial universities, the Carr-Saunders Report of 1948 provided

Hong Kong with an example of the possible development of extra-mural activities in the context of the Far East.

Hong Kong followed other British colonies in reviewing its higher education system in the years after the end of the War. There had been high-level discussions within the Colonial Office throughout the final years of the War regarding the post-War educational development of Hong Kong, and the University of Hong Kong in particular. This planning eventually led to the full re-establishment of the University in 1948, but at that time the job of reconstruction had only just begun. It would not be until 1952 that the Main Building would be fully restored and extended, and throughout this time student numbers remained low because of the severe restrictions imposed by buildings, budget and staff. By the late-1940s, however, a full development plan had been drafted and a number of recommendations for development were agreed in March 1950. In April 1950 the London-based Inter-University Council for Higher Education in the Colonies (IUC), an advisory body of the Colonial Office, sent two of its members, Mr Walter Adams and Dr Mouat Jones, to Hong Kong to study the HKU development proposals. These proposals were approved by the Colonial Office, and later in 1950 work began at HKU on both construction projects and the hiring of new staff. It is worth noting that the recommendations of March 1950 focused almost entirely on HKU's re-establishment costs and did not include any proposals for the introduction of extra-mural studies, even though such provision was now enshrined in imperial adult education policy. Already in the late 1940s it was becoming clear that a major review of university education in Hong Kong was needed, but this review did not occur until 1951.

In October 1951, the Governor of Hong Kong, Sir Alexander Grantham, appointed Mr John Keswick and several community leaders to form a Committee on Higher Education. John Keswick was the taipan of Jardines and had only recently returned from Shanghai where he had supervised the final days of the firm's existence on the Mainland. He had also worked with the Special Operations Executive in Chungking, and towards the end of the War had been appointed political advisor on Chinese affairs to Lord Mountbatten in South East Asia Command.[32] Keswick's Committee was asked to consider:

> (a) what demands there are in the Colony for general and professional higher studies, how far these demands are at present being met and planned for, and what further faculties would be required to satisfy these demands;
> (b) what measures are recommended to satisfy such requirements as are determined under (a) above, and whether the measures could best be applied through existing institutions and organizations or through the establishment of new ones;
> (c) to what extent the scheme could be self-supporting and self-accommodating, and from what sources any additional support or accommodation necessary may be obtained.[33]

In the following months, the Keswick Committee invited members of the public to submit their opinions about the Hong Kong higher education system, and consulted local and overseas specialists for their suggestions.[34] The concept of extra-mural education aroused some interest among the members of the committee and the general public. The Hong Kong Teachers' Association, for instance, expressed its support for the University to 'take an active part in adult education by developing its extra-mural activities and giving courses or lectures as is done in many countries'.[35] Sir George Allen, Vice-Chancellor of the University of Malaya, met the Keswick Committee in February 1952 to share his experience from Malaya and his ideas more generally on the provision of extra-mural studies in the colonial university setting.[36]

It was the University itself, however, which made the most detailed suggestions for the implementation of extra-mural studies. Bernard Mellor, the University Registrar and a member of the Keswick Committee, submitted a memorandum to the Committee in early 1952 outlining his belief that the University should target adult education at the highest level within the broader adult education system. He defined the role of a department of extra-mural studies in terms of (1) the training of tutors and lecturers (in co-operation with the Professor of Education), (2) the provision of 'academic-type evening courses and summer schools', and (3) giving advice on and help in the organization and co-ordination of adult education generally.[37] Mellor recommended that a Council for Adult Education be established on the lines of the Singapore model. The University and other public or private adult education agencies would be members of the Council which would have the role of co-ordinating and developing adult education in the colony. The government would be responsible for providing the necessary funding for establishing the Council and its initial operations. Furthermore, Mellor recommended that a department of extra-mural studies should be established at the University with a director and one or two full-time tutors, both of whom would be funded by the University. It was proposed that the University should take over the Government Evening School of Higher Chinese Studies and use it as 'the nucleus of its Department of Extra-mural Studies'.[38] With the exception of the proposal for a Council for Adult Education, the Keswick Committee adopted most of Mellor's proposals and included them in the final report.[39]

The Keswick Committee submitted its report to the Governor of Hong Kong on 28 July 1952 and the report was tabled in the Legislative Council on 17 September 1952. The Committee was in general reluctant to recommend a significant extension of higher education to the local Chinese population. It felt that the academic standards of the University of Hong Kong needed to be safeguarded and, in order to achieve this aim, the Committee maintained that 'the standards of degree courses in Hong Kong should be closely related to English standards'.[40] Nevertheless, it recognised that:

> The development of Arts studies in Chinese would serve a valuable purpose in redressing a certain disbalance within the University; yet there is the attendant risk that the consequent increase in the number of students would reduce the value of the contribution which the University has to make to the corporate life of each student. We value very highly the part a residential university can play in fostering a sense of community service and in developing tolerance and human understanding. We want to see the University of Hong Kong extending its scope without in any way lowering the quality of its graduates.[41]

These statements implied that university education in Hong Kong should continue to be limited to a small number of students. Such a statement is not surprising given the educational background of the members of the Committee and the prevailing belief in elitist university education at that time both in Hong Kong and elsewhere around the world. Moreover, although some new degree courses in the medium of Chinese were being considered, the medium of instruction at Hong Kong University would continue to be English, thereby excluding the vast majority of school-leavers.

Despite its elitist views on university education, the Committee recognised the need to provide further education opportunities to secondary and post-secondary Chinese students, no matter whether they had lived in Hong Kong for a long time or had arrived in the colony more recently:

> It has always been the traditional policy of the British Government to give whatever help it could to political refugees, a policy which, though dictated in the first place by humanitarian motives, has nevertheless brought many material benefits in its train . . . Hong Kong must certainly accept responsibility for providing for these students in so far as it can do so without reducing the opportunities of its own students . . . If Hong Kong really believes in the value of education and in the importance of its role in the Far East, it will go beyond a bare minimum, and will adopt a positive policy to assist these students . . . They form a select group of intellectuals coming in the main from influential families, and it may be expected that their intellectual ability and advanced training will win for them influential positions. To neglect them would be to lack vision and to miss an opportunity to do what we know to be fundamentally right.[42]

The Committee also understood the fact that there was a large demand for post-secondary part-time courses among graduates of secondary schools and people already in full-time employment. This demand had arisen for a number of reasons. While many students hoped to equip themselves with professional or technical knowledge and skills, which might finally enable them to obtain a recognised diploma or degree, some students wanted to foster their general knowledge during their leisure time. The Committee observed that:

> The great demand for evening commercial courses of lower than university standard, in particular for courses in shorthand, book-keeping, and commercial English, is indicated by the 1,195 applicants last year [1951] for entry to the commercial classes run by the Government Evening Institute . . .
>
> Verbal evidence given before the Committee also confirmed the considerable demand from a variety of people already in employment for evening courses in Accountancy, Commerce and English. Many witnesses dwelt on the need for courses of university diploma standard, for courses to cover the examination syllabuses of established professional bodies, and for courses of somewhat lower standard such as could be given by a Technical College.[43]

There also appeared to be a demand for a greater variety of courses for girls, especially in nursing, secretarial work and domestic subjects; there was also a need for cultural courses, with keen interest being shown in language, literature, social studies, art, drama, and music:

> The breadth and intensity of the demand for higher education so far expressed is all the more striking because of the absence of facilities for study and the scarcity of organizations through which desires for self-improvement can be fostered. Nor is the Chinese community often vociferous in putting forward its claim. The evidence so far produced is therefore without doubt an under-statement of the true demand.[44]

Such huge demand for post-secondary education contrasted sharply with HKU's lack of involvement in education at the community level. While the Keswick Committee appreciated the corporate spirit within the University, it stated that the functions of a modern university should be 'to advance knowledge, to pass its knowledge to its students and to serve the community'.[45] Just as the Asquith Commission had stated seven years before, the Keswick Committee also emphasised the importance it attached to the idea that the University should serve the community by promoting a wider provision of post-secondary education through a department of extra-mural studies:

> It seems to us a natural development of its functions that a university foster the intellectual life of the community through a department of extra-mural studies, which could arrange part-time courses on a wide range of topics to meet popular demands. By doing this, the University could bring within its sphere of influence that very important group of people whose minds continue to be active long after their formal studies have been completed. And the traffic would be two-way, for the University would draw strength from such a close and continuous contact with the general public.[46]

The Committee was aware that opponents of adult education might use the spurious argument that Hong Kong was 'a cultural backwater', and that any demand for extra-mural courses 'would be limited and would not justify expenditure upon them', so it argued that such a view was unwarranted:

> There has been evidence in recent years of a very marked increase of interest in education generally and cultural studies especially. We have no doubt that the time is ripe for the opening of an Extra-mural Department [in the University].[47]

The Keswick Committee believed that the new department should not be just another institution offering evening courses, but that it should eventually emerge as a centre for the co-ordination and development of adult education in Hong Kong, a view which was in sympathy with Mellor's original suggestion:

> There is not only a need for additional courses, but also for an organization that can institute them and co-ordinate them with existing courses, advise the community on their comparative standards and values, and maintain contact with professional and technical examining bodies elsewhere in the Commonwealth.[48]

Perhaps it is not surprising that Keswick and his committee adopted such grand and far-reaching recommendations. Keswick had witnessed at first hand the disastrous imposition of Communist rule in Shanghai, and all the members were aware of both the flight of capital from the Mainland to Hong Kong and the massive influx of refugees. In this world turned upside-down, Hong Kong had the potential to become a major centre of both trade and education in East Asia.

It was probably because of this grand vision that the functions of the new department of extra-mural studies proposed by the Keswick Committee were more ambitious than those envisaged by the Asquith Commission. Both the Asquith Commission and the Keswick Committee realised the importance of a department of extra-mural studies to enable adults to develop intellectually and acquire knowledge after leaving school, but the Asquith Commission did not pay much attention to the qualifications to which these extra-mural courses led. In comparison, the Keswick Committee emphasised that most of the courses provided by the new department should lead to certificates, diplomas or other recognised qualifications. This stipulation was made necessary by the demand from potential students for qualifications which might help them in their efforts to secure better employment. Also, the lack of technical colleges and polytechnic institutes, which would otherwise have offered technical or professional courses, compelled the University to consider offering a form of extra-mural education which would cater for the public's need of technical and professional education, but on a temporary basis until other 'technical' institutions could be established or extended. As a result, the Committee recommended:

> . . . to include within the scope of the Extra-mural Department of the University a number of courses that would normally be provided at a Technical College or a Polytechnic Institute. We refer to courses in professional and commercial subjects leading, it may be, to a certificate or diploma or other recognized qualification, as an example of which we would suggest a course for the training of auditors of Chinese accounts . . . We assume that other institutions such as the Technical College will extend their scope and will gradually take over the courses temporarily provided by the University Extra-mural Department.[49]

There were, therefore, two thrusts to the Keswick proposal for a new department of extra-mural studies. On the one hand, the department would provide liberal and cultural courses. These included literature, music, and drama, as well as courses 'whose claims to be included in the University curriculum as full degree courses have not been firmly established', such as Fine Arts and Portuguese.[50] On the other hand, the department should also offer professional courses which would lead to a university certificate, diploma or other recognised qualifications in areas such as accountancy and journalism. There should also be some courses of 'university standard though limited in breadth and depth', which might be 'taken to a standard similar to that of the same subject in a pass degree course', such as English and Economics.[51]

The Keswick Committee had high hopes for the proposed department of extra-mural studies, and recommended that the government divert considerable resources to this new development. The Committee followed the recommendation in the Asquith Report that a 'fully staffed department of extra-mural studies should be regarded as one of the normal features of a Colonial university'.[52] The capital expenditure required to establish the department was not significant. The Committee recommended appointing a director of professorial status, an assistant director and two clerks. The new staff would require three offices but no other permanent accommodation because extra-mural classes could be given in existing classrooms on campus or in schools.[53] It should be noted that all departments at HKU were relatively small at this time, but Extra-Mural Studies was to be by far the smallest, so the financial burden of the proposal seems to have been kept to a minimum by Keswick and his fellow committee members.

The Committee's underlying commitment to extra-mural studies was, however, shown in the financial arrangements for the provision of courses and the lecturers' salaries. The Keswick Report suggested that:

> Most of the lecturers will be part-time staff who will be paid by the lecture or by the course. The salaries will be partly, but probably not entirely, met by the income from fees, and a subsidy will be necessary to meet this deficit and to pay the incidental charges incurred in planning and promoting the courses.[54]

The tentative annual subsidy for part-time staff salaries for the first year amounted to $30,000 while the total annual subsidy was set at $95,080. Although the proposed expenditure to be incurred by the department accounted for only a small percentage of the entire budget of the University, it was an impressive figure when compared with expenditure under other proposals in the Keswick Report.[55] The Keswick Committee also recommended absorbing into the new department the existing Evening School of Higher Chinese Studies. This recommendation was made mostly for practical reasons. It would be the best way to ensure that a high standard of studies was maintained, the diploma to be given would be a recognised University diploma, and the School was already housed in University premises.[56]

The Keswick Report of 1952 was the first official proposal to establish a department of extra-mural studies in the University of Hong Kong. It represented an attempt by the colonial government to put Hong Kong University at the centre of adult education in the colony and it succeeded in attracting some public support. For example, Dr S. N. Chau, a long-time champion of the University, made a sympathetic speech on extra-mural studies in the Legislative Council in March 1953.[57] However, the enthusiasm of the Keswick Committee to implement this ground-breaking idea did not elicit a corresponding welcome from the University, so the establishment of the Department of Extra-Mural Studies did not materialise until 1957.

The University's Responses to the Keswick Report

The University's responses to the concept of extra-mural studies as suggested in the Keswick Report of 1952 were varied. On the one hand, a few academic departments acknowledged the popular demand for extra-mural or evening courses and began to develop courses to meet the public need. On the other hand, some sectors of the University raised serious doubts about the wisdom of expending so much effort in providing education to the general public, and reservations surfaced about entering into commitments with outside examination bodies. The whole matter of extra-mural studies also became mixed up with other more political issues within the University, and therefore became a touchstone for wider changes which were being discussed at that time. It therefore took more than three years before the University came to a decision to set up the Department of Extra-Mural Studies.

Positive Reactions

Several members of the University responded positively to the idea of extra-mural studies. Bernard Mellor, who had proposed a department of extra-mural studies to the Keswick Committee in early 1952, was a firm supporter of implementing the Report's recommendations. A positive response also came from the Vice-Chancellor, Sir Lindsay Ride, soon after the release of the Report, even though he had many other development issues waiting to be resolved at the time. Although the Keswick Report was heavily concerned with the development of HKU, it was not officially forwarded to the University for consideration until 1 February 1955, more than two years after it had been submitted to the governor.[58] Nevertheless, Ride pre-empted the government by appointing a working party in the early months of 1953 'to advise him unofficially on matters in the Keswick Report affecting the University'.[59] The working party produced three reports, in which it agreed 'heartily' with the Keswick Committee's recommendation to create a department of extra-mural studies and for the new department to absorb the Evening School of Higher Chinese Studies.[60] There are strong indications that the Vice-Chancellor was keen to make an early start at addressing the various issues raised by the Keswick Report, including the establishment of a department of extra-mural studies.

Other positive responses came from the teaching departments of the University. Since its restoration in the late 1940s, the University had begun part-time or evening courses in several subjects. The University had even co-operated with the Government in running a course on trade unionism before the Keswick Report was submitted in 1952.[61] Faculties and departments also offered a number of evening courses to professionals and the general public, and from early 1953 to the end of 1956, at least twenty-four evening courses were approved by the Senate and Council.[62] Most of these were 'liberal' courses, such as language courses, or refresher courses for professionals, and were conducted in English. Apart from the course in trade unionism jointly organised by the University and the government, these courses were financially self-supporting.[63] The course fees were usually around $100–$150, much higher than the junior-level adult courses offered by the government.[64] The enrolment figures for these courses varied a great deal. A course in Spanish, for example, attracted twice as many applicants than the quota in 1953, while a course in French Literature and Language had to be cancelled in September 1955 because of low enrolment.[65]

The most fundamental change in the nature of extra-mural courses provided by the University was the introduction of evening courses in 'Accountancy and Secretarial Practice' in June 1955. This was the first programme to be introduced which would lead to the acquisition of a qualification granted by an external professional body. The programme was supervised by Professor E. S. Kirby and taught by lecturers of the Economics Department and other teaching units within the Faculty of Arts. The first seven-month course covered subjects in economics, book-keeping and accountancy, law and 'company secretarial practice'. The syllabus was designed to meet the professional expectations of the Intermediate Examination of the Association of Certified and Corporate Accountants (ACCA) and the

Chartered Institute of Secretaries (CIS).[66] Professor Kirby intended to provide courses for the corresponding Final Examination of these professional bodies and in future 'to broaden the coverage to take in some more of the professional and institutional examinations; extending especially, perhaps, into the field of Cost of Works Accounting, which is likely to be growing in importance and demand henceforward'.[67] The public response to the University's first courses in Accountancy and Secretarial Practice was impressive. It was reported in September 1955 that 'there were over five hundred applicants for these courses, of whom between thirty and forty would be selected for enrolment in each of the four courses'.[68] The increasing efforts of teaching departments in starting evening courses and their enthusiastic reception by the public indicate that parts of the University readily accepted the idea of extra-mural studies suggested by the Keswick Report.

Negative Reactions

These positive reactions were not, however, entirely representative of the University's response to the call for extra-mural studies in the years after the submission of the Keswick Report. In fact, there were several occasions on which the University showed doubts and reluctance in committing itself to the establishment of a department of extra-mural studies. Despite its readiness to provide extra-mural courses, the Faculty of Arts appeared to be unenthusiastic about formally establishing a department of extra-mural studies. The Faculty failed to give any priority to the creation of a department of extra-mural studies in its five-year development plan which was approved by the Faculty Board in September 1953.[69] It is difficult to account for the Faculty's lukewarm attitude towards the project, as some of the greatest supporters of the Department after it had been established were members of the Faculty of Arts. Perhaps there was a feeling that existing evening courses were working well and hence there was no need for a new department. Alternatively, there may have been a fear that the Faculty would lose these courses to a University-level department beyond its immediate control. Resources were almost certainly a worry too, with a common fear at the time among academics at HKU that any new development must necessarily mean a reduction in existing programmes.

The higher administration of the University also appeared to be less keen than the Keswick Committee with regard to establishing a department of extra-mural studies. The Vice-Chancellor and Registrar had in fact suffered an embarrassing setback after the visit in March–April 1953 of two Inter-University Council officials, Sir Alexander Carr-Saunders and Professor D. G. James, who had been invited to report on the progress of developments at HKU. Carr-Saunders and James were shocked by the 'urgent and difficult problems' faced by the University, and in their draft report of 10 July 1953 they were mildly critical of Ride and Mellor, particularly in their handling of financial matters.[70] While the visitors acknowledged that most of the problems facing the University were unavoidable, they were nevertheless firmly of the opinion that 'the University should aim at the proper housing, equipment and staffing of existing departments and should not venture into new fields until this has been accomplished'.[71] This seemed to rule out the implementation of Keswick's recommendations regarding extra-mural studies, and the Carr-Saunders James Report did not even mention the provision of extra-mural courses at the University.

The uncomfortable recommendations of Carr-Saunders and James were never formally published, but in August 1953, the Governor, Sir Alexander Grantham, set up a new committee to examine the problems facing HKU. He invited Sir Ivor Jennings, Vice-Chancellor of the University of Ceylon, and Mr D. W. Logan, Principal of the University of London, 'to examine and make recommendations on the constitution, function and financial requirements of the University in the light of the Cox and Mouat Jones/Adams Reports and any reports and developments since'.[72] Their report, known as the Jennings-Logan Report, was submitted to the Council and the Senate on 9 February and 2 March 1954 respectively. Although their primary objective was not to produce a detailed study of the Keswick Report, Jennings and Logan were nevertheless requested by the governor to comment on the earlier report. In the last paragraph of their report, Jennings and Logan therefore mentioned the provision of extra-mural courses in the University. They adopted a rather sceptical tone which reflected the main findings of Carr-Saunders and James:

> First, we doubt the wisdom of asking the University to undertake courses of a polytechnic character. The belief that universities can tackle any job that is handed over to them is a tribute to their efficiency, but our experience is that academic staff do not excel in matters outside their normal sphere. Secondly, we doubt if adequate space can be found in the University until a Library building is erected. Thirdly, this new Department would require considerable funds, not only to employ tutors, but also to provide equipment for art, music and the drama. . . . Finally, the long list of recommendations set out in [the Keswick Report] alone suggests a fear that the Department of Extra-Mural Studies would be asked to do too much too quickly. We suggest that it take over the General Arts courses at the Evening School of Higher Chinese Studies and then feel its way, within the limits of the available funds, towards further developments. We are strengthened in this view because some Departments of the University are already embarking on individual activities, which, if there were an Extra-Mural Department, could be more readily organized under its umbrella.[73]

The Jennings-Logan recommendation implied that, despite the overwhelming demand for adult education in the colony, there was no urgent need to expand the scale of the extra-mural courses in the University, nor was it practical for the

University to divert any of its scarce resources to facilitate the development of extra-mural studies. The writers of the report also felt that it would be dangerous for the University to absorb the commerce courses being run by the Evening School of Higher Chinese Studies. Taking over such courses would mean that the University might have to award certificates or diplomas to students in these courses even though they did not receive any formal instruction in the University. But hidden behind the findings of the Jennings-Logan Report was a concerted attempt by certain sections of the University to thwart any plans for a significant development in extra-mural studies before these plans had time to mature and gain widespread support. The University was at this time very short of funds and there was enormous competition for these resources among the four faculties. The University Treasurer had budgeted for a $1.1 million deficit in 1952–53, and a long-term shortfall of $650,000 per annum was predicted if new recurrent funds could not be found.[74] The financial climate was not therefore particularly conducive to new developments of this type.

The administration of the University was aware of the possible danger of an over-commitment to extra-mural courses which would lead to increased expenditure, but they were also worried about interference from external bodies in the academic standards of its courses. When the Council approved in principle the introduction of evening courses in Accountancy and Secretarial Practice on 17 March 1955, it noted clearly that 'the University should not at present commit itself to a firm policy on the question of its responsibility for organised Extra-mural courses leading to professional examinations run by outside bodies'.[75] The Senate also turned down extra-mural classes in English for members of the general staff in April 1955 because 'the present resources of the University were not equal to such a commitment'.[76] Despite a great deal of discussion within the University, by mid-1955 the Council and the Senate were still not eager to implement the recommendations of the Keswick Report regarding the provision of extensive extra-mural courses.

Establishment of the Department of Extra-Mural Studies

Preliminary Work

In spite of doubts by Jennings and Logan about the timing of developments in extra-mural studies, they did not actually oppose the establishment of a department. Discussions about a department of extra-mural studies therefore began soon after the release of the Jennings-Logan Report in early 1954. On 3 March 1954 the Senate considered the desirability of setting up committees, including an 'Entrance Control and Qualifications, University Examinations and Extra-mural Studies Committee'.[77] A working party was formed and eventually submitted its report to the Senate on 20 October 1954. While the report advised against forming the committee mentioned above, it nevertheless recommended that the Senate form an ad hoc committee to report on the place of extra-mural studies in the University.[78] The Senate approved this proposal and set up a Committee on Extra-Mural Studies chaired by Professor K. E. Priestley with a membership of three other Senate members.[79] The Committee on Extra-Mural Studies made its recommendations in a report to Senate in April 1955. The principal recommendations were that (1) a department of extra-mural studies be formed and a director appointed, (2) the director be given an assistant and a stenographer, and (3) existing evening courses offered by the University and the General Arts Course of the Evening School of Higher Chinese Studies be transferred to the department as soon as the director could be appointed.[80] The Senate and Council received and adopted the report at their meetings of 7 and 23 June 1955 respectively.[81]

During the same period, the Joint Establishments Committee of the University also considered requests from faculties and departments for additional teaching staff in the years from 1955 to 1957. Its report, submitted to the Senate on 4 January 1955, recommended that the post of Director of Extra-Mural Studies with the status of Professor 'should be instituted forthwith and attempts made to recruit to it by the summer of 1955'.[82] The Court finally resolved on 29 June 1955 that, pursuant to the Senate and Council recommendations, the directorship of Extra-Mural Studies should be established immediately.[83] Thus, the proposal to establish a department of extra-mural studies was put on hold while the search for a full-time director began in mid-1955.

The selection and appointment of a Director of Extra-Mural Studies did not proceed as smoothly as expected. The Vice-Chancellor at first recommended Mr R. L. Marshall and this recommendation was approved by the Council on 24 January 1956, but Marshall declined the offer.[84] The University later appointed Mr Gerald H. Moore to the post for an initial period of two years.[85] Before working in Hong Kong, Moore had taken part in extra-mural work for the University of London and had been a Resident Tutor at University College in Ibadan, British West Africa.[86] He arrived in Hong Kong on 28 October 1956 to take up the new post.[87] Moore was not however appointed at professorial level, so this immediately ensured that Extra-Mural Studies would have a lesser profile than other departments headed by a professor. The Department was also anomalous in that it was not put under one of the four faculties but was responsible directly to the Senate. Moreover, at this stage the establishment of the Department had not even been approved by the Council or the Court.

The 1955 report of the Committee on Extra-Mural Studies had proposed that the administrative work of the Department should be shared with an assistant to the director. It was expected that Mr J. H. Gransden, head of the University's Department of Modern Languages, would be seconded as Assistant to the Director during Moore's first year of office.[88] However, this plan was never realised and the administrative work of the Department had to be borne entirely by the Director himself and a secretary who was appointed on 1 January 1957.[89]

The second step in establishing the Department was to find suitable accommodation. The University was at that time chronically short of teaching and office space so it was difficult to spare any rooms for the new Department. Moore requested an office soon after he arrived in Hong Kong. Professor F. S. Drake, Dean of the Faculty of Arts, at first suggested that Moore could temporarily use a vacant room in the Department of English in the Main Building.[90] But this provisional arrangement did not solve the problem because there were no vacant rooms in the Main Building 'until the extension on the roof is completed, which can hardly be before the spring [of 1957]'.[91] The new extension was not however made available to the Department of Extra-Mural Studies because it had already been allocated to other staff members. Drake suggested asking the Department of Social Medicine to move from Room 102 in the south-east quadrangle of the Main Building to the Medical Research Building, so that the vacated rooms could be used as a permanent office for the Department of Extra-Mural Studies.[92] The Senate expressed its concern about this issue and asked the Vice-Chancellor to investigate the question further.[93] By January 1957, Moore and his clerk still had to be temporarily housed at Eliot Hall. This accommodation was described by the Senate as 'unsatisfactory, because of its temporary nature and its very poor access to outside visitors', hardly an appropriate home for a department which was intended to play such an important role in extending the University's work into the community.[94] It was to be some time before the Department would move into its more permanent home in the Main Building.

Moore's Memorandum of January 1957

Moore's work as Director of Extra-Mural Studies began soon after his arrival in Hong Kong in late October 1956. He submitted a memorandum on extra-mural studies to the Senate on 25 January 1957 aiming to 'give members of Senate an account of my immediate impression of the extra-mural field in Hong Kong, my comments on various recommendations which have been made in previous reports, and finally, my own recommendations as to the immediate measures that should be taken to develop extra-mural activity'.[95] This memorandum contained the first detailed plan for the administration, courses and finances of the new Department and indicates very clearly the quality of the appointee.

Moore's proposal appears to have been developed from the recommendations of the previous reports. While the Senate had already accepted the Committee Report of April 1955 and had determined to set up the Department of Extra-Mural

Studies, Moore further proposed the creation of a Board of Extra-Mural Studies (BEMS) as an intermediate body between the Department and the Senate. This was necessary because the new Department would not fall under the control of one of the four faculty boards in the same way that all other departments did. The BEMS was therefore similar to the boards of the faculties and the Board of Social Study. The Board's intended function, under powers delegated by the Senate, was to 'overlook the whole work of the Department and to improve in detail the proposals of the Director. This will both relieve Senate of an unnecessary burden and enable the Director to get ahead with urgent arrangements for courses, etc'.[96] It was also recommended that the Department be provided with a clerk (who had already been appointed) and an assistant to the Director.

The absorption of the Evening School of Higher Chinese Studies was the first major problem which Moore faced in the administration of the new Department. There were divergent opinions expressed in the Keswick and Jennings-Logan reports about the extent of absorption which was desirable. The Keswick Report supported a full-scale take-over of the Evening School while the Jennings-Logan Report recommended absorbing its general arts courses only. Moore did not think that the separation of arts and commerce courses between his department and the Evening School was beneficial to the University:

> It seems to me that there would be no advantage whatever in the University's taking over the General Arts courses only. Such an arrangement would merely bisect something which is already working as a unit: it would be administratively clumsy, and academically it might be taken to imply a denigration of the Commerce course which could only be resented among tutors and students in that group. The Technical College has neither the means nor the ambition to tackle commercial courses of this nature at present. Furthermore, I submit that the teaching of commercial subjects at a sufficiently high level is a legitimate activity for a University, whether intra-murally or extra-murally. Such education is really no more 'vocational' than the training of doctors, teachers, architects, or engineers. The University should either take over the whole Evening School or leave matters as they are.[97]

He further supported transferring the Evening School to the Department because:

> It would provide the new Department with a substantial volume of higher education in Chinese which is already established and already well-known in Hong Kong. A certain amount of accumulated public good-will would go with the transfer and this could only benefit the public relations of the University and of the Department. From an academic point of view, the quality and status of the School's diploma (which the University might wish to reclassify as a Certificate) would benefit greatly from the control and recognition of the University.[98]

Moore also insisted that the absorbed Evening School should retain its character, 'which is that of an institution offering higher education as far as possible in the medium of Chinese. This legitimate and serious need would not be met if the emphasis upon proficiency in English were greatly increased, either in the admission or tuition of students'.[99] He recommended that, instead of taking over only the general arts courses, the whole Evening School should be transferred to the Department with effect from 1 July 1957.[100]

The arrangement of courses was another important aspect of Moore's memorandum. At the time when Moore came into post, the University provided evening courses in Accountancy and Secretarial Practice, education, and languages. The Committee on Extra-Mural Studies suggested in 1955 that these part-time courses be brought under the umbrella of the Department of Extra-Mural Studies. Moore did not see much advantage in taking over courses which had been operated efficiently by other departments. He therefore recommended leaving the existing courses in education and Chinese language where they were.[101] In spite of his recommendation to transfer courses in Accountancy and Secretarial Practice from the Department of Economics and Political Science to his own Department from the 1957–58 academic year, Moore suggested that the University should not make any future commitment to these commercial courses 'so that the way is still open for the University to transfer these courses to another body (such as a Polytechnic or Higher Commercial College), should the opportunity arise in future'.[102] This is a rather surprising recommendation considering the popularity of these courses, but it perhaps indicates that the commercial courses were at that time not considered to be quite right for a university to offer, even under the umbrella of extra-mural studies. It also seems that there was a real expectation that other post-secondary institutions would soon be established in Hong Kong.

While Moore did not wish to take over all the existing part-time courses, he recommended that in future all extra-mural courses would be 'conducted under the auspices of the Department of Extra-Mural Studies (and of the Board of Extra-Mural Studies if it is set up), in full co-operation with the interested Departments of the University, the Government and other bodies. Administrative responsibility will then rest squarely with my Department'.[103] He proposed that experimental extra-mural courses should be provided along the following lines:

(i) 3 year Tutorial Classes following a consecutive course in one subject, with twenty-four meetings in each year (e.g. Portuguese Language, Economic Geography of the Far East, Nuclear Physics, Higher Mathematics, Chinese Art and Architecture, Western Music, The Novel since 1870);
(ii) Sessional Classes of twenty-four meetings occupying one academic year (subjects similar to (i) but less ambitious in scope);
(iii) Short or Terminal Classes of six to twelve meetings, some of them of a specialised type (e.g. a course for Art Teachers in Matriculation classes);

(iv) Short Summer Schools of an intensive character, lasting from five to ten days with several meetings each day, visits, field and practical work, etc. These would take place normally in the Summer or Easter vacations.[104]

Moore expected that a great variety of courses would be offered by the Department in the future. The Department would not only provide courses which would lead to recognised qualifications, but also 'liberal' courses for self-improvement. Moore accepted the recommendation of the Keswick Report that there should be two broad types of courses in the new Department, one type aiming at providing professional training, and the other to provide a more cultural and 'liberal' education. He stated clearly in the memorandum that 'it is my desire to provide as many such "liberal" courses as possible, in order to counter-balance the number of more utilitarian courses which the Department will also be requested to run'.[105] This initial concern for balance remains at the core of HKU SPACE's educational philosophy today, with programmes ranging from 'short courses for personal development', through professional and diploma courses, all the way up to degree and postgraduate programmes. Moore also expressed his particular concern with the language used in the courses. As the Department was set up for improving the provision of general higher educational opportunities in Hong Kong, he made it clear that some courses, depending on the public demand and the enrolment, should be conducted in Cantonese or Mandarin.[106]

The financing of extra-mural courses was Moore's other main concern. In comparison with the Keswick Report's recommendation of an annual budget of $95,080 including an allowance of $30,000 for the salaries of part-time lecturers, Moore's expectation of the University's financial commitment to extra-mural studies was much less ambitious. He thought that liberal courses should not be run on a profit-making basis and that the University should contribute a large share of teaching costs of these courses as an 'important social service'.[107] He noted that in Britain the Ministry of Education bore about three-quarters of the teaching costs for these extra-mural courses.[108] He recommended that the liberal courses should have a registration fee of no more than $6 per course and a further charge of $1 per meeting. The annual fee paid by a student in a one-year 24-session class would therefore be $30, which was considerably lower than the fees previously charged for evening courses.[109] Even so, Moore expected that the total cost of 180 teaching hours in these liberal courses would remain at $9,000. This sum could be recovered partly from fee income, varying from $2,150 to $5,400 per course depending on the enrolment in individual courses.[110] Expenditure on these extra-mural courses was therefore to be much lower than envisaged in the Keswick Report.

The financial position of the Accountancy and Secretarial Practice courses and the courses offered by the Evening School of Higher Chinese Studies were even better. Moore assumed an annual profit of $4,000 to $5,000 arising from the commerce courses previously offered by the Economics Department.[111] The original deficit of $33,745 from the Evening School could also be balanced by a reduction of the teaching hours without affecting academic standards. These figures showed that the courses might even be expected to bring in a surplus and thus help reduce the overall financial burden of the Department.[112] It is with this suggestion that we see the genesis of the University's later policy of ensuring that both the DEMS and SPACE were profit-generating activities rather than a drain on University resources.

Formal Establishment of the Department of Extra-Mural Studies

Moore's memorandum on extra-mural studies provided a feasible plan to initiate the work of the Department. The memorandum did not face any significant challenges when it was submitted to the Senate on 5 February 1957. While the Senate noted that there were many points of detail which would require consideration later, it recommended that virtually all of Moore's suggestions be sent to Council for approval. These included:

1. The establishment by the Senate of a Board of Extra-Mural Studies, with a constitution and terms of reference to be decided by the Senate.
2. The formal institution of a Department of Extra-Mural Studies.
3. The transference of the Evening School of Higher Chinese Studies to the Department of Extra-Mural Studies as from July 1, 1957.
4. The experimental provision of 3-Year Tutorial, 1-Year Sessional, Terminal and Short Courses and Summer Schools.
5. Chinese and English to be considered equally as possible languages of instruction for extra-mural classes.
6. The registration of all students.[113]

Senate's approval was followed by a Council resolution on 21 February 1957 authorising the Senate to 'establish a Board of Extra-Mural Studies, with a constitution and terms of reference to be decided by the Senate', and requesting the Court to institute a Department of Extra-Mural Studies.[114] The Council also referred 'various other recommendations concerning Extra-Mural Studies to the new Board for detailed consideration'.[115]

At its meeting on 3 March 1957, the Senate resolved that a Board of Extra-Mural Studies be established under the Senate. The functions of the Board were set out in its terms of reference:

> Subject to the provisions of the Ordinance and the Statutes,
> (a) to advise the Senate on any question relating to higher adult education, [and]
> (b) to do all such other acts and things which may be requisite to perform any duty which the Senate may delegate to it.[116]

Interestingly, at this stage the Senate did not delegate any specific powers to the Board, but simply made provision for future delegation. The Senate later confirmed the membership of the Board. Its chairman was to be the Director of Extra-Mural Studies and its secretary was the Registrar, Mr Bernard Mellor. The Vice-Chancellor (Sir Lindsay Ride) and Librarian (Mrs Dorothea Scott) were members, there were two representatives from the Senate (Professors K. E. Priestley and F. S. Drake), and two members drawn from the community (the Hon. Kwok Chan, OBE, JP, and Mrs Ellen Li Shu-pui). The Director of Education was represented by Mr W. J. Dyer.[117] The Board of Extra-Mural Studies therefore included representatives of all the principal stakeholders, both from within and outside the University, and created a model which is still in use fifty years later. HKU SPACE's activities are currently governed and advised by three boards with balanced memberships reflecting University, School, and community stakeholders: a Board of Directors with thirteen members, a Board for Continuing and Professional Education and Lifelong Learning with thirteen members, and the School Advisory Board with twenty-one members.

The final step towards the formal institution of the Department of Extra-Mural Studies was gaining the Court's approval. At its meeting on 21 May 1957, the Court 'CONSIDERED a recommendation of the Senate and Council and, on the motion of the Vice-Chancellor seconded by Professor K.E. Priestley, RESOLVED that a Department of Extra-Mural Studies be instituted'.[118] The first meeting of the Board of Extra-Mural Studies was held on 22 May 1957, the day after the Court had approved the formation of the Department.[119] This represented the official start of the work of the Department within the University of Hong Kong. The Vice-Chancellor, one of the members of the Board, delivered a congratulatory message to the Director highlighting the significance of the new-born Department:

> Your Department [of Extra-Mural Studies], which was instituted by the Court yesterday, is the most important of all our departments as far as public relations are concerned. Planned aright and if given full scope, your work will touch every section of the community, every stratum of our society; it is the most important means of explaining or making available to the masses the knowledge accumulated by the few.[120]

The Vice-Chancellor's message illustrated clearly that a golden opportunity existed for the Department of Extra-Mural Studies to act as a vital link between the University and the community from the first day of its existence. The degree to which this fond hope of Sir Lindsay Ride would be achieved in the next fifty years could not be predicted in 1957, but as the subsequent history of the Department and HKU SPACE has shown, his words proved to be prophetic.

Conclusion

The arrival of Gerald Moore on 28 October 1956 and the institution of the Department of Extra-Mural Studies on 21 May 1957 symbolised the formal commencement of extra-mural studies within the University of Hong Kong. It is beyond dispute that the Department started on a very humble scale: one director and one secretary settling into a room in the remote fastness of Elliot Hall. It was arguably the smallest department in the University at that time and would continue for many years to be understaffed and underfunded. The Department probably inherited nothing from the University's tradition of external studies before the War, except perhaps a belief that non-matriculated students of any variety were inferior to 'proper' undergraduate students. The University continued to accept external students throughout the period in which its extra-mural courses were being established. However, the formation of the Department in 1957 reflected the convergence of several important phenomena underlying the changing role of the University in Hong Kong society. HKU followed the general post-War policy of higher education in British colonies in responding to the society's need for higher adult education. The colonial government, the University and the community at large recognised that a university was no longer entirely an 'ivory tower' for academics and a privileged class of students alone, but it was also an institution which could and should transfer knowledge to the wider population, and foster the intellectual and cultural life of the general public. It was also recognised that the public had a role to play in governing the activities of the Department and in shaping the University's policies on adult education, roles which were to be reinforced and expanded as the years went by. Despite the fact that the development strategies and teaching modes of the Department have changed considerably over time, and the scale and range of its provision of adult educational opportunities have expanded far beyond the original vision of Sir Lindsay Ride and Gerald Moore, the Department's mission to serve the community has remained largely unchanged fifty years later under the University's School of Professional and Continuing Education.

CHAPTER THREE

Early Years in the Department of Extra-Mural Studies, 1957–1965

THE YEARS BETWEEN 1957 AND 1965 were a crucial period for the development of the Department of Extra-Mural Studies (DEMS). The newborn department, small and poorly equipped, now took complete charge of extra-mural courses at the University. In spite of the considerable demand for adult higher education in Hong Kong, the concept of 'extra-mural studies' was still new to society, and especially to many in the University. The University had previously concentrated its attention on internal students and often perceived extra-mural studies as a secondary, marginal, insignificant, or even irrelevant activity. One consequence of this ambivalence was that the DEMS had to fight hard to get the recognition and resources it needed from the University in order to establish itself in the way that it wished. The Directors of Extra-Mural Studies, initially Mr Gerald Moore (1956–60) and later Mr Ieuan Hughes (1960–67) had to start from almost nothing and faced a number of academic, administrative and financial problems from the inception of the Department. Their leadership in developing policies to deal with the twin problems of increasing student demand and severely limited resources was a key factor in the rapid development of the DEMS within such a short period.

Administration of the Department — Setbacks and Development

Evening School of Higher Chinese Studies

The first important step in establishing the Department was to absorb the Evening School of Higher Chinese Studies as proposed in previous reports and memoranda. Negotiations between the University and the government were initiated during the first year of operation of the DEMS, but the transfer of the Evening School was ultimately not realised because of disagreements between the two sides over financial arrangements and the declining significance of the Evening School in adult higher education. The University had already invited the government in late March 1957 to discuss the possibility of transferring the Evening School. At that time the Evening School was composed of General Arts and Commerce sections, but had a relatively small enrolment of students.[1] The Board of Extra-Mural Studies (BEMS) decided at its first meeting on 22 May 1957 to set up a sub-committee to come up with recommendations within six months as to whether the University should enter into formal negotiations with the government, and, if absorption of the Evening School was recommended, to suggest operational arrangements for the transfer.[2] The sub-committee, which included members of the BEMS, University academics, and a government official from the Education Department, held two meetings and invited Professor F. S. Drake and Mr E. F. Szczepanik to prepare memoranda on the General Arts Section and the Commerce courses of the Evening School.[3] The sub-committee was not, however, able to reach any firm decisions within the scheduled six-month period, and the Board had to ask the Director to give his own views.[4]

On the basis of a memorandum prepared by Professor Drake, the Director submitted his proposal on the transfer of the Evening School on 2 December 1957. He proposed that the whole Evening School be transferred to the Department of Extra-Mural Studies with a new name — The Evening School of Arts and Commerce — from 1 July 1958. There were to be no major changes to the character, organisation, syllabus, entry standards, length of terms and fees during the first three years after the takeover, but the remuneration of Evening School teachers would be increased from the standard $25 per hour fee to a new scale of fees ranging from $25 to $50 per hour, reflecting the pay-rates of extra-mural tutors. When the students finished their studies in the Evening School, they would be given certificates issued by the 'Evening School of Arts and Commerce, University of Hong Kong'.[5] The Senate and the Council approved Moore's proposal in February 1958, subject to the necessary financial arrangements being completed.[6]

The proposal for HKU to absorb the Evening School at first found favour both with the community and the government. It was reported in the Chinese press that, in both educational circles and among students, it was anticipated that the academic status of the Evening School would be greatly enhanced and that everyone 'looked at this issue very seriously, and hoped for an early merger'.[7] In May 1958, the government agreed in principle to transfer the Evening School to the University from 1 July 1958 for an experimental period of three years.[8] Unfortunately, the negotiations between the University and the government reached a deadlock in subsequent months. There was serious disagreement over the proposed level of government subsidies to the Evening School after the transfer. The University expected that it would recover from the government the entire recurrent deficit of the Evening School by means of a subvention of $70,000 per annum.[9] This amount exceeded the Evening School's existing annual deficit of $40,000 because the University claimed that many of the expenses associated with the Evening School's activities had not been included in past financial statements.[10] The University's proposal for an increase in salaries also implied additional expenditure, estimated by a government official at around $80,000 per annum.[11] The government did not agree with the University's estimate and was only willing to offer an annual subsidy of $40,000 for the Evening School's continuing operation under HKU supervision.[12] The government's offer was further lowered to $30,000 per annum in June 1958 when the Evening School decided to phase out its commerce courses from the next academic year.[13] The divergence of opinion on the financial arrangements prevented both sides from realising the transfer of the Evening School on the scheduled date of 1 July 1958.

Behind the financial disagreements there was an even more compelling reason for the failure of these drawn-out negotiations between the University and the government. The position of the Evening School in 1958–59 was in many ways inferior to the situation which existed when the Keswick Committee reported its findings in 1952. The development of various post-secondary colleges, the Technical College and HKU's own extra-mural courses provided many more options than had previously been available for secondary graduates who wanted to further their studies without matriculating to the University. The diploma qualification awarded by the government's Evening School was also of comparatively low value for career progression.[14] The enrolment at the Evening School dropped from 344 in September 1955 to 125 in June 1959, and the attrition rate among first-year students was astonishingly high.[15] Two of the three sections of the Evening School had already been cut because of poor enrolment, and the School ran a deficit of $40,000 in 1956–57 in contrast to a surplus of $11,000 five years earlier.[16] The sharp divergence between the initial success of the extra-mural courses of the Department and the decline of the Evening School led Gerald Moore to conclude in May 1959 that 'the time has gone when the University might usefully have taken over the School'.[17] The Board of Extra-Mural Studies finally confirmed the termination of negotiations with the government in December 1959.[18] The University continued to allow the Evening School to use its classrooms until July 1965, but from that time the Department of Extra-Mural Studies requisitioned all HKU classrooms in the evenings.[19]

The Status of the Department of Extra-Mural Studies in the University

The failure to transfer the Evening School was just one of the setbacks which the Department faced during its early development. More worrying was the fact that the Director found it extremely difficult during the first few years to gain proper recognition within the University for the work achieved by his Department. There were worries in the Senate about academic standards but the most obvious manifestation of the poor standing of the Department could be seen in resource allocation. The fundamental problem was constitutional in nature. Throughout the first two years of its operation, the DEMS was locked in a heated dispute with the University over its refusal to grant the Department the status of a 'Teaching Department' and its Director the status of a 'Teacher'. The Director was consequently excluded from membership of the Senate, which meant that he could have no say in the academic governance of the University. This policy was at odds with the normal practice in the United Kingdom and continued to be a sore point at HKU until the policy was changed in 1960. The problem had not arisen when the Department was first instituted in May 1957 because 'Teaching Departments' and 'Teachers' were not well-defined in the Statutes at that time. The University had in fact stated that the Director would be a member of the Senate when it advertised the post in early 1956, and it was also expected that the Director would be appointed with the status of a professor.[20]

The new University Ordinance of 1958, which was making its way through Senate and Council at the same time as the proposal to establish the Department of Extra-Mural Studies, introduced a very strict definition of 'Teaching Departments' and 'Teachers' which is still in force in 2007. 'Teaching Departments' were defined as the teaching units under the faculties, and 'Teachers' were the academics who worked within these Teaching Departments. The Department of Extra-Mural Studies and its Director, who came under the Senate's supervision through the Board of Extra-Mural Studies, were excluded from holding either status. These exclusions would have significant implications for the representation of the Department at Senate meetings because the Director was not entitled to a seat in Senate. This created an impression that the University did not regard the Department and its Director as genuine academic members of the University because they did not teach matriculated university students. Gerald Moore was very discontented with this provision and protested in October 1958:

> It is a little hard to understand why my department should not be classed as a teaching department, since the whole purpose and function of it is to teach. To that end I employ thirty or forty tutors (many of them non-members of the University staff) and enrol several hundreds of students in a wide range of subjects. Some of these subjects are not professed by the University at all, and the whole initiative for launching them has to come from me . . . The planning and conducting of the whole extra-mural programme is thus an academic — not purely an administrative — function.[21]

Moore's own role as Chairman of the Board of Extra-Mural Studies, which was responsible to Senate in much the same way as the faculty boards were, made his position:

> . . . a little invidious when I am not even a member of the parent body . . . It is customary for Directors of Extra-Mural Studies at British Universities to be members of Senate. A 'spot check' of University Calendars had confirmed this fact. The principle has therefore been fought and settled on other battle grounds.[22]

Sir Lindsay Ride, the Vice-Chancellor, turned down Moore's request discreetly. He denied in his reply on 12 February 1959 that Moore's terms of service included a seat on the Senate because Moore was not an applicant for the directorship in 1956, nor was he appointed under the original terms of that advertisement. Furthermore, Professor Ride suggested that Moore was not eligible to be a Teacher for the following reason:

> I think you will find there is a strong feeling that 'Teachers' means *those teaching degree courses*; and by this reading the same restriction would apply to the meaning of 'Teaching Department' . . . I do not want to be discouraging, and I do not pretend that in this letter I have exhausted all argument on the subject, but I do think that at present there are very real difficulties in the way of your becoming a member of Senate, and I would not advise you to press the question just now.[23]

Moore found the Vice Chancellor's reply 'extremely discouraging' and it is not difficult to sympathise with the predicament in which the Director found himself. The University's position seemed to be based on administrative obstinacy and was clearly out of step with developments in Britain. Besides insisting that he was appointed under the original terms of advertisement, Moore protested against the University's demeaning attitude towards him and his Department:

> As the first Director of Extra-Mural Studies, I feel it is up to me to win a position of respect for my department within the University. Its continued exclusion from Senate cannot fail to create the impression that it is something of a 'poor relation' which must be kept at arm's length academically. The fact remains that my whole work is teaching — and teaching for which Senate is ultimately responsible. In this respect my position is quite different from that of other departments not represented on Senate. Yet I am not seated there to explain my policies or hear them debated.[24]

The Vice-Chancellor's denial that Moore had been appointed according to the original terms of the recruitment advertisement also implied that his career prospects in the University were dim. He complained to the Vice-Chancellor that he found himself 'without prospects either of promotion beyond Senior Lecturer or of admission to Senate'.[25] This situation did not bode well for the future of the department nor for the more general acceptance of extra-mural studies as a mainstream educational activity within the University.

When the Senate discussed this issue at its meeting on 2 June 1959, the senior administrators of the University still maintained their views. The Registrar, Bernard

Mellor, suggested that there were common characteristics which Teaching Departments shared with each other, such as 'a curriculum leading to a University qualification controlled by Senate regulations' and 'students matriculated under authority delegated by the Senate, for the purpose of admission to follow the curriculum'.[26] This was a very clear restatement of the philosophy which had been adopted from the earliest years of HKU's existence, when only matriculated students were given full membership of the institution and 'external students' were tolerated but given very little status or respect. Mellor went even further, however, and declared that the position of the University on this issue had hardened somewhat because of the recent statutory changes:

> Mr. Moore asks the question, in his letter of April 4 [1959]: 'does this mean that the University has now changed its policy?' The answer must be 'yes', insofar as there is a new Ordinance which, along with other major changes, defines more closely the organization and functions of the University and its statutory bodies.[27]

Mr. Mellor was perhaps wrong in this assertion. While it is true that the new Ordinance had brought about a great many changes, it did not alter the traditional view taken by the University with regard to non-matriculated students. What was new, of course, was the idea that the teachers of non-matriculated students should have a lesser status than other lecturers in the University. This problem had not arisen before the formation of the DEMS because non-matriculated students had always been taught together with matriculated students by the University's professors and lecturers.

Despite Moore's strong protest, the Senate still rejected his application for the Department to be recognised as a Teaching Department and the Director a member of the Senate.[28] The Senate's decision had a detrimental effect on the newborn Department. Moore resigned from the University and left in January 1960 to direct extra-mural studies for Makerere University College in East Africa.[29] Although there is no clear evidence to link Moore's departure with the arguments of 1958–59, it is obvious from his correspondence with the Vice-Chancellor and comments from his former colleagues that he was not satisfied with the University's policies on extra-mural studies.[30] Moore's resignation did, however, bring about a change in university policy. By the time the University began to advertise for Moore's successor in January 1960, a decision had been taken to make the Director of Extra-Mural Studies a member of the Senate in accordance with common British university practice.[31] However, the academic status of the Director was still unclear, until the Development and General Purposes Committee confirmed in June 1969 that the Director of Extra-Mural Studies was in future to be accorded the status of a Teacher under the Statutes.[32]

The inferior status of the extra-mural branch of the University's activities was also illustrated well in the Board of Extra-Mural Studies. The original objective of the Board was to 'approve policy and programmes' with powers delegated by the Senate.[33] However, it soon emerged that in practice the Board was to be an advisory rather than decision-making body, and its terms of reference defined its role as being to advise the Senate on adult education affairs. The Senate refused the Board's request for delegation of powers to approve individual courses, even when such approvals were in line with previously established policies regarding fees and other course arrangements, or in case of emergency.[34] This policy was upheld for the first four years of the Department's operation and was not finally revoked until April 1961. This perhaps indicated that the Senate did not wish to delegate too much power to a Board which was experimental in nature, chaired by a non-Teacher, and which included in its membership non-University people. The impact of this policy in the first few years was to reduce the flexibility of the Department in organising courses to meet public demand.[35]

The status of extra-mural students in the University was also very low. Although extra-mural students were required to register for enrolment and attend classes regularly, they were not really considered to be proper students of the University. This practice is perhaps understandable because extra-mural students were neither full-time nor were they attempting to acquire university qualifications and, as was explained in the previous chapter, the University had long discriminated against non-matriculated students. What is less easy to explain is the University's reluctance to allow extra-mural students to use facilities which were necessary for effective study. Extra-mural students became eligible to apply for readers' tickets to use the University Library during the 1958–59 academic year, but they were not allowed to borrow books until after 1963.[36] The Department had to gain financial support from outside bodies and the Library Fund of the University in order to establish its own book-box system for extra-mural students. This problem with library facilities illustrates very clearly the University's inadequate commitment to extra-mural students. The argument was made that University resources were scarce and should be used first and foremost for matriculated undergraduate students, but the restrictions enforced by HKU were certainly not in keeping with policies adopted in British universities at the same time.

Staff

The Department had to contend with a shortage of staff throughout its early years of development, and in many cases staff shortages posed the major obstacle to any expansion in extra-mural activities. The Department was initially established with a Director, an Assistant to the Director, and a clerk. The post of Assistant to the Director was not filled until the appointment of Mr T. C. Lai, a part-time English tutor in the Department, in November 1958.[37] The University was satisfied with this three-man team and it did not attempt to increase the Department's staffing levels until a review of University development in 1957–58. The Department soon found that the University's expectations of what could be achieved by such a small unit were far too optimistic, however, and calls for more staff were soon heard.[38] The Director and his Assistant formulated extra-mural policy, communicated with part-time tutors, prepared programme booklets and co-ordinated enrolment, as well as having to deal with all other administrative matters. It soon became clear that the small complement of staff directly affected the quality of the activities of the Department. Moreover, there were some questions raised as to the Director's ability to lead the unit effectively. A government official commented that Moore was 'a very woolly man' and unlikely to be able to organise courses properly with so few staff to assist him.[39] The expanding workload soon proved that there was an urgent need to increase the staff of the Department.

The staff problem was aggravated by frequent changes of personnel during the early days. Moore left the University after just three and a half years' service in January 1960. The administration of the Department had to be carried on by T. C. Lai for about ten months until the new Director, Mr. Ieuan W. Hughes, arrived in November 1960.[40] Educated in Law at the University College of Wales, Hughes had taught extra-mural courses in the University of Manchester for nine years. He had also served for three years as tutor to the Rochdale 'Economic Class', the first of the 'tutorial classes' to be established in Britain under R. H. Tawney in 1908. He was therefore a very strong advocate of the post-War movement to extend the provision of extra-mural studies in British colonial universities, and was seconded to East Africa to be the only extra-mural tutor in Makerere College in Kenya between 1955 and 1960.[41] His arrival in Hong Kong did not solve the staffing crisis in the Department. T. C. Lai decided to take study leave in Manchester for one year from September 1961 and Hughes was left to co-ordinate the work of the Department on his own. It was difficult to lay solid foundations for extra-mural studies when staffing was so unstable.

Hughes was determined to develop the extra-mural activities of the University and strove for an expansion of the Department's staff establishment throughout his tenure of the directorship. Within weeks of arriving in Hong Kong, Hughes delivered a 'University lecture' in which he outlined his policy for the Department. This policy statement, which was subsequently published as a supplement to the *University of Hong Kong Gazette*, the official publication of the University, set out clearly the ways in which Hong Kong needed to respond to the worldwide call for adult education to be accepted as a normal part of educational provision in every country.[42] Hughes was very much a man of his time, with a social conscience which reflected advances in government policy and educational theory in the United Kingdom after the War. In Britain, adult education was the financial responsibility of the state, but Hughes realised that things were different in the colony of Hong Kong. A certain amount of educational and social propaganda would have to be deployed in order to create a sympathetic environment for measures which were commonplace in Britain. His main concern was with staff. He believed that an effective department of extra-mural studies had to be staffed by a combination of resident and staff tutors. Resident tutors were those responsible for extra-mural studies in particular geographical areas. Hughes defined a resident tutor in the context of his experiences in England and East Africa as:

> . . . the antenna of the department and should live and work in the area he serves, thus being part of the community and at the same time a sort of built-in adult education Geiger counter. He must get to know the people thoroughly, their needs and their wants. He must therefore be sympathetic, perceptive, and approachable. He should maintain a close constructive contact with the educational, cultural, and social institutions and groups within his area and with commercial and industrial undertakings, at all levels. He must learn to divert to the appropriate quarter those needs and demands which do not fall within the province of a university and be ready with further help if required. Occasionally, he may have to assist in the formation of a new organization to fill an exposed gap. His main work however must be to pioneer, establish, and maintain extra-mural classes. This includes not only bringing potential students together and welding them into a group, but also finding suitable tutors, meeting places, *etc.*[43]

While residential tutors divided their work into geographical regions, staff tutors would oversee extra-mural courses within their own particular subject areas across the whole region. Hughes defined the work of a staff tutor as being:

> . . . to organize and teach subjects for which there is a particular local need . . . The staff tutor should also maintain close constructive contact with all interested in his field, develop extra-mural teaching (by helping both tutors and classes) in his subject, and be constantly alert for new and improved ways of making the university's contribution. He should also be able to conduct and/or organize research and produce (or ensure the production of) books, papers, and pamphlets that would help the study and teaching of his subject.[44]

Hughes felt that 'a corps of resident and staff tutors' was indispensable in establishing a thriving extra-mural studies culture in Hong Kong. Together they were 'the tools to do a vital and urgent job' and inasmuch as extra-mural studies could be defined as a 'social service', any delay in advancing the cause would lead to the suffering of those who were being deprived of the adult education opportunities that society should be providing for them. Hughes felt that of extra-mural education 'it may truly be said that nowhere in the whole field of education can so much be done for so many for so little'.[45] This was a message which he returned to time and again during his directorship. In 1965 he told his students:

> Adult Education must not be regarded as a luxury for a few exceptional persons here and there, nor as a thing which concerns only a short span of early manhood, but that adult education is a permanent national necessity, an inseparable aspect of citizenship, and therefore should be both universal and lifelong. The opportunity for adult education should be spread uniformly and systematically over the whole community, as a primary obligation on that community in its own interest and as a chief part of its duty to its individual members.[46]

The challenge was to convert these high ideals developed during a career devoted to adult education in England and East Africa into a practical plan for Hong Kong.

Hughes drew up a proposal for staff expansion based on these ideas soon after he assumed office in November 1960. He finished and submitted the plan to the Board of Extra-Mural Studies in March 1961. He proposed that the University should immediately provide one resident tutor who would be responsible for extra-mural courses in Kowloon. By the academic year 1965–66, there should be three resident tutors supervising courses on Hong Kong Island, Kowloon and the New Territories as well as two staff tutors specialising in various subjects.[47] Hughes anticipated that residential tutors would be appointed locally. They should be able to speak Cantonese and Mandarin in order to be able to communicate directly with members of the community. Before making their appointment permanent, residential tutors should get 'practical experience of the work, its possibilities and problems' in the first year of work, study in an adult education training course in the second year, and apply these experiences to their work in the third year.[48] Staff tutors would not necessarily be local appointees in these early days due to a lack of experienced staff in Hong Kong, so he 'would welcome the possibility of experienced specialist adult tutors coming here on loan or secondment'.[49] The Board agreed to Hughes's proposal, commenting that the DEMS was 'severely handicapped' in having no full-time tutors, and that the Department might have to reduce its activities in the next few years if it could not soon appoint more permanent staff.[50] The Senate and the Council agreed with these sentiments and supported Hughes's expansion proposal in April 1961.[51]

Although the University agreed to upgrade the Director's salary from the senior lecturer scale to the professorial scale and had added two clerical staff to the Department's establishment by 1962, any substantial expansion of staff could not be implemented without additional financial support.[52] The University had not taken account of the need for more staff in the DEMS within its Seven Year Plan for 1959–66, and this meant that it had no funding to employ new full-time tutors for the Department. The University managed to secure a grant of $48,450 from the Asia Foundation in October 1961 to sponsor the appointment of the Department's first staff tutor for one academic year and Miss Priscilla Mark (Mrs Priscilla Tso) was appointed under this scheme in the 1962–63 academic year.[53] The Foundation, however, stated clearly that it would not finance such an appointment thereafter and that the post would ultimately have to be funded by the government.[54] The government's financial commitment to extra-mural tutors was therefore crucial for the future development of the DEMS.

The government initially had no consistent policy on extra-mural university studies. The Education Department was certainly keen to help the University because the DEMS would complement the government's own endeavours to promote adult education. The Director of Education, Mr Peter Donohue, advised the Government to 'give sympathetic consideration' to Hughes's request for additional finances at a Government House conference in April 1961.[55] The Education Department promised to help the DEMS in various ways, such as permitting the University to use government school buildings for extra-mural classes and assisting with the recruitment of part-time extra-mural tutors from schools. It also supported the University's proposal for the secondment of Mr K. K. Chan from its Adult Education Division to the DEMS during T. C. Lai's study leave, virtually without charge.[56]

The higher echelons of the government administration were, however, much less generous than the Education Department. The Colonial Secretary, Mr Claude Burgess, insisted that the secondment of any government official to the DEMS should be funded by the University itself.[57] This dispute became 'tiresome and undignified' in the opinion of the government because K. K. Chan had to work for the DEMS without any substantive agreement on the terms of his secondment for three more months from September 1961.[58] The problem was not solved until the Vice-Chancellor personally intervened in January 1962 and the Colonial Secretary permitted the secondment to continue under the terms originally proposed, commenting bitterly that 'there seems to be nothing to do but to accept the consequence of our failure'.[59] The colonial government had long been niggardly in its treatment of the University, and this was simply the latest example of government authorities failing to see the value of investing in higher education initiatives proposed by HKU.

The government was even more reluctant to consider a revised Seven Year Plan in order to provide a larger staff for the DEMS. The University officially requested the government to include Hughes's expansion plan in a revision of the Seven Year Plan in May 1961.[60] In spite of support from the Education Department and an appeal from several community leaders, it took the government until June 1962 before it assented to the inclusion of Hughes's scheme. It gave no definite answer on the matter, however, until May 1963, two years after the University's original submission of the Hughes plan to the government.[61] The reason for such a long delay is not clear, but it is certain that the University and the DEMS were annoyed at the government's tardiness in coming to a decision. They expressed their discontent at the delay on a number of occasions, some of which led to unfortunate repercussions. Hughes, for example, noted in a speech to the Hong

Kong Rotary Club in February 1962 that 'there has been no reply' from the government to his expansion plan but 'we live in hope'.[62] Local newspapers gave wide coverage of Hughes's critical speech.[63] The *China Mail* in particular was sympathetic to the plight of the DEMS:

> It is to be hoped that assistance along the lines suggested, will be given by Government . . . And if the deficiency is not to be remedied until 1966 when the current [seven-year] plan ends, valuable opportunities are going to be thrown away . . . Government should mark the beginning of the University's second-half century with an encouraging grant to carry on the good work already started by the Department.[64]

It was reported that the wide media coverage given to Hughes's pleas irritated the Governor, who himself 'warned off' the newspapers for giving the issue too much publicity 'on the grounds that the University's contribution to adult education was trifling by comparison with the Government's adult and technical education provision'.[65] It is true that the *China Mail* had to moderate its earlier commentary five days later by stating that 'the charge of neglect that we levelled at Government must be revised in so far as adult education generally'.[66] But the specific charge about the government's reluctance to support extra-mural university adult education as opposed to other more technical and vocational forms of post-secondary education had clearly hit a raw nerve.

The Vice-Chancellor, Sir Lindsay Ride, who had earlier rejected Moore's request to give full departmental status of the DEMS, also took the Department's side in demanding government approval of the expansion plan. Ride, on the advice of the BEMS and Hughes, criticised the government's prolonged indecision during the Department's Student Rally on 30 March 1963:

> Your Director worked hard behind the scene to win Government support, but the only positive response was a request from the Secretariat in June 1962 for the University to include these proposals in their review of the 7-year plan due in 1963. This was done in November [1962] with a request for an answer by 1st March [1963], which was the latest date that would give us time to plan any authorised changes with anything like efficiency.[67]

More astonishingly, Ride warned that the activities of the DEMS would in all likelihood have to shrink back to the scale of 1960–61, when Hughes first took over the Department, unless something was done soon:

> Obviously we must cut our coat according to our cloth; if Government does not approve our proposals, then when our present funds are exhausted we shall have to reduce our activities to something of the order of 60 courses. . . . I know such a drastic action would be a great disappointment to you as it would be to us also, and we shall do all we can do to avoid it. I proposed therefore that we should have in

> readiness for 1962/63 operations, a full one based on hopes, an alternative one based on 1960, and which [one] will come into operation will depend wholly on what funds are at our disposal.[68]

Ride's criticism attracted widespread press attention. The Student Rally and Ride's speech received broad coverage in the *South China Morning Post*, with the editorial comment that the 'scope [of extra-mural studies] may be cut unless needed help is given' to the DEMS.[69] The speech and the news report no doubt caused further embarrassment to the government.

The staff expansion programme of the DEMS had, in fact, already been approved by the government in May 1962.[70] The revised scheme did not fully adopt Hughes's recommendation to appoint resident tutors in different geographical areas, but it allowed for the DEMS to appoint three staff tutors in the following two academic years, and two more staff tutors in 1965–66 if necessary.[71] The government funding not only made the permanent appointment of Priscilla Mark possible, but it also enabled the Department to appoint four half-time staff tutors in September 1963, namely Mr Y. C. Jao, Miss Ina Kwok, Mr Perry Siu, and Miss Nana Wong.[72]

Unfortunately, the personnel situation in the Department in the next few years was far from stable. Hughes suffered a heart attack in early 1965 and had to retreat from work for three months.[73] The Assistant to the Director, T. C. Lai, resigned from the University in order to take up the post of Deputy Director of Extra-Mural Studies at the new Chinese University of Hong Kong (CUHK) on 1 April 1965.[74] Lai's resignation was a great loss to the Department as he was the longest-serving member of staff. For the Chinese University, of course, it was a great boon. The situation became even worse when three of the half-time staff tutors left the Department in the 1964–65 academic year.[75] Although the vacancies were gradually filled, their departure suddenly left the DEMS 'with only very inexperienced staff'.[76] Although, as will be shown in the following discussion, the DEMS was still able to achieve impressive development during these years, frequent changes of personnel greatly reduced efficiency, and hampered further development in the Department.

International Co-operation

Despite the continuous shortage of staff, the Department took an active role in sharing its experience with overseas extra-mural institutions and in seeking opportunities for international co-operation. It frequently invited overseas scholars to visit the Department in order to study the development of extra-mural studies in Hong Kong. The first prominent visitor was Mr Philip Sherlock, Director of Extra-Mural Studies and Vice-Principal of the University College of the West Indies, invited by Gerald Moore to visit HKU in 1959.[77] Thereafter, a number of overseas scholars and adult educationalists paid visits each year to the Department. A more formal and comprehensive visit was made in March 1962 when Ieuan Hughes invited Mr W. E. Styler, Director of the Department of Adult Education at the University of Hull, to visit the DEMS and other local adult educational organisations for about a month.[78] Styler's visit was an important opportunity for the Department:

> During the month he was here he undertook an arduous and intensive programme of interviews, committees, conferences and visits of classes and kindred organisations. He gave many informal talks and spoke personally to great numbers of students and most of the tutors, proving an unfailing source of encouragement and inspiration. He conducted a number of extremely helpful training conferences for class secretaries and tutors and delivered a memorable address at our second, and again highly successful, Annual Rally. Finally, he presented an immensely useful Report which was searching, shrewd, and constructive and had been accepted in principle by the Senate.[79]

Hughes cited three principal reasons for the success of Styler's visit. First, the advice and practical assistance that Styler gave on the day-to-day running of extra-mural work and the 'refreshing stimulation' he provided for staff, tutors and students were invaluable. Second, he was able to set the work of the Department in its international perspective and also brought HKU staff up to date with ideas, developments and trends elsewhere. Finally, the visit provided HKU with an opportunity to recruit an ambassador to adult education colleagues and organisations in Britain, and it was felt that Styler would be able to provide them with first-hand knowledge of the possibilities and problems in Hong Kong.[80]

Styler's Report, completed on 6 April 1962 and accepted in principle by the Senate in June 1962, made a number of comments and suggestions on the administration, courses and finance of the DEMS. Many of his recommendations were similar to those already suggested by Moore and Hughes. The most significant recommendations touched upon thorny issues such as the University's failure to recognise the academic status of DEMS staff, the need for a residential tutor and several staff tutors, and the now unavoidable calls for an increase in subsidies for extra-mural courses.[81] Styler also commented on 'the danger of unnecessary duplication and even competition' among extra-mural courses offered by post-secondary colleges, especially after the forthcoming opening of the Chinese University of Hong Kong. Styler suggested:

> Some effective scheme of coverage will need to be worked out which will ensure co-operation between the two universities. The idea that has occurred to me is that the new University should confine its organising in extra-mural work to the New Territories and that its lecturers should continue to help the older University in Kowloon and Hong Kong in so far as their services can be made available . . . In the early stages, therefore, perhaps such organising of extra-mural work as is carried

> on in the New Territories should be undertaken by the Extra-Mural Department of the University of Hong Kong, on the understanding that at an appropriate time it should be handed over to the new University.[82]

It is important to note that in spite of the Senate's acceptance 'in principle' of many of Styler's recommendations, his report was never regarded by the University as an official policy paper for extra-mural studies, and there was no substantial follow-up action arising from the report. However, the Senate and the Council agreed with the idea of periodical visits by overseas scholars as a means of improving the quality of extra-mural activities, and in early 1963 they agreed that the DEMS should formally invite an external visitor every three years.[83] In fact, Styler maintained a close relationship with HKU over the next few years, visiting again in 1964 and 1965, and co-operating with Hughes in promoting extra-mural activities in Southeast Asia.[84]

Apart from inviting external visitors, Hughes also represented his Department and the University on visits to overseas institutions. He participated actively in international conferences on adult education, and his sociable character helped the DEMS to establish connections with its regional counterparts.[85] Hughes attended the UNESCO conferences on Adult Education in Asia, first in Saigon in April 1962, and later in Sydney in January 1964. Hughes observed in his report on the Saigon conference that HKU appeared to be the only Asian university equipped with a department of extra-mural studies.[86] The Sydney Conference succeeded in creating the Asian-South Pacific Bureau of Adult Education (ASPBAE). Hughes was elected to the executive committee of this organisation and became editor of its newsletter and journal.[87] He also visited universities, adult education organisations and educational foundations in the United Kingdom, the United States, Canada, New Zealand, Australia, Denmark, the Philippines, Singapore, Malaysia, Indonesia, Vietnam, Thailand and India to learn more and give advice on extra-mural studies between 1960 and 1967.[88]

The highlight of these international activities was the Leverhulme Conference on Extra-Mural Studies organised by the Department at HKU between 26 and 31 October 1964. The idea of organising such a conference in Hong Kong originated at the Association of South East Asian Institutes of Higher Learning (ASAIHL) biennial conference of university heads in Jakarta in 1963. Sir Lindsay Ride drew the attention of other participants to the work of his Department of Extra-Mural Studies, and this prompted the ASAIHL heads to ask HKU to organise the next conference with the intention that it would focus on extra-mural studies.[89] ASAIHL did not carry through with this plan but HKU continued to organise the conference independently, with financial support from the Leverhulme Trust.[90] The Conference aimed to:

> Provide an opportunity for frank, factual and clarificatory presentations of a variety of university adult educational activities and experiences and for a free interchange of ideas concerning the possible roles of universities in adult education, so as to assist the universities in the South East Asian region to determine for themselves what part, if any, they felt it appropriate for them to play in their own communities.[91]

The Conference was opened by the governor, Sir David Trench, and was chaired by Sir Lindsay Ride. There were thirty-seven participants, including delegates from some twenty universities in Hong Kong, Malaya, the Philippines, Singapore, Thailand and Vietnam, and a number of consultants, specialists, and representatives from ASPBAE and ASAIHL. During the six-day Conference the participants presented papers, discussed the report adopted at the Sydney UNESCO Conference earlier in 1964, visited the HKU and Chinese University campuses, and met with local extra-mural students.[92] The Conference itself was described enthusiastically as 'an invigorating success', and it was particularly beneficial to the University because the Department of Extra-Mural Studies consolidated its leading position in the development of extra-mural studies in Southeast Asia.[93] Unfortunately, the promising resolutions of the conference were not all implemented.

One of the most significant resolutions of the Leverhulme Conference, despite its ultimate failure, was a proposal to set up in Hong Kong a regional institute for adult education with 'training, research, library and clearing house functions'.[94] Hong Kong was perceived by Hughes as a suitable place for establishing this institute because it was politically stable and easy of access. It also had an active Department of Extra-Mural Studies at HKU, which could start the work of the institute more or less immediately.[95] This suggestion was initially welcomed by institutions in the region. The follow-up visit by Hughes and Styler to Southeast Asian universities and educational authorities, as agreed by the Conference, in November 1964 also confirmed that there was general support in the region for this resolution.[96] ASPBAE confirmed its wish for the establishment of the institute at HKU.[97] Hughes drafted plans for an 'Institute of Adult Education for South East Asia' after the Conference, and contacted foundations, authorities and institutions around the world as a prelude to implementing these plans in the following years.[98] The establishment of such an institute was, however, never realised. This was due partially to the fact that the necessary financial resources could not be raised, but politically there was disagreement among the countries in the region about setting up the Institute in a British colony.[99] The whole proposal eventually lapsed when Hughes left HKU in November 1967. Hughes's attempt was nevertheless a clear example of active leadership by the early DEMS in international co-operation in the field of higher adult education, and was the only time that such ambitious proposals for international co-operation were made or led by HKU.

Extra-Mural Courses — Policies and Practice

The Number of Courses and Enrolment

The first courses directly supervised by the Director of Extra-Mural Studies were organised even before the establishment of the Department in May 1957, with the Senate approving Moore's proposal for three evening courses at its meeting on 8 January 1957.[100] All of them were literary or cultural courses:

1. The Chinese Literary Tradition (February to May 1957): 12 lectures in English by Mr. James J. Y. Liu, B.A. (Peking), M.A. (Bristol), Assistant Lecturer in the Department of Chinese,
2. Chinese Art of the Sung and Yuen Periods (February to March 1957): 6 lectures in Mandarin by Professor F. S. Drake, B.A., B.D., Dip.Ed., Dip. Geo. (Lond.), and
3. Shakespeare and the Elizabethan Theatre (February to May 1957): 12 lectures in English by Mr. G. H. Moore (Cantab.), Director of Extra-Mural Studies.[101]

Enrolments in these three courses were quite impressive. There were 139 applicants, of whom 125 came to lectures and 73 attended at least two-thirds of all the lectures.[102] While this number seems remarkably small by today's standards, it must be remembered that the undergraduate population of the University stood at only 800 in 1957, so this represented an encouraging start to extra-mural studies.[103] The first extra-mural courses officially offered by the DEMS were courses in commercial subjects which had been organised by the Department of Economic and Political Sciences since 1955. Moore took over responsibility for these evening courses in April 1957, and this move was followed by the creation of a supervisory sub-committee under the Board of Extra-Mural Studies on 22 May 1957.[104] The Department commenced its first full term with eight courses in Accountancy, Law, Economics and Company Secretarial Practice on 28 May 1957. A total of 172 students enrolled in these eight courses.[105]

The number of courses offered by the Department increased rapidly in the next few years, from twelve in 1956–57 to 281 in 1964–65. The enrolment figures were also encouraging. The total number of students registered for extra-mural courses in 1956–57 was 330. The annual enrolment had climbed to 6,341 registered students in 1964–65, a twenty-fold increase (see Appendix 2). At this time the population of undergraduate students at HKU stood at 1,735.[106] Approximately three-quarters of the students enrolled in DEMS courses were considered to be 'effective students', those who attended at least two-thirds of the classes. W. E. Styler was quite confident that there would be a steady increase of extra-mural students. He commented in his 1962 Report that 'given the necessary resources I should not be in the least surprised if the work of the Department continued to expand until the number of students attending its classes increased from the present 3,000 to perhaps even as many as 10,000'.[107] The public demand for extra-mural courses appears to have been even larger than the actual enrolment figures suggest. Courses were often oversubscribed and the Department consequently had to reject many applications, and it was also acknowledged that there were many subjects which the Department was unable to offer but for which a demand existed.

Subjects

Despite the small full-time staff, the DEMS managed to open courses in a wide range of subjects with the help of an army of part-time tutors. In the 1958–59 academic year, the second full year of operation, the Department organised forty-four courses in two streams with nine subject areas. The first stream, Liberal Studies, was comprised of courses in six subject areas: Oriental Studies; Philosophy, Psychology and Education; Economics, Sociology and Law; Geography, History and International Affairs; Mathematics, Science and Medicine; and Arts, Music and Architecture.[108] Some of these courses aimed at providing the students with general knowledge, while others were refresher courses for professionals. The Liberal Studies courses did not lead to specific qualifications although attendance certificates were issued to 'effective students'. The second stream, Languages and Vocational Courses, had a different function. They were intended to help students acquire specific vocational or semi-vocational skills or professional qualifications. This stream offered three broad subjects: English Language, Other (mostly European) Languages, and Vocational and Higher Commercial Subjects. The classification of courses changed from time to time, but these basic categories indicate the types of subjects which the Department offered in its first few years of operation.

The early DEMS invested much effort in seeking a balance between Liberal Studies courses and Vocational courses. While British extra-mural studies programmes had traditionally emphasised the non-vocational nature of their courses and the broad aim of intellectual development for its own sake, there was an expectation within Hong Kong society that extra-mural studies would equip students with vocational skills and empower them to secure better jobs. In fact, the Keswick Committee had very clearly expressed this view in its 1952 report when it recommended that HKU should start extra-mural studies with courses which were of a vocational or semi-vocational nature. This divergence of aims and expectations compelled successive directors to consider carefully these restrictions to DEMS activities during the planning of their extra-mural programmes.

The first two directors, Gerald Moore and Ieuan Hughes, shared similar views on the purpose of extra-mural studies but adopted slightly different policies. Both of them appreciated the traditional value attached to enriching people's intellectual and cultural lives, and were eager to apply this vision in the local context. However, they also recognised the necessity of catering to the needs of local society which demanded advanced vocational training through the University's extra-mural studies programmes. Moore acknowledged that although traditional liberal classes were the bedrock of all extra-mural education, vocational training was also a legitimate concern in colonial societies:

> I have the greatest admiration for the traditional type of extra-mural course, a small tutorial group following a course of study under the same tutor for two or three years, without any other motive than the enrichment of their minds and their citizenship. But to hold up this type of course as the ideal, or even the only legitimate, extra-mural activity does not make sense in the sort of situation in which we now find ourselves . . . The colonial working-man usually wishes to make adult education a means of changing his whole economic and social position as rapidly as possible . . . Consequently there is a great demand for adult education which will afford some material, as well as intellectual, self-improvement.[109]

Moore observed that there was no reason why extra-mural courses 'should be any more inherently "illiberal" than an intra-mural degree course' when many degree programmes were of a vocational or professional nature.[110] This was certainly the case at HKU where Medicine, Engineering and teacher training had long been recognised as the University's major goals in assisting the modernisation of the colonial economy and society.

Moore was certainly not reluctant to propose vocational courses or certificate courses. The first courses the DEMS offered in May 1957 were the commercial courses which assisted students in preparing for external examinations. Additionally, there were a number of refresher courses which helped professionals, such as teachers, police and engineers, to acquire new information and skills in their own professions. There was also a failed attempt by Moore in November 1959 to start a practical course in the Phonetics of English which would lead to 'a written examination and the award of a properly recognised University certificate'.[111] Although most of the extra-mural courses remained in the 'liberal' category throughout the early period, these endeavours nevertheless demonstrate clearly Moore's willingness to respond to the needs of Hong Kong society and organise a limited number of vocational and certificate courses.

Ieuan Hughes's preference for Liberal Studies courses was initially stronger than Moore's. Hughes was perceived by one of his colleagues as a man who had a 'missionary spirit' and who was determined to serve his extra-mural students, who were often seen as an underprivileged group in society.[112] In March 1961, Hughes emphasised to the Senate that the different types of liberal studies were 'a matter of prime concern to Universities' and 'the backbone of a University's Extra-Mural contribution'.[113] He recommended that the University should avoid running vocational training courses, especially those aimed at teaching technical, commercial or language skills, unless the 'liberalizing influences' in them predominated. He suggested in a public lecture in December 1961 that the purposes and functions of an extra-mural department included 'to serve the community and area as a whole by providing a well-balanced programme of courses' and 'constantly and in every class to help to develop the whole man'.[114] Extra-mural courses should therefore not aim solely at vocational training, but should always provide opportunities for self-improvement and intellectual development for those who enrolled in them. While his predecessor had acknowledged that a citizen's demand for material self-improvement was not 'in any way a criminal desire', Hughes lamented this tendency in the attitudes of the local population when it came to adult education and extra-mural studies:

> Instead, people tend to live in and for the present, and seek to make the most of here and now, wanting quick and definite results as soon as possible. People do not build for tomorrow, even the investor expects to get his full outlay in three to five years. In such an atmosphere, adult education is more likely to be seen as a valuable facility for meeting immediate ad-hoc needs rather than a movement rooted in the community or a permanent strand in the lives of individuals.[115]

Hughes's inclination towards 'liberal' courses during the period of his directorship can also be demonstrated through course statistics. In the 1964–65 academic year, for example, there were 4,542 students registered in the 133 Liberal Studies courses, while only 1,799 students took the 98 Languages and Vocational Courses.[116]

In his early reports and essays, Hughes showed that he did not want to give vocational training a high priority in the Department, but he soon acknowledged the benefit of vocational courses to society. He played an active role in starting professional courses in law and librarianship, which will be discussed in the next chapter. It was also agreed at a Board of Extra-Mural Studies meeting in June 1964 that more courses which followed the syllabuses of recognised examinations should be provided in the future.[117] Hughes, therefore, did not intend to eliminate entirely vocational courses in the Department, but tried to accommodate the needs of the community for vocational courses within his traditional vision of what extra-mural courses were designed to achieve.

Types of Classes

There was an amazingly diverse selection of extra-mural courses offered by the Department in its formative years. The majority of courses were conducted as regular weekly evening classes. These courses normally held one meeting per week though some courses met twice weekly. Most courses lasted for several months with between six and thirty meetings per course.[118] The starting dates of the courses were staggered, depending on the availability of tutors. Weekly classes were usually held on the University campus or at other borrowed premises across the city between 5:45 p.m. and 6:45 p.m. While vocational courses were generally conducted only as lectures, the DEMS encouraged the liberal courses to be conducted as 'tutorials' which emphasised active questioning and discussion among tutors and students. As the one-hour duration of each lesson was sometimes not enough for both teaching and discussion, suggestions were made to extend the duration of classes to one and a half hours, but it is not known to what extent this recommendation was adopted.[119]

Apart from these conventional classes, the Department started other types of courses, some of which were fairly innovative at the time. Public lectures and seminars had been organised outside the campus for some years and elicited impressive responses. The Department's first attempt at a series of public lectures was in Tsuen Wan in the New Territories in October and November 1958. The aim of these lectures was to 'add activities with a strong local and social emphasis to the more general and academic work of the Department'.[120] The 1959 Departmental Report gave the following description of this lecture series:

> One of the most interesting courses of the year was an experimental one held at the Rural Committee Headquarters in Tsuen Wan. This bilingual Study Group on the Development of the Township attracted a varied local audience, including the Chairman and the Rural Committee, Village Representatives, farmers, landowners, mill managers and headmasters. The Director of Extra-Mural Studies acted as Chairman, assisted by Mr. Robert Ting (Headmaster of Tsuen Wan Government School) as Interpreter. A team of [HKU] lecturers visited Tsuen Wan to address the group successively on the history, geology and topography, economic growth and physical development of Tsuen Wan, as a background to some final lectures on the engineering and architectural problems of development in the new town.[121]

The Department published a report on this study group in September 1959, in which Moore concluded that the series of lectures was 'of value to the Department in indicating the special approach which will be needed for spreading extra-mural work in the New Territories — vernacular, pragmatic and local in emphasis'.[122] It was a small start to work in the New Territories, but the enthusiastic response indicated that the University might eventually extend its extra-mural activities beyond the traditional liberal and vocational fields and help people in Hong Kong deal with real everyday issues associated with questions of livelihood and rapid economic development.

The DEMS eventually started to extend its activities beyond the established early-evening classes, organising a series of day-time and late-evening classes, the latter of which were mainly held in the new City Hall, beginning in 1962–63.

Single-lecture programmes and high-level conference-seminars were also occasionally held during that year.[123] Public lectures and seminars on a variety of topics were promoted by the Department in the following years. For example, in the 1966–67 academic year, the Department organised at least four different seminars on various industries and on history education in Hong Kong, and its free evening lectures on the 'Hong Kong Economic Scene' also received a good response.[124]

The DEMS also tried to deliver its message and conduct open lectures through the mass media. Moore gave a radio address through Rediffusion (the first cable radio and television service in Hong Kong) in September 1958 to explain the objectives and work of the DEMS.[125] In 1960–61, Hughes chaired the University's Jubilee Radio Committee and was responsible for co-ordinating a 'Town and Gown' series of seven broadcasts 'in which the work of the University and its place in the community was widely discussed and illustrated'.[126] In the next academic year he participated in cultural programmes on Radio Hong Kong and was a regular member of critics' programme on television.[127] T. C Lai and Y. C. Jao also hosted a series of courses on Economics over Commercial Radio in 1964–65.[128] Apart from being a convenient means to deliver lectures and other information, radio proved to be a powerful way of widening the audience base which the DEMS was able to reach.

Residential courses were another major area which the Department intended to develop. These courses required students to reside together for more than a day, usually a weekend, for a series of activities. Styler's 1962 report emphasised the advantages of this type of course. They were able to provide 'a means of deepening personal contacts between students and between tutors and students' in an environment where they could not be disturbed by the outside world.[129] Public responses to residential courses varied greatly. For example, Moore's proposal for a 'Summer School on Condition of Life and Work in Hong Kong', a one-week residential school for government officials to be held in August 1959, was bluntly rejected by the government because it was considered impractical to release government staff for such a long period.[130] The Department nevertheless achieved significant success in jointly organising with the Royal Hong Kong Police Force a weekend field trip with lectures on Lantau Island in 1961–62.[131] In general, residential courses did not have a great appeal in most cases 'because of lack of suitable accommodation and the strangeness of the idea of sleeping away from home which, anyway, is only about thirty to forty-five minutes of travel'.[132] Successful residential courses were therefore relatively few in the early 1960s.

Other types of courses were arranged by the Department occasionally. Specific lectures, courses or training sessions were organised at the request of public bodies or professional organisations, aiming at training specialised groups of people. During the early 1960s, the Department succeeded in co-operating with the Police, the Standing Committee of Youth Organizations, the Hong Kong Federation of Youth Groups, Caritas, and the Hong Kong Library Association in conducting both refresher courses and examinable courses according to their needs.[133] The first overseas study tour, accompanied by a ten-week preparatory course, was organised by Priscilla Mark in July and August 1963. About twenty-five participants travelled to Angkor Wat, Saigon, Thailand, Malaya and Singapore for three weeks.[134] It seems extraordinary that the Department was able to offer such a diversity of courses when such limited resources were available during the initial years of its development.

The Language Problem

Contrary to the original recommendations of both government and University reports, the majority of extra-mural courses were conducted in English although the student population was overwhelmingly Cantonese-speaking. In the 1964–65 academic year, 80 per cent of courses offered by the Department used English or other European languages as their medium of instruction, while only 14 per cent of courses were conducted in Cantonese and 6 per cent in Mandarin.[135] It was not appropriate for some courses to use languages other than English, especially those leading to external examinations, but the main reason for the extremely high proportion of classes which were taught in English was more obvious. Most of the tutors were expatriates and it continued to be difficult to recruit experienced and qualified Chinese tutors at that time.

The Department was concerned about this language problem. Styler's 1962 report, for example, observed that there was a serious need for more courses to be conducted in Chinese, especially Cantonese:

> There must be many intelligent people who know no English or insufficient English to be able to benefit from classes conducted in that language. It is certain that discussion in the classes is made more difficult for students when they have to be conducted in English. There is a view, expressed to me once or twice, that the University should confine its extra-mural work to classes in which the English language is the medium of instruction. I feel myself that this would be a bad mistake and would reduce both the benefits which the University gives through its extra-mural work and also the advantage it may hope to gain in making itself more widely appreciated and understood by the community.[136]

Hughes also noted a rather surprising phenomenon in the responses of students who had finished English-language courses in the Department:

> Many of the English students return, some for more English, virtually none for literature, but quite a number to other courses, their interest having been kindled in the English classes or because they now feel they can get more out of them with their improved comprehension.[137]

Despite the fact that the DEMS had early recognised this language problem, it was not able to find an easy solution. More local tutors were eventually recruited during the 1960s, but the courses conducted in English still outnumbered those conducted in Cantonese or Mandarin until the mid-1980s.

Students

Extra-mural students came from all walks of life. The largest occupation groups were teachers, clerical workers, businessmen, government servants and 'students'.[138] Most of them were Chinese and aged below 40, the majority being between 20 and 29 years of age.[139] Despite the paucity of reliable statistics available to him, Gerald Moore observed that many extra-mural students had received some previous higher education and enrolled in extra-mural courses to broaden and deepen their knowledge.[140] The occupational and age profiles of those enrolling in DEMS courses reflect the fact that most of the classes were conducted in English. Only people with a sound education in English were able to benefit from these courses. It must also be noted that some courses were designed as refresher courses and therefore required some background knowledge or qualifications prior to enrolment.

The characteristics of student groups varied in each of the subject areas. Courses in Oriental Studies, for example, attracted 'a devoted band of followers, mostly the middle-aged to elderly with scholastic affinities, anxious to acquire all they can from their rich cultural inheritance'.[141] Refresher courses, due to their specific teaching objectives, were attended predominantly by students who were practising in related professions. There were more young students in vocational and language courses, many of whom wanted to acquire particular skills or qualifications for career progression.

In spite of the generally high education level of the students, their qualities and motives did not always satisfy the Director. Hughes was critical of his students in terms that have been repeated many times in higher education circles in Hong Kong:

> Students are generally diligent, keen, and friendly, as intelligent as elsewhere, and take their studies rather seriously. They are not, as a rule, inclined to participate . . . A variety of attitudes contribute to the reluctance to question or comment — traditional genuine respect for the teachers; implied loss of face — by the student if it is a foolish question, by the tutor if he cannot answer, difficulties of comprehension and expression due to strangeness of language or cultural concepts (this is a major problem); the belief that a question is a waste of time, as the other students may know the answer or because it reduces the tutor's lecturing time, and you have paid to hear what the tutor has to say; the utilitarian view that education consists not in teaching you what to think, let alone how to think, but in the acquisition of approved answers — especially those required for examinations.[142]

Hughes, a great believer in the humanising potential of his work, also worried about the motives which led students to undertake extra-mural courses:

> Student motives are as varied as anywhere else but, as will have been gathered, a considerable emphasis is placed on meeting immediate, specific, utilitarian needs, especially by the younger English-speaking Chinese who want to establish themselves or are on the climb in a highly competitive environment. Many therefore apply for certificates of attendance.[143]

Once again, his worries about younger extra-mural students seem to reflect a side of the Hong Kong character which other commentators have interpreted as being central to the Hong Kong success story. That these younger learners with such pragmatic aims might eventually mature into Hughes' ideal adult learner was also acknowledged:

> Those in their thirties have wider and deeper motives and stronger human and social interests and, together with a more forward looking element in the early twenties, may well provide . . . a leavening, constructive, and stabilizing core — much needed in Hong Kong society . . . The over-forties predominate in the Classical Chinese Studies courses. They have the loyalty, character, and liveliness of mind one associates with veteran tutorial-class students in Britain.[144]

A major difference between extra-mural studies and full-time university studies was the fact that it was much more difficult for extra-mural students to develop a true sense of identity and 'belonging' than it was for HKU undergraduates. Extra-mural students, most of whom worked during the day time and rushed to attend their classes in the evenings, found little time and few opportunities to establish relationships with classmates and tutors. Lack of premises specifically for the use of the Department also retarded the growth of a sense of belonging among extra-mural students. The DEMS therefore worked hard to strengthen ties among students and improve communication between students and tutors. Apart from encouraging tutors to hold tutorial discussions during classes, the Department attempted to enhance communication among students and tutors in other ways:

> For the first time [in 1961–62] we have had class secretaries, elected by the students in each class, and they have proved a boon not only with their comments and suggestions at our several Secretaries' Conferences, but also as essential links between the Department and the Tutors on the one hand and the students on the other; this could well provide an embryonic student organisation. Another vitalising contribution has been the out-of-class activities arranged by Secretaries and/or Tutors in a number of classes: these have usually led to a marked improvement in atmosphere and morale — the class becoming a group of individual personalities instead of a series of isolated names — and hence in the work done.[145]

The Department organised regular meetings with tutors and class secretaries. The first Tutors' Conference took place at St John's College in June 1961. Hughes and more than twenty participants discussed the theory and practice of adult education, including the best techniques for organising classes and maintaining good relationships with students.[146] Conferences for class secretaries were also held, beginning in 1961–62. During these conferences the Director and guest speakers gave talks about extra-mural education and the class secretaries were invited to express their own views.[147]

The highlight of student participation in the 1960s was the annual student rally. The first student rally was held in Loke Yew Hall on the afternoon of 18 March 1961 as a part of the University's Jubilee celebrations. The Vice-Chancellor, Sir Lindsay Ride, was present at the occasion and gave an address of welcome. About 750 participants, including tutors and extra-mural students, gathered together to take part in a number of activities, including exhibitions, special lectures, tea and dances. They were even able to join the internal undergraduate students in an open-air evening gathering and barbecue, organised by the Students' Union, at the University Sports Field.[148] The first rally, which was described as the extra-mural students' 'first opportunity to come together as a body' was, from all accounts, a remarkable success.[149] Annual student rallies were organised over the next few years, with the Vice-Chancellor or his representative attending together with other guests from the University and the wider community, tutors and extra-mural students. The rallies contributed to the development of the Department in numerous ways. First, they provided a good opportunity for staff, tutors, extra-mural students, and other members of the University to communicate with each other in an informal and friendly atmosphere. Second, they allowed students to experience a taste of the extra-curricular activities of internal students, something which had been impossible to imagine previously. Third, the attendance of the Vice-Chancellor and other senior members of the University at the rallies demonstrated the University's support for the DEMS and its activities, thereby strengthening the extra-mural students' sense of belonging to the University. Finally, the rallies demonstrated to the wider Hong Kong society that the Department was developing a strong extra-mural student population which it hoped would one day make great contributions to the community.

Accommodation

One of the major practical problems faced by the DEMS in the initial years was a lack of accommodation for both its general office and its classes. The first department office in Eliot Hall was very inconvenient for visitors and poorly equipped for the needs of staff. The situation was not much improved until the Department moved its office to the basement level in the north-west corner of the Main Building, an area which had been used as a students' canteen until the 1961–62 academic year.[150] The Departmental Report for 1961–62 provides a brief description of the new office:

> [The new office] makes us more easily accessible and gives us room to welcome and deal with callers. The porch has become a self-service bureau: we have a small lecture/conference room; the reception area can be used for exhibition and as a seminar room at night; there is an area to house our growing library and alcoves for private study and for the use of visiting tutors and class secretaries or committees.[151]

Unfortunately, finding meeting places for extra-mural classes still posed a great challenge. As the Department had no premises beyond its new administrative office, it had to borrow rooms in different places, both within the University and in town, in order to deliver its courses. In the first full academic year (1957–58) the Department's courses were held in three venues: the University campus, the Club Lusitano in Central, and the Grantham Training College in Kowloon.[152] The venues used for extra-mural courses changed every year, but all of these venues were arranged on a temporary basis and none of them except the University campus could provide a full range of supporting facilities, such as a library and study areas. Even the on-campus accommodation was not very satisfactory. The University was quite distant from the city centre and was not in a convenient location for most working people. The period during which the University could spare rooms for extra-mural classes each day was also short: approximately one hour from 5:45 p.m. to 7 p.m. The restricted availability of teaching rooms on campus made the arrangement of extra-mural classes very inflexible.[153]

The Styler report of 1962 emphasised the importance of establishing an extra-mural centre closer to the places where most students worked:

> A meeting place in or near the centre of the city at which most of the classes could be held would be a great improvement. Centres for adult education are now a feature of University extra-mural work in Britain . . . and experience in running them is everywhere the same, i.e., they are soon using all available accommodation. In their favour is not only the fact that their geographical location may be more convenient than the local university but also the fact that as they are designed for adult education they are more attractive to students than borrowed or hired accommodation.[154]

Hughes echoed this view and suggested what sorts of facilities an extra-mural centre should include:

> The accommodation position is desperate; what we most urgently need are premises of our own, preferably in Hong Kong and Kowloon, such as the extremely successful

> adult colleges which British universities are establishing in city centres. Besides rooms for classes and seminars, such a building, designed and equipped for adults, should contain a library, a reading and study room, a multi-purpose hall with audio-visual and exhibition equipment, and social and eating facilities, and if (as is the case here) there is no residential college, a residential section.[155]

This was a tall order indeed at a time when the University was attempting to expand the provision of classrooms and laboratories for its undergraduates on the main campus. Hughes must have known that his expectations were unrealistic, but he nevertheless attempted to find whatever ways he could of realising his dream of a proper town centre for extra-mural classes.

The Department had in fact been looking into various possibilities of acquiring buildings in urban areas of Hong Kong and Kowloon for much of its short existence. Without any possibility of further financial support from the University, Gerald Moore tried to find outside financial support in the late 1950s to buy a small hut in the Argyle Street camp in Kowloon so as to 'create a more concentrated interest in our work in the Kowloon area'.[156] The hut in question had a floor area of only 550 square feet so it would indeed have required a rather concentrated approach to make it suitable as a centre for extra-mural studies. It was not, however, ultimately acquired by the University. In March 1963, Mr R. C. Lee, a notable Hong Kong businessman and philanthropist, told Hughes that he had approached a well-known donor asking for $1 million for the extra-mural centre. Lee agreed to find a plot of land to allow the development to proceed.[157] In July 1964, Sir Lindsay Ride wrote to the Jockey Club asking for $2–3 million for the development of an extra-mural centre after the BEMS had resolved that 'every effort should be made to enlist support' to buy or rent property in commercial buildings for extra-mural studies.[158] Despite the continuing efforts of the Vice-Chancellor and the directors of the DEMS, none of these plans were successful. The Department set up a temporary town office in September 1964 in order to simplify the process of enrolling students, but this office was not intended to provide accommodation for courses and was closed after the two-week enrolment exercise was completed.[159] The proposal for an extra-mural town centre did not come to fruition, in fact, until the government decided to give additional subsidies to the Department so that it could start extra-mural courses for the University of London external LLB degree programme in 1964. This development will be discussed in the next chapter.

Finance

The University was generally not generous in financing extra-mural studies during this period. As has already been mentioned, the University refused to support any extra-mural staff outside the budget agreed by the government. It also avoided committing itself to capital investment in extra-mural studies. In fact, the DEMS was so poorly equipped that Moore reported in April 1959 that his Department had only one cheap portable gramophone and one slide projector for teaching.[160] Nevertheless, it is also true that the University subvention to extra-mural studies increased substantially throughout the period. Most of the subvention went to cover the salaries of the permanent staff, with salaries paid to senior staff increasing more than fourfold from $40,000 to $181,937 between 1957 and 1965. The increase in wages to clerical staff was also impressive: from $4,580 to $32,191 between 1958 and 1965. The annual subvention of the DEMS by the University rose from $69,669 in 1957–58 to $269,850 in 1964–65. It ought to be noted, however, that this increased figure for 1964–65 represented only one per cent of the total University expenditure for the year. From December 1963, the University also provided modest additional subsidies, amounting to around $500 per annum, through the Library Fund for the purchase of books.[161]

The University's spending on extra-mural studies never covered any more than the staff salaries and administrative expenses of the Department of Extra-Mural Studies. Extra-mural courses were expected to be run on a self-financing basis. All direct course expenditure, including tutors' salaries, teaching materials and rental fees for off-campus classrooms, were to be met by course fees. The DEMS enjoyed greater flexibility in controlling its resources from the 1962–63 financial year when the University set up an Extra-Mural Studies Fund and allowed the Department to accumulate its surplus in the Fund for meeting ad-hoc expenditure in the future.[162] This was a prudent move by the University which allowed it to avoid any future call for financial assistance from the Department. The practice at HKU perhaps reflects the application in a colonial context of fundamental policy changes taking place in the United Kingdom during the 1950s and early 1960s. Where once the British government had led the world in financing liberal adult studies through the extra-mural departments of its universities, by the late 1950s the emphasis had swung round to technical adult education and the funding of liberal studies was falling behind. There was no denial of the importance of adult liberal studies in this policy shift, but rather a re-assignment of priorities in a rapidly developing technological age.[163] It does seem, however, that HKU did not finance its fledgling extra-mural studies activities as generously as its British counterparts.

The requirement for self-financing of extra-mural courses at HKU inevitably led to high course fees. The standard fee of liberal courses was initially set at $1 per meeting with a registration fee of $6, but in 1958 was increased to $1.25 per meeting with no registration fee.[164] The course fee did not appear to be very high for students with decent jobs, but it was already more than twice the level of the fees charged by British extra-mural courses and was not always affordable for middle- and lower-class citizens.[165] In the absence of stable subsidies from the University, the DEMS soon found difficulty in maintaining a single fee structure for all courses and had to adopt a complicated system to determine course fees and finance extra-mural courses. Higher fee levels might be set in different courses, depending on the duration of the particular course, the anticipated enrolment, the target student group, and particularly the 'saleability' of the course. Chinese Language courses, for example, were charged at $4 per meeting, and arts courses at $4 or $5 per meeting in 1958–59.[166] Vocational courses were often charged at a higher rate because many students were willing to pay higher fees with their employers' sponsorship or the expectation of economic benefit from the vocational skills learnt from the courses. The surplus generated from these courses was used to subsidise the liberal cultural courses which attracted smaller enrolments. The Department was forced to increase course fees in order to meet the rising costs of administration and accommodation. By 1967–68, the liberal courses were charged at $2.50 to $3.50 per meeting, approximately double the fees paid by students in 1957–58. Fees for professional, refresher and arts courses were mostly set within a range of $3 to $5 per meeting.[167]

The Directors had long been eager to convince the University of the necessity for direct subsidies to extra-mural courses. From the time of his arrival in 1956, Moore suggested that three-quarters of course expenditure should be subsidised by the government.[168] Hughes and his colleagues also tried their best to point out the problems of the financial system at HKU in further developing extra-mural studies. Styler, for example, noted in his 1962 report that:

> The present method of financing classes contains many unsatisfactory features. To cover its costs each class has to recruit at least twenty-five students and the fees asked from students are very high compared with most other countries. Experience in Britain suggests that the best results are achieved with a class membership of between twelve and twenty students . . . To make it possible for smaller classes to be organized the Department should have at least a reasonable assured income which is independent of students' fees and is known before the commencement of each session.[169]

Hughes also used the benchmark of British practice in voicing his dissatisfaction with the financing of extra-mural courses at HKU:

> In Britain, where education is regarded as a public service . . . students' fees cover only one-sixth of this expenditure, the lion's share being contributed by central and local government subsidies . . . Tutors' fees, by Hong Kong standards, are a modest flat rate and compare reasonably with the United Kingdom. Students' fees . . . are among the highest in the world (from five to nine times the United Kingdom hourly rate) . . . The high fees undoubtedly reduce enrolment in the liberal studies courses and unfortunately make extension courses conducted by University specialists particularly liable to founder. They also discourage the middle — let alone lower — income groups, which are dominantly Chinese speaking and contain fine student material.[170]

Hughes was very concerned that the operation of his Department and its provision of educational services tended to be based upon financial imperatives rather than sound educational policy:

> The decision to allow many of our courses to run is based, not merely on the fees received for the courses concerned, but on the overall fee-income balance. Consequently during the opening months complicated mathematical and financial calculations have to be made daily in order to arrive at what essentially is an educational decision.[171]

Their efforts were, however, in vain. Apart from a few exceptional occasions, such as the pilot programme for the external law degree of London University, the government and the University maintained the self-financing policy for extra-mural courses, and this set an unfortunate precedent for all extra-mural programmes developed throughout Hong Kong in the next four decades. The Hong Kong government did not recognise a duty to provide extra-mural educational opportunities to its citizens, and focused instead on technical and vocational programmes which seemed to be more pragmatic ways of improving the economic and social conditions of its escalating population.

As the University was reluctant to provide additional funding to make up for the shortfall in government subsidies for extra-mural studies, outside bodies played an active role in supplementing the finances of the early DEMS. The Carnegie Foundation and the Asia Foundation, two American educational foundations, were particularly generous in financing the Department during this early period. The Carnegie Corporation of New York helped the Department to start a book-box scheme for extra-mural students in the first year of the Department's operation.[172] Without the Asia Foundation's grant of $48,450 in 1962–63 (equal to approximately 30 per cent of the University's subvention to the DEMS in that year), the DEMS could not have appointed its first staff tutor. The Asia Foundation also financed field trips, study leave, and other activities of the Department. Other bodies such as the Leverhulme Trust helped the DEMS from time to time with grants for special purposes. They provided the DEMS with crucial resources which the University was not prepared to offer at that time.

Conclusion

The early days of HKU's Department of Extra-Mural Studies were marked by marginalisation from the University's mainstream educational activities and severe financial restrictions. As one of the newest and smallest units in the University, the Department was marginalised in various ways. Constitutionally its director was not initially recognised as a 'Teacher' and was excluded from the Senate.

Administratively it was never accepted as a fully functioning 'Teaching Department' and was instead tied to the Senate under a Board of Extra-Mural Studies which had power only to advise and not to determine policy in extra-mural matters. It was relatively understaffed and suffered frequent changes of personnel, making a fuller development of its activities impossible. Financially the Department enjoyed neither direct subsidies nor dedicated premises designed specifically for the extra-mural classes. It is not surprising, therefore, that this seriously impaired department failed to function in the ways envisaged by the Keswick Committee. However, the performance of the DEMS during this period was in many ways astonishing under its first two directors, Gerald Moore and Ieuan Hughes, and the number of extra-mural courses available to students expanded rapidly during the first decade of the Department's operation. Many activities organised by the Department were indeed ground-breaking. Residential courses, student rallies and overseas trips for non-matriculated university students were completely new elements of HKU's mission. Regional co-operation in adult higher education was in its earliest stages, but the Department and HKU were among the leaders in this movement.

More importantly, however, the Department of Extra-Mural Studies acted as a very visible link between 'gown' and 'town', providing much-needed educational opportunities for university-standard education to non-university students. While this was in some ways a continuation of the University's previous commitment to providing educational opportunities for 'external' students, the new arrangements were on a scale which soon attracted a huge number of students. From the early 1960s HKU would always have more extra-mural students on its books than undergraduates. The problem of the lack of recognition suffered by the DEMS in this period was not unlike the difficulties which were emerging in the provision of extra-mural liberal education in the United Kingdom. Already there were calls for a more balanced policy to ensure that liberal adult studies would be safeguarded against the emergent demands for extra-mural teaching of a more professional and vocational character.[173] Unlike the situation in Britain, however, where it was believed that the overarching ideal of attaining an enlightened democracy could be achieved through the provision of continuing liberal education for the masses, in the colonial context of Hong Kong there was no such priority in political development or educational provision.[174] Therefore, in the years that followed the opening up of extra-mural studies at HKU, the focus would quickly shift from liberal studies to professional and vocational education.

CHAPTER FOUR

From Retrenchment to Resurgence, 1965–1982

THE DEPARTMENT OF EXTRA-MURAL STUDIES experienced a period of phenomenal growth and activity in the first years of Ieuan Hughes's directorship, but continuing funding difficulties, staff departures, and a decline in the Director's health brought this growth to a halt in the second half of 1965. Several years of retrenchment followed and a new Director, Roger Williams, presided over the Department during a period when many problems had to be addressed. Funding difficulties and space shortages continued, but to these were added new concerns over competition from the extra-mural department at the Chinese University of Hong Kong, pressure from the University Grants Committee for closer co-ordination of extra-mural activities between the two universities, and even an attempt to merge the two departments in 1968. It was during these difficulties that the University began to show a stronger commitment to the Department, culminating in the acquisition of a permanent extra-mural Town Centre at great cost to the University in 1982. By this time the days of retrenchment in the mid-1960s were long past, and a series of new extra-mural professional programmes had been introduced which has prompted one writer to describe the Department of Extra-Mural Studies as the 'cradle of professional studies in Hong Kong'.[1] This chapter will deal with the major institutional developments affecting the Department of Extra-Mural Studies between 1965 and 1982, while Chapter 5 will examine in more detail the new professional programmes offered by the Department between 1964 and 1985. These programmes were instrumental in changing the face of professional education in Hong Kong.

Retrenchment in the late 1960s

The development of extra-mural studies at HKU reached its first peak in the mid-1960s. Due to Ieuan Hughes's enthusiasm and the government's increase of funding for its programmes, the Department achieved record-breaking enrolments in 1964–65. During that year 6,341 students enrolled in 281 extra-mural courses. The rapid expansion, however, brought with it an enormous workload which fell on the shoulders of the small core of full-time staff. Without any significant increase in staff and resources, the Department had reached its maximum capacity and was no longer able to sustain such rapid expansion. It was about to face a choice between two policies: continuous expansion of extra-mural studies at a lower standard, or retrenchment of its activities to sustain the overall quality. The Department ultimately chose the latter course.

The staffing problems already encountered by the Department remained unsolved throughout the late 1960s. The departure of T. C. Lai and a number of other staff tutors in 1964–65 greatly impaired the smooth operation of extra-mural courses. Ieuan Hughes's heart attack in 1965 was an even greater blow to the development of the DEMS for he had been the originator of most of the new initiatives. By July 1965 the Department's activities were being maintained by only three members of staff: two full-time and one temporary.[2] Although the full-time staff gradually increased to eleven in 1967–68, this was still far from sufficient to maintain the high-quality operation of the Department. Staff tutors were forced to take on a wide range of duties, from academic responsibilities such as teaching, course development, contacting tutors and formulating the syllabus, to administrative tasks such as collecting statistics and dealing with student registration. Each staff tutor supervised twenty to thirty extra-mural courses in September 1967, a far heavier load than their counterparts in British universities.[3] Mr W. E. Styler commented on the seriousness of the staff shortage when he visited the DEMS in 1966. He suggested that there was a need to increase the staff establishment of the Department to eighteen full-time appointments by 1969 in order to 'achieve stability and to begin to consolidate its work'. He emphasised the importance of a stable and adequate full-time staff for the future of extra-mural studies at HKU:

> They would provide the central professional element in the University's extra-mural work, building up a solid core of local expertise and experience, and, not having to disperse their talents over too wide an academic programme as at present, would be able to work steadily at improving the quality of the work undertaken and be able to build relations with other departments which should draw more members of the teaching staff into extra-mural work.[4]

Styler's recommendation for more staff involved large financial commitments, and this could not be achieved without the blessing of the funding authorities. Unfortunately, both the government and the University maintained their lukewarm attitude towards financing extra-mural studies. The new University Grants Committee (UGC), set up in 1965 to supervise the government subvention for the two universities, favoured a tightening of the budget for extra-mural studies. When the UGC held its first meetings with the universities in March and April 1966, Professor M. J. Wise of London University, who was one of its members, suggested a retrenchment in the activities of HKU's Department of Extra-Mural Studies.[5] The UGC imposed on the University the view that there should only be a 'very modest increase of the staff in the Extra-Mural Department' as it prepared its first triennial plan for 1967–70.[6] More gravely, the UGC attempted to defer proposals for the further expansion of extra-mural studies in order to compel the DEMS to follow a policy of co-operation with the Chinese University of Hong Kong (CUHK).[7] Moreover, the University tightened its control over DEMS expenditure under the new UGC funding system. The financial flexibility of the Department was further eroded in October 1967 when the Council reorganised the Extra-Mural Studies Fund and excluded the payment of full-time staff salaries from the Fund.[8] The University's reluctance to provide additional resources for the Department remained unchanged during the next ten years. The Development and General Purposes Committee (DGPC), for example, in 1969 dismissed the Department's proposal for teaching subsidies of $50,000 per annum in the 1970–74 quadrennium, fearing that these might be spent on balancing deficits incurred by extra-mural courses.[9] In 1977 the Senate also reiterated its commitment not to expand extra-mural activities 'at the expense of other University developments'.[10] The lack of financial support from the Hong Kong government and the University left the Department unable to sustain extra-mural activities on such a large scale as had been achieved in the mid-1960s.

Despite his keenness to expand extra-mural activities, Ieuan Hughes realised that his poor health, staff shortages and a lack of additional funding left the DEMS with virtually no choice but to reduce its activities. Retrenchment began in the 1965–66 academic year, with a decrease in the number of courses from 281 to 231, and a drop in enrolments by 600. This retrenchment policy was extended after Hughes resigned and returned to Wales to take up the wardenship of Coleg Harlech (the Welsh National Residential College for Adult Education) in November 1967. He was succeeded as Director by his deputy, Mr Roger Arthur Williams.

Roger Williams was also a specialist in extra-mural studies and had joined the Department at a time when it was seriously understaffed and desperate for experienced full-time professionals. He was a graduate of the University College of Wales and held two bachelor's degrees, one in Modern History and another in Economics and Political Science. He obtained his M.A. degree at the University of Wales in 1951. Before taking up his original appointment at the University of Hong Kong, he had fourteen years of experience in extra-mural studies at the University of Glasgow.[11] Williams was initially seconded from Glasgow to HKU in October 1965 for two years.[12] He was originally scheduled to return to Glasgow after these two years of service, but the DEMS badly needed his experience and asked him to stay in Hong Kong for a longer period.[13] Williams finally decided to continue at

HKU and was appointed, on Hughes's recommendation, as Deputy Director early in 1967.[14] When Hughes resigned from the DEMS later in the same year, Williams became Acting Director, but on 1 March 1968 he succeeded as Director of Extra-Mural Studies.[15]

While Hughes was an ardent supporter of extra-mural studies and was determined to expand his Department as quickly as possible, sometimes to the detriment of staff whose workload consequently expanded far beyond 'normal' levels, Williams was less ambitious and more realistic about the strengths and weaknesses of the DEMS. He was perceived by one of his colleagues as a meticulous and talented administrator who attempted to maintain good relationships with other parts of the University.[16] Williams's prudent attitude perhaps made him even more open than Hughes to the necessity of retrenchment for the good of the Department. He made his position clear in 1968 in a review of past development in his department:

> The need for consolidation arises from the Department having sought over the past decade to meet the needs expressed by the Hong Kong community for adult education provision. In so doing, it disclosed a very large need for such provision, unsatisfied by other institutions, and this forced the Department to push ahead faster than the resources at its disposal justified. The result was that the Department became overloaded, with its staff stretched beyond their capacity.[17]

The scale of activities organised by the DEMS therefore continued to contract during the first years of Williams's leadership. In the five years from 1965, the number of courses and students dropped by over 30 per cent, returning to the same levels as 1962–63.[18] Many of the extra-curricular activities which had taken place outside the classroom and had illustrated the creativity and diversity of extra-mural studies at HKU were abandoned. The annual student rally was not organised again after the eighth rally on 16 March 1968.[19] Mid-day lectures were discontinued and public lectures were curtailed. The Department's overseas contacts were also kept to a minimum. Study tours to neighbouring countries were suspended.[20] A summer school for an American college had to be held in alternate years with what had previously been an annual police course.[21] While Hughes was very active in international associations and travelled around the world to establish contacts with other adult education agencies, there is little evidence to suggest that Williams felt this to be an important part of his job. It was widely recognised that in spite of his excellent administrative skills and his Herculean efforts to build up the Department over the next two decades, Williams was a less charismatic leader than Ieuan Hughes and had a very different management style.

The policy of retrenchment allowed the Department a period of consolidation and improvement. Enrolments were limited in more than one-third of extra-mural courses with the aim of maintaining smaller class sizes.[22] Staff tutors and part-time tutors therefore had fewer duties so that they could spend more time dealing with the needs of individual students. Despite the decrease in the number of courses and students, the total teaching hours soared by 44 per cent between 1966 and 1970.[23] About half of all extra-mural courses in 1968–69 had teaching sessions which lasted one and a half hours or more, allowing more wide-ranging discussions within the classes.[24] The period of retrenchment lasted for about five years and ended in 1970, after which the Department returned to growth in terms of course and student figures.

The Department, the University and the UGC

The role of the Department of Extra-Mural Studies within the University and the broader higher education system was not yet fully settled in the late 1960s. The University had come to recognise the DEMS as a key auxiliary academic unit, even though it refused to give it full 'Teaching Department' status, but controversy continued between the University and the UGC over the development policy for the Department. Disagreement over collaboration between the extra-mural studies departments of the two local universities, resource allocation matters, and the academic status of the Department were the sources of this controversy.

Collaboration with the Chinese University of Hong Kong

Hong Kong's second department of extra-mural studies was established at the Chinese University of Hong Kong (CUHK) in April 1965.[25] This new department was directed by Mr T. C. Cheng, President of United College, but its activities were in fact organised by the Deputy Director, Mr T. C. Lai, who had gained an excellent training in extra-mural activities during his years at HKU. He was therefore able to guide the new extra-mural department at CUHK very effectively and it grew rapidly over the next few years. Enrolment figures indicate the enormous success of the new extra-mural department: in 1966–67 it admitted 7,413 students in 262 courses, a level of activity which its counterpart at HKU had not achieved in a whole decade of operation. It continued to be the largest extra-mural department in Hong Kong in terms of enrolments for the next twenty-five years.

While CUHK's new extra-mural department had its own merits and benefited the community in many ways, it was felt by some that the extra-mural activities of the two universities needed more co-ordination to avoid unnecessary duplication. Both universities had already foreseen the problem of course overlap and unnecessary competition even before the second extra-mural department began its work. Such worries were first addressed by W. E. Styler in April 1962, a year before the opening of the Chinese University. Styler suggested that the new university should concentrate its extra-mural work in the New Territories rather than in the urban areas of Hong Kong and Kowloon.[26] The leaders at CUHK would have been aware of this recommendation after the appointment of T. C. Lai, but they were hardly likely to impose this restriction upon their own university when such a large market for extra-mural studies existed in Kowloon. CUHK did recognise the danger of duplication between the two extra-mural departments but concluded in July 1964 that any problem was restricted to vocational and language courses.[27] CUHK was no doubt correct in adopting this view. First, public demand for higher adult education in Hong Kong was so large that even two departments could not satisfy all the needs. Second, duplication was not likely to exist in most liberal or cultural courses because there were no fixed syllabuses in these areas. The essence of these non-examinable courses was that they provided participants with opportunities to discuss and cultivate their intellectual needs, rather than merely learn a predetermined set of facts. Third, the extra-mural students targeted by CUHK differed from those at HKU. Most of the extra-mural courses at CUHK were conducted in Cantonese while, as has already been noted, the majority of courses at HKU were in English. The two institutions therefore attracted different types of students. It was recognised, however, that there was still a need for the two universities to co-ordinate vocational and language courses which were generally taught using similar syllabuses.

Despite acknowledging the need to avoid duplication of courses, the two universities were reluctant to co-operate in extra-mural activities until the intervention of the public authorities. Even then, co-operation remained indirect and informal. Some courses were administered jointly by both departments and a third party, there was some informal liaison between the two departments on course offerings, and there was also some co-operation in usage of accommodation and in the recruitment of tutors.[28] Further co-operation was encouraged by the UGC. One of the UGC's first initiatives was to promote co-ordination between HKU and CUHK in auxiliary academic activities such as libraries, teacher training and extra-mural studies.[29] In April 1966, the UGC visited HKU and suggested setting up a joint board of extra-mural studies which would aim at 'providing the institutional means for making this co-operation effective'.[30] This suggestion would not have had much force if the UGC had not had control over public funding to the universities. The UGC Chairman made it clear in February 1967 that the UGC intended to push the universities towards co-operation by using its fiscal powers to impose a joint board to take control of extra-mural activities in the colony:

> The Committee [UGC] although it recognises that Extra-Mural work in Hong Kong is of great importance believes that it would not be justified in recommending substantial additional funds until a Universities' Joint Board of Extra-Mural Studies has produced, after consultation with other organisations who were providing facilities for broadly similar audiences, a plan for Extra-Mural Studies in Hong Kong which stated clearly the aims of the Joint Board and its proposed methods of attaining them.[31]

Pressure from the UGC succeeded in drawing the two universities to the negotiating table. Arrangements for informal consultation between the two extra-mural departments on 'collaboration, co-ordination and demarcation possibilities' were not realised, however, because of Hughes's illness.[32]

Other UGC initiatives bore more fruit. Dr A. A. Liveright, Director of the Center for the Study of Liberal Education for Adults at Boston University, visited Hong Kong and submitted a memorandum in April 1967 on a *modus operandi* and tasks for the proposed joint board. He had no intention of turning the joint board into a supervisory body for local extra-mural studies, nor did he suggest merging the two extra-mural departments. Instead, Liveright commented that 'the major purpose of the Joint Board shall be to offer the educational and research facilities of the two Universities to the community of Hong Kong', and that it 'should operate more as a cooperative planning and development body for the two Universities rather than as a rigid and inflexible Board of Control'.[33] He also identified areas in which the two universities should not compete with each other and those in which healthy competition should take place, as well as the necessary steps to achieve greater co-ordination of extra-mural courses between the two departments. Liveright's recommendations were transmitted to the two vice-chancellors, who were preparing to form a Joint Committee on Extra-mural Studies (JCEMS) through the Liaison Group of the Vice-Chancellors' Meeting. The Liaison Group considered the terms of reference for the Joint Committee at its meeting on 14 April 1967 and, after some amendment, the terms of reference were approved by the vice-chancellors in the subsequent weeks.

While the DEMS was not opposed to co-operation with Chinese University, it initially had some reservations about the proposal to establish the Joint Committee. Hughes raised his doubts about the Joint Committee's powers and duties and its relationship with the extra-mural departments in a letter to the Vice-Chancellor in May 1967. He claimed that he was 'not at all clear as to the backgrounds, aims, hopes or objectives of the proposals or where we in the Department and the University stand in all this'.[34] He was worried that his Department would be placed in an inferior position in the Joint Committee because the HKU delegates were less experienced in extra-mural studies than their counterparts from CUHK. Roger Williams also had serious concerns about Liveright's recommendations, and felt that 'there is much in it which we cannot accept — unreservedly, anyway'.[35] The hesitations of Hughes and Williams were partly relieved by a discussion with the Registrar in which some principles were agreed with regard to the future position of the DEMS in the Joint Committee. It remained impossible at this early stage, however, to foresee the outcome of negotiations within the Joint Committee.[36]

The JCEMS came into existence in June 1967 under the chairmanship of Professor J. B. Gibson, Professor of Pathology and Pro-Vice-Chancellor at HKU, and its first meeting was held on 21 September 1967.[37] The revised terms of reference stated that the Joint Committee aimed, at this initial stage of co-operation, to 'prepare and present . . . plans for Extra-Mural Studies in Hong Kong (during the triennium 1967–70)' after consultation with other adult education agencies.[38] The two universities exchanged information about staff, finances and development plans at the initial meetings. Both departments agreed at an early stage in discussions that the unification of the two extra-mural departments 'was neither practical nor, in the end, economical' as no manpower could be saved by creating a single department of extra-mural studies. Some members also suggested that what Hong Kong needed was diversification, rather than unification, of adult education.[39] This view in fact reflected the opinion put forward by Liveright in his report of April 1967.

The main achievement in the early months of the JCEMS was an agreement reached on 9 November 1967 on 'principles or guide-lines for co-operation' over future certificate and examinable courses.[40] Both departments agreed to 'stay out of areas in which the other is already solely engaged' and seek the Joint Committee's guidance in case of overlap. They also agreed to meet with each other two or three times each term to ensure that these agreements were being honoured. According to this undertaking, HKU agreed not to offer examinable or certificate courses in Hotel Management, Advanced Translation, Tourist Guiding and Chinese History, while CUHK would not enter a wide range of fields, such as Law, Housing Management and most of the subjects in Engineering. There were some exceptions, however, which allowed the two extra-mural departments to offer the same courses. Social Work Certificate courses, for example, would be offered by both HKU and CUHK in alternative years. Certificate courses in Art and Design could be taught at the two universities concurrently, but in different languages.[41] In spite of the absence of official endorsement by the Joint Committee, this proposal was 'accepted as a very satisfactory indication of co-operation between the departments'.[42]

In February 1968 the JCEMS produced its first report for the two parent universities, outlining a number of directions which the extra-mural departments could follow in the future.[43] The Joint Committee recommended the purchase of extra-mural town centres, the introduction of part-time degree courses, the expansion of professional and vocational courses, and exploration of opportunities for conducting adult education through radio and television.[44] There is no evidence to indicate whether this report led to the production of a concrete working plan for joint programmes, but even without such a plan the report was still significant as it represented the first policy paper on extra-mural studies agreed by both universities.

The UGC, however, had more ambitious plans for collaboration between the two extra-mural departments. In July 1968 HKU submitted a proposal for further development of its Department of Extra-Mural Studies which was in line with recommendations in the Joint Committee report. The reply from the UGC was surprisingly negative. In blocking the proposal the chairman of the UGC,

Mr M. A. R. Herries, asserted on 2 October 1968 that 'the Committee [UGC] believes that something more than relatively loose collaboration is required and that at the very least there should be close dove-tailing of the activities of the two Departments and that preferably they should be merged'.[45] A week later the UGC's secretary confirmed this view, stating that UGC would have 'great difficulty in recommending substantial funds for the Extra-Mural Departments unless a reorganisation is carried out'.[46]

The UGC's reply led to strong protests from the universities. Roger Williams, who had by this time been promoted to Director of Extra-Mural Studies, was furious at the UGC reply and wrote to the Vice-Chancellor outlining his concerns:

> It seems to me that the two Vice-Chancellors, and the Joint Committee established by them, have been led completely up the garden path and that the negative and unconstructive UGC reply can only be construed as a vote of no confidence in the Departments of Extra-Mural Studies of the two Universities. . . . UGC is obviously not prepared to support two individual Departments. Having only recently established an Extra-Mural Department in the Chinese University, without consultation with Hong Kong University, the two Universities are now being asked to unscramble an egg that is well and truly scrambled . . . It would seem that the position of the UGC has been ill thought out and it should be asked directly its views. Indeed, the logic of the UGC position is that both Extra-mural Departments should be closed down.[47]

Professor Gibson was also discontented with the UGC's attitude and concluded that 'it is probable that nothing less than a complete merger will satisfy the U.G.C.'. He believed that the merger would do little to reduce public spending because the merger plan entailed even larger capital investment and more complex management arrangements.[48] The Vice-Chancellor, Professor K. E. Robinson, lodged a formal protest to the UGC on 15 October 1968:

> I am however very apprehensive that an attempt to compel these two departments to engage in even closer cooperation, so far from leading towards the joint operation which the Committee wishes to promote, would be almost certain to have the reverse effect . . . The suggestion that the two departments should be merged seems to be quite impracticable, nor do I see why the Extra-mural Studies Department should be singled out for such treatment.[49]

The University later clarified its viewpoint on collaboration between the two extra-mural studies departments in its 'Statement of Development Policy 1970–74':

> It has always assumed, indeed, that one reason for the existence of two rather small universities in Hong Kong was precisely that they should be different, not identical, in their methods and organisation, and it believes this to be no less so in those spheres of activity with which both are concerned than in any others. It has,

> however, in common with the Chinese University, always sought to foster the fullest cooperation between the two universities and it believes that the proposals [on extra-mural studies] it now submits to the Committee [UGC] are as fully in conformity with those objectives as the circumstances of the case permit.[50]

The Chinese University also articulated its equally strong opposition to the merger of extra-mural departments. CUHK's Vice-Chancellor, Dr Li Choh-ming, felt that 'the merging of the two departments would kill their initiative and have the effect of discouraging or even abandoning' extra-mural work in Hong Kong.[51] The message from the two vice-chancellors was very clear — there should be no merger of the two extra-mural departments.

Such vigorous opposition from the two universities had perhaps not been foreseen by the UGC. Faced now with such a strong rebuff from the universities, the UGC tried to moderate its stance on the issue. It reserved its decision for several months until further discussion at the next plenary session of the UGC. At a meeting with the members of the Department of Extra-Mural Studies on 20 March 1969 during a formal visitation of HKU, Herries raised the merger issue again and invited the Department to explain why a merger was not possible. The HKU delegates listed a number of disadvantages from both educational and administrative points of view. After the meeting, Williams felt that the UGC was likely to 'retreat on [the] merger front'.[52] In fact, when Herries gave his concluding speech at the end of the visitation a week later, he claimed that 'while the Committee [UGC] was not wrong to urge the closer collaboration between the two departments, we need not for the moment press the suggestion made in 1968 that there should be a merger of the two departments'.[53] The statement brought an end to the UGC's attempt to merge the two extra-mural departments, an issue which was never raised again.

Despite the retreat of the UGC, the merger controversy had already undermined the existing arrangements between the two universities on extra-mural co-operation. Both universities became cautious about addressing the issue, fearing that the public might perceive that they were willing to give up their independence or invite external intervention in their respective domains of activity. The general atmosphere of mistrust and rivalry between the two universities also prevented the leaders of the two extra-mural departments from taking any further steps towards co-operation. It was later argued that the lack of co-operation between the two departments was partly due to personal conflicts between Roger Williams and T. C. Lai, but the wider institutional mistrust must surely have been the real reason.[54] The Joint Committee continued to function for the next few years, but no substantial action was taken.[55] There were at least fourteen HKU extra-mural courses, most of which were non-examinable but of a vocational nature, which were identified as being similar to those offered by the CUHK.[56] There was even an occasion in the early

1970s when there was a conflict between the two departments in organising an extra-mural medical programme, which had been traditionally within the sphere of HKU.[57] It was not until the government proposed a new Open Learning Institute in the 1980s that the two universities, together with the polytechnics, actively co-operated in extending adult education in Hong Kong.[58]

Resource Allocation

Resource allocation was closely connected with the dispute over the merger of extra-mural departments at HKU and CUHK. HKU had long hoped that it might be possible to increase public funding for extra-mural studies and had made this request to government continually during the 1960s. The merger controversy between the UGC and the universities illustrated very clearly that UGC support for extra-mural studies was half-hearted. While the UGC said it was willing to increase financial support for extra-mural studies if the two universities agreed with its merger proposal, a rejection of the proposal was likely to put extra-mural studies funding at risk. The UGC's reluctance to support an expansion of extra-mural activities at HKU was clearly revealed in its Chairman's controversial letter of 2 October 1968. Herries noted that it 'would not be acceptable' to the UGC for the University to finance an expansion of DEMS activities by using surpluses from the public block grant voted to HKU.[59] The UGC secretary, Mr S. F. Bailey, further explained that while the University was free to use the Extra-Mural Studies Fund, which was in essence supported by student fees, it should not divert any public money outside the approved budget for extra-mural activities.[60] This restrictive policy meant that any attempt to finance extra-mural courses using public funding was banned even if no increase of government subvention was involved.

The University of course agreed with the UGC that it should not spend too much public money on extra-mural studies because such an increase might diminish the funds available for other academic activities which had higher priority. However, the University was not satisfied with the UGC's intervention in its internal operation through threats over resource allocation. The Vice-Chancellor issued a stern reply:

> Any such action would, it seems to me, spell an end to the University's freedom of decision in the expenditure of its total income during the Triennium subject to the terms of the recurrent grants memorandum and would, in my judgement, entail a complete departure from the principle of the University Grants Committee system.[61]

The University repeated its request for more funding from the government for extra-mural studies in its 1969 quadrennial development plan:

> The University is concerned at the restriction and indeed reduction of the activities of the Department [of Extra-Mural Studies] which have resulted from the Committee's injunctions, and in particular from its understanding that 'substantial additional funds' would be provided if the Committee was satisfied with the measure of coordination envisaged in the Report [of the Joint Committee] . . . it believes that some further development is now long overdue, if these activities are even to be maintained, and the morale of the Department not to deteriorate rapidly.[62]

In contrast to the compromise on the merger issue, the UGC stood firm in its policy of making minimal provision of public money for extra-mural studies. The UGC chairman responded to the University's request for more resources for the DEMS during the visitation in March 1969:

> As far as the Committee [UGC] is concerned there would appear to be no need to limit the development of this work if the fee income could be made to cover staff costs, including perhaps those of the Extra-Mural Department Staff itself. To the extent this is not possible the work in this field of the Extra-Mural Department will, of course, be in competition for resources with other University activities. We would however be ready to consider financial proposals for modest expenditure on this particular area of work for the next quadrennium.[63]

Professor Gibson was at first optimistic about the UGC Chairman's address. He told the Vice-Chancellor that he wished to revise the plans for increasing extra-mural teaching if the UGC really acknowledged the contribution being made by the DEMS and if it could approve more than 'modest expenditure'.[64] His hopes were unlikely to be realised, however, as the UGC chairman's statement implied that the self-financing policy for extra-mural activities would continue, and that public funding would remain as low as possible. It later emerged that the UGC expected even the administrative expenditure of the DEMS, if possible, to be paid for out of fee income rather than by grants from the government.[65] The Joint Committee was more realistic in its assessment of the situation. It expressed 'total dissatisfaction and disagreement' with the government's suggestion that all staff of the extra-mural departments should be funded through student fees alone. Although Bailey reassured the members of the Joint Committee that the UGC had no intention to cut budgets for extra-mural studies, he did not make any firm promise regarding the funding of extra-mural departments.[66]

Both the government and the University continued to follow a policy of minimal financial commitment to extra-mural studies throughout the 1970s. The University recognised this policy when preparing its triennial plan for 1978–81 in January 1977, stating that the University 'should not be expected to underwrite a further expansion of extra-mural activity at the expense of other University developments' unless 'sufficient funds can be available' from the UPGC.[67] By this time the UGC had been transformed into the University and Polytechnic Grants

Committee (UPGC). The UPGC also declared in April 1977 that it would not 'wish to see ever-increasing calls being made on full-time teachers, nor does it support the appointment of a number of additional staff tutors'.[68] The financing of the Department therefore remained little changed during this decade. The ratio of publicly-funded expenditure to self-financed remained approximately even.

Academic Status of the Department

The academic status of the Department of Extra-Mural Studies within the University improved significantly during the 1960s. The Director of Extra-Mural Studies had occupied a seat in the Senate since Hughes's arrival in 1960, and from 1966 all staff tutors were classified as 'Teachers' and were therefore allowed to sit on faculty boards.[69] The 'Teacher' status of the Director and his deputy and assistant were also confirmed in June 1969.[70] The Department's teaching role was therefore fully recognised as being a legitimate part of the academic mission of the University, even though the DEMS was not officially considered to be a 'Teaching Department' under the Statutes.

While staff tutors were constitutionally recognised by the University as members of the academic staff, in reality too they were now assuming more academic duties along with their administrative role in the Department. During the early 1960s, staff tutors undertook most of the academic and administrative duties of the Department because of inadequate secretarial support. One of the staff tutors, for example, spent only about twenty hours teaching in a semester but had to spend considerable time on non-academic duties like arranging accommodation and assisting with the printing of brochures.[71] The routine or even tedious clerical work which the staff tutors were required to do left them open to criticism for not fulfilling the duties expected of HKU academics or British extra-mural staff. This problem was gradually rectified from 1965 by appointing 'Specialist Staff Tutors' who participated heavily in teaching and co-ordinating courses in their subject areas.[72] Mr Jon Prescott, for example, joined the DEMS in October 1966 to take care of subjects in Art, Architecture and Planning.[73] Mr Joe England was appointed in the 1968–69 academic year to supervise courses in Management Studies, and Dr S. G. Redding assumed similar duties from the 1973–74 academic year. Existing staff tutors were also shifting their roles and began to put more emphasis on teaching and less on routine administration. This transformation of roles was completed by 1973 and by the 1975–76 academic year the staff tutors worked nearly ten hours per week on teaching and other academic matters, a load which was considered normal for other University teachers.[74] This development strengthened the academic position of both the staff tutors and the Department within the University.

The three-tier management structure of extra-mural studies was also reformed to strengthen the connection between the DEMS and other parts of the University. By 1964 the Board was still chaired by the Director of Extra-Mural Studies but had expanded to consist of fourteen members including the Vice-Chancellor, the Registrar, Senate representatives, all staff tutors and several community leaders.[75] From time to time the contribution of external members was impressive as they helped the DEMS establish contacts with society and enlist public support. Hughes's illness in 1965, however, brought the operation of the Board of Extra-Mural Studies to a virtual halt for two years.[76] In June 1967 the Vice-Chancellor and Hughes agreed to reform the existing Board in order to meet the changing needs of the Department and to take account of the establishment of an extra-mural department at CUHK. It was felt that wider participation from other parts of the University was desirable in the next phase of development for extra-mural studies.[77] The Senate resolved at its meeting on 3 October 1967 that the BEMS be renamed the Committee on Extra-Mural Studies (CEMS) 'to advise the Senate on any question relating to extra-mural policy' and 'subject to Council regulations, to administer the extra-mural studies subvention'.[78]

The new CEMS was similar to the committees of management which the University used to manage other non-faculty units and became responsible for both academic and administrative affairs. The chairmanship was transferred from the Director of Extra-Mural Studies to the Pro-Vice-Chancellor. The number of seats for Department staff on the new Committee was restricted to three, and there was initially to be no membership from outside the University.[79] The transformation of the BEMS into the Committee on Extra-Mural Studies therefore marked something of a change of approach to extra-mural studies, involving a tightening of University control, a reduction of representation from those with expertise in adult education, and a rejection of outside involvement from the community. While the DEMS and its Director came under closer scrutiny from the Senate through the new CEMS, the structure was also designed to facilitate more efficient decision-making and closer liaison between the DEMS and the faculties. A chairman from outside the DEMS might also provide more objective advice and certainly ensured that the Senate's wishes for extra-mural affairs were more actively pursued.

While the Department was able to achieve greater academic recognition within the University in the late 1960s, the UGC had a quite different view. The chairman of the UGC was adamant in 1968 that 'although any Extra-Mural Department may need to undertake some teaching it should be mainly administrative in function'.[80] The UGC's concept of an extra-mural department was the exact opposite of what the DEMS had been struggling to achieve at HKU as it sought to improve its academic status. The UGC's policy therefore drew strong protest from HKU. Williams argued that 'whatever else UGC is talking about it is not university adult education' as it was not possible for administrators lacking a strong academic background to plan and co-ordinate high-quality extra-mural courses.[81] Professor Gibson was disappointed at the UGC's attempt to go beyond its powers and interfere with the academic development of the University.[82] The Vice-Chancellor's long reply to the UGC perhaps best reflects the University's point of view on the academic status of the DEMS:

> [The remark of the UGC] seems to imply that the Hong Kong University Grants Committee believes that all extra-mural studies departments of the United Kingdom universities are working on a fundamentally mistaken basis and that we should adopt the American system under which 'university extension' staff are I believe administrative rather than academic . . . I take it to be an essential feature of that pattern that the staff of the Department should mainly consist of what are called 'Staff Tutors', usually at Lecturer level or above, who are themselves well qualified academically in some subject in which the University is concerned to maintain or develop extra-mural teaching, but who besides teaching themselves are also largely concerned with the organisation of classes, lectures, short term residential courses and Summer Schools, the planning of new courses and the selection of part-time teachers (including members of the academic staff of the University) for extra-mural work in their particular area . . . In other words, a staff tutor in an extra-mural department, like other University teachers, is expected to engage in teaching, in administration, and in research . . . It is no doubt for such reasons that the Statutes of this University expressly include in the category of *teachers* of the University staff tutors in the Extra-mural Studies Department.[83]

Although the UGC continued in its attempt to turn the DEMS into an 'administrative machine' during the last months of 1969, it chose not to provoke the University again and made no response to the Vice-Chancellor's assertion on the academic status of the DEMS.[84] The disagreements between HKU and the UGC over the academic status of extra-mural studies, collaboration between two extra-mural departments, and resource allocation highlighted the fact that the University's aims and those of government and government-sponsored bodies often conflicted when it came to extra-mural studies. Resourcing was a particularly difficult issue, with both government and UGC being reluctant to commit themselves financially to developments in extra-mural studies. This attitude was the opposite of what the Keswick Committee had advocated in the early 1950s, but was entirely consistent with the Hong Kong government's established policies in higher education.

Growth of Professional and Vocational Courses

Despite disagreements over a variety of extra-mural policies, the Department, the University and the UGC agreed that the main focus of the DEMS should now be to provide more opportunities for professional training in order to assist with the economic development of Hong Kong. This policy development represented a departure from the original principles of extra-mural studies supported by Moore and Hughes, who believed that there needed to be a balance between liberal and vocational courses. The DEMS had, of course, organised vocational courses from the outset and kept developing them throughout the early 1960s, but the new Director, Roger Williams, was even more ready than his predecessors to expand vocational courses. From the beginning of his directorship he was aware of the increasing demand for professional and vocational courses in Hong Kong.[85] In considering recent developments in extra-mural studies in Hong Kong and Britain, he observed a shift of emphasis from liberal and cultural courses to a wider spectrum of professional and vocational training. He attributed this shift in emphasis to the 'increasing complexity of modern life, with its rapid industrial and technological changes' which had in turn increased the demand for 'vocational' subjects.[86] He noted that in order to cater for this demand in areas where there were no recognised courses of training, many British extra-mural departments had begun to organise diploma and certificate courses. In Hong Kong there was also a 'marked demand' for such courses: 'Long past are the days when vocational and craft subjects were the province of the local authority, while liberal studies were the preserve of the University. This division, never absolute, is now much blurred.'[87] He was a realist when it came to assessing the changing role of extra-mural studies in a modern industrialised society. To him the need for such courses was clear and immediate and his Department would have to do something to address this demand.

Roger Williams's inclination to introduce more extra-mural courses of a vocational nature was declared in his proposals for the 1970–74 quadrennuim:

> Whilst seeking to continue the earlier British University tradition of offering many courses in the liberal arts, the main emphasis of the Department's programme lies in the field of vocational and professional education. This reflects a world-wide trend in adult education provision and is particularly appropriate in the circumstances prevailing in Hong Kong, where the opportunities for higher education are limited or even non-existent in some subjects.[88]

Some members of the University had an even greater desire for vocationally-oriented extra-mural courses than Williams. Professor Gibson, for example, frankly referred to liberal extra-mural courses as 'those activities in the leisure field' and concluded that 'I don't think this is a first priority in Hong Kong and I doubt if it is really an activity to which the University should honestly devote much support'.[89] The liberal courses were, in the eyes of Gibson and many others in the University, not essential and should therefore remain as only a minor part of extra-mural studies in Hong Kong. Vocational courses, on the other hand, should in future be the mainstay of the DEMS.

Hopes for an expansion of vocational training in extra-mural studies were also apparent outside the University. Mr Tang Ping-yuan, a Legislative Councillor, voiced his concerns about vocational training in March 1968 and suggested extending extra-mural studies in the vocational field and placing emphasis on the practical side.[90] The UGC also recognised the potential of extra-mural studies for training professionals for various industries. Its members shared Gibson's view on vocational extra-mural courses and pronounced clearly which type of extra-mural courses it was going to support when the chairman addressed the University in March 1969:

> Committee Members noted with interest that these [part-time evening courses of a vocational nature], as at present provided, were in such demand that they could be financially self-supporting at any rate for direct costs. They were also clear that many of these courses fulfilled a real need in Hong Kong. They therefore believe that priority should be given, within the Extra-Mural Department [to these courses] . . . With regard to general or non-vocational courses the Committee believes that, although no doubt valuable, it would not be right to devote high priority to them. The test which might be applied is that of demand and broadly speaking only those courses in this field which can meet at least their own direct expenditure should be continued for long as a University activity.[91]

While vocational courses were being more emphasised in extra-mural studies, both the UGC and the Department were careful not to extend these activities to low-level technical training which was within the remit of other institutions, especially the projected Polytechnic. The UGC, while supporting the development of vocational training at the DEMS, envisaged that 'some broad demarcation line between the activities of the Polytechnic and of the Universities in this field' should be established. In general, the DEMS should 'concentrate upon teaching at University level', while lower level courses could be offered by other institutions.[92] Those involved in extra-mural studies at HKU repeatedly expressed their lack of interest in these technical subjects.[93] The Joint Committee also welcomed the UGC's suggestion of drawing a demarcation line between the Polytechnic and the extra-mural departments.[94] This self-limiting policy seems to have worked quite well in practice and HKU never attempted to expand into purely technical training. Despite the fact that the DEMS did not establish strong contacts with the Polytechnic, there were very few conflicts between the two institutions in the area of vocational training in the following years.

While the distinction between 'vocational' and 'liberal' courses was never absolute and there are no reliable statistics to illustrate the changing emphasis in extra-mural course provision, some observations will be helpful in understanding the emerging trend.[95] It was reported in 1973 that '80 to 85% of the courses run by the Extra-Mural Department were of vocational or professional nature and only 15% of general cultural interest'.[96] The percentage of students in subject areas mainly for vocational purposes reached 81 per cent of the total enrolments in the 1984–85 academic year.[97] An increase in the number of certificate courses also indicates the rising tide of interest in vocational qualifications. In 1964–65, the DEMS inaugurated its first Extra-Mural Certificate courses in Librarianship in collaboration with the Hong Kong Library Association (HKLA). Twenty years later in 1984–85, a cohort of 1,275 students completed their studies in twenty-seven courses at different levels and were awarded corresponding qualifications. All but three of these qualifications were primarily for vocational purposes.[98] An even larger number of students took DEMS courses to prepare for external examinations, most of which were vocational or professional in nature. The majority of new staff tutors recruited during the 1970s were responsible for vocational rather than non-vocational courses. In 1968–69, there were seven staff tutors working in the Department, five of whom were responsible for professional and vocational courses.[99] By the 1983–84 academic year, the number of staff had increased by thirteen, most of whom were involved in new courses in professional and vocational subjects such as Social Work, Librarianship and Computer Science.[100]

The DEMS therefore provided a wide variety of professional and vocational courses by the mid-1980s, many of which were being offered for the first time in Hong Kong. Many of these courses were able to provide high quality vocational training and built a solid foundation for the expansion of professional education at the tertiary level. A number of these new programmes will be discussed in greater detail in the next chapter.

The Extra-Mural Town Centre

One of the outcomes of the steady introduction and development of new professional and vocational programmes was a rising demand for office and teaching space. The shortage of accommodation on the main campus of the University had been a problem since the Department was established in 1957, but various short-term solutions were always found as new demands arose. While the Department's various activities continued to be administered from cramped accommodation in the basement of the Main Building and other non-university premises were rented in different parts of Hong Kong and Kowloon for teaching purposes, it nevertheless quickly became apparent that the University would soon have to invest in purpose-built accommodation closer to its student base. In the mid-1960s, therefore, it was finally decided that an extra-mural Town Centre would be established to cater for students who worked in and around Central. After securing rented premises for a large Town Centre in 1967, the Department's new teaching facilities in the heart of the city gradually became the venue for most extra-mural courses and the true centre of extra-mural teaching at the University of Hong Kong.

When the Department inaugurated the full-time University of London external law degree in 1964, it became necessary to secure an appropriate venue for teaching and offices for reasons that are explained in the next chapter. The Extra-Mural Law Centre in the Chiao Shang Building was rented with government support from March 1965. Although the Law Centre was primarily utilised as accommodation for law courses, the DEMS was allowed to use the facilities for its own extra-mural courses when it was not occupied for law teaching. The Department therefore offered experimental day-time courses for 'housewives, retired people, a.m. and p.m. teachers, visitors here for a short stay, shift workers, and others in the community who were not necessarily occupied in the day, as well as those who could be specially released from their work to attend refresher classes that would heighten their working ability' in the Extra-Mural Law Centre.[101] In 1965–66, ninety-two courses (including both law and non-law courses) were held in the Extra-Mural Law Centre, and it thus became the principal venue for extra-mural courses.[102] The advent of the government-sponsored Centre therefore led to a considerable improvement in the facilities available to the Department in delivering extra-mural courses.

The five-year lease of the eighth floor of the Chiao Shang Building was broken for uncertain reasons after less than three years of occupancy in 1967. The lease in fact allowed the DEMS to vacate the building after three years, a necessary clause because in 1964 the Department did not know for how long the government would continue to sponsor the London LLB scheme. But in June 1966 the government extended its support of the project through to 1969, enabling the completion of the five-year lease without difficulty. It is therefore likely that the lease was broken as a result of the political riots which occurred in Hong Kong in 1967. A pro-Communist emporium had long been located in the Chiao Shang Building and it became a notorious leftist stronghold during the riots. It seems that the DEMS, fearing that the presence of communist agitators in the building would have an adverse effect on its courses, decided to find other premises.[103] In fact, after the removal, Roger Williams suggested that if the DEMS had not left the Chiao Shang Building, enrolments would have suffered significantly, with a drop of perhaps 50 to 75 per cent.[104] The Department succeeded in moving into a new Extra-Mural Town Centre on the eleventh floor of Universal House, 151 Des Voeux Road Central, and recommenced teaching activities there on 9 October 1967.[105] The new Town Centre had a floor area of approximately 9,000 square feet, and by 1970 the Department was paying a rent of about $140,000 per annum.[106] The Centre consisted of seven lecture rooms, two seminar rooms, two art studios and music rooms, one library and several offices which had a capacity of around 300 students at any given time.[107]

Even though the DEMS had secured a well-equipped and modern teaching facility, the Department and the University felt that the rented premises represented a far from ideal solution to the Department's space problem. A permanent Town Centre owned by the University was considered as being essential for the future development of extra-mural studies. The DEMS continually asked the University for a permanent Town Centre for its increasingly numerous courses and to facilitate future development. For instance, already in 1968 Roger Williams was seeking more space than was available at the new Town Centre, reporting that:

> The pressure on the existing accommodation there is already intense, all the available lecture-room accommodation being fully used on every week-night and with increasing use being made of the Centre for courses during the day and at weekends. Next session [1968–69], some courses which are perfectly proper offerings in themselves but which do not rank high in the Department's priorities are being excluded from the programme because of this pressure on accommodation.[108]

The pressure on space had become even more critical because the DEMS had agreed to accommodate the staff of the new Law Department until 1969. It was also noted that space which had previously been available for teaching in alternative venues such as City Hall and the United States Information Service was being reduced because of other demands on those bodies.[109]

The University acknowledged the desirability of a permanent Town Centre and the Joint Committee on Extra-Mural Studies 'stressed the solid advantages to be gained if the Extra-Mural Town Centre were to be purchased outright' in its report of February 1968.[110] The University kept the matter high on its list of priorities, and in June 1970 the Senate agreed to list a Town Centre for the Department as one of the building projects on the University's Capital Building Programme for the 1972–75 triennium.[111] Although the University ultimately failed to include this proposal in the final Capital Building Programme submitted to the UGC in July 1970, it nevertheless described the projected Town Centre to the UGC in detail: the gross floor area would need to be approximately 22,500 square feet, including additional teaching space, music rooms, a dark room and common rooms. The expanded Town Centre would cost $1.7 million to build or $5.6 million to purchase.[112] The UGC offered no objections to the purchase of such a facility when consulted in 1968 and 1973, provided that any such purchase did not require additional resources from public funds.[113]

The issue of a permanent Extra-Mural Town Centre even attracted the attention of the Convocation of the University, a statutory body consisting of the University's graduates. Convocation wrote to the University in July 1973 to express its support for the expansion of the Department of Extra-Mural Studies, in particular the establishment of a permanent Town Centre, observing that:

> It is the stated policy of both the Government and the University that no one should be barred from taking a place in the University because of financial need.

> But have we ever thought of those who even though they are fully qualified but who in spite of support from bursaries and loans, could still not be in a position to take his rightful place in the Citadel of Higher Learning because he has to earn money to support his immediate family? And if such persons were to wish to better themselves after working hours in order to quench their thirst of learning, does the University not feel obliged and morally obligated to provide facilities to satisfy their needs? That is why Convocation strongly advocates the University to expand the Extra-Mural Department and to urgently request Government to provide this department with a permanent town centre. The existence of a permanent centre for the Extra-Mural Department will symbolise by a physical presence the concern of the University in the community it serves, and emphasises the fact that the University is part of the community.[114]

Despite such general support from across the University community, the plan for a permanent town centre was not realised until the early 1980s. The University originally envisaged the new town centre as part of a larger building project shared with other users, and several different proposals were considered over the years. There was even a suggestion in 1972–73 that the town centre could be housed in a purpose-built floor on top of another government building or multi-storey car-park in Central or Wanchai.[115] When the Town Centre lease at Universal House (renamed Nanyang Commercial Bank Building in 1977) expired in August 1978, however, there was still no substantial progress on the acquisition of a permanent town centre.[116] The University was therefore forced to find other leased premises for the Town Centre.[117]

After 'a long and difficult search', the University managed to secure a six-year lease of the entire eighth floor of the new Wing On Centre at 111 Connaught Road Central from July 1977. The annual rent in the first three years was a staggering $720,000. Of this amount, the University agreed to pay $280,000 in the first year and $400,000 in each of the second and third years. After a short period of internal decoration, the new Town Centre went into operation in January 1978.[118] The new Town Centre had a much larger capacity than the old premises at Universal House. Its floor area was about 15,250 square feet (60 per cent more than at the old building) and there were fourteen lecture rooms accommodating 600 students, compared with seven lecture rooms for 300 students in the previous centre.[119] After moving to the Wing On Centre, the number of courses conducted in the Town Centre soared from 144 in 1977–78 to 268 in 1978–79. By the end of the 1970s, nearly half of the extra-mural courses offered by the Department were being taught in the new Town Centre.

The University became more serious in its efforts to secure a permanent home for its operations in Central once the Town Centre moved to the Wing On Centre. The Committee on Extra-Mural Studies advised the University in April 1979 on the space required for a permanent Town Centre in terms of quality and quantity.

The Committee recommended that the Town Centre should be 'as centrally located as possible in proximity to public transport terminals and to car parks' in order to cater to the needs of part-time adult students. It believed that the best location would be on the fringes of the Central district, near 'the Hong Kong waterfront in an area bounded by the Macau Ferry Pier on the West and by Asian House on the East'.[120] The space requirement of the permanent Town Centre was estimated at around 18,000 square feet. This would allow for a larger number of lecture rooms and a music room, all of which were to be fitted with modern facilities suitable for adult education.[121]

The senior management of the University also reached a consensus that a permanent Town Centre for its extra-mural activities was preferable to temporary leased premises. Among the numerous advantages of a permanent centre were the avoidance of (1) irregular and uncontrolled increases in annual costs due to rental variations; (2) periodic restoration and refurbishing costs made necessary by changes of accommodation; and (3) wasting substantial amounts of staff time in moving premises, which entailed complicated course planning and timetabling 'which themselves also have an adverse effect on morale'.[122] More importantly, the University's Finance Committee agreed in October 1981 to the criteria for a permanent Town Centre which had already been suggested by the CEMS in 1979. They even proposed that the floor area of the Town Centre should be increased to 20,000 square feet.[123]

After years of searching, an opportunity to secure a suitable site emerged in May 1981. The developer of Shun Tak Centre, a new commercial complex which was scheduled for completion in 1985, agreed to sell an entire floor with an area of 22,000 square feet for about $60 million.[124] The site matched the criteria already set by the CEMS and the Finance Committee: it was located in the Central district above the Macau ferry terminal, which was also planned to be connected with the Mass Transit Railway; there were to be multi-storey public car-parks in and adjacent to the building; the floor area of 22,000 square feet met the University's requirements exactly; and the internal partitioning and the related infrastructure could be custom-built for the purposes of extra-mural studies. The more remarkable fact was that although the University had to use its own Endowment Fund to buy the premises, it was expected to enjoy a financial advantage of about $22 million from the purchase of the premises at Shun Tak Centre compared with rented space at the Wing On Centre over a ten-year period.[125] The Council was impressed by the recommendation presented at its meeting on 25 February 1982 and authorised the Finance Committee to negotiate with the developer for the purchase to proceed.[126]

The proposal to locate the permanent Town Centre in the Central district was, however, not without opposition. When the Finance Committee finished its negotiations with the developer and proposed in April 1982 to acquire the property for about $45 million, a Council member expressed doubts about the purchase of premises in a quarter of Central where such high property prices prevailed. Instead, he suggested relocating the Town Centre to the new reclamation area in Tsim Sha Tsui East. The rationale for such a counter-proposal, which seemed to go against all the previous decisions relating to this matter, was later explained by C. G. Large, the University's Finance Officer:

> The essence of his [the Council member's] question will I presume be the postulation that extra-mural needs might more economically be satisfied by a provision of classes in Tsimshatsui East, where property prices are known to be cheaper; and the recognition that the University does not have to advertise or, 'sell' its product in order to attract students. They will seek it out of their own volition; even make some sacrifice of personal time and convenience to get to extra-mural classes. The popular area in Central is an undesirable location for an extra-mural studies operation as the University is here competing with commercial tenants for space.[127]

This counter-proposal was sternly opposed by the Department. Roger Williams emphasised that the premises in the new Shun Tak Centre could be custom-built according to the actual needs of the Department and would provide space for extra-mural courses for a very large number of students. He considered that the Shun Tak Centre was much more accessible than the site in Tsim Sha Tsui East, thus minimising the travel time of students and tutors who were unlikely to be willing to take more than two forms of public transport to reach the Town Centre. He used statistics to show that students living or working in Kowloon were quite willing to attend lessons on the other side of the harbour while many of those living or working on Hong Kong Island were reluctant to travel to Kowloon. Tutors, one-third of whom were University staff, were also unwilling to travel from Hong Kong Island across the harbour to teach. A Town Centre in Kowloon would also increase logistical problems, restrict the usage of the Town Centre by the University itself, and make enrolment exercises more difficult. It was noted that the Chinese University had already set up an extra-mural town centre near Tsim Sha Tsui East, and Williams wanted to avoid having two town centres in the same district. He felt it was important that the two centres be able to develop their own identities and having them in such close proximity was problematic. Finally, Williams warned that if the Town Centre was moved to Kowloon, the Department of Extra-Mural Studies would lose at least one-third of its extra-mural enrolments, approximately 7,500 students.[128] These were very strong reasons for the Council to stick with the original plan and purchase the Shun Tak Centre premises.

After a long discussion at its meeting on 28 April 1982, the Council finally supported Williams's arguments and approved the Finance Committee's proposal to purchase the premises in the Shun Tak Centre for about $45 million.[129] It was expected that the existing Town Centre would be moved to the Shun Tak Centre after the expiry of the lease at the Wing On Centre, which had been extended for two more years from 1983. The long-held hopes of the Department for a permanent Town Centre would therefore be realised after nearly three decades of waiting. This represented a very considerable investment in the future of extra-mural studies, and shows how far the fortunes of the DEMS had revived under the directorship of Roger Williams.

Conclusion

Despite the retrenchment policy of the mid-1960s and the government's continuing reluctance to provide additional resources for extra-mural studies, the DEMS was able to develop and extend its activities steadily until the early 1980s. The shift in focus from liberal studies courses to more vocationally-oriented programmes strengthened the role of the Department in providing professional studies to adult learners. The expansion of the Town Centre throughout the period also enhanced the capacity of the Department to organise more courses for more students. During the twenty years from 1964 to 1985, the numbers of courses doubled and the number of registered students trebled. In the year 1984–85, the DEMS organised 950 extra-mural courses with an enrolment of 28,417 students. The total number of lecture hours in the year had risen to 36,948. It should be noted that these figures were far above the enrolments and teaching hours of the University's full-time undergraduate programmes.[130] In 1984–85 the Department was awarding a range of qualifications to successful students: a diploma, three University certificates, and twenty-three Extra-Mural Certificates were awarded to 1,275 students. This was indeed an impressive contribution to professional and continuing education in Hong Kong, but it was only a start to the extraordinary growth that would take place in the 1980s and 1990s, and which will be examined in Chapters 6, 7 and 8.

The Department of Extra-Mural Studies facilitated personal and career development for thousands of individuals. The extra-mural courses gathered people from all walks of life and allowed students to widen their social networks and intellectual horizons while working towards qualifications that were of very real benefit to their careers. The vocational programmes were designed principally to assist students in acquiring the necessary professional skills for improving performance at work and enhancing their career prospects. Some of the extra-mural students even launched new careers after the completion of their studies at the DEMS, and others later returned to acquire further professional qualifications. Many extra-mural students were therefore motivated by their studies with the DEMS to keep on studying for the rest of their lives. Some of these stories will be examined in the next chapter which aims at surveying in greater detail some of the more important areas of vocational and professional studies offered by the Department from the mid-1960s until the mid-1980s.

Photo 1 An examination in Loke Yew Hall for the Evening School of Higher Chinese Studies, 1953. (Courtesy of HKU Libraries)

Photo 2 Awards ceremony in Loke Yew Hall for the Evening School of Higher Chinese Studies, attended by the Governor, Sir Alexander Grantham, in1953. (Courtesy of HKU Libraries)

Photo 3 Mr Ieuan Hughes, Director of Extra-Mural Studies (1960–67). (Courtesy of *South China Morning Post*)

Photo 4 A South-East Asian study tour led by Miss Priscilla Mark arrives in Kuala Lumpur in July 1963. (Courtesy of Mrs Priscilla Tso)

Photo 5 Mr T. C. Lai and his students departing Hong Kong for a study tour of Japan, 1963–64. (Courtesy of Mr T. C. Lai)

Photo 6 Participants in the Leverhulme Conference on Extra-Mural Studies held at HKU, 26–31 October 1964. The Vice-Chancellor, Sir Lindsay Ride, sits in the centre of the front now, with Mr W. E. Styler to his right. Mr Ieuan Hughes is at the centre of the back row, with staff tutors Y. C. Jao to his left and Perry Siu to his right. (Courtesy of HKU Libraries)

▲ **Photo 7** Members of the Department of Extra-Mural Studies with members of the Hong Kong Government Education Department, October 1966. Front row: Mrs Nana Tsao is on the far left, Mr T. C. Lai is third from the left, Mr Ieuan Hughes is second from the right, and Mrs Priscilla Tso is on the far right. Back row: Dr C. K. Leung is second from the left and Mr Perry Siu is third from left. (Courtesy of Mrs Priscilla Tso)

◀ **Photo 8** Red star atop the Chiao Shang Building, October 1967. It was soon after this political stunt by Communist sympathisers that the Department of Extra-Mural Studies moved out of its first Town Centre. (Courtesy of *Sing Tao News Corporation*)

Photo 9 Mr Roger Williams, Director of Extra-Mural Studies (1968–86), receiving a cheque for $10,000 from Mr Hilton Cheong-Leen of Lions International, May 1969. This donation was used to support the diploma course in management studies. (Courtesy of *South China Morning Post*)

Photo 10 Head Office of the Department of Extra-Mural Studies in the Main Building in 1978; this space is now the University's Faculty of Arts Office. (Courtesy of HKU External Relations Office)

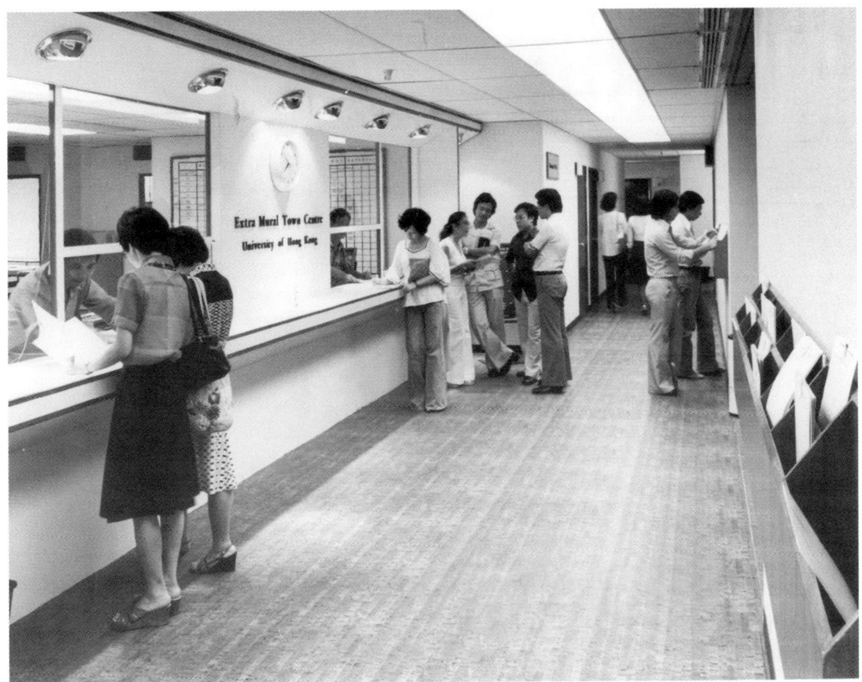

Photo 11 The new Town Centre of the Department of Extra-Mural Studies in the Wing On Centre, 1978. (Courtesy of HKU External Relations Office)

Photo 12 Students using the Library in the Town Centre, 1978. This was a popular place for after-work study. (Courtesy of HKU External Relations Office)

Photo 13 An art class in the new Town Centre, 1978. (Courtesy of HKU External Relations Office)

Photo 14 A Putonghua class in the new Town Centre, 1978. (Courtesy of HKU External Relations Office)

Photo 15 By 1986 the Department's Town Centre was relocated to the newly-constructed Shun Tak Centre in Sheung Wan. (Courtesy of the *South China Morning Post*)

Photo 16 Presentation Ceremony for the London School of Economics Diploma in Economics, September 1991. Front row (left to right): Dr R. Gosling (LSE); Professor Rosie T. T. Young, HKU Pro-Vice-Chancellor; Dr Christine Challis (LSE); Professor Lee Ngok, Director, School of Professional and Continuing Education. (Courtesy of HKU SPACE)

Photo 17 A Chinese calligraphy class at the SPACE Town Centre, 1992. (HKU SPACE)

Photo 18 University of London Graduates Reception in HKU Convocation Room, January 1992. Professor S. Sutherland, Vice-Chancellor of London University is addressing the graduates while Professor Wang Gungwu, Vice-Chancellor of HKU, Professor Lee Ngok, Mr John Cribbin, Dr R. Gosling (LSE), and Professor Tom Nossiter (LSE) look on. (Courtesy of HKU SPACE)

Photo 19 Graduation ceremony for the Curtin University Bachelor of Business degree, 1992. (Courtesy of HKU SPACE)

Photo 20 Students of the Master of Housing Management course on a field trip to Singapore, 1993. (Courtesy of HKU SPACE)

Photo 21 Students in a practical class at Queen Mary Hospital for the Medical Laboratory Science course, 1995. (Courtesy of HKU SPACE)

Photo 22 Professor Lee Ngok, Director of Extra-Mural Studies (1986–91) and Director of the School of Professional and Continuing Education (1992–95). (Courtesy of HKU SPACE)

Photo 23 Mr Bill Howarth, Acting Director of SPACE addressing a graduation ceremony for accountancy graduates in 1995. (Courtesy of HKU SPACE)

Photo 24 The T. T. Tsui Building, headquarters for HKU SPACE since May 1996. (Courtesy of HKU SPACE)

Photo 25 A class in the Admiralty Learning Centre. (Courtesy of HKU SPACE)

Photo 26 Student group, HKU SPACE Community College. (Courtesy of HKU SPACE)

Photo 27 Professor Enoch Young, Director of HKU SPACE (1997–2007), making an address at the 2007–08 commencement ceremony of the HKU SPACE Global College in Suzhou. (Courtesy of HKU SPACE)

Photo 28 The Kowloon East Campus (2007), the newest and most advanced of HKU SPACE's learning centres in Hong Kong. (Courtesy of HKU SPACE)

Photo 29 Professor C. F. Lee, Director-designate of HKU SPACE. Proessor Lee will take up full-time duties from February 2008. (Courtesy of HKU SPACE)

Photo 30 Mrs Selina Tsang as Honorary Patron of the HKU SPACE Alumni, 21 May 2007. Mrs Tsang is with Professor Enoch Young and Dr Peter C. Y. Lee, inaugural president of the HKU SPACE Alumni. (Courtesy of HKU SPACE)

CHAPTER FIVE

The Cradle of Professional Studies in Hong Kong, 1964–1985

THE DEPARTMENT OF EXTRA-MURAL STUDIES enjoyed a period of sustained growth from the end of the 1960s until the early 1980s. This growth was to a significant extent due to the introduction of a number of new extra-mural professional programmes which have been discussed in outline in the last chapter. It is not possible within the confines of this book to provide an exhaustive account of these new courses which did so much to satisfy the huge demand for high-quality vocational and professional training courses which the accelerating economic development of Hong Kong created. This chapter will therefore focus on the development of selected programmes which made significant contributions to the training of professionals in Hong Kong, beginning with the full-time London University external Bachelor of Law programme introduced in 1964. Later, a Diploma in Management Studies was launched in 1968. These programmes complemented existing vocational courses in librarianship, and a whole host of courses in Social Work and language studies which aimed at improving the skills of professionals as Hong Kong began to aspire to an international role in the globalising economy of the 1980s.

Some professional programmes were tailored to meet needs which were particular to Hong Kong, and the Housing Management Certificate course was one such programme which will be discussed. Other courses did not aim at any particular vocational group, but nevertheless allowed alumni to begin new careers in areas where they had little previous experience. While it has not been possible to give more than a handful of examples of the ways in which these vocational and professional programmes assisted in the career development of extra-mural alumni, it is hoped that these will at least point to the ways in which the Department's work assisted students to achieve their career aspirations and at the same time contributed to the educational development of the wider Hong Kong community. It was during this period that particularly strong bonds were forged between 'town' and 'gown', especially now that around half of the University's extra-mural courses were held in its Town Centre, which had been located in Universal House from 1967 until 1977, and then in the Wing On Centre from 1978 until the completion of the new Shun Tak Centre in 1986

The University of London LLB External Degree

The first full-scale professional training programme organised by the DEMS was the three-year preparation course for the University of London's external Bachelor of Law (LLB) degree. Prior to the introduction of the programme in 1964–65, the Department had already offered some courses to assist students who were attempting qualifications from external bodies such as the ACCA and CIS, but the LLB external degree programme was a much more important undertaking. First, the government was actively involved in this programme. For the first time, the government invested a large amount of public money in an extra-mural programme because it hoped that this would be the initial step in developing legal education in Hong Kong. Second, this was the first extra-mural programme which could assist students in gaining an external bachelor's degree. Third, in spite of various academic and administrative changes over the decades since it was introduced, the external London LLB remains one of the major professional training courses offered by HKU SPACE, and continues to be an important means of training lawyers and other professionals who need a solid foundation in legal knowledge.

Legal education at HKU can be traced back to the pre-War period. In 1924, George W. Keeton was appointed by the University as Reader in Law and Politics, but the focus of his teaching was primarily on the academic rather than the professional side of the law and his three-year stay in Hong Kong was too brief to achieve any significant development in legal education.[1] The demand for lawyers in Hong Kong was negligible and remained so for many years, so the government was not keen on developing local legal education even during the 1950s. Those graduates of HKU who wished to become solicitors or barristers in the pre-War years were therefore forced to pursue their legal training in Britain, usually at Oxford or in London. Early HKU students who followed this route to legal training in England included William Thomas (B.A. 1920), Leo D'Almada (Arts 1919–22), Oswald Cheung (Science 1938–41) and Patrick Yu (Arts 1938–41). The Keswick Report of 1952 recognised this situation as being acceptable to the legal profession at the time and stated clearly that there was 'no sufficient reason' for establishing a school of law in the University. A few evening courses in the branches of the law which were related to accountancy and other professional subjects were considered sufficient for the needs of the colony.[2]

This view, however, was no longer appropriate in the Hong Kong of the 1960s. A huge demand for lawyers had arisen in Hong Kong as the economy developed, but the supply of lawyers was limited and no local institution provided a proper legal education. Local students could still only pursue their legal studies overseas, and Hong Kong barristers continued to be called to the bar in England. It was, in theory, possible to become a solicitor locally through examinations of the Law Society of England and Wales, but there were few facilities in Hong Kong to help students prepare for these examinations. Correspondence courses, which were offered by overseas institutions, were available, but their effectiveness was greatly reduced by postal delays and insufficient communication between tutors and students.[3] The DEMS recognised the demand for legal courses very early on and from 1957 offered introductory courses in legal studies.[4] Unfortunately, these courses were not designed for professional examinations and were not a viable alternative to a proper legal education programme.

In view of the growing need for a supply of local legal practitioners, Mr Peter A. L. Vine, President of the Incorporated Law Society of Hong Kong, made a request early in 1962 for the University to consider offering a law degree. At the subsequent annual meeting of the Law Society he publicly expressed his wish that a faculty of law should be established at HKU to provide a degree programme in law. The graduates of this programme would be partly exempted from the qualifying examinations of the Law Society.[5] The DEMS quickly responded and began giving courses covering the syllabus of Part I of the Solicitors Examination from 1962–63.[6] W. K. Thomson, Registrar General of the Hong Kong government, sent a memorandum to the Colonial Secretary in May 1963 supporting Vine's call for a law faculty at HKU. He observed that the ratio of solicitors to the population was much smaller in Hong Kong than in other places and that such a ratio made it impossible for the legal profession 'adequately to safeguard the rights of the poor'. Thomson suggested that, for the sake of economy, HKU could organise a part-time degree programme and appoint part-time teachers from the legal profession.[7] A similar system had operated in the University's Faculty of Medicine for fifty years and represented a 'quick fix' for the problem.

The University responded to Thomson's proposal enthusiastically, confirming to the government its interest in establishing both a law programme and a new faculty, but it was not in favour of teaching law courses on a part-time basis. Instead, it suggested that the DEMS could develop a pilot project offering a full range of part-time courses for the University of London LLB external degree before the new faculty came into existence.[8] The Department, the University and the government all supported this proposal and preliminary planning work began in the following months. The Senate approved the extra-mural law programme in April 1964. The DEMS would organise courses covering a full curriculum for the external LLB degree of London University from September 1964 for an experimental period of five years.

A small number of students (ten to fifteen) would be admitted annually in the first three years. They would study as full-time external students of London University and were expected to finish their studies in three years. They would be taught by full-time staff tutors and part-time tutors, many of whom would be practising in the legal profession. Classes were to be conducted in Central, and would be supported by the Supreme Court Library. A review would be undertaken after three years to decide whether the new Faculty of Law should be established.[9]

The responses of various bodies to the plan were quick and encouraging. London University was willing to make special arrangements with the Department so that HKU could directly admit external students to the London degree and allow them to finish their examinations within three years, instead of the normal five years.[10] It also appointed Professor George Keeton, who had taught at HKU from 1924 to 1927 and was now Head of Law at University College London, as adviser to the programme.[11] While the Supreme Court Library was not ultimately made available for extra-mural students, the Attorney General agreed that students could use the Legal Department Library after office hours.[12] The University Council agreed on 18 June 1964 to the proposal for the London University LLB external programme to be organised by the DEMS.[13] The Finance Committee of the Legislative Council approved the government's financial commitment to the extra-mural law programme on 10 July 1964, promising to support the net cost of the programme, amounting to approximately $1.4 million in the first three years.[14]

The most difficult part of the preparation work was finding suitable premises for the new Extra-Mural Law Centre. Everyone agreed that it was necessary for the premises to be in Central. Many of the proposed part-time tutors would be practitioners who would not be prepared to teach if they were forced to travel too far from their workplaces for classes. Central would also be more convenient for students who needed to make use of the Legal Department Library. The University first hoped in April 1964 to lease the old guard house facing the Hilton Hotel on Garden Road.[15] It soon emerged that the proposal was impractical as the building might have to be vacated at short notice in the future for redevelopment.[16] It then proved difficult to find an alternative building which was large enough to house all the law classes at a reasonable price.[17] The University finally secured a five-year lease in October 1964 on the entire eighth floor of a newly constructed building at 92–94 Queen's Road Central (later known as the Chiao Shang Building) which had a gross floor area of 5,028 square feet.[18] After a short period of refurbishment, the new Extra-Mural Law Centre came into operation and was the venue for all law classes from March 1965.[19]

The extra-mural LLB programme started even before the Central premises were ready for use. When the introduction of the programme was announced on 7 August 1964 it attracted 194 applicants, about 30 per cent of whom were already university graduates. An Advisory and Selection Committee consisting of University members and legal professionals was formed and it eventually admitted thirty students to the programme.[20] Classes commenced in late October 1964, and four subjects were taught in the first year. These aimed at helping the students prepare for the Intermediate Examination to be held in June 1965. Each subject was taught in thirty evening lectures by part-time tutors, and these lectures were supplemented from December 1964 to May 1965 with tutorials led by Dr Clifford Pannam of the University of Melbourne and several local tutors.[21] The LLB programme continued growing in the next couple of years. Two additional batches of students, thirty in the second year and twenty-eight in the third, were admitted. Three full-time law teachers, Dafydd Evans, John Rear and Vincent Shepherd, were appointed in 1966. Dafydd Evans was the first to be appointed and was to become a driving force in the development of legal education in Hong Kong. He had been a lecturer in Law at London University and was ideal for the task ahead when he was seconded to the DEMS in January 1966. He later became the first Professor of Law at HKU when the Department of Law was established in March 1969.[22] More part-time tutors, including Professor Zelman Cowen and Miss Mary Hiscock of the University of Melbourne, were invited to assist in teaching the programme in the years that followed.[23]

The large number of applications for the London University LLB preparation programme indicated that there was a great demand for legal education in Hong Kong. A special review committee appointed by HKU in February 1965 found that the extra-mural law courses were so popular because 'for the first time, legal studies are made available to persons who do not have the economic resources to study abroad or the disposition to spend five years in articles with no guidance or assistance in preparing for the Law Society examination, which must be passed as a condition of admission'. This committee also recommended that a Faculty of Law should be established at HKU immediately.[24] A plan for a Department of Law was adopted by the University Council in April 1965.[25] In July 1966, the government agreed to continue its support for the extra-mural law degree programme for two further years until the end of the project in September 1969 in order to allow the students enrolled in the programme to complete their studies. The government's financial commitment to the programme was enlarged to around $2.1 million.[26] Two commissions were appointed, one by the University and the other by the Judiciary, to report on the progress of legal education in Hong Kong. Both acknowledged the success of the experimental project undertaken by the Department of Extra-Mural Studies, and recommended the introduction of a three-year internal LLB programme and one year of postgraduate professional training for law students at HKU.[27] The involvement of Professor Zelman Cowen of Melbourne University (a future governor-general of Australia) and Mr L. C. B. Gower of the Colonial Office's Inter-University Council ensured that the move from extra-mural legal education to a full-time programme was informed by advice from leading international experts in legal education, while local opinions were championed by Sir Ivo Rigby.

While the extra-mural law programme had proven the practicability of local legal education, the performance of the extra-mural law programme itself was far from perfect. Among the first thirty students admitted in September 1964, only four eventually finished their studies and received their degrees within the required three-year period.[28] When the scheme came to an end in 1969, only fifteen of the eighty-eight students obtained their degrees.[29] Most of the remaining students failed in examinations or else simply abandoned their studies for one reason or another. The programme was thought to be far too demanding for part-time students to finish within three years. The London University LLB curriculum, which was based solely on the laws of England and Wales, did not necessarily fit the Hong Kong legal context and was not entirely appropriate for potential practitioners.[30] Part-time tutors from the legal profession were, in spite of the high professional expertise they possessed, not the best teachers for a full law degree programme. Gower and Cowen therefore commented in their April 1967 report that the extra-mural law programme was 'clearly not a satisfactory means of meeting the long-term need' for legal education in Hong Kong.[31]

The demonstrated demand for legal education and the weakness of the extra-mural law programme offered by the DEMS finally convinced the government in 1968 to approve in principle the establishment of a Department of Law at HKU.[32] The Department of Law was set up in March 1969 with the appointment of Professor Dafydd Evans from the DEMS to guide its early development, and the first students were admitted in September 1969.[33] The first cohort of law graduates in 1972 moved on to take the Professional Certificate in Law (PCLL) course at HKU in the 1972–73 academic year. The year 1973 therefore saw the first group of graduates who were fully qualified to enter the legal profession with a HKU qualification.[34]

In spite of the cessation of the government-sponsored pilot scheme in 1969, the DEMS continued to run courses to prepare students for the London University LLB examinations. These courses were no longer organised as a rigid three-year programme exclusively for London University external students, but as individual courses which would prepare students in the subjects examined.[35] Extra-mural students registered as external students with London University directly and enrolled in the DEMS preparation courses according to their needs. The Law courses offered by the Department therefore underwent a number of changes in the following decades. The University of London External Programme was on the verge of closure in the early 1980s because of the dwindling demand for the scheme in Britain. It was saved only because of the continued demand from overseas students, including those in Hong Kong.[36] From 1982–83, the Department co-operated with the *Hong Kong Law Journal* to invite experienced United Kingdom law lecturers to deliver a series of revision lectures over the Christmas and Easter periods each year.[37] In 1983, the DEMS re-organised the programme and introduced a full range of courses specifically designed for the London University LLB examinations.[38] Although the number of successful students in the LLB external courses remained fairly low throughout this period, it provided an important path for part-time students in Hong Kong to pursue their legal studies and acquire qualifications recognised by the local legal profession.[39]

The value of the London University LLB courses and other extra-mural law courses was not confined to the legal profession. Many people found the law courses of the DEMS useful for their non-legal careers or simply for their own personal development. Dr Patrick Wong Lung-tak, for example, enrolled in a non-examinable company law course in 1969 while he was a full-time accounting student at the Hong Kong Technical College (which later became the Hong Kong Polytechnic). He was initially not very interested in the subject and considered it as no more than a remedial course for his day-time studies. The course was, however, well taught and it aroused Wong's interest first in company law and later in legal studies as a whole. Dr Wong therefore sought to change his studies from accountancy to the law and enrolled in preparation courses for the first-year London University LLB external examination. Although Dr Wong did not continue with this plan and eventually qualified as an accountant in 1974, he remained dedicated to study and research in company law, taxation and other legal subjects, becoming a specialist in these fields within the accountancy profession. Apart from teaching him the relevant subject matter, the extra-mural law courses also provided Dr Wong with opportunities to improve his listening and oral English skills.[40] The professional expertise and general skills he learned from the law courses helped his career development in many ways. His story is just one of many that could be cited to show how extra-mural legal studies through the DEMS has allowed successive generations of businessmen and professionals to supplement their training with legal knowledge in specific fields.

The Diploma of Management Studies

The Diploma of Management Studies (DipMS) programme was the flagship professional course of the Department of Extra-Mural Studies for two decades between the late-1960s and mid-1980s. Despite having a relatively small annual intake, which was kept at around thirty-five, it was the Department's first and only programme leading to a HKU Diploma qualification during this period. The academic standards expected of students and the recognition given to this programme were therefore greater than other extra-mural courses which led to lower qualifications such as University Certificates or Extra-Mural Certificates.

Before introducing this Diploma programme in 1968, the DEMS had run courses in business management and related subjects for some years. In the initial years of the Department, for example, courses in 'Higher Commercial Studies' provided a structured programme helping students to prepare for the external examinations of the CIS and ACCA. These courses were not, however, necessarily able to meet the new demands of a society undergoing rapid economic change. As early as 1963 the Department was aware of the need for a middle-management course to train managers and supervisors in up-to-date management techniques.[41] From 1964–65 the Department organised several management courses in Business Administration, Business Management, and Personnel Management for mid-level managers of companies.[42] The DEMS, with the aid of the Carnegie Foundation and the Canadian government, invited Professor A. J. McIntyre, Director of Extension at the University of Western Ontario, to visit HKU from September to November 1964 in order to 'survey the fields of business management and related social and economic studies in Hong Kong'.[43] He held discussions with community leaders and members of the University, and finally recommended that a two-year middle management diploma course should be organised by HKU.

Before proposing the Diploma of Management Studies programme to the University, the Department tried to negotiate with the Hong Kong Technical College to offer a Joint Diploma programme in Management. From 1966, the staff of the Department participated in the Technical College's part-time three-year evening diploma course, which was taught at a lower academic level than that envisaged by the Department for its own diploma. However, they failed to make any satisfactory arrangements for co-operation. The Director of Education, who supervised the Technical College, finally suggested in October 1967 that the University should offer its own diploma course in Management Studies and that the Technical College should discontinue its diploma course in Management.[44]

The Committee on Extra-Mural Studies (CEMS) discussed the plan for a HKU DipMS at its first meeting in November 1967.[45] In a subsequent paper prepared by the Committee it was stated that 'the course planned lays emphasis on Production Management and is expected to be of value to many junior executives including some of our own graduates who have gone into industry and commerce'.[46] The programme was, therefore, designed to lead to a postgraduate qualification rather than an undergraduate or post-secondary diploma. It required applicants to have a university degree or to have reached a 'minimum age of 27 and with at least four years of experience in an executive capacity'. The proposed course was for three years, instead of the two-year programme suggested by Professor McIntyre, and would lead to the award of a University Diploma. It would consist of thirty weeks of tuition, 'giving a minimum total of 210 hours tuition per year, from 7:00 to 9:00 p.m. three nights a week. It will be incumbent upon all students to undertake a period of full-time residential study (two week-ends) in each year of the course'. More importantly, the Diploma qualification was expected to be recognised by the United Kingdom authority established by the Department of Education and Science in 1961 in consultation with the British Institute of Management. The HKU qualification would therefore enjoy a high academic and professional status.[47]

The proposal was eagerly supported by the University. The Senate adopted the plan in January 1968, and approval by the Council and the Court was given in March and June 1968.[48] The course received impressive responses from government and business sectors, and it attracted more than two hundred applicants in its first year, many of whom were sponsored by their employers. The DEMS admitted thirty-five students for the first DipMS course which started in October 1968.[49] The majority of the first batch of students were men in their mid-twenties or early-thirties, working as mid-level executives in the government or major firms in Hong Kong.[50] The curriculum covered subjects in economics, accounting, statistics, industrial relations, production and engineering control, case studies and a final-year project. A revised curriculum was introduced in 1970–71 to allow the DEMS to conduct its classes in day-release sessions and shorten the study period of the programme from three years to two.[51] Mr J. W. England was responsible for the initial development of the programme but, from 1973, Dr S. G. Redding was appointed Staff Tutor in Management Studies. He had previously taught at the London School of Economics and the European Institute of Business Administration (INSEAD), and during his time at the DEMS earned a growing reputation for his research on the differences between Asian and Western approaches to management.[52]

Being one of the first local university-level management programmes, the Diploma in Management Studies was vitally important to the development of business management education in Hong Kong. When the DipMS programme commenced in October 1968, the University was already setting wheels in motion for a review of the opportunities for introducing management studies at university level. The Senate appointed a working party in December 1968 which was asked 'to report through the Vice-Chancellor on ways of improving the case for Management Studies (including business administration and industrial management) on a University basis'.[53] Roger Williams and Mr J. W. England were among the eleven members of the working party which submitted its report to the Senate on 4 February 1969.[54] Although the report concluded that the University should emphasise the development of 'Industrial Management Studies', which was based on the technological disciplines, it also underlined the importance of 'Business Management Studies' in the University, especially the part-time postgraduate diploma and refresher courses organised by the DEMS. There seems to have been a realisation even in the late 1960s that the Hong Kong economy did not rely solely on its industrial output and that training was also required for the business sector. The working party recommended that the University should commence undergraduate teaching in management studies in a new Department of Management Studies headed by a chair professor within the Faculty of Social Science, but agreed that the DEMS should continue to offer its DipMS programme to postgraduate and part-time students.[55]

The recommendations of the Working Party were, however, questioned by Tom Lupton, Professor of Industrial Sociology and Deputy Director of the Manchester Business School. Lupton was appointed by HKU in 1969 to advise on 'the overall development of Management Courses within the Department of Extra-Mural Studies', and 'the possible development of Management Studies in teaching departments, having due regard to current plans'.[56] He observed that 'Hong Kong manufacturing firms have, with few exceptions, little ideas of how to make use of University Graduates and will certainly not pay competitive salaries to recruit them'.[57] He doubted whether there was a need to develop undergraduate programmes in 'Industrial Engineering' (or even 'Industrial Management' as recommended in the previous report) or Management Studies.[58] His comments on the undergraduate programme which the proposed Department of Management Studies was to offer were not very encouraging:

> Management Studies or Business Studies are quite different [from Industrial Engineering]. At undergraduate level, even when imaginatively taught, they can never be much more than a fairly superficial introduction to a large number of disciplines, professional procedures, and organisational problems . . . The Faculty of Social Sciences is at present too small to embrace all the disciplines and subjects required for management studies if these are to be done well. To attempt to introduce them in a fairly new faculty would divert attention from the essential task of building up work in the disciplines, from which future interdisciplinary studies may fruitfully grow.[59]

While he opposed the establishment of a Department of Management Studies and the provision of an undergraduate programme in management studies, Lupton nevertheless recommended developing postgraduate and post-experience education through a new Centre for Studies in Administration and Management. As a short-term policy, he advised the University to strengthen the role of the DEMS in the provision of courses in management studies:

> The Extra-Mural Department should be encouraged to develop courses in Production Management, Financial Management, and Sales and Marketing Management, on a part-time basis, for managers-in-post . . . As these specialised courses develop, the Diploma in Management Studies should gradually shift its emphasis towards general management, both in the persons recruited and in the subjects taught and the methods of teaching.[60]

The Department of Extra-Mural Studies was seen by Lupton as a 'developer of post-graduate part-time vocational and professional work' where managers could enhance their management knowledge and skills without interrupting work in their businesses.[61]

The academic standard of the DipMS programme was stringently maintained at university level by following the same practices and regulations as the University. The Senate set standards for admissions, approved regulations and syllabuses, and appointed external examiners to maintain the academic quality of the DipMS programme. Tutors were generally HKU faculty members, staff tutors of the DEMS, or practising professionals or senior managers in major firms, hence the teaching quality was high.[62] External examiners from overseas universities appreciated the high academic standards expected and the corresponding excellent performance of students.[63] The DipMS courses remained the only academic programme in management studies at HKU until the Department of Management Studies came into being in February 1976. The new Department started a Master of Business Administration (MBA) programme from 1977–78 which allowed students to finish courses on a full-time or part-time basis. In the first few years, students who possessed the HKU DipMS qualification were eligible to enrol in the MBA programme even though they did not hold a first degree and were exempted from the entire first year of the curriculum.[64] The Department's DipMS was therefore given high recognition as a professional qualification at a time when no other programme was available in Hong Kong.

The DipMS programme finally came to an end when the teaching of management studies at HKU was gradually taken over by the internal Department of Management Studies. In the early 1980s the University initiated a review of the relationship between the DipMS and MBA programme, and especially the practice of admitting DipMS holders to the MBA programme. In March 1982, the Committee on Extra-Mural Studies made a compromise by not insisting on the 'first-degree' status of the DipMS qualification with regard to admission to the MBA programme, while the Department of Management Studies continued to allow non-graduate DipMS holders to enter the programme under special exemption.[65] In March 1983, the MBA regulations were tightened to exclude non-graduate DipMS holders from entering the part-time MBA programme.[66] Dr A. J. Berry of the Manchester Business School, who was invited to advise the University on part-time management studies, recommended in April 1983 that a three-year part-time programme be introduced in which students would spend two years enrolled in the DipMS and one year in the MBA, but his proposal did little to improve the situation.[67] When the Department of Management Studies decided to offer from 1984 its own three-year part-time MBA programme, in which the first and second years of study were similar to the curriculum of the DipMS, the DEMS realised that there would no longer be any demand for its two-year diploma course and so decided to phase out the DipMS programme.[68] In January 1984 the Senate approved the suspension of admissions to the DipMS course in the following academic year, and finally cancelled the DipMS programme after the last group of students completed their studies in 1985.[69]

Dr Darwin Chen and Professor Stephen Ho Wing-chiu were early graduates of the DipMS programme who benefited from their studies in the DEMS. Dr Chen enrolled in the second DipMS cohort in 1970 when he was the manager of Hong Kong City Hall. He expected that he would improve his skills in managing financial information, personnel affairs and marketing, all of which were requirements of his job at the time. In fact, what he actually gained from this course went far beyond his expectations. Through interaction with tutors and classmates, the programme strengthened his lateral thinking, and this allowed him to initiate innovative projects in various government departments, such as the URBTIX ticketing system and the three-tier film classification system. It also enhanced his human relationship skills, which were essential in managing his subordinates, communicating with senior officials, negotiating with public or commercial organisations, and co-operating with officials from China on political issues. The excellent results which Dr Chen attained in the DipMS programme, in conjunction with his performance at work, attracted the attention of senior officials and helped his career progression within the government. Before retirement from the Civil Service he had risen to the position of Director of Building and Lands. He was also Chairman of the Hong Kong Arts Development Council and continues his association with the University as Chairman of the Advisory Board of HKU SPACE.[70]

The DipMS programme had an even more profound impact on Professor Stephen Ho. Professor Ho's local school education was disappointing and ended with poor results in the Hong Kong Certificate of Education Examination (HKCEE) in 1967. He continued his studies in Scotland in 1970 and, without any financial support, managed to finish a Scottish Higher National Certificate programme in Business Studies at Napier University. The uncertainty of future employment opportunities because of insufficient academic qualifications and professional training made him realise the importance of continuing education for his career development. His formal part-time studies commenced with the DipMS programme in 1974. The programme helped him widen his social network through frequent discussion with his classmates who came from diverse backgrounds. This networking was valuable to Ho as his classmates shared their experiences with each other, inspired new business ideas, created opportunities for career development, and helped to change his own mindset. Some of his classmates became close personal friends during the course. More importantly, the course broadened his mind and further aroused his thirst for learning. After completing the course, he persisted in continuing education and acquired a number of professional qualifications, which in turn assisted him in meeting challenges in his career in logistics. He is now the president and CEO of Ferguson International Freight Forwarders, Vice-Chairman of the Hong Kong Branch of the Institute of Exporters, and Vice-President of the Chartered Institute of Logistics and Transport.[71]

The DipMS pioneered by the DEMS was one of the first qualifications in management studies to be offered by a higher education institution in Hong Kong. From 1968 to 1985, the programme trained nearly four hundred executives and managers, many of whom later became leading figures in major companies and public organisations. The up-to-date management knowledge and skills which they learned in the programme did much to enhance the efficiency and management quality of businesses in Hong Kong. The programme also had a profound impact on the individual students in their career and personal development, and ultimately led to the establishment of a fully-fledged Department of Management Studies at HKU in 1976. Gordon Redding, the senior staff tutor in management studies within the DEMS from 1973, was eventually appointed as Professor of Management Studies in 1982 and led the Department of Management Studies with great distinction for many years.[72]

Librarianship

Librarianship courses are a good example of the efforts taken by the DEMS to initiate vocational training courses in co-operation with local professional bodies. There were no proper training programmes for librarians in Hong Kong before the 1960s. In fact, the demand for such workers was relatively small because there were no public lending libraries in the colony until the opening of City Hall in 1962.[73] An expansion of government libraries and those run by other institutions in the 1960s created a demand for more properly trained librarians, so the DEMS tried to fill this gap in the provision of training for librarians. It started the first 'Library Techniques' course in 1960, with 52 people enrolling and 40 finishing the course.[74] In the early years, the Department provided two types of librarianship courses, one for basic training in Chinese libraries and one for advanced and professional training leading to the British ALA Intermediate Examination. By 1963, about 160 students were enrolled in the two courses.[75]

These pioneering courses were replaced by an English-language certificate course organised in co-operation with the Hong Kong Librarians Association (HKLA) in September 1964, with Miss Kan Lai-bing as the tutor-in-charge.[76] The course was further revised in 1967 into two identical sub-professional certificate courses for library assistants, one in English and the other in Cantonese. The revised syllabuses aimed at giving 'basic training in librarianship' and helping library assistants and clerical staff already working in libraries 'to be more complete in the practical work in their own libraries'. This course also equipped those who wanted to become professionals in librarianship with background knowledge of the profession.[77] The HKLA, through its Education Sub-Committee, supervised the academic and professional standards of the course. The Association arranged visits and textbooks for the students, and its Chairman moderated the examinations. The DEMS was responsible for the administration of the course, including recruitment of tutors and students, and arranging tutorials and examinations.[78]

Most of the tutors were experienced full-time staff in local libraries. Students were taught the basic theories and practices necessary to run libraries, and this knowledge was supplemented by library visits and practical sessions. The tailor-made curriculum fitted the situation of libraries in Hong Kong, particularly in areas such as Chinese cataloguing and the special needs of school libraries. One hundred and eighty-five students took the examinations during the five years from 1964. Over half of them passed and received the Joint Certificate awarded by the HKLA and the DEMS.[79] The first enrolments in this course came from two groups of students: library workers, who were given priority to enrol in order to improve their skills, and other individuals who were not working in libraries but who hoped to enter the career. In the mid-1970s, however, the percentage of students in the first category rose as demand for such training courses grew among existing library workers. In the 1979–80 academic year, all the students in the Certificate Course were working in libraries.[80]

More professional and advanced courses appeared gradually from the mid-1960s. A course which prepared students for the United Kingdom Library Association Part I Examination was organised between 1967 and 1974. Two hundred and twenty-four students took the course during these seven years.[81] Courses in advanced reference, bibliography and classification were also inaugurated in the 1970s. The Department extended its librarianship courses to the postgraduate level in 1980–81. In response to calls from the Urban Council for more locally-qualified, Chinese-speaking staff in public libraries, the Department started a three-year part-time postgraduate diploma in librarianship specifically for these library staff. Local professionals in librarianship worked together to devise and manage the course. The course was managed jointly by the DEMS and the HKLA. Dr Kan Lai-bing, Librarian of the Chinese University at that time, and Mr T. A. Chow, Chief Librarian of the Urban Council Libraries, directed this postgraduate diploma course. By 1982–83, twenty-two students had completed the three-year diploma programme.[82]

Apart from the HKLA, the DEMS also maintained close contacts with other bodies which had an interest in the librarianship courses. Librarianship was one the first subjects in which co-ordination was needed between the extra-mural departments of the two universities to avoid duplication. In October 1967, CUHK started a librarianship certificate course in Cantonese without the support of the HKLA.[83] When the two extra-mural departments discussed the co-ordination of certificate and examinable courses in November 1967, it appeared that neither department wanted to abandon its own librarianship certificate course and this matter was described as 'much more complicated and bedevilled' than other problem areas.[84] The HKU Department was nevertheless willing to open triangular negotiations between HKU, CUHK and the HKLA, and an agreement was finally reached in 1973. From September 1973, HKU's certificate course would specialise in English, while CUHK's extra-mural department followed the same curriculum but it was taught in Cantonese. The HKLA would ensure that similar academic standards were maintained in both courses by appointing the same tutor-in-charge and devising the same examination questions, but in different languages.[85] While the two extra-mural departments taught their courses separately, they maintained some co-operation by sharing the same syllabuses under the auspices of the HKLA.

The DEMS also co-operated with the government to provide various other extra-mural courses for semi-professional librarians. In 1979 the Education Department introduced the teacher librarian scheme aiming to appoint one teacher in each school to supervise school libraries on a full-time basis. As these teacher-librarians needed training to carry out the new tasks, from September 1979 the Education Department sponsored various short day-release or long courses for teacher-librarians to enhance the quality of school libraries.[86] This co-operation continued in the following years. The Postgraduate Diploma in Librarianship programme, launched in 1980, was another way in which the DEMS responded to the government's expansion of public libraries. Co-operation between the Department, the HKLA, the Chinese University and government departments in providing a full range of librarianship courses in Hong Kong demonstrates how HKU's Department of Extra-Mural Studies eventually had to come to a *modus vivendi* with Chinese University in areas of extra-mural studies which HKU had pioneered. Such competition would only increase as the years passed.

Mr Frederick Ng Yip-lap is a DEMS alumnus who succeeded in developing his career as a librarian through participation in the librarianship Certificate course. In the mid-1960s, he was working at HKU as a clerical officer looking after the reference library in the Language School. He joined the Librarianship Certificate course in 1966 to improve his technical knowledge of librarianship and as a possible means to gain a proper library job. The course made a strong impression on him: the tutors were devoted to their teaching and his classmates were helpful and willing to share their experience in library work. The benefit of the course was in some ways immediate, as the course enabled him to find a job in the HKU Library where Dr Kan Lai-bing was his first supervisor, but the course also had a long-term impact on Ng's career and personal development. The course helped him to establish a personal network with other library workers, some of whom later became his work colleagues, and others kept contact with each other after the course. More importantly, the Certificate course gave Mr Ng the confidence to enrol in a master's degree in Library Studies at the University of Hawaii in 1975. The Certificate course which he took in the Department was therefore the first step in a new career which saw him secure the post of Senior Associate Librarian at the Hong Kong Baptist University, where during retirement he continues to share his expertise and learn as a library and archives consultant.[87]

Continuing Professional Education: Social Work

The professional and vocational courses offered by the DEMS in the 1970s and 1980s were highly diversified. The DipMS programme, for example, provided executives who had received little academic training in business management with a proper and structured means to learn theory and practice in management. Some courses prepared students for professional examinations in order to enter particular professions such as law and librarianship. There were also a number of courses which aimed at providing refresher or post-experience training for professionals who had been working in their particular field for some time. Examples of such courses may be found in Architecture, Art and Design, Commerce, Education, Engineering, Law, Science, and Medical Services. It is not possible to explore the features of programmes in every subject area, but the Department's description of its courses in Social Work in its Annual Report for 1975–76 provides a good example of how diversified continuing professional education was in the 1970s and how it benefited Hong Kong society.

Social Work was a relatively small area for the DEMS, with 432 students in twenty-one courses in the 1976–77 academic year. In fact, Social Work is one of the extra-mural subject areas which is often overlooked, possibly because of the larger full-time programmes which were already well established at the universities. But as has been mentioned in an earlier chapter, Social Work was one of the first areas in which HKU offered an extension course as early as 1946, and it was an area in which the government was particularly keen to secure qualified and experienced workers. The huge influx of refugees from China in the late-1940s and 1950s created numerous social problems which needed to be addressed urgently, and it was for this reason that the Diploma in Social Studies and Certificate in Social Studies were launched in the Faculty of Arts in 1950. Another diploma course was offered by Chung Chi College from 1958 but these programmes produced only a very small number of graduates. Undergraduate Social Work programmes were established at CUHK in 1964 and HKU in 1967, but still there was an increasing demand for qualified social workers and refresher courses as voluntary agencies and government welfare programmes expanded to meet the growing needs of Hong Kong.[88] Extra-mural courses in Social Work therefore appealed to a wide range of people working in community and charitable organisations, and the knowledge and skills learned in these courses had an immediate impact on the lives of those who did not share all the benefits of Hong Kong's economic boom. The range, variety and complexity of extra-mural offerings in social work is just one example of the work being done by the DEMS at the time, but it also suggests how much was being achieved in other subject areas not examined here.

Extra-mural courses in Social Work fell into three main categories. The first category included all the post-experience courses in social work for social workers.

These were organised at a number of different levels with different audiences in mind, and the DEMS in 1976–77 classified them into three sub-categories:

> (a) First, there are those courses which are designed for experienced social workers in order to keep them abreast of recent research findings. The recent courses on 'Some Current and Local Researches related to Social Welfare' and on 'Current Issues in Psychology' would clearly fall into this sub-category.
> (b) Secondly, there are in-depth studies of particular problems, skills, or approaches, that could not possibly be fully covered during basic social work training. The course, 'Supervision in Youth Work', designed for youth work supervisors, would be a case in point.
> (c) Thirdly, there are introductory courses for those who have recently entered the field, such as 'Residential Social Work', 'Understanding and Helping the Mentally Handicapped Child', 'Understanding Adolescence' and so on.[89]

These continuing professional education courses deepened and broadened the knowledge base of practising social workers and were particularly useful in keeping them up to date with the latest developments in their own fields or in newer fields of work. The second category of Social Work courses were those designed for 'non-Social Workers':

> These are largely appreciation courses designed to assist other professional people in their daily work. Courses for Housing Officers on 'The Social Services in Hong Kong' and on 'Social Welfare and Community Work', come into this category, as do courses on School Social Work for Teachers, or the course on 'Working with the Terminally Sick' for nurses and other medical people.[90]

The third category included a whole range of extra-mural courses which were not focused on social work, nor were they specifically designed for social workers. These were nevertheless courses which had proven to be of great assistance to social workers in the field and consisted of courses in such diverse fields as law, sociology, social psychology, and management studies:

> Some of these courses are likely to be of more obvious assistance to Social Workers than others — the course on 'Sensitivity to Human Needs' being a good example — but all are capable of providing Social Workers with stimulus and with a broader perspective, enabling them to see their immediate tasks in a wider setting.[91]

This third category of courses was an example of what educational jargon at the time referred to as 'role education', a form of lifelong learning which differed from the purely refresher or post-experience courses for professionals.

The Department of Extra-Mural Studies therefore carved out a special role for itself in the field of Social Work. It saw this role as being 'the provision of continuing professional education: not in basic training, nor just by providing refresher courses, but by providing post-experience courses for those already in employment, by engaging in so-called 'role' education, and by giving those in allied professions an appreciation of the theory and practice of Social Work'.[92] This role therefore neatly complemented the basic training courses provided by the university Social Work departments and the advanced degrees that were later introduced. In later years HKU SPACE would collaborate with the Department of Social Work in creating training packages on service quality standards for NGOs and developing a joint diploma programme for mainland social workers.[93]

Language Courses (English, Japanese and Putonghua)

Language courses are worth considering because they formed the largest section of the vocational courses offered by the DEMS throughout this period. Language courses attracted 1,173 students or about 18 per cent of extra-mural enrolments in 1964–65. Two decades later, enrolments in language courses had risen to 7,035 and accounted for nearly a quarter of the extra-mural student population. At first sight, the language courses appear to be much less 'vocational' in nature than many other courses offered by the Department. Indeed, many students enrolled in language courses for leisure, and most of these courses did not have an examination or lead to a specific qualification. They had nevertheless been categorised as vocational courses from the early years of the Department because it was widely acknowledged that they could greatly improve the communication abilities of students, and effective communication was an essential tool in the commercial world. The courses therefore attracted many people whose primary objective was to improve their performance at work.

The changing numbers enrolled in different language courses also reflected this trend. There had always been a large number of students taking extra-mural English courses, mainly because English had long been perceived as 'the passport to success' for very many people in Hong Kong.[94] The provision of such a large number of extra-mural English courses was, of course, entirely consistent with HKU's role as an English-language university, and a staff tutor, Mr Duncan Macintosh, was specifically assigned to this large area of the Department's work. However, when commercial and cultural contacts between Hong Kong and Japan or Hong Kong and the Chinese Mainland became more frequent in the 1970s, enrolments in Japanese and Putonghua courses soared. Not surprisingly, the demand for other foreign language courses remained low in Hong Kong because these languages were less likely to be useful in the workplace.

From the mid-1960s, English language courses became the second largest subject area among courses offered by the DEMS. In 1964–65, there were 842 students taking 34 'English Language and Literature' courses, most of which aimed at teaching practical skills in English.[95] The topics ranged from practical communication skills to advanced training in writing. Apart from these courses there were also English language courses specially designed for different student groups, such as English refresher courses for teachers, English courses in an integrated programme for external examinations, and English courses for employees of particular commercial firms or government departments. The general objective of all these courses was to improve the students' English standards, but the different categories of English language courses had no apparent connection with each other. They were offered on an ad hoc basis without any clear over-arching structure. Curriculum design and teaching standards for these courses largely depended on the individual tutors employed to teach them. The courses were conducted in ten to twenty weekly lessons and the topics they covered were comparatively narrow. Extra-mural students' improvement in English therefore tended to advance in a piecemeal fashion rather than through a carefully-designed progression of courses.

In 1967, the DEMS consolidated various English language courses and began offering a two-year Extra-Mural Certificate course in 'Use of English'. This course aimed to 'develop and improve skills in written and oral English'.[96] The first-year 72-hour curriculum included 'remedial teaching' which allowed students to re-learn basic English sentence structure and improve their reading, writing, listening and oral skills. In the second year the emphasis shifted to more complex matters, such as newspaper reading and report writing. There were a number of sub-classes conducted in various places in Hong Kong and Kowloon. Most of the part-time tutors were native speakers of English and many were teachers from the University or in local schools. Individuals who passed in English at the HKCEE were eligible to apply for the courses, but the DEMS commented that such a prerequisite was a 'totally unreliable guide' and it ultimately had to introduce an entrance test and a supplementary preparatory course in 1970.[97] Students used a variety of textbooks and these were supplemented by materials specially designed by the DEMS. Students were required to pass examinations in both years to qualify for the certificate at a level similar to that of the Hong Kong Advanced Level Examination (HKALE) qualification. Grade 'A' and 'B' were considered by the Department to be 'highly valued and accepted by employers as representing a fairly solid achievement'.[98]

The 'Use of English' programme received a modest public response in the first year of operation but it soon became very popular in the following years. The number of students increased from 140 in 1967–68 to 307 in 1969–70. When the Department expanded the programme by introducing a special stream in 'Commercial Practice' in 1970–71, the result was even more impressive: 797 students enrolled in twenty-eight courses in various streams and at different levels.[99] While the backgrounds of the students were by no means uniform, a typical student would be an office-worker, male and in his twenties, and would have received a Form Five or Lower Sixth education.[100] The average performance of the students in classes was not always encouraging and Duncan Macintosh commented that the students, who were exhausted from their daytime work, tended to be 'passive learners, content to sit in his class and not to participate more than [they have to]', but many of them realised the 'functional importance of English' and were keener to learn.[101] Employers responded positively to the certificate course, as more than one third of the students during the 1970–71 academic year were sponsored by their employers, most of which were major firms in Hong Kong.[102] A total of 1,930 students completed the 'Use of English' course in the decade between 1975 and 1985. By 1984–85, the DEMS had organised four additional Extra-Mural Certificate programmes in English Studies.[103] In that year, there were 3,596 students, or 12 per cent of the University's total extra-mural student population enrolled in 'English Studies' courses. This was the largest single subject area offered by the Department in terms of enrolment.[104]

It is difficult to quantify the value of these courses for the students who took them, but Mr Kenneth Yim Chi-keung is one DEMS alumnus who benefited from his English language certificate courses. Mr Yim joined the 'Use of English' and 'English for Business' courses from 1973 to 1975 because he found that his English language standard was not sufficient for his job in the shipping industry. His post required him to deal with many legal documents in English, and he found that the courses he took improved his business English and helped him to improve his career prospects in another large commercial firm. In particular, the course enabled him to deal with different situations in a business environment efficiently and politely, such as replying to customers' complaints and preparing business letters and other documents. All of these skills were essential for him to become a successful manager.[105]

Apart from the programmes in English studies, Japanese and Putonghua language courses also became increasingly popular during this period. Initially, however, demand was low. Throughout the 1960s, courses in Japanese and Putonghua remained a very small percentage of the total enrolments in the Department: in 1968–69, there were only thirty-five students in two Japanese language courses and twenty-two students in two Putonghua courses.[106] These courses, like other foreign language courses in the early days of the DEMS, were designed as two-year programmes. The second-year course in Putonghua was, however, seldom organised and that in Japanese had never drawn sufficient applicants to be offered in the 1960s.[107] In the mid-1970s the situation changed rapidly. There was a significant increase in demand for courses in both languages, and in October 1974 the DEMS started a Certificate course in Japanese. The course aimed to 'increase the vocational qualities' of learners and 'help students understand another culture'.[108] The course was divided into three levels and each level lasted for half a year. Students who finished the advanced level were expected to be proficient in using the Japanese language in daily life. Classes were mainly conducted in Cantonese or Putonghua, depending on the mother tongue of the students, so that there would be no language barrier between tutors and students.

The DEMS also launched a new scheme in 1974 to conduct a course in Putonghua through Radio Hong Kong. The idea was so successful that there were nearly 1,000 participants and the Department therefore had to restructure and expand its existing Putonghua courses from 1975. When the Chinese mainland began economic reforms during the late 1970s, the DEMS offered further Putonghua courses specially designed for business communication. While all these new attempts in Putonghua courses were mainly for local Chinese students, the DEMS inaugurated an Extra-Mural Certificate course in Elementary Mandarin for English-speakers in 1981–82. The rapid expansion and diversification of language courses reflected the keen interest of local people in learning these two languages. In fact, the 'Oriental Language' subject area, which consisted mainly of Japanese and Putonghua courses, continued to be one of the three areas which had the largest enrolments throughout the early 1980s. In the 1980–81 academic year, there were 1,473 students in Japanese courses and 1,378 students in Putonghua courses.[109] Even after the courses in Japanese and Putonghua were reorganised in 1982–83 resulting in a loss of 900 students and 30 courses, Oriental Languages still continued to be the subject area with the second largest enrolments and the highest number of lecture hours for that year.[110] The provision of such a large number of language courses to so many students provided numerous Hong Kong people with an opportunity for career advancement in businesses and industries where a second language was vital.

Special Courses: The Housing Management Certificate Course

Apart from the large range of public extra-mural courses in the area of continuing professional education, the DEMS also organised tailor-made courses for, or in conjunction with, public or commercial organisations. Many of these courses aimed at improving employees' vocational skills or assisting them to acquire specific professional qualifications. A comprehensive list of organisations which the DEMS co-operated with in these years is not available, but a few key figures indicate that the DEMS maintained fairly strong connections with local organisations in the 1970s and the 1980s. In 1976–77, the DEMS ran in-house courses for at least fifteen organisations in the public and commercial sectors, and organised extra-mural courses in collaboration with eight organisations.[111] In 1984–85, the Department organised at least 43 courses for 1,198 employees of the Hong Kong and Shanghai Banking Corporation, the Chartered Bank and other European banks to prepare their employees for Stage I or Stage II examinations of the Institute of Bankers.[112]

The three-year part-time Certificate course in Housing Management was possibly the Department's most successful and long-standing training course specially designed for an outside organisation. The profession of housing management only emerged in Hong Kong after the government became involved in the provision of accommodation for lower and middle income earners in the 1950s. A large number of public housing estates were built and the government needed housing managers and assistants to maintain a satisfactory living environment in these estates. Housing management was, however, a new vocation in Hong Kong and few local professionals had been trained in this area of management. Recruitment of qualified housing managers relied mainly on expatriates trained in Britain, but this solution to the problem was expensive and could not keep pace with the growing demand for trained housing managers. It was difficult for locals to become qualified in this profession as they needed to rely on correspondence courses and pass the examinations of British professional institutes. These study programmes were often not very appropriate for Hong Kong managers as the curriculum for the British professional examinations did not reflect the situation that existed in the public housing sector in Hong Kong.

The Hong Kong government realised that the solution to the shortage of trained officers in housing management was to develop its own training scheme for local recruits. In 1963, it started the first two-year training programme in Housing Management for housing assistants of the Urban Services Department in co-operation with the DEMS.[113] Mr Simon Li was one of the young housing assistants who received this training as a part of his initial employment contract. The subjects in the programme fell into two categories. Professional subjects in Building and Housing Management were developed and taught in-house by the government using expatriate housing managers who taught the subject according to the special needs in Hong Kong, while the DEMS was responsible for the other courses in law, accountancy and socio-economic studies. Although the DEMS courses allowed outside enrolments, they were usually filled by government housing assistants, and these courses therefore became virtually exclusive to the Housing Management programme. The part-time tutors recruited by the DEMS were of high quality: Leo Goodstadt was the tutor for the 'Housing Problems in Hong Kong' course, and the 'Landlord and Tenant' course was taught by experienced crown counsels recruited from the government. Simon Li commented that he and his colleagues had little difficulty in comprehending the concepts taught in the classes because they had hands-on experiences in the field, but the lack of free time posed a major obstacle to their studies. The training was conducted fairly intensively. There were typically two evening classes and a daytime session every week. Although students received support from their supervisors and could be released from their normal duties for study, they needed to use all their leisure time for evening classes and revision.[114] Such dedication to their part-time studies was a common feature of working professionals in Hong Kong during the 1970s and 1980s, and Simon Li and his classmates are just a few of numerous examples that could be cited in this regard. Examinations were held at the end of each year and the qualification was recognised by the government.

The success of the programme led the government to consider taking a further step to formalise and expand the training scheme in housing management. In 1969, a three-year part-time Certificate course in Housing Management was introduced by the DEMS. Apart from the Housing Authority and the Urban Services Department, the Resettlement Department also became involved, hoping that the additional training would allow its officers to 'bring a more professional approach to the concept of estate management within this department' and 'increase control and efficiency in resettlement estates'.[115] A small number of employees of the Hong Kong Housing Society and large commercial firms were also admitted from time to time with sponsorship from their employers.[116] The government departments were not involved heavily in teaching, but they co-operated with the DEMS and the Hong Kong Branch of the Institute of Housing Managers in course design and by recognising the qualification.[117] The curriculum of the Certificate course was similar to that of the previous training programme but with some additions and improvements. The subjects offered included Building, Law, Accountancy, Social Services, Politics and Government, and English. The Certificate qualification was soon recognised as the equivalent of the Diploma in Housing Management sponsored by the United Kingdom Institute of Housing Managers.[118]

Although nearly all students in the Certificate courses came from public authorities, the characteristics of the students were far from identical. Such variation can be illustrated by the experiences of three alumni of the Certificate course. When Mr Joseph Lee King-chi enrolled in the first Certificate course in 1969, he was working in the Housing Division of the Urban Services Department as a housing assistant. Apart from his interest in the profession of housing management, he considered the course as a way of qualifying himself for further career progression. Studying at the DEMS provided him with a sense of being a university student and gave him a chance to enjoy some campus life.[119] Mr Michael Fok Po-choi, who was also a young housing assistant in the early 1970s, shared a similar experience with Joseph Lee. Mr Fok remembered that he was not very enthusiastic about the course when he began his part-time studies in 1971, and it was not until he finished the first year of studies that his interest in the profession bloomed.[120]

The students from the Resettlement Department had a rather different profile. Mr Mok Yiu-kwong had been working in the Resettlement Department for fifteen years when he commenced his housing management course. The Resettlement Department initially had little concern for housing management as a profession, and Mr Mok was one of the first officers in the Department to show an interest in developing his career in this specialty. He was therefore one of the first twelve students from the Resettlement Department to enrol in the Certificate course in Housing Management in 1969. The students from the Resettlement Department found that they had to work very hard in the course because two-thirds of the curriculum was virtually unrelated to their daily work. On the other hand, as they were working in the more senior ranks of the civil service and were generally more mature than the students from the Urban Services Department, they seem to have been better prepared for hard work.[121] They formed study groups after lectures and maintained frequent communication with the tutors. Such extra-curricular activities were rare among the younger and less-experienced students from the Urban Services Department.

In spite of these differences, all three alumni appreciated that the tutors were extremely knowledgeable in their fields and supportive of their students. Many tutors were 'the best in town', drawn from all possible sources including the University, the government and outside bodies.[122] Well-known tutors from the government included Mr Jeremy Fell Mathews, a crown counsel in the early 1970s who later became Attorney-General from 1988 to 1997, and Mr Fung Tung, who became the Director of Housing in 1990. Senior HKU teaching staff, such as Professor W. G. Gregory of the Department of Architecture, and Professor J. M. Robertson of the Department of Social Work, also taught in the Certificate course. The high teaching standards of these tutors deeply impressed the students and encouraged them in their studies.

The impact of the Certificate course on the profession of housing management in Hong Kong was vast. The government considered the Extra-Mural Certificate awarded by the DEMS to be a key requirement for promotion from Housing Assistant to Housing Manager. The course not only equipped the students with professional expertise, but also developed their management and leadership skills as well as personal qualities which enabled them to perform their duties at a higher level of efficiency in future career postings. On the other hand, those who did not take the course were less likely to be promoted to higher ranks in the government service. All four DEMS alumni from the Housing Management courses who were interviewed by the authors were promoted to senior management positions in the Housing Authority. Mr Simon Li was the Business Director (Management) before his retirement in 1998 and now works in consultancy, project management and voluntary services. Mr Joseph Lee retired in 2002 as Senior Assistant Director of Housing and joined the Urban Renewal Authority in 2003 as District Development Director. Mr Mok Yiu-kwong was the Assistant Director of Housing when he retired in 1993 and is now the District Development Implementation Strategist of the Urban Renewal Authority. Mr Michael Fok has recently retired from the post of Senior Housing Manager of the Housing Authority. The course was therefore very popular among junior officers in these government departments. The annual intake rose from about 30 in 1969 to 160 in 1975. In the 1975–76 academic year, there were 425 housing management students in eighteen courses which were further sub-divided into thirty classes.[123] The number of eligible applicants became so great that many had to wait several years before being admitted to the course.[124]

The DEMS programme was one of the foundations of modern housing management in Hong Kong and accelerated the professionalisation of housing management in the colony. The expansion of public housing under the Ten Year Building Scheme in the 1970s led to an even greater demand for professional housing managers and the Certificate course was one of the Government's mainstays in supplying qualified local officers. The development of multi-storey buildings and private housing estates also boosted the demand for housing managers in the wider workforce. From 1975 to 1985, more than 900 students were awarded the Certificate and many more enrolled in the course without eventually acquiring the qualification. After their training, these students worked not just in government departments, but also in other public authorities and commercial firms. It is estimated that at least half of the professionals in housing management in Hong Kong today have received some sort of professional training from the Department of Extra-Mural Studies or HKU SPACE.[125] As the first and only professional training programme in Hong Kong for two decades, the Certificate course helped to train the bulk of housing managers in Hong Kong. Even today, HKU SPACE continues to train professionals in housing management in several of its programmes.[126]

Conclusion

It has only been possible in this chapter to survey a few of the many areas in which the Department of Extra-Mural Studies provided vocational or continuing professional adult education from the mid-1960s to the mid-1980s. The focus has been on extra-mural professional education because that was very much the policy of the DEMS at the time, and these programmes were receiving strong support from both the University and the government. Some of the new areas initiated by the DEMS, such as Law and Management Studies, even became fully-fledged university departments in the late 1960s and 1970s. This does not mean that the Department of Extra-Mural Studies began to focus entirely on professional studies and ceased to offer the old 'liberal' courses which were held in such high esteem in the 1950s and 1960s by Gerald Moore and Ieuan Hughes. The liberal courses nevertheless began to take a secondary role in the work of the Department from the late 1960s, but even those courses which aimed only at personal intellectual development were sometimes of use to students who learned new skills that could be used as a means of supporting themselves. The DEMS produced several artists in this period, including the very successful Liu Ming who came to Hong Kong from Guangdong in 1973 and soon enrolled in several fine arts and sketching courses. By 1986 he had mounted his first solo exhibition in Macau and over the last twenty years has earned both local and overseas recognition for his oils and watercolours. While some alumni took DEMS courses with clear career goals in mind, numerous others enrolled only for pleasure or intellectual stimulation and yet their working lives were enriched by the experience.

The small number of individual graduates whose experiences as students of the DEMS have been examined in this chapter can hardly be presumed to be representative of the tens of thousands of students who enrolled in one or more extra-mural courses in this period. They do, however, give a hint of what their studies at the DEMS allowed them to achieve in their professional careers. Every alumnus interviewed by the authors of this book was extremely grateful for the opportunities for professional development and career advancement which HKU's extra-mural courses provided at a time when full-time professional qualifications were either not available in Hong Kong or very limited in their student intakes. It is perhaps not surprising, therefore, that one of the outstanding features of extra-mural studies programmes for working professionals during the 1970s and 1980s appears to have been the extraordinary dedication and dogged determination of a whole generation of Hong Kong workers to improve their professional skills. The Department of Extra-Mural Studies therefore benefited countless Hong Kong workers and certainly deserves the title of 'cradle of professional studies in Hong Kong'. That the DEMS became involved in professional education in the 1960s would no doubt have pleased the founders of the University, whose main aim in establishing HKU was to provide professionals trained in medical sciences and engineering for the modernisation of China. What is seldom realised in HKU, however, is that the University's extra-mural activities were in some ways far more successful in achieving this goal in Hong Kong during the 1970s and 1980s than its undergraduate programmes which were so limited in their intake of students and output of graduates. The sheer number of DEMS students also reinforces an earlier observation that the Department had, by the 1980s, become the University's principal means of connecting 'gown' with 'town'.

CHAPTER SIX

From Department of Extra-Mural Studies to School of Professional and Continuing Education, 1985–1991

THE YEAR 1985 IN MANY WAYS marked a turning point in the development of the Department of Extra-Mural Studies. The construction of Shun Tak Centre was completed and the first University-owned Town Centre was nearly ready for occupation. Roger Williams, Director of Extra-Mural Studies since 1967, decided to retire after twenty years of service with the Department and a new Director, Professor Lee Ngok, was appointed in 1986. The government also moved towards adopting a more progressive adult higher education policy in 1985, and both the University and the Department took ground-breaking steps to engage actively in these changes. The Department initiated or participated in various academic developments in the areas of open and distance education. The University also reviewed its role in adult higher education within Hong Kong and initiated reforms in the management structure of the DEMS to equip it better to deal with the changing demands in society. These developments indicate that the University at last recognised the need for a thoroughly up-to-date Department of Extra-Mural Studies to ensure that future development in this field of the University's work would meet the expectations of society and the highest international standards. These changes finally led to a restructuring of the Department into the School of Professional and Continuing Education (SPACE) in 1992.

The Evans Report and a New Director

By the mid-1980s, the Department of Extra-Mural Studies had accumulated nearly thirty years of experience in providing a full range of extra-mural programmes to people in Hong Kong. It devised and executed its own development plans with a degree of independence that had not been envisaged by Senate in 1957, and continued to report its work to the Senate through the Committee on Extra-Mural Studies (CEMS). The three-tier governance structure of Department, CEMS and Senate had served the Department well throughout this long period of development. However, by the mid-1980s this simple structure was showing signs of stress and some senior university administrators began to doubt that it could continue to cope with the increasing academic and administrative demands in the still-expanding area of extra-mural studies. Having served the DEMS for twenty years, Roger Williams was due to retire from the directorship at the age of sixty in June 1986. As a result, the University decided to take advantage of Williams's forthcoming retirement to review the current status and future development of the DEMS.

There had already been quite some discussion in Hong Kong about the future of post-secondary and technical education as the 1980s began. The Topley Committee had been appointed in November 1980 to advise the government on the expansion of existing tertiary institutions, the creation of new institutions, the relationships between institutions and the use of distance learning.[1] It reported to the Governor in June 1981 and recommended an expansion in the provision of tertiary education, particularly in key areas of skills shortages so as to assist in the development of the economy. The number of first-year undergraduate degree places needed to be trebled by 1989–90 (to 4,900) and quadrupled by 1994–95 (to 6,500), and first-year non-degree places should be doubled to 26,700 by 1989–90.[2] Moreover, the Topley Committee recommended that distance-learning techniques should be developed 'within regular courses of instruction that made use of classroom teaching' and the government should explore 'the greater use of home-study packages, of correspondence courses and of radio broadcasts within adult education'.[3] These were sweeping changes and although the Topley Report was never formally published, many of its recommendations were taken up and implemented in later reports such as the Llewellyn Report of 1982 and the Education Commission Report of 1984.[4]

In January 1985, the University's Development and General Purposes Committee (DGPC) set up a Working Party to 'consider the future role and development of extra-mural studies in University, for advice to the Senate and/or the Council'.[5] The Working Party was chaired by Professor Dafydd Evans, who had participated in the London University LLB pilot programme in the mid-1960s but was by this time Dean of Law. The other four members were Professor M. A. Brimer, chairman of the Committee on Extra-Mural Studies, Professor Gordon Redding, a member of the CEMS, and Professors W. S. Leong and K. F. Shortridge, but it did not have any representation from the Department of Extra-Mural Studies.[6] The Working Party met for more than two years, collecting opinions from the Director and staff tutors of the DEMS on the future of extra-mural studies at HKU, and finally submitted its report in August 1987 for discussion by the Development and General Purposes Committee in September 1987.[7]

The Working Party recognised that the underlying rationale for extra-mural studies in Hong Kong had changed significantly in the three decades since the DEMS had been established, but was confident that the Department should continue to play a role in the development of continuing and 'open' education in Hong Kong.[8] The Evans Report made twelve recommendations covering administration, finance and the courses offered by the DEMS. The most significant recommendation of the Report concerned the selection of the new Director of Extra-Mural Studies. The Report confirmed the full academic status of the directorship, stating that 'the leadership of Extra-mural Studies must be academically, rather than managerially, oriented; the Director must be given opportunities to engage in teaching and research'. The Working Party suggested that the University should designate the Director as a 'Teacher' according to the Statutes in order to confirm the full academic status of both the Director and the Department.[9]

The University took note of the developing opinions within the Working Party and appointed an academically-oriented Director well before the final report was submitted. Professor Lee Ngok was named Director-designate in April 1986 with his appointment to take effect from 1 January 1987.[10] Professor Lee was a well-known scholar in the humanities and was already an experienced and talented university administrator at the time of his appointment. A HKU graduate in History (B.A. 1963, DipEd 1964, M.A. 1967) with a doctorate from London University, he had taught in the University's Department of History since 1968 and was promoted to Reader in 1984. His research was principally in the area of strategic defence with a special focus on the case of China, but he had also written in the fields of Chinese Communist Party history and the history of Chinese migration.[11] He was therefore an established scholar with a strong background in teaching and research. Professor Lee's administrative capabilities were also well proven during his long tenure of the deanship of the Faculty of Arts between 1976 and 1985, a period when three new academic departments had been established.[12] The appointment of a senior and respected academic as the new Director of Extra-Mural Studies was a clear acknowledgement by the University that the DEMS had come of age as a teaching unit and that it was time to enhance its status with a strong academic leader. It was not long before Professor Lee proved himself more than capable of leading the Department as it began to face increasing challenges and opportunities.

Lee Ngok's directorship proved to be very different from that of Roger Williams. The gradual development of the department's activities between 1967 and 1985 changed pace under the new Director and a flood of new programmes were added to the University's extra-mural offerings. Enrolments rose from 28,416 in 1984–85 to 57,985 in 1994–95 (see Appendix 2), and fee income sky-rocketed from $10 million to $168 million in the same period (see Appendix 3). Lee Ngok early recognised the potential for continuing higher education in Hong Kong, and in his inaugural lecture delivered in 1992 (playfully titled 'Opportunity Knocks') he elaborated on a number of policies which he had already implemented with incredible success. His central policy during his ten years as Director was to make SPACE a major contributor to 'human resource development' in Hong Kong, especially in the area of 'knowledge-intensive service industries' through increasing the supply of graduates.[13] He felt that the only way for Hong Kong to plug the graduate gap was to embark on a massive expansion of part-time higher education to satisfy the demands of a large and highly motivated pool of up to 536,000 students.[14] This would require 'bridging strategies' and co-operation between local and overseas partners, an area in which Lee Ngok and SPACE would take a lead in the second half of the 1980s.[15]

Apart from the question of the new Director, the Evans Report also suggested a number of general principles to guide the development of the DEMS. For example, there was a strong recommendation that the governance of the Department should be reformed. The Report observed that the Committee on Extra-Mural Studies 'is not an academic governing body (nor is it a committee of management), and does not provide for a forum equivalent to a Faculty Board for teachers in the Department of Extra-mural Studies to participate in academic planning and the formulation of academic policies, nor does it promote any sense of identity and cohesion'.[16] It was felt that the CEMS should therefore be transformed into a 'board of extra-mural studies' which would include all 'Teachers' in the DEMS and enjoy powers and duties similar to those of the boards of the faculties. This new board would be complemented by another small administrative body to 'look after the non-academic and managerial aspects of extra-mural studies operations, such as the determination of course fees and the management of the Extra-mural Studies Fund'.[17] The Working Party believed that this bicameral structure would provide the Department with a more comprehensive and effective governance structure.

The Evans Working Party acknowledged that the DEMS should continue to 'play a role in the provision of continuing and open education in Hong Kong'. The Department should not only organise non-examinable or sub-degree programmes, but should also now begin to seek possibilities of collaboration with faculties within the University in order to offer courses leading to a University degree. It also encouraged the DEMS to develop, in collaboration with overseas institutions, 'courses leading to the award of degrees by these institutions under their distance-learning or external studies scheme'.[18] These policy directions soon proved to be central to the future development of the DEMS and became its main academic endeavour during the directorship of Lee Ngok.

The Evans Report was the University's first attempt at a full review of the organisation and governance of its extra-mural activities in the three decades since the establishment of the Department. Despite the fact that the recommendations of the Report were not adopted by the University as official policy until the very last stage of the Department's restructuring in 1991, the Report made a very strong case for the University's support of continuing education. Moreover, it provided a set of general guidelines for the development of the Department when it was faced with a number of challenges and opportunities in the subsequent years.

The Open Learning Institute and the DEMS

The need for reform of the Department of Extra-Mural Studies became more pressing when a number of challenges and opportunities arose in adult higher education in the mid-1980s. The most significant change during this period was the emergence of the concept of 'open education'. The Education Commission defined 'open education' in its 1984 report as:

> ... education which is conducted outside the formal institutional system . . . open education is non-age specific, covering basic literacy to tertiary level studies. It ranges from specialised vocational studies to general interest studies which may be recreation or leisure-oriented. The aims of open education are manifold and include remedial learning, providing second chance opportunities for obtaining qualifications, updating and keeping abreast of developments in fields where knowledge is expanding rapidly, and fulfilling individual personal development needs.[19]

It was clear that the extra-mural activities which the DEMS had long organised were part of 'open education' as defined by the Education Commission, but the delivery of open education was slightly different from that of conventional extra-mural studies departments. Post-secondary open education was often, although not necessarily always, related to 'distance learning', which was defined as 'a form of tuition and study in which the principal element is pre-prepared course material on which the student works off campus to complete assignments or prepare for examinations'.[20] The technological advances of recent decades enabled adult learners to undertake effective part-time studies even without the traditional face-to-face contact with tutors. Students could learn through written and audio-visual materials as well as via television or radio programmes. They could maintain interaction with tutors through occasional tutorials, teleconferencing, telephone conversations and written assessments. Distance learning had its advantages, particularly in enhancing the flexibility with which institutions organised courses and the ways in which students learned. This approach was not novel for the DEMS as it had for a long time been offering extra-mural courses to students who were preparing for correspondence courses or external degree examinations. This was a relatively low-level form of distance learning, however, and the Department had little experience in initiating courses which were conducted chiefly through the distance learning mode. This contrasted with other universities in the British

Commonwealth which were establishing very large distance learning programmes, such as at the Open University in Britain and the University of New England in Australia.[21] The two new adult educational concepts of 'open education' and 'distance learning' compelled the DEMS to prepare itself academically and administratively in order to cope with the perceived change in the needs of adult higher education in Hong Kong.

The need for change and engagement with these new concerns in adult education became more urgent for the Department in the mid-1980s because a new institution in post-secondary open education was being formed with government support. After many decades of playing a minimal role in adult higher education, the government was increasingly aware of its potential role in encouraging developments in this sector and therefore became more active in seeking new ways to develop open and distance education. Its endeavours finally led to the establishment in 1988 of the Open Learning Institute (OLI), an institution which aimed at providing post-secondary open education to all members of the public. Being one of the key providers of adult higher education in Hong Kong, the DEMS participated actively in the early development of the Institute. It also realised through this engagement that it had to reform its own extra-mural programmes in order to counter the challenges which the Institute would inevitably bring to the field.

Participation by HKU in the Open Learning Institute

The Hong Kong government's active involvement in proposals for open education began when a government-appointed visiting panel headed by Sir John Llewellyn, formerly Director-General of the British Council and Vice-Chancellor of Exeter University, reviewed the Hong Kong education system in 1981. The panel published its report in the following year, suggesting the possibility of a joint venture to promote continuing education supported by different organisations in the community.[22] In July 1983, the government commissioned the University and Polytechnic Grants Committee (UPGC) to study the possibility of establishing an Open University in Hong Kong, modelled on the British university of the same name. The UPGC did not support this proposal, but it did support the idea of 'open education' and recommended that all higher educational institutions should develop open education as 'a co-operative and collaborative venture'.[23]

A comprehensive plan for the government's participation in open education was subsequently considered by the Education Commission, a new body created in April 1984 as a result of the Llewellyn Report. In August 1986, the Education Commission published its 'Report No. 2' (ECR2), in which various aspects of the education system in Hong Kong were examined. The Report observed the inadequacies of adult higher education in Hong Kong and stated that 'there is a *prima facie* case, both social and economic, for an open education programme which will supplement conventional education and provide opportunities for those who otherwise would be denied them'.[24] The Education Commission recommended that the programme 'should encompass the full-range of post-secondary studies, starting at a level related to school leaving qualifications and extending to second degree level', providing 'central cores of academic and vocational studies allowing development into specialist areas leading to recognised qualifications'.[25] The open education programme was to be open to all adults, and because many adult students could not attend conventional classroom teaching sessions, it was suggested that a distance learning approach should be adopted to maximise the accessibility of the programme to adult learners.[26]

One of the key recommendations of the Education Commission's Report was the establishment of a consortium of institutions to carry out the open education programme. The Commission was convinced that the open education programme could not be carried out effectively through co-operation between autonomous institutions, an opinion which is supported by the competitive nature of relations between HKU and CUHK in adult education since the mid-1960s. Instead, the Commission recommended inviting all five government-subsidised post-secondary institutions to form a consortium specifically for open education.[27] The consortium would be an independent academic entity, responsible for devising the open education programme, organising courses of various types, and conferring degrees and other qualifications on its students. This type of collaboration ensured that the existing institutions would give the necessary support for the new venture without endangering the distinctive identity of the type of open education which the Education Commission had envisioned.

HKU first received the Education Commission's proposal for an open education consortium with caution. Any commitment to the consortium carried educational, administrative and financial implications, and the University believed that 'it may be thought best for the University to reserve its position' until the government began detailed planning for the new consortium.[28] HKU's attitude towards the government's plans eventually became much more positive, however, for the University was familiar with plans to widen public access to part-time higher education and had itself already begun to increase the number of part-time places available at postgraduate level in various disciplines.[29]

The University's most serious attempt to widen access to higher education was a proposal for part-time or external degrees awarded by the University. Discussion on this issue had occurred intermittently within the University since the late-1960s. In 1968, the Joint Committee on Extra-Mural Studies suggested that part-time degree courses should be offered by both HKU and CUHK.[30] During the 1970s, the Convocation, the UPGC and overseas visitors all suggested the possibility of introducing part-time or external degree programmes at HKU.[31] In January 1979, following the publication of the *White Paper on Senior Secondary and Tertiary Education* (October 1978), the UPGC formally asked the two local universities to submit proposals for 'part-time degree courses, designed mainly for mature students'.[32] In October 1981, the Senate and the Council approved an external degree programme which would admit external undergraduates in the faculties of Science, Arts and Social Sciences from September 1982.[33] It was expected that the University would 'develop distance teaching materials, largely in print form, and provide an off-campus study centre where external students could have access to tutors, library facilities, audio-visual facilities and study space'.[34] However, the Sino-British talks on the future of Hong Kong and the advent of economic recession in the territory compelled the UPGC to postpone and finally terminate the plan in 1984.[35] Despite having to abort this programme, the University had made all the necessary preparations for providing part-time studies for adult learners. As a result, when a working group of the Education and Manpower Branch clarified many of the uncertainties concerning the new Open Learning Institute in July 1987, the Senate approved HKU's participation in the proposed consortium.[36]

The University envisaged that its contribution to the OLI would happen at two levels. It would participate in the OLI in a formal sense by having representation on the governing body of the Institute. Meanwhile, it would also be involved in the actual operation of the OLI, 'involving direct contribution by way of preparation of course materials and delivery of teaching', in particular the distance education materials.[37] While HKU's involvement at these two levels assisted the early development of the new Institute, the University also benefited from the opportunity to gain experience in offering distance learning courses, which might prove to be useful in its own degree programmes.

The DEMS and the Proposed HKU-OLI Collaboration

Having been the major provider of part-time university-level courses in Hong Kong for three decades, the Department was eager to develop open and distance education even while the University was still hesitant about accepting the government's proposals concerning the OLI. Professor Lee Ngok told a Senate meeting in January 1987 that 'the University might be able to undertake its own individual initiative in the field of continuing education, following the favourable public response to the proposals of the Education Commission for developments in open education'.[38] The participation of the DEMS in the development of open education was also endorsed in principle by the Committee on Extra-Mural Studies in March 1987.[39] The Evans Report, released in the month before the Senate's formal agreement to participate in the Open Learning Institute, acknowledged the Department's role in continuing and open education in Hong Kong.[40] The active involvement of the

Department in the OLI initiative was also reflected in the appointment of Professor Lee as the University's representative on the OLI Planning Committee in January 1988. He was later also appointed to the Council of the Open Learning Institute.[41] Nevertheless, the exact role of the Department in the HKU-OLI collaboration and in the University's expansion of open education was at that time still unclear. It was obvious that the DEMS could not by itself fulfil the University's commitment to participate in the OLI because it did not possess the necessary academic expertise. The existing governance and administrative structures for extra-mural studies at HKU were also not robust enough to deal with the massive expansion in open and distance education. The Senate, therefore, established a new Committee on Open Education (COE) in October 1987, chaired by a Pro-Vice-Chancellor (Professor R. T. T. Young), and consisting of eight other members including the Director of Extra-Mural Studies.[42]

The Committee on Open Education was asked to 'advise the Senate on the academic areas in the University in which there is interest and capability for developments in continuing and open/distance education'. It was also to advise on 'the necessary framework of administrative and academic support services' required to implement the University's plans.[43] The implementation of these plans was to prove far more complex than anyone had imagined, however, and the new Committee's task was complicated by the fact that its functions overlapped with those of the Committee on Extra-Mural Studies. This meant that the DEMS came to have two masters in matters concerning the Department's involvement in open and distance education. The administration of open and distance education was further complicated by the participation of the various teaching departments and administrative units of the University. Closer co-ordination among so many different bodies within the University was therefore needed before any effective action could be taken.

The External Studies Unit / Distance Learning Unit

Before the Committee on Open Education came into full operation, the DEMS was already prepared to provide its own blueprint for future expansion in open and distance education. The Department's 'Proposals for Development in Open, Distance and Continuing Education 1988–1994', commonly known as the Six Year Plan, was released in February 1988. This paper was the Department's first attempt to go beyond the University's conventional triennial planning system and outline its plans for longer-term development. One of the major initiatives of the Six Year Plan was the introduction of external degree programmes in Chinese Language and Translation, Law, Medical Laboratory Science, and Social Sciences.[44] All HKU external degree programmes would be supported by a new External Studies Unit

(ESU) under the supervision of the Department. The Six Year Plan envisaged that the ESU would become a university-wide unit for 'the provision of distance teaching material and the administration of degree courses for students off-campus'. It would cater for both the DEMS and other departments which managed external degree courses.[45] The proposed unit would be administratively responsible for managing the records of external students and tutors, distributing teaching materials, and monitoring costs, budgets and financial information. It would provide academic support for distance education, giving 'advice to academic colleagues on the presentation of material for distance learning' and 'drawing up a production schedule and monitoring material production processes'. Programme Development Officers would be needed to form 'the nucleus of a team of educational technologists/course designers in the Unit'.[46] The Department hoped that the External Studies Unit, in collaboration with other service units such as the Centre for Media Resources and the Hong Kong University Press, would become the support centre for all distance learning programmes provided by the University. Both the Committee on Extra-Mural Studies and the Committee on Open Education supported in principle the Department's proposals for an External Studies Unit. The CEMS, despite recognising the uncertainty of HKU's participation in the Open Learning Institute, supported the Six Year Plan, including the establishment of the ESU, at its meeting on 7 April 1988.[47] The Committee on Open Education also agreed to the initiatives proposed by the DEMS in open and distance education and encouraged the Department to 'make temporary appointments to support the development of distance teaching materials'.[48]

Unfortunately, responses to the proposal for an External Studies Unit were not completely positive outside these two committees. The Committee on Open Education sent a consultation paper to the faculties on 25 October 1988 inviting them to comment on the role of the DEMS in open and distance education, and particularly the proposed establishment of the External Studies Unit.[49] While faculties and departments had no fundamental objection to the University's commitment to open and distance education, some of them expressed doubts about the role of the DEMS and were sceptical about an External Studies Unit under the auspices of the Department. The Faculty of Education was particularly sceptical, noting that 'a University Committee or Unit, not within the Department of Extra-mural Studies, could be established as the liaison and policy-making body for the University's links with the OLI; and that Faculties should be allowed to work out details of courses directly with the OLI'.[50] The Dean of Education criticised the Committee on Open Education for going beyond its jurisdiction in presuming that the DEMS and the External Studies Unit should be the co-ordinating body between HKU and the Open Learning Institute.[51] The Science Faculty also voiced similar views, saying that 'there was a need for the establishment of an External Studies Unit in the University, but independently of the Extra-Mural Studies Department, to look after the details of the University's direct and indirect associations with the OLI programmes'.[52] Although the two faculties did not specify exactly why they were opposed to the plan, it seems clear that they were worried that the External Studies Unit might monopolise liaison between the University and the Open Learning Institute and might even become a supervisory body with control over the faculties' work in open and distance education.

Some departments in the Faculty of Social Sciences also expressed their reservations about the role of the DEMS in the new open and distance education programmes. In spite of its support for the co-ordinating role of the DEMS in future development, the Management Studies Department emphasised that the DEMS should only have 'the resources for administration and not academic development across the fields envisaged'.[53] The Department of Psychology was not even in favour of 'a strong role for the EMS Department'.[54] All these negative comments indicated a widespread doubt and suspicion about the nature of the role to be played by the Department of Extra-Mural Studies and the External Studies Unit in the University's increasing efforts in open and distance education.

Faced with such open opposition to their proposal, the DEMS was quick to clarify the supportive, rather than supervisory, role of the proposed External Studies Unit to the academic departments of the University:

> It should be emphasised that the EMS proposal to establish an ESU does not intend to infringe on the rights of the faculties to develop their degree courses and communicate with the OLI. Rather, the ESU would provide the necessary support in education technology and related academic expertise of the EMS Staff Tutors in adult and continuing education.[55]

The Committee on Open Education, after considering the different views expressed by the various University bodies, continued to feel that the DEMS was a suitable organisation to provide educational technology support. The Department had experience of teaching adult students across a wide range of academic subjects; it also had experience of operating in a self-financing milieu; and it was further felt that education technology specialists would fit better into a multi-disciplinary academic environment like the DEMS rather than a purely service or administrative unit.[56] The External Studies Unit, as defined by the Committee on Open Education, was to be an advisory and administrative unit, providing advice 'on instructional design and the development of distance education packages' and organising the financial and operational arrangements for the planned academic programmes.[57] Although the Committee on Open Education supported the establishment of an External Studies Unit under the control of the DEMS, they seem to have realised that the ESU would ultimately have to be supervised by the Committee itself in order to overcome the suspicions of the faculties:

> It is important to stress the Unit's reporting role which is proposed to be to the Committee on Open Education through the Director, EMS and that this will not mean that the EMS Department will control or have a lien on its facilities. The External Studies Unit (ESU) will serve a University wide function and could, conceivably, be an independent unit. Nevertheless, in view of the fact that its activities will start on a modest scale on the basis of fixed term contracts, of the undoubted interest and enthusiasm in EMS for open and distance education, and of the fact that initial funding will be from resources arising from EMS activities but set aside by the Council for the development of open and distance education, it is appropriate for the Unit to be located in the DEMS department initially.[58]

Following the Senate's approval of the Committee on Open Education's Interim Report on 6 June 1989, the External Studies Unit was established within the DEMS but under the supervision of the Committee on Open Education (see Figure 6.1). The functions of the new Unit were much less extensive than the Department had proposed initially and were essentially limited to production of distance learning materials. The ESU was therefore renamed the Distance Learning Unit (DLU) in the 1989–90 academic year 'since it was felt this better described its functions'.[59] The Unit was staffed by two contract-term Programme Development Officers and a small team of clerical staff.[60] The Unit's two initial projects were commissioned by the Open Learning Institute for the development of distance learning materials. The first project, a Social Sciences Foundation Course, was commissioned by the OLI in August 1990.[61] Led by Dr Peter Bradshaw who was on secondment from the Open University (UK) from April 1990, the project team included four staff tutors from the DEMS and three teachers from the departments of Political Sciences, Sociology and Economics. The team completed a 'camera-ready copy' set of materials which it delivered to the Open Learning Institute in January 1992.[62] The second project for a Chinese Studies Foundation course was organised by Dr Y. W. Liu on secondment from the University of Western Australia. It was agreed that the University should retain the copyright in this course package which would be sold to the OLI on a per capita basis in 1992.[63] These two projects represent the most concrete examples of the University's early operational participation in the Open Learning Institute, but such involvement fell far short of the consortium principle which the Education Commission had originally favoured for the OLI.

While the Distance Learning Unit gained experience from production of distance learning materials through the first two projects commissioned by the OLI, it tried not to overlook its primary function 'to provide a service to the University'.[64] The Distance Learning Unit planned in 1990 to work closely with other units, especially the Centre for Media Resources, to expand its services to extra-mural and University courses which adopted distance learning as one of their modes of

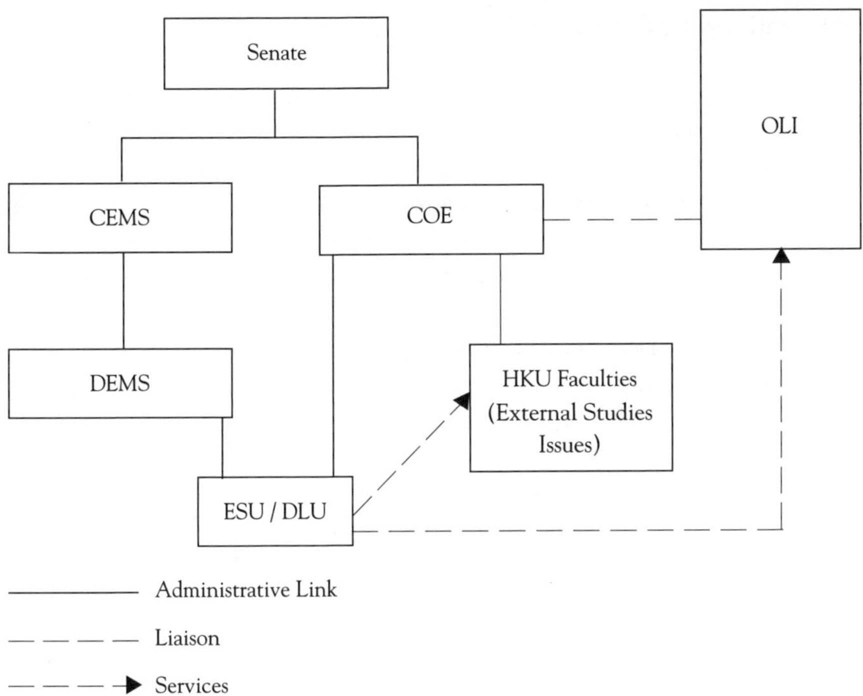

Figure 6.1 Organisation chart of extra-mural studies and open education at HKU, 1989

teaching. However, its role in the University's development of distance education should not be overstated. No large-scale distance-learning scheme was ever implemented by the DLU within the University.[65] The University's mode of participation in Open Learning Institute courses also shifted and soon rendered the DLU peripheral to the main areas of collaboration. The University tended to encourage its staff to collaborate with the OLI in areas such as course development, academic consultation or teaching on an individual basis. The Council approved in June 1989 that the work of HKU teaching staff for the Open Learning Institute should not be regarded as 'outside practice', for which prior permission had to be obtained and from which the remuneration had to be shared with the University.[66] The University came to prefer this type of involvement by staff because it provided more flexibility in the types of collaboration which could occur. Collaboration with the Open Learning Institute through contractual agreements with the Distance Learning Unit was less flexible, hence less preferable and ultimately far less significant in the expansion of the Department's activities than the other major development of the late 1980s — international collaboration.

International Collaboration for Degree Programmes

The involvement of the Department of Extra-Mural Studies in international degree programmes from the mid-1980s was closely connected with new concepts of open and distance education. But this development was initiated primarily by the DEMS itself, rather than by government or University policies. From the late-1980s, the Department established and strengthened its collaboration with overseas institutions in offering both undergraduate and postgraduate degree programmes for local adult learners.

Although the Department had developed a wide range of extra-mural courses by the mid-1980s, there were still many opportunities for expanding the types and modes of programmes being provided. First, most extra-mural courses were devised and conducted by the Department's own tutors. These courses were taught very traditionally through lectures, seminars and tutorials. While this conventional face-to-face mode of learning had its own merits, it was not necessarily able to provide a highly flexible scheme for course developers, tutors, part-time students and assessors. Moreover, with the exception of the London University LLB programme, none of the extra-mural courses led to a formal degree qualification. This weakness became more apparent when professionals in some industries wanted to formalise or upgrade their qualifications, but found that there were no degrees or other advanced programmes of study available locally. The lack of higher education opportunities in Hong Kong had been noted several times in the 1980s, and perhaps most embarrassingly for the government during an honorary degrees ceremony at HKU in March 1983.[67] Hong Kong's brain drain problem in the mid-1980s, which accelerated after the June Fourth Incident in 1989, also intensified the demand in society for more opportunities for 'local people to be trained and educated to fill those gaps and to prepare them for the exigencies of the post-1997 experience'.[68] Part-time degree programmes developed by overseas institutions and conducted jointly with the DEMS through diversified teaching methods from face-to-face contacts to distance learning were therefore thought to be a suitable solution for these working adults.

Collaboration between local and overseas institutions in offering open education and distance learning courses was also in line with government policies. The second report of the Education Commission argued that local initiatives in open education were 'unlikely to be so comprehensive as to cover all possible specialist requirements, and external institutions may well be able to fill such gaps'.[69] In particular, the Commission recommended that overseas institutions be encouraged to co-operate with local post-secondary institutions in order to avoid courses being offered in an uncontrolled way by sub-standard overseas institutions. Such co-operation would also help to improve the standards of similar programmes being offered by local institutions.[70] As the need for such part-time overseas degree courses was so pressing and the government had no apparent objection to collaboration between local and foreign institutions, the DEMS formulated a policy to develop overseas degree programmes and declared this initiative in its Annual Report for 1987–88 as part of its contribution to open and distance education in Hong Kong.[71]

University of London External Degree Programmes

Extra-mural courses leading to overseas degree qualifications were in fact not completely novel to the Department of Extra-Mural Studies. The preparation courses for the LLB external degree of the University of London had, for example, been running for more than twenty years. One of the features of these preparation courses was that they did not constitute a formal part of the London University external degree structure. These external degrees were designed for distance education, and London University provided its external students with specially designed study materials and assessed their performance through examinations or assignments. The role of the DEMS was to assist students to prepare for examinations according to the London syllabuses, but not to maintain or control the academic standards of these external degrees. Although the external students were perfectly eligible to sit examinations without having attended any lectures or tutorials, the preparation courses offered by the DEMS still appealed to many external students in Hong Kong because the courses supplemented the distance learning materials with intensive lectures, tutorials, and exercises. It was acknowledged that these might help students obtain better results in their examinations. In 1988–89, there were 2,874 students enrolled by the DEMS in the preparation courses for the London University LLB external examination.[72] Priscilla Tso had originally managed these courses but Bill Howarth was recruited in the 1980s to oversee the external law programme.

The highly successful London University LLB preparation courses provided a good model for the Department's development of overseas degree programmes. As the DEMS was able to enrol only about one-third of the newly registered LLB external students in Hong Kong in 1988–89, it was obvious that there was a huge unsatisfied demand for its preparation courses. It therefore decided to expand the number of places available for new students from 400 to 650 in the next academic year.[73] Mick Fisher, who had been a visiting lecturer from Manchester Metropolitan University since 1988, was appointed in 1991 to run the law courses with Edith Browne, and Professor Chris Sherrin taught as a visiting lecturer in the programme before being appointed to HKU's Faculty of Law. Carole Peterson and Bronwyn Davies were appointed in succession to develop the Department's PCCL programme.[74]

The DEMS also extended the variety of preparation courses available to help students who were sitting for the various other London University external degree examinations. In the autumn of 1987, it ran two preparatory courses for the London University Bachelor of Arts in Philosophy examination in collaboration with the Hong Kong Philosophy Society and later HKU's own Philosophy Department.[75] The course was a success and was further expanded in the next few years. In 1988–89, the Department started another scheme of preparation courses for the London University Bachelor of Science in Economics external examination. This two-year programme consisted of ten courses which assisted the students to prepare for the Part I and Part II examinations. There was a remarkable public response to the programme. It was well oversubscribed in the first year with 398 students admitted, and 688 in the second year.[76] More preparatory courses for the London University external examinations were offered in the next few years. These included courses for diplomas in Economics and Law, a Bachelor of Arts in Geography, and the Master of Law.[77]

In spite of a lack of any official academic partnership, the External Division of London University and the DEMS had developed 'a close working relationship' with each other in 'providing for the welfare a large number of Hong Kong students'.[78] From the 1988–89 academic year, the DEMS publicised the London University external programmes and its preparation courses by organising an annual London University Open Day at its Extra-Mural Town Centre, the first year of which attracted several thousand potential students. The Department also operated a joint information counter with London University at the British Education Exhibition in the Convention and Exhibition Centre to answer questions from the public.[79] Moreover, the DEMS also began to bring experienced overseas lecturers to Hong Kong in order to offer intensive short courses of one or two weeks' duration. The law courses taught by Mick Fisher and Chris Sherrin have already been mentioned, but another good example of these types of courses were those offered in conjunction with the London School of Economics preparation course starting in 1989–90. The London School of Economics external co-ordinator, Rosie Gosling, recruited Professor Tom Nossiter from LSE's Department of Government to teach the sociology component of the programme, while Teresa Bradley from Limerick Institute of Technology taught the courses in mathematics and statistics. Jennifer Ng from the DEMS gave administrative assistance. Teresa Bradley has been involved with the programme ever since and still travels to Hong Kong every spring to teach the statistics preparation course.[80]

The existing working relationship between the DEMS and London University was not, however, robust enough to cater for the increasing number of Hong Kong students wishing to enrol in the external courses. The registration procedure which required students to deal with London University directly was considered 'time consuming, expensive and detrimental to the students' interest'.[81] London

University therefore approached the DEMS and suggested transferring a number of tasks from London to Hong Kong, including the processing of applications, publicity, student recruitment and general enquiries.[82] An agreement was reached between the two institutions in April 1989 which allowed Hong Kong students (whether or not they would also enrol in a DEMS course) to register for the London external degrees at a special office operated by the DEMS.[83] In its first few months of operation in mid-1989, the office was temporarily located in the Extra-Mural Town Centre which had opened in the new Shun Tak Centre in August 1986.[84] In mid-September 1989, it moved to a new extension of the Town Centre on the fifteenth floor of the Shun Tak Centre.[85] Staff in the local registration office were assisted by a team from London University during the initial period, and they were also despatched to London to receive short-term technical training.[86] The new scheme was a great success. During the first registration exercise up to the end of December 1989, the office processed over one thousand new applications, about four hundred more registrations than had been completed in Hong Kong in the previous year.[87] While the new office attracted more registrations for the London University external degrees, it also strengthened the image of the DEMS among students in Hong Kong as a 'principal locus of courses to prepare students for the London examinations'.[88] During the next two decades, London University would remain one of the closest partners of the DEMS and HKU SPACE in the provision of programmes leading to overseas qualifications.

New Partnerships

While the DEMS was strengthening its administrative co-operation with London University, it also sought new partnerships with other overseas universities, mainly in Australia and New Zealand, in offering both undergraduate and postgraduate programmes. Unlike the London University model which required the DEMS to have very little participation in the academic governance of degree qualifications, most of the new partnership arrangements allowed both the Department and the overseas partner universities to play an active role in academic and administrative matters. These new partnerships soon outperformed the London University model and eventually became the most common form of collaboration between the DEMS and overseas institutions.

The first feasible proposal for a non-London University overseas degree programme emerged in early 1987 when Professor Lee Ngok met with a representative from Curtin University of Technology, an Australian university located in Perth. Together they came up with the idea of jointly delivering one of Curtin's business degrees in external mode in Hong Kong.[89] A proposal was drafted in April and May 1987 to offer a three-year part-time programme leading to Curtin's

Bachelor of Business (BBus) degree in Accounting or Marketing from February 1988. The target students were adults who had received some post-secondary education in business studies and had a minimum of three years of work experience, at least one of which had to be at the managerial level. The students were required to finish eighteen courses in three years, with two intensive preparatory courses beforehand, one in Hong Kong for twelve days and the other at the Curtin campus in Australia for nine days. The programme was mainly conducted in distance mode, meaning that students relied primarily on course materials supplied by Curtin University. There were no regular lectures during the period of study. However, the programme supplemented distance learning with a limited amount of face-to-face teaching in workshops, seminars and consultation sessions, as well as by requiring written assignments. The degree programme, like other extra-mural courses, was self-funded and hence charged its students at full cost: about $66,500 for the entire three-year programme.

Both the Department of Extra-Mural Studies and Curtin University made significant academic and administrative commitments to the programme. The preliminary proposal delineated the division of responsibilities between the two universities as follows:

> Curtin would be responsible for the academic contents of the programme, as the degree would be awarded by Curtin. In particular, Curtin would have the duty to prepare and produce the teaching and reading materials for the programme. In addition, the exercise of continuous assessment and examination as well as the conduct of course seminars would also be the responsibility of Curtin. . . . [DEMS] would be responsible for the conduct of tutorials. It would also have the responsibility to provide an input in relation to matters arising from the teaching arrangements in Hong Kong. The duties of [D]EMS would include, inter alia, operational support of the programme such as arrangement of tutorials and the provision of local teaching facilities.[90]

The financial arrangements were that Curtin University would receive the entire student fee and the DEMS would charge Curtin for conducting tutorials, providing accommodation for teaching and examinations, and for all administration and publicity. The ratio by which Curtin University and the DEMS would share student fees was expected to be approximately 55:45 in the first year.[91]

Apart from managing the programme, the DEMS also took on heavy academic responsibilities for the Curtin project. Workshops and seminars were conducted by three full-time staff members of the Department, and they also supervised part-time tutors in consultation sessions. The programme was co-ordinated by an Academic Committee consisting of an equal number of members appointed by Curtin and HKU. The HKU representatives were to be chosen from the DEMS, academic departments in related subjects such as Industrial Engineering and

Management Studies, and from outside the University. The Academic Committee would supervise all academic matters to do with the programme, such as course regulations, the standard of course materials, assessment and examination, and management of students and tutors. The DEMS therefore played an active role in the academic side of the programme from the very beginning.

This ground-breaking proposal for a degree programme in collaboration with an overseas institution led to controversies within the University. A debate took place in a Committee on Extra-Mural Studies meeting on 25 May 1987, in which Professor Lee explained that this type of joint venture 'would improve the standard of some of the courses offered by the Department' and would not affect the existing activities of the DEMS. The proposal was in line with the government's attempt to develop open education, and would satisfy the community need for adult higher education in the business area at a reasonable fee level.[92] However, doubts and concerns were raised by other members of the Committee. Professor Gordon Redding, who had worked as a staff tutor in the DEMS for nine years from 1973 to 1982 and was now Head of the Department of Management Studies, was one of those who expressed reservations about the programme. While he 'supported the proposal in principle', he requested the Committee on Extra-Mural Studies and the DEMS to clarify several points, including whether the financial arrangement whereby HKU would work for Curtin University to earn fees was appropriate for a university of HKU's standing. He also wondered whether the academic standards, professional recognition, student fees, and managerial structure of the programme were completely satisfactory. Perhaps more importantly, he asked whether there was any overlap or conflict between the proposed Curtin programme and the proposal of the Department of Management Studies for a full-time HKU Bachelor of Business Administration (BBA) programme which was due to start from September 1988.

Professor Redding's concern for protecting the interests of his own department was the first of many subsequent criticisms of the DEMS and SPACE. This issue would arise many times in the next twenty years in relation to external programmes which were similar to internal HKU degree programmes, both undergraduate and postgraduate. Apart from Professor Redding's doubts, the Committee on Extra-Mural Studies was told that 'there were expressions of caution by some members in the Department of Extra-mural Studies on the proposed joint venture with Curtin University'.[93] Despite these reservations, the Committee finally agreed that 'it would be desirable for the Department of Extra-mural Studies to be involved in distance education and part-time degree programmes in the long run, and supported in the meantime its collaborative effort with established, accredited overseas institutions leading to the award of degrees by those institutions', and supported in principle the proposal.[94]

The proposal was debated again when it was referred to the Senate for approval. While the Senate recognised the increasing need within the community for open and distance education, members expressed their concern that the new partnership would compel HKU to commit itself to a degree programme over which it could not exercise very much control. At its meeting on 2 June 1987, the Senate asked the Committee on Extra-Mural Studies to 'identify such additional safeguards as might be needed to secure the essential interests of the University'.[95] The DEMS produced a detailed paper for Senate which attempted to answer eight of the principal concerns raised by Senate. It was noted that Curtin University already had a high academic reputation and that the proposed programme would in any case be reviewed in five years' time. It was proposed that a Bachelor of Business Academic Committee be set up to monitor the programme and assure academic standards. Staffing and co-ordination problems would be reduced by hiring two or three tutors by 1990–91. On the question of conflict of academic interest and the risk of saturating the market, it was noted that the Curtin programme and the Department of Management Studies programme targeted different student groups and therefore no conflict in fact existed. Moreover, the Curtin degree was only a pass degree while the HKU degree was a higher-status honours degree. On the matter of fees and the division of earnings, there was no consensus, but the fees were nevertheless not considered to be excessive.[96]

The DEMS did everything it could to convince the Department of Management Studies to support the proposed DEMS-Curtin partnership, but these efforts were fruitless. In a letter dated 15 September 1987, Professor R. I. Tricker, Acting Head of the Management Studies Department, worried that the Hong Kong business community would confuse the Curtin degree, a pass degree requiring lower entry standards, with a HKU honours degree. He also refused to 'undertake any commitment to provide staff or other resources for the Curtin degree'. Finally, Professor Tricker attacked the fundamental policy behind the proposal:

> Whilst the proposal raises a number of matters of detail, the key issue can best be stated as a matter of university policy: should the university offer degrees by distance learning, accredited by overseas universities, in subject areas, where the University is already offering full time courses? The reaction from the Department of Management Studies is in the negative. The principal reason lies in the potential confusion in the minds of the Hong Kong community and potential students, the impossibility of adequately differentiating between the degrees that are offered, and the resultant loss of reputation and lowering standards … I do not think they can be overcome by appointing members of the Department of Management Studies to your [Curtin degree] advisory board.[97]

Unable to convince the Department of Management Studies to endorse the proposal, the Director of Extra-Mural Studies had no alternative but to try and reassure Professor Tricker that the DEMS was not 'in competition or conflict with the BBA programme'.[98] He explained that the DEMS had long maintained close co-operation with London University in the external degree programmes, and that the DipMS previously organised by the DEMS co-existed with the MBA programme of the Department of Management Studies. The external degree programmes should therefore not damage the interests of other academic departments of the University. It may well be that the earlier difficulties between the DEMS and the Department of Management Studies over the MBA programme was at the root of this new dispute. It appears that Professors Redding and Tricker did not trust the DEMS, and no amount of reassurance from the Director of the DEMS would set their minds at ease.

The Senate did not agree with the objections raised by the Department of Management Studies. It considered that the benefits of an external degree programme in distance learning mode in collaboration with an overseas institution overwhelmed the risks. It finally agreed on 6 October 1987 to allow the BBus (Curtin) programme to be 'mounted initially for a period of five years, subject to review'.[99] The enrolment figures for the programme were very encouraging in the initial years. One hundred and forty-five applicants competed for about 20 places in the first intake in January 1989. The number of applications remained at the same level in the following years, causing a gradual expansion of the annual enrolment to eighty-eight by 1992.[100]

The success of the joint venture with Curtin University encouraged the DEMS to inaugurate external degree programmes with other overseas universities. By September 1989, there were thirteen part-time degree or equivalent level advanced professional courses, most of which were offered in collaboration with overseas universities, serving about 2,100 students.[101] These partnerships continued to develop with many other overseas universities over the next fifteen years and are summarised in Appendix 6. Meanwhile, the University was increasingly aware of the need for a more comprehensive policy in this area. The Senate, for example, expressed its concern in May 1990 regarding a proposal for a Master of Pharmacy degree with the University of Otago. It noted that:

> . . . there was an urgent need to formalize the University's policy regarding to the part that external educational institutions might usefully play in its plans for open and distance education, bearing in mind inter-alia experience already gained by the Department of Extra-mural Studies in such collaborative ventures.[102]

HKU's academic departments and faculties were beginning to worry about competition from the increasingly successful DEMS programmes, but it also seemed clear that the University's existing structure and processes of academic governance 'were no longer entirely satisfactory in the new context of rapidly developing extra-mural activities'. It was felt that clarification was needed concerning 'the overall role of the academic departments of the University in relation to courses operated by the Department of Extra-Mural Studies'.[103] A proposal to offer a joint M.A. programme in Contemporary China Studies with the Departments of History and Geography had already failed to gain approval because of worries about the loss of faculty control over such programmes.[104] Concerns such as these from the faculties, the rapid expansion of external degrees and the University's participation in the Open Learning Institute together constituted a pressing need for an in-depth review and reform of the structure of extra-mural studies at HKU. The task of reviewing extra-mural studies began in 1988 and finally led to the transformation of the Department of Extra-Mural Studies into the School of Professional and Continuing Education in 1992.

From the DEMS to SPACE: Restructuring and Transformation

As the establishment of the External Studies Unit and the introduction of overseas degree programmes led to an extensive change in the way in which the DEMS provided continuing education to the community, it was necessary for the University to consider restructuring the administrative and academic governance of the Department. In the period between 1988 and 1991, various proposals on the future of the Department were discussed within the administrative and governing committees of the University. These discussions, the most important of which took place in a Joint Working Party from late 1989 and the Davies Working Party in 1990–91, finally came to fruition in late 1991 when it was decided to transform the Department of Extra-Mural Studies into the School of Professional and Continuing Education from 1 January 1992.

The Department of Extra-Mural Studies Ten Year Plan

The first proposal to restructure the DEMS was the Department's own 'Academic Development Proposals to 1996–97', commonly known as the Ten Year Plan, which was released in November 1988. The Ten Year Plan was a reworked version of the Six Year Plan which had been approved by the Committee on Extra-Mural Studies earlier in 1988. The Ten Year Plan did not make any substantial revisions in terms of academic development. However, the Ten Year Plan proposed an ambitious series of structural changes for the DEMS which involved upgrading the Department into a School of Extension Studies (SES) in 1991. It was proposed that the new School should consist of two core departments, the Department of External Studies (DES) and the Department of Continuing Education (DCE).[105] The School would be led by a dean and assisted by two directors, each of whom would head a department. The foundation of the Department of Continuing Education would be the existing DEMS, which had long provided traditional extra-mural courses in liberal studies and vocational subjects. The Ten Year Plan argued that the change of name to Department of Continuing Education would express 'a move away from the relatively traditional thinking in the development of adult learning, towards a concept of optimal provision of life long education for adult learners, the change in name reflecting the prevailing trend in Commonwealth Universities'.[106] The goal of the Department of Continuing Education would be to 'continue to provide "lifelong" education for adult learners, especially via the award of Diplomas which will have secured accreditation/articulation by overseas tertiary institutions and hopefully by HKU itself'.[107] It was conceived that the annual enrolment of the Department of Continuing Education would reach 50,000 by 1997, compared with about 33,800 extra-mural students enrolled in 1987–88.

The Department of External Studies would be constructed around the core personnel in the External Studies Unit, which was at that time still in the initial planning phase. It would be staffed by programme development officers, teaching consultants and some staff tutors. The Department of External Studies would be responsible for the expansion of part-time external degree programmes offered by the School, through collaboration with the Open Learning Institute, other local or overseas universities, and HKU's own academic teaching departments. The long-term objective of the DES was to 'offer its own degree programmes via external studies in certain disciplines [in] which it will have established academic standards equivalent to those in other Faculties'.[108]

There would be a Board of Studies for each department to ensure the maintenance of high academic standards. The boards would consist of academic staff from the School of Extension Studies, members of the wider University, and community representatives. A Finance Committee would also be set up to supervise the finances of the School and it would report directly to the University Council. The members of boards of studies and the Finance Committee would also be members of a Board of the School, the highest governing body of the School which would be responsible for overseeing the academic governance of the School and reporting to the Senate. The School would be supported by a modest new Research Centre, which was expected to be set up in 1991, 'in order that certain research projects relating to open and continuing education as well as other subject areas can be undertaken'.[109] The project results would be made available to a wider public through the publication of in-house journals.

The DEMS Ten Year Plan was included in the University's larger plan for the 1991–94 Triennium, and was received by the Senate in June 1989. The proposal to establish a School of Extension Studies did not however receive official approval from the University at this time and hence the plan was not implemented.[110] Instead, the Committee on Open Education and the Committee on Extra-Mural Studies adopted some of the principles underpinning this plan and took their own initiative in planning for a completely restructured Department of Extra-Mural Studies. This process took more than a year to achieve the original goals of the Ten Year Plan.

The Hawkridge Report

One of the responsibilities of the Committee on Open Education was to consider the University's development in open, distance and continuing education. The COE therefore worked actively from its establishment in evaluating the role of the DEMS and devising a suitable reform plan for the Department. The first step in the review was to invite Professor David Hawkridge of the Open University (UK) to come to Hong Kong sponsored by the Committee for International Co-operation in Higher Education to look into the University's overall development plan for open and distance education. He made his visit to the University in January 1989.[111] In early February 1989, Professor Hawkridge completed his report entitled 'External Studies and Distance Education at the University of Hong Kong', in which he listed and analysed seven non-mutually-exclusive options which the University could choose for the development of open and distance education. A summary of his recommendations is given in Table 6.1. The University did not at this time choose any particular option from the Hawkridge Report, but its subsequent policies in open education corresponded with some of the options identified by Hawkridge.[112]

Hawkridge understood that if HKU adopted any of his options which involved provision of external studies and/or distance education using its own academic resources (options A, B or E), it would need to expand the DEMS and give it a new structure. Agreeing in principle with the School of Extension Studies model proposed in the Ten Year Plan, he was more interested in the administrative structure needed to provide distance education. He proposed that if the University decided to develop its own external degree, the Distance Education section should be subordinate to the Department of External Studies and be further subdivided into two units of Production and Teaching (see Figure 6.2). The Distance Education (Production) Unit should be staffed by educational technologists who would design courses and methods of student assessment.[113] Furthermore, he felt that the Committee on Open Education and the Committee on Extra-Mural Studies should be combined into a new Senate Committee on Extension Studies so as to rationalise the supervision of extension work and make one committee responsible for all policy in this area. Such a restructuring of the Senate-level committees was considered necessary before the Board of the new School could be established to take over the administration of open and distance education at the University.[114]

The Hawkridge Report was not an official University policy document, but it nevertheless provided a basis for the Committee on Open Education and the University to conduct further discussion on the development of open and distance

Table 6.1 Summary of Options in the 1989 Hawkridge Report

Option	Recommendation
A Offer sub-degree extra-mural courses	Expand present programme as resources permit.
B Offer extra-mural courses to degree level	Expand offerings within limits set by Senate after negotiation between the Faculties and the new EMS.
C Offer London-type external degree	Ignore.
D Produce degree courses for OLI	Do so if terms from OLI are suitable and staff resources can be found within HKU's priorities.
E Produce courses for HKU degree-at-a-distance programmes	Do so only if economies of scale can be achieved in producing courses that do not compete with OLI. Avoid costly small-scale pilot projects.
F Allow staff to work direct for OLI on course production	If D, E and/or G are not endorsed, endorse F and clarify terms, otherwise consider priorities in using staff for distance course production.
G Join other institutions in producing OLI courses	Do so if terms from OLI and other institutions are suitable, and joint staff resources are required.

(*Source:* HKUSM 6 June 1989, 32, Appendix T, Annex 2, document 316/489; 'External Studies and Distance Education at the University of Hong Kong', 4 February 1989, p. 10.

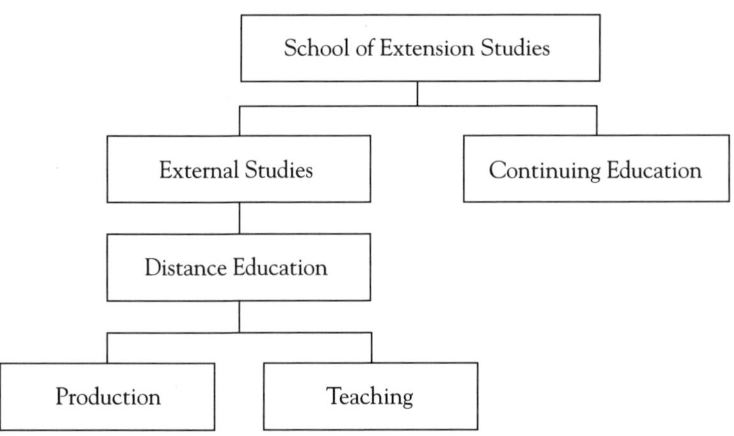

Figure 6.2 School of Extension Studies proposed by Professor Hawkridge, 1989

(*Source*: HKUSM 6 June 1989, 32, Appendix T, Annex 2, document 316/489; 'External Studies and Distance Education at the University of Hong Kong', 4 February 1989, p. 8.)

education in general, and the future of the DEMS in particular. In its Interim Report of May 1989, the Committee on Open Education did not support Hawkridge's proposal to merge the COE and the CEMS immediately because they felt that 'there is a distinction between University-wide policy on open and distance learning, which will include the role of [DEMS], and the management and financial of overview of the 'traditional' EMS activities which will be a continuing area on which the Senate will need advice'.[115] However, the Committee on Open Education held the view that the DEMS had the best potential of all existing units within the University to develop open and distance education courses and therefore recommended that the University support 'the initiatives in this area along the lines proposed in the Hawkridge Report'.[116] It also recognised the need to review the powers and duties of the Committee on Open Education and the Committee on Extra-Mural Studies. The Committee on Open Education therefore recommended creating a 'Joint Working Party of the Committee on Open Education and the Committee on Extra-Mural Studies' under the Senate with a view to 'draw up firm proposals' for the above recommendations. The Senate approved the formation of the Joint Working Party at its meeting on 6 June 1989.[117]

The Joint Working Party and the Director's New Proposal

The Joint Working Party was composed of the chairmen of the Committee on Open Education and the Committee on Extra-Mural Studies, a member nominated by each Committee, and the Director of Extra-Mural Studies.[118] Its first task was to discuss a new restructuring proposal put forward by the Director of Extra-Mural Studies. The new proposal abandoned the original two-department model because 'complexities in financial arrangement and statutory independence enjoyed by Heads of Departments would make the original plan unworkable'.[119] Instead, the School of Extension Studies would be headed by a Director and would consist of two divisions. One of these would be called the Continuing Education Division and the other the External Studies Division (see Figure 6.3). Each of these divisions would be led by a deputy director. The deputy directors would be appointed at the rank of Senior Lecturer or Reader in order to 'signify the University's recognition of the valuable contribution that experienced and well-qualified academic staff made to the well-being of EMS work'.[120] The duties of the two divisions would be similar to the two departments proposed in the Ten Year Plan. The Continuing Education Division would be mainly responsible for adult courses on a face-to-face basis. The External Studies Division would aim at organising courses 'linked to accreditations by overseas and possibly local institutions in the form of either first and second degree or professional offerings'. These external studies courses would be conducted in face-to-face teaching or distance learning modes, or a mixture of both.[121] The new School of Extension Studies would be supervised by a Board of Studies with an elected chairman. Each division would also establish several Academic Committees for maintaining the academic standards of particular programmes, especially those leading to qualifications offered by HKU or overseas institutions. The Academic Committees would report their work to the Board of Studies.

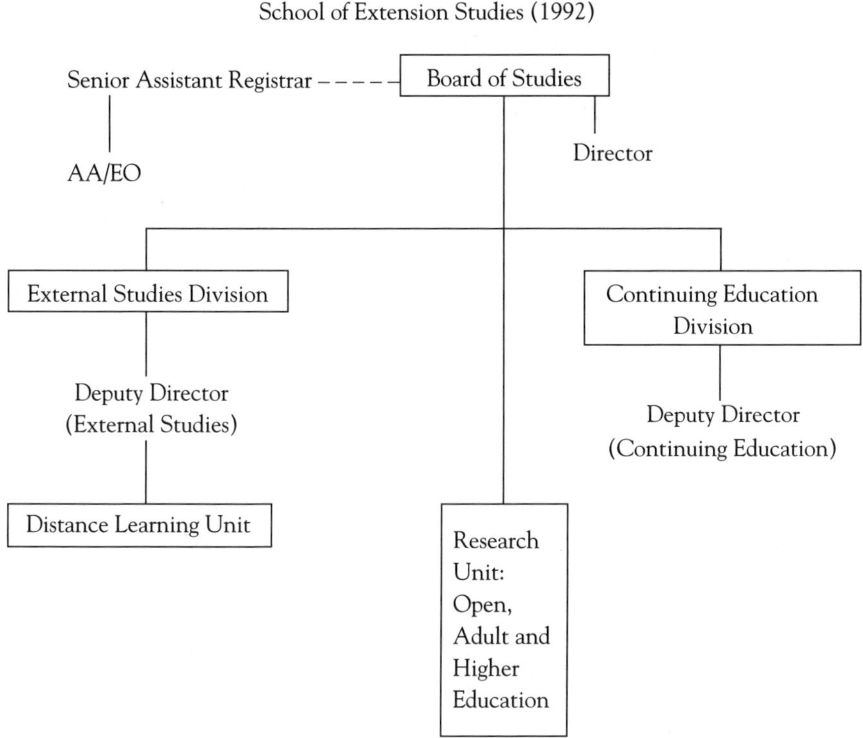

Figure 6.3 School of Extension Studies proposed by the Joint Working Party, November 1989

(*Source:* HKUCM 22 Feburary 1990, 21, Appendix P, Annex I, document 236/1189; 'Proposals for the establishment of two Deputy Directors in the Department of Extra-Mural Studies in 1990–92 and the School of Extension Studies (tentative title) in 1992', p. 10)

It was suggested that the new School of Extension Studies should be created in 1992. During the transformation period from 1990 to 1992, the proposal recommended that the two deputy directorships, a Senior Assistant Registrar post and the Board of Studies be established to strengthen the structure and experience of both divisions. The deputy directors during this transition period would be appointed from among the existing staff of the DEMS. The eventual plan for when the School was fully established in 1992 was for the Director of Extra-Mural Studies to become the Director of the School of Extension Studies, and the two deputy directors would be 'recruited by means of either standard international advertisements or competition within the EMS department'.[122] All the administrative and academic operations of the DEMS would then be transferred to the new School of Extension Studies.

The Joint Working Party held only one meeting on 20 November 1989 before it was reorganised into the Davies Working Party in June 1990.[123] At that meeting it agreed with the general principles of the Director's proposal but suggested that the new School be given another name, such as 'Institute', in order to 'convey the wide ranging nature of the Centre's activities and allow for a more flexible structure than the School title'.[124] The Joint Working Party also came to the conclusion that there should be two supervisory boards instead of one within the proposed School. One would be a Policy Board which 'would discuss matters of academic policy development in much the same way as Senate or Faculty Boards did in their respective areas', and the other would be a Management Board which 'would allocate resources, oversee the financial position and act in much the same way as Council and its committees did for the University generally'.[125] The School Director would be the chairman of the Policy Board and an ex-officio member of the Management Board. The responsibilities of the Committee on Extra-Mural Studies were expected to be taken over by the two new School boards, while it was agreed that the status of the Committee on Open Education should be reviewed as soon as the new School was established. The recommendations of the Joint Working Party were soon endorsed by the Committee on Extra-Mural Studies and the Committee on Open Education.[126] The General Purposes Committee (GPC), a new joint Council and Senate committee which had been established to share the original powers of the Development and General Purposes Committee (DGPC) with the Academic Development Committee (ADC), also agreed in January 1990 to a DEMS proposal for the appointment of two deputy directors, Mr Duncan Macintosh for Continuing Education and Mr Bill Howarth for External Studies, for two years from July 1990.[127]

The General Purposes Committee was not entirely happy with the situation, however, and decided to flex its muscles and influence the ongoing discussions about the future of extra-mural studies in a more direct way. Despite the existence of a Senate Joint Working Party, the General Purposes Committee insisted on examining the future of extra-mural studies itself, and established its own GPC Working Party with a brief to 'review the policies, governance, organisations and practices' so as to ensure that the new School of Extension Studies would be the most appropriate vehicle for the University's activities in adult higher education.[128] In April 1990, it decided to give the new GPC Working Party extensive powers and duties which would 'subsume the work' of the Senate's Joint Working Party.[129] The planned composition of the new Working Party also showed the intention of the GPC to take the lead in deciding the University's future extra-mural policy.

The GPC decided to appoint Professor Ian Davies, a Pro-Vice-Chancellor, to the chairmanship of the Working Party. It also invited all the former Senate Joint Working Party members and the deans of four faculties to sit on the new Davies Working Party. The wider representation in the new Working Party diluted the influence of members drawn from the Department of Extra-Mural Studies and its two parent committees and therefore gave it greater authority than the previous Joint Working Party in determining the future of extra-mural policy at the University.[130]

The Committee on Extra-Mural Studies and the Committee on Open Education were reluctant to allow a Working Party of the General Purposes Committee to run in parallel with its own Joint Working Party. The Committee on Extra-Mural Studies expressed regret that it had not been consulted on this issue by the GPC.[131] Professor Lee Ngok felt that the arrangements made by the GPC created 'potential for duplication of, and conflict with, the Senate-endorsed review which was already under way'.[132] Finally, the Vice-Chancellor, Professor Wang Gungwu, intervened at the request of the GPC and broke the deadlock by recommending to the Senate that the original Joint Working Party should be reorganised. Despite the continuing supervision of the Committee on Open Education and the Committee on Extra-Mural Studies, the reorganised Joint Working Party under Professor Davies had both its terms of reference and its membership changed to reflect the wishes of the GPC. The Senate approved the Vice-Chancellor's proposal at its meeting on 5 June 1990 and the second Joint Working Party (hereafter referred to as the Davies Working Party) came into existence in July 1990.[133]

The Davies Working Party and a Final Proposal for the School of Professional and Continuing Education

The seven-member Davies Working Party met on three occasions in the next nine months and produced its report in March 1991.[134] The Davies Working Party used the Evans Report of 1987 as the basis of its discussions, and asked the University to adopt 'the spirit of intent' of the Evans proposals as University policy. The main task of the Davies Working Party was therefore to come up with a new academic and administrative structure for the DEMS. The Working Party had detailed discussions about the identity of the new organisation. A 'School', defined as 'a unitary structure with an executive Dean who combines the role of Head and Chairman of the Board of Studies', had been agreed to be the most appropriate structure for the University's new extra-mural unit. The Director of Extra-Mural Studies nevertheless expressed doubts about the suitability of the proposed 'School' model. He was unwilling to be both the executive director and the academic head of the School concurrently and was worried about the possible confusion with other 'schools' of the University.[135] However, the Working Party found that the 'School' model remained the best in comparison with other alternative forms of organisation and nomenclature. The term 'Faculty' was not deemed appropriate because there was no precedent at that time for an executive faculty head. The other problem with the term 'Faculty' was that it did not fit the unitary structure of the new organisation because a faculty at that time normally had a number of departments as its constituent parts. 'Institute' was not a good option because it usually referred to a research unit. 'Unit' was also not suitable as it implied 'a relatively small scale of operation' which the DEMS clearly was not. 'Centre' was inappropriate because it was normally used within HKU for organisations primarily aimed at providing administrative services or conducting research activities. The term 'College' seemed to be a good choice but 'this suggested to us [the Joint Working Party] too much of a separateness to be used for EMS since we prefer to see an emphasis on EMS as an integral part of University activity'.[136] As a result, the Joint Working Party agreed to use the 'School' model for the new extra-mural studies unit.

The Davies Working Party also paid considerable attention to the name of the new School. The phrase 'Extra-Mural Studies' was perceived as 'somewhat dated' and it was agreed that it had to be replaced with something more up to date. Both the Department and the Working Party considered that 'Professional and Continuing Education' would be more appropriate as a name because it explained the activities of the new unit exactly.[137] In comparison, the term 'Extra-mural Studies' was somewhat ambiguous and tended to describe 'the target of the courses rather than the content'.[138] While there was little dispute over the use of 'Continuing Education' to describe the activities of the new School, the addition of 'Professional Education' to the new name had to be justified because some felt that it would 'intrude on the preserve of Faculties' which already provided professional education. The Davies Report was at pains to point out that the term 'professional' was used 'in a general sense' and should not be thought of as being specific to any particular profession. In fact, there had already been many extra-mural courses offered by the DEMS which led to professional qualifications.[139] The Davies Working Party was therefore in favour of the name 'School of Professional and Continuing Education' for the new extra-mural unit.

The other recommendations of the Davies Report were generally similar to those proposed by the previous working parties on extra-mural studies. The Davies Report agreed with the suggestion of the Evans Report that the new School should adopt a bicameral structure, with a Board of Studies and a Management Board. The existing Committee on Extra-Mural Studies and the Committee on Open Education would be abolished and their powers and duties absorbed by these two boards. The Board of Studies would act in a similar way to a faculty board. It would be responsible for ensuring the overall academic standards of the School and providing a place for discussion of the School's academic policy. The membership would include all staff tutors, representatives of the faculties and community representatives. The Board of Studies would have under it a number of Academic Committees to supervise programmes which were to be classed in three categories. The first category included all the old Extra-Mural Studies certificate and diploma courses; one Academic Committee would be established for all the existing certificate courses, and other academic committees would be formed for each of the diploma courses. Courses leading to a University qualification awarded by a Faculty fell into the second category; a joint Academic Committee would need to be established for each one of these programmes and they would include staff from the School and the relevant faculty. The third category consisted of all courses leading to qualifications awarded by external institutions. Each programme would have a joint Academic Committee consisting of members from the School, the relevant Faculty and the overseas institution.[140]

The nature of the Management Board would be similar to that proposed by the first Joint Working Party. The Management Board would report to Council and be 'a small, senior group to provide the necessary management and financial overview of EMS activities'.[141] The membership would include lay members of the Council and its Finance Committee, and the Director of the School. The Davies Report also mentioned the possibility of turning the School into a limited company as part of its long-term development strategy. The Report recommended that the structure of the new School should follow the existing development policy. There would be two Divisions, namely Continuing Education and External Studies (see Figure 6.4), and the Report outlined the subject areas which ought to be included under each division.[142] The two divisions would function as described in the previous proposals. The Distance Learning Unit would be placed under the supervision of the External Studies Division, while a new Teaching and Research Unit (TRU), which aimed at 'promotion and support of research and scholarship related to adult learning and development', would be set up as an independent unit within the School.[143]

In order to emphasise the academic status of the School, the Davies Working Party proposed the re-titling of key school staff. Staff holding the titles of 'Staff Tutor' and 'Programme Development Officer' could, for example, be re-titled as 'Lecturer'. This was a very important suggestion because it gave extra-mural staff the same title, and therefore the same academic status, as their colleagues in the University's internal teaching departments. It was also noted that more administrative support was required within the School to enable the lecturers to focus more fully on academic matters. Steps had already been taken by this time to strengthen the senior management of the department and John Cribbin had transferred from his post as Secretary of the Faculty of Arts in late 1990 to be Senior Assistant Registrar in the DEMS. Cribbin had originally joined the University from the Open University (UK) in early 1982 to work on the ill-fated external degrees programme and had been at various times secretary of the CEMS, secretary

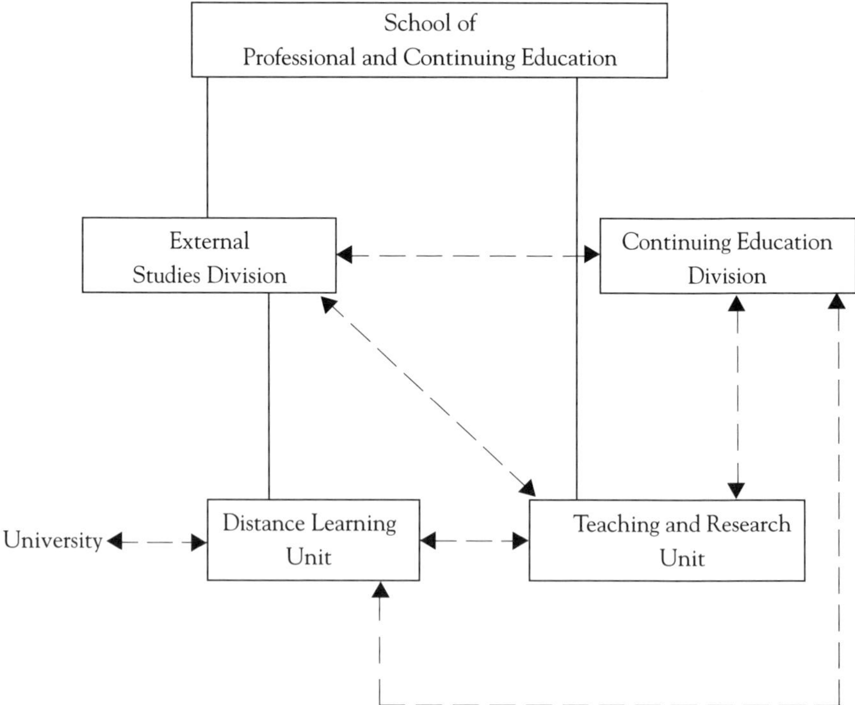

Figure 6.4 School of Professional and Continuing Education proposed in the Davies Report, March 1991.

(*Source:* HKUSM 20 December 1991, 17, Appendix K, Annex I.V, document 208/1190; 'Joint Working Party of the Committees on Open Education and on Extra-Mural Studies: Extra-Mural Studies Organization', Annex A.)

of the External Studies Committee, and secretary of the Committee on Open Education.

After three years of extensive discussions and preparation, the plans for transforming the Department of Extra-Mural Studies into the School of Professional and Continuing Education were ready for adoption by late 1991. The Academic Development Committee and the General Purposes Committee supported the recommendations of the Davies Report with only a few minor amendments.[144] The Senate approved on 5 November 1991 the recommendation of the Davies Report that the DEMS be disestablished and reconstituted as the School of Professional and Continuing Education from 1 January 1992.[145] The Court and the Council approved the proposal on 19 and 20 December respectively and less than two weeks later SPACE came into existence.[146]

Conclusion

During the seven years between 1985 and 1991, the Department of Extra-Mural Studies underwent significant transformations on a number of fronts. The Department quickly responded to the government scheme to expand open and distance education by assisting the formation of the Open Learning Institute and providing it with pedagogical support. The Department also established partnerships with overseas institutions to provide part-time degree-level programmes in subjects to which local tertiary institutions had never or seldom paid attention. These new attempts had great academic, administrative and financial implications for the Department and the University and therefore generated a certain amount of controversy within the University. Some members of the University worried that collaboration with external institutions might compel HKU to compromise on academic standards and therefore damage its reputation, while others were uncomfortable with the fact that these programmes helped partner institutions to generate large profits. It was also obvious that the existing management structure of the Department was not capable of dealing with the increasingly complex operations of the University's extra-mural activities, and reform was needed to enable the Department to overcome the challenges facing it. Formulating these reform proposals and gaining the University's approval were difficult tasks, and even the composition of the Working Party to discuss these matters became an issue which brought the four committees involved in extra-mural education policy and the Senate into conflict. The recommendations of the 1991 Davies Report enjoyed general support, however, and led to the transformation of the DEMS into the School of Professional and Continuing Education (SPACE) from 1 January 1992. The new School was already a formidable organisation with an able director, but it was now set up to operate with even greater academic, administrative and financial efficiency in the remainder of the 1990s and beyond.

CHAPTER SEVEN

The School of Professional and Continuing Education, 1992–2007

THE RESTRUCTURING OF THE DEPARTMENT OF EXTRA-MURAL STUDIES into the School of Professional and Continuing Education in January 1992 not only involved a change of name and structure, but also marked a significant transformation in the School's status and identity both within the University and the wider society.[1] Its enhanced status as a 'School' within the University placed SPACE in a better position to proceed with its academic development. In the 1990s the School was granted financial autonomy and a corporate status so that it could plan its activities with greater flexibility and respond to the continuing and professional education (CPE) market in flexible, prompt and pro-active ways. Partnerships with overseas institutions continued to be an important part of its overall strategy, and there were serious attempts to strengthen working relationships between SPACE and other parts of HKU. The School now offers courses covering an even wider spectrum of fields than ever before at many different levels. It has a number of permanent learning centres across Hong Kong, and is increasingly involved in projects on the Chinese Mainland. This chapter will discuss the remarkable development of SPACE over the last fifteen years and its various interactions with the University, the local community and the surrounding region in a period of rapid expansion in the continuing and professional education market.

SPACE and HKU: Autonomy and Control

One of the crucial factors leading to the success of the Department of Extra-Mural Studies and SPACE was the support they received from their parent institution. The University had played an active role, albeit with limited financial commitment, in adult higher education since 1957, and this support continued during the SPACE era. The University provided SPACE with assistance both directly and indirectly, and the School was quick to acknowledge that it 'could not be as successful as it is without the University in terms of its historical development, the facilities, the reputation for quality and the resource of staff expertise'.[2] On the other hand, the School began to enjoy greater freedom in its CPE activities once its operations became fully self-financing and market-driven after 1992. While SPACE succeeded in making use of these advantages to develop itself into a large enterprise capable of facing ever-changing market trends during the 1990s, the School's unconventional structure and financial arrangements in comparison with other parts of the University made it seem, at least to some, like an autonomous entity rather than an integral part of HKU. In the 1990s, therefore, both co-operation and suspicion existed between the University and the School. A contradictory relationship such as this was difficult for both parties to negotiate, but it quickly became evident that if SPACE was to continue expanding and using the University's name, the relationship between SPACE and the University would have to be strengthened.

The First Years of SPACE, 1992–1995

The first four years of SPACE witnessed a gradual increase in its autonomy and the complexity of its operations. The School no longer operated on the modest scale of the old DEMS, and it was becoming larger year by year. Its new status placed SPACE in a special position within the management hierarchy of the University, and the School even had its own brand name and logo from the outset of operations. A ten-year strategic plan was completed in March 1993. This included a mission statement emphasising co-operation with HKU's faculties, other institutions in Hong Kong and overseas institutions.[3] SPACE had already been establishing partnerships with various overseas institutions, and locally it became one of the founding members of the Federation for Continuing Education in Tertiary Institutions (FCETI), of which Professor Lee Ngok was elected the first Chairman in May 1994.[4] The School provided its students with subjects in six major clusters, and enrolment figures rose by 50 per cent in the four years from 1991–92. In 1994–95, there were 57,985 registered students or 10,293 full-time student equivalents (FTE) contributing over $168 million in course fee income, equal to about 5 per cent of the total expenditure of HKU.[5] Both the academic and support staffs were strengthened during the first years of operation. In 1996, SPACE had a full-time academic staff of thirty-seven, supported by 825 part-time tutors, and an administrative, clerical and auxiliary staff of 117, which was larger than most internal faculties.[6] These figures demonstrate that in the first years after its restructuring, SPACE was already developing into a large and distinctive entity with a special identity that was significantly different to the identity which HKU was pursuing as a research-led university.

Despite the obvious benefits of close co-operation, communication between SPACE and other parts of the University was not very strong in the early 1990s. At the management level, a faculty-type Board of Studies was created by the Senate to oversee academic policy within the School. A separate body, the Management Board, existed under the Council to supervise the management and finances of SPACE.[7] This was a unique arrangement which arose out of the expectation that the new School would operate in a more flexible and market-oriented way. The conventional unicameral structure found in most units within the University was not thought sufficient to handle the needs of SPACE. Since the faculties and the senior management of the University were represented on the two boards, it was originally hoped that the boards would act as channels through which the other parts of the University could participate in the development of SPACE.[8]

The reality never lived up to this expectation. The Board of Studies was dominated by members from the teaching staff of SPACE who outnumbered the representatives from the faculties, and the Director of SPACE was also the chairman of the Board of Studies. The Management Board was much smaller, limited to a few senior officers of the School and the University who were bound to work closely with each other even without such a Management Board. Participation of other academic departments in the policy-making process of SPACE was therefore minimal. The relationship between SPACE and other parts of HKU at the operational level was also limited and not without conflict. University departments generally recognised the School's administrative expertise and some of them were willing to co-operate with SPACE on part-time courses for non-university students. In fact, the Department of Extra-Mural Studies had established connections with academic departments and teachers from the very first extra-mural course in 1957. Between 1968 and 1991, at least 289 HKU staff members taught in DEMS courses at different levels.[9] Major examples of such co-operation included the Ordinary/Higher Technical Certificate in Medical Laboratory Science programmes in collaboration with the Medical Faculty, and various certificate courses organised with the Faculty of Engineering from the early 1970s.[10] In most cases, however, the HKU teachers participated in these courses on an individual basis, and departmental participation in extra-mural programmes was only occasional.

The faculties never seriously considered organising higher level programmes with the DEMS until the late 1980s when the government expanded higher education and supported part-time postgraduate programmes at local universities. HKU began offering part-time taught postgraduate programmes in 1971–72. Many of the departments preferred to run these programmes by themselves, but some others acknowledged the capability of the DEMS/SPACE to manage overseas degree programmes, and co-operated with the School in organising part-time programmes at higher levels. The first step towards greater co-operation came in 1991–92 when the DEMS started its first HKU postgraduate course leading to a Postgraduate

Certificate in Laws (PCLL) qualification. This one-year full-time course was operated in parallel with that offered by the Law Faculty. While it was organised and taught largely by the DEMS/SPACE academic staff, the course content, structure, methods of teaching, assessment and examinations were made to 'duplicate exactly' the HKU internal course. The HKU Law Faculty was indirectly but significantly involved in the School's PCLL programme by 'giving academic and professional guidance' through various channels, such as participation by individual lecturers in teaching and formal representation in the specific Academic Committee.[11] Co-operation between SPACE and the Law Faculty was extended to include joint programmes in PCLL (part-time) and the Hong Kong Common Professional Examination Certificate (HKCPEC).[12]

The first HKU degree course jointly organised by SPACE and the University was the Master of Housing Management programme in 1992–93. It was developed from the existing Extra-Mural Diploma in Housing Management and was a two-year part-time programme targeting working professionals in housing management who wished to upgrade their academic qualifications and university graduates who wanted to join this profession. The Centre of Urban Planning and Environmental Management (CUPEM) and the Faculty of Social Sciences formally participated in this programme.[13] SPACE started its first HKU part-time undergraduate programme with the Medical Faculty in January 1994. The programme recruited registered nurses with at least two years of experience for a Bachelor of Science in Nursing Studies degree which required three years of study. By the end of the project in 1998, nearly 270 registered nurses had been admitted to the course in three batches.[14] In 1998–99, SPACE collaborated with twelve HKU faculties and other units on courses at different levels.[15] By 2006, at least twenty-three undergraduate or postgraduate programmes had been offered jointly by SPACE and the various faculties of the University.[16]

These joint programmes worked in a similar way to the courses offered with overseas institutions. SPACE was responsible for enrolment, teaching venues, logistic arrangements and other administrative matters, while both the School and the participating HKU departments shared academic responsibility for the programmes. In many cases there was at least one full-time teacher appointed at SPACE to manage the programme and perform teaching duties. An Academic Committee or Academic Advisory Committee was established under the Board of Studies to supervise academic matters and the general management of each programme. Membership of these academic advisory committees included representatives from SPACE, and representatives of the participating HKU departments and other relevant bodies.[17] These supervisory bodies ensured academic standards and acted as communication platforms to bring the different partners together.

In spite of the various joint projects undertaken in the early 1990s, the relationship between SPACE and other parts of the University remained precarious throughout this period. There was an unspoken suspicion within the University about the standing of SPACE as an academic partner in the organisation of higher level programmes. Constitutionally, SPACE was an academic unit of the University with 'School' status, and its full-time teachers had been re-titled from 'Staff Tutors' to 'Lecturers' in order to acknowledge their academic status. Unfortunately, many HKU departments maintained a view that SPACE was academically inferior and they therefore refused to co-operate with the School. In fact, it was difficult in the early 1990s to see how the School could ever hope to function as an academic unit in the way that the University's academic departments worked. First, research had become essential in all academic departments, but was rare if not completely non-existent in the School. While SPACE was initially keen to encourage a culture of academic research, the various proposals were not implemented well and the research environment in the School remained weak.[18] Second, there were criticisms that the overall academic standards of SPACE degree courses were weakened by lower admission standards and shorter periods of study than those normally required by the University. For example, during negotiations for the proposed Master of Housing Management programme, a department in the Faculty of Social Sciences asked whether the lower admission requirement would 'affect the academic/professional standard of the programme itself'.[19]

Apart from academic considerations, the relationship between SPACE and some parts of the University remained bitter because of the School's close connection with foreign institutions. Some HKU departments had long believed that SPACE, in collaboration with overseas institutions, was their competitor rather than their partner in the local continuing and professional education market. Sometimes they even overtly opposed the School's academic proposals to safeguard their own interests. The most serious clash of this type occurred in 1993 when SPACE planned to offer a Master of Business in Accounting programme in collaboration with Monash University. The Business School and the Faculty of Social Sciences protested vigorously against the proposal. The Board of the Faculty of Social Sciences discussed the proposal at its meeting on 15 February 1994 and recorded, with a strong sense of suspicion, its concerns:

> (a) about the University appearing to be acting as a broker for foreign Universities in their ventures of mounting joint degree programmes with the School as well as the lack of apparent benefits to the University;
> (b) whether the use of University accommodation and facilities such as the Library by the School was adequately costed; [and]
> (c) whether the mounting of degree programmes by S.P.A.C.E. would have effects on future proposals to introduce similar programmes on the University's part . . .[20]

Stronger opposition came from Professor Gordon Redding, who was now the Director of the Business School. It was he who had represented the Department of

Management Studies in criticising the collaboration between SPACE and Curtin University in 1987. Professor Redding wrote to the Senate on 25 February 1994 to 'register a protest on behalf of the Business School at the plan for SPACE to teach of Master of Business (Accounting)'. He listed three reasons for his objection, challenging the legitimacy of SPACE's plan to run any degree programme:

> (a) I do not accept that SPACE has an appropriate structure for the management of degrees, and that is based on nine years of experience working in Extra Mural. The 'ownership' of a degree by an entire faculty is a prerequisite for its proper management.
> (b) I consider that this university demeans itself, and weakens its reputation, by brokering the degrees of other universities whose prime concerns are cash flow.
> (c) I do not think that SPACE should compete with other units of this university in degree work when it could be doing so much else.[21]

SPACE naturally rejected these allegations, especially the insulting assertion that it was acting as a degree 'broker'. Professor Lee Ngok explained that the academic standards of SPACE programmes were well maintained by the system of academic advisory committees. He also declared that SPACE did not work for its own self-interest, but to help the University in serving the community:

> As part of the University, I have always regarded the School as being the 'window' of the University, committed, on the University's behalf, to the servicing of community needs in providing high quality professional and continuing education programmes to the Hong Kong society. For the 'benefits' enjoyed by the School, they are in fact 'benefits' of the University.[22]

Despite the evident annoyance of its senior managers, SPACE made a conciliatory gesture in order to settle this question. Bill Howarth, the Acting Director of SPACE, assured the faculties at the Senate meeting on 1 March 1994 that 'SPACE had no intention of competing with any departments in their programmes and was willing to withdraw the proposed programme with Monash University if and when the University decided to offer [a] similar programme on its own'.[23] The Senate approved the proposal upon this understanding which subsequently became the guiding principle in introducing all new SPACE programmes.[24] Opposition to the proposed SPACE-Monash joint venture reflected the view of many HKU academics in the early 1990s that SPACE was neither entitled nor sufficiently competent to manage degree-level courses. Such disapproval intensified when the School's partnerships with foreign institutions seemed likely to endanger existing or future activities of HKU's academic departments.

Financial Independence

The University's financial support for both the Department of Extra-Mural Studies and the School of Professional and Continuing Education had for decades remained one of the most substantial connections between the two parties. Despite the fact that the SPACE programmes were meant to operate on a self-funded basis, the University subsidised its extra-mural activities through the payment of full-time academic staff salaries and the provision of University facilities. Before 1985, the University contributed about half of the total expenditure of the DEMS every year. From the mid-1980s the proportion of the University subsidy to the total expenditure of the Department kept decreasing because of the expansion in self-funded activities. The Department's improved funding position in turn meant that it could begin to contribute financially to the University. It shared the cost of the Town Centre and implemented a 'buffer system' which returned any surplus beyond a fixed amount back to the University.[25] Nevertheless, the block grant support from the University was still not insignificant. In the 1991–92 financial year, HKU spent about $19.7 million on the new SPACE, accounting for about 21 per cent of the School's total expenditure.[26] Such huge subsidies represented a significant commitment by the University to continuing and professional education as a service to society.

The newly-established SPACE was eager to increase its control over the annual surplus it was generating in order to provide some protection from possible market fluctuations, and the school also needed to retain funds to finance new projects, especially the provision of high-quality teaching accommodation.[27] In spite of the considerable operating surpluses each year in the late 1980s and early 1990s, the School was not reluctant to warn the Management Board and the University Council of the possibility that the SPACE Fund might dry up in the foreseeable future. This was the basis of the School's request for a relaxation of the 'buffer requirement'.[28] In 1992 and 1993, the School succeeded in obtaining the Council's approval to raise the ceiling of the SPACE Fund from $1.5 million to 5 per cent and then 10 per cent of the School's annual gross income. It was expected that there would be approximately $6.6 million in the SPACE Fund by June 1993.[29]

Allowing SPACE to have greater control over its surplus was acceptable as long as this did not hinder the University from receiving a share of the financial benefits from continuing and professional education activities. This understanding soon faced a challenge, however, in view of the School's very rapid development. SPACE came into conflict with the University over the appropriation of the SPACE Fund several months after the introduction of the 10 per cent buffer rule. The dispute arose from a proposal in December 1993 for the purchase of a new teaching centre in North Point at a cost of about $70 million. The purchase was to be entirely financed by the School itself through the SPACE Fund balance, the School's operating surplus for that year, and a bank mortgage which would be repaid by the

School.[30] The University Council had no objection to the purchase of the proposed teaching centre, but it was very concerned about the substantial reduction in financial contributions from SPACE to the University which would result from the commitment of large capital and interest to the project. The Council resolved on 30 December 1993 that the proposal for the new teaching centre be approved, but that the size of the buffer should be reviewed in June 1994 to 'ensure that contributions back to the block grant would not be unacceptably diminished'.[31]

In the following months, the University's Finance Office tried to enforce the Council resolution and negotiated with the School on another set of rules to regulate the appropriation of the SPACE Fund. It sent two proposals to the School in April 1994. The first was that SPACE would not need to return its surplus to the university for one year, but after this first year the SPACE Fund would be limited to only 1 per cent of the net surplus after deducting the projected capital expenditure. This meant that in 1994–95, SPACE would pay $11.21 million to HKU and keep only $1.55 million in the SPACE Fund. The second proposal was that the balance of the SPACE Fund would be fixed at approximately $2 million, and the remaining surplus would be returned to the University. Under this proposal, SPACE would contribute $1.07 million to the University in 1994–95.[32] As both proposals meant that an extremely small balance would be kept in the SPACE Fund, they were strongly opposed by SPACE. The School Secretary, John Cribbin, wrote to the Finance Office to protest against these proposals, emphasising a number of indirect contributions from SPACE to the University which he estimated at around $10 million per annum.[33] In this light, Cribbin argued, the University's support for continuing education was not overly generous, and any penny-pinching in the short-term did not augur well for long-term development:

> After all, it should not be forgotten that this contribution represents the University's provision of educational opportunity to the community at large. . . The School's operation and development should also be looked at in 5–10 year framework rather than merely in an end of year balance sheet approach.[34]

The Finance Office was not convinced by Cribbin's argument. The Director of Finance insisted in May 1994 that the School should not reduce its financial contribution to the University drastically because of its own capital expenditure. He also dismissed Cribbin's 'indirect contribution' argument and asserted that it was reasonable for SPACE to pay for the University's services and facilities because SPACE was a self-financing body with a large surplus, but he made two new proposals for the future of the SPACE Fund. The first proposal was to set the SPACE Fund buffer at a particular level in advance, from $2.5 million in 1994–95, rising to $8.5 million in 1997–98. The alternative proposal was that the University would withdraw all direct subsidies from the school within three years and SPACE would become an entirely self-financing unit.[35] The Finance Office gave SPACE ten days to consider these two options.

Such a hard-line reply from the Finance Office irritated the School's management. John Cribbin replied bluntly to the ultimatum:

> If you wish to put these [proposals] to the Finance Committee at its meeting on 31 May 1994, so be it, that is your prerogative as Director of Finance. . . Neither Professor Lee nor I believe that there is at present an urgent need for these policy decisions to be resolved by the end of this month since there are a number of imponderables . . . [36]

However, the School could do nothing further except to restate its argument about possible financial instability due to market fluctuations and the insufficiency of its reserves. The Finance Office was uncompromising on this issue. The Director of Finance countered the School's worries by suggesting that:

> If the School does foresee a downturn in demand in the future, I suppose the School would reduce the number of rented teaching accommodation and also to defer any planned capital project in order to reduce its total expenditure under the circumstances.[37]

The message from the Council and Finance office was clear — contributions from SPACE to the University should not be reduced, even at times of economic downturn and decreasing financial surpluses.

The skirmish between the School and HKU's Finance Office was finally settled by the senior management of the University. The School's Management Board first discussed this matter on 27 May 1994, at which time the members generally opposed the University's proposal to cut the SPACE Fund buffer and the University's subsidies to the School. Some of them considered that the cut in funding would reduce staff numbers and the volume of teaching activities, and would also endanger the quality and competitiveness of SPACE activities. The Management Board resolved to advise the University's Finance Committee that no surplus could be returned to the University in the 1993–94 financial year, and that in the following years, the SPACE Fund balance should be set at 3.5 per cent of the fee income instead of the surplus. It was forecast that under this arrangement approximately $5.4 million would be kept in the SPACE Fund and $7.3 million returned to HKU in 1994–95. The Management Board also stated that SPACE was willing to bear a reduction of resources caused by any cut in external funding.[38] The Finance Committee met on 31 May 1994 and maintained its view that the School's protests were not completely justified. They reaffirmed the Council's resolution that financial contributions from SPACE to the University should not be diminished. However, it agreed to the proposals of the Management Board that the SPACE Fund buffer should be set at 3.5 per cent of fee income, and that SPACE would not be asked to transfer its surpluses to the University in 1993–94.[39] This recommendation was approved by the Council at its meeting on 30 June 1994.[40]

This was not, however, the end of disagreements between SPACE and the University over the School's funding system. After the Council's resolution in June 1994, there were rumours within SPACE that the University intended to cut funding to the School by 60–80 per cent, a reduction which would have a devastating effect on the School.[41] At that time, the University was providing the largest subvention to continuing and professional education among the other local tertiary institutions. In 1994–95, HKU's subvention to SPACE was 0.88 per cent of the University's total expenditure whereas the average for the other four universities was only 0.18 per cent.[42] There was therefore a worry that the disproportionately large subvention from HKU to SPACE might attract the attention of the UGC and trigger a review of funding to SPACE which might in turn eventually lead to a reduction in the School's subvention. Such speculation was not entirely groundless because the UGC was in fact about to implement a policy of reducing its financial support for continuing and professional education in Hong Kong. By the early 1990s, it was clear to the UGC that continuing and professional education operations in local universities had achieved the objective intimated in 1969 and were now virtually self-financing. The UGC therefore no longer saw the need to continue its subvention to these adult education activities.[43]

The dispute over the use of the School's financial surpluses resurfaced when the SPACE Fund came under review again in June 1995. The University's Finance Committee, aware of the new UGC policy, took advantage of the review and at its meeting on 15 June 1995 adopted a recommendation to reduce the funding of SPACE from the block grant. According to the new scheme, the University's funding of academic posts at SPACE would be changed from an 'establishment' basis to a 'one-line budget' basis from the 1995–96 financial year. Moreover, the University's subvention to the School would be reduced by $5 million every year from 1995–96 until it supported only the 'core staff' of SPACE. In return, SPACE would be allowed to cross-subsidise its own programmes, and keep its surplus in a new reserve fund.[44]

The lack of prior consultation with SPACE over this proposal for reducing the block grant created fierce opposition from the School. The Director, Professor Lee Ngok, wrote to the Council on 27 June 1995 to protest against virtually the entire proposal. He insisted that SPACE deserved 'better treatment than a proposal to halve the resources allocated with no reason given' when the School boasted 5,000 to 6,000 FTEs, equal to half the total student population of the University.[45] The Director also criticised the Council for its lack of 'transparency and accountability' in making this decision and admonished it for conjecturing about possible future changes in policy by the UGC. Moreover, he did not feel that the cross-subsidisation system would guarantee the financial viability of the School, nor was he happy about the lack of definition as to who the 'core staff' of SPACE might be.[46] The Finance Office again stood its ground. The Director of Finance rejected the use of FTEs in connection with SPACE because the School was not a UGC-funded institution. He also rejected the idea of consulting the Senate because financial matters fell outside the Senate's terms of reference. SPACE was asked to follow the new one-line budget system because this policy had been introduced by the University on an institution-wide basis in 1992–93.[47] The Council agreed with the Finance Committee's recommendations this time, and decided on 29 June 1995 that the University's subvention to SPACE would be reduced gradually from the next financial year.[48]

The cut in subsidies to the School started in 1995–96. During the first year the subvention to SPACE fell by about $4.44 million to $24.09 million. In June 1996, the Council decided to push forward with the plan by again reducing the level of block grant subsidy in 1996–97 to $15 million, and allowing SPACE to keep up to $20 million from its operating surplus as a reserve fund. Any remaining balance would be utilised to repay outstanding bank mortgages, and in future all indirect costs for the use of University facilities would be charged to SPACE.[49] However, the actual pace of the reduction of university subvention to SPACE was much faster than expected. The government introduced a Non-Local Higher and Professional Education (Regulation) Bill to the Legislative Council in February 1996 which was to come into effect on 20 June 1997.[50] This ordinance prohibited programmes leading to overseas qualifications being offered in Hong Kong without government permission. Under the new legislative framework, SPACE could be exempted from registration on the condition that the University would guarantee that these courses satisfied certain requirements, including a provision 'that no government funding is allocated to such courses'.[51] The provision of a subsidy to SPACE from the government block grant clearly went against the requirements of the ordinance. The Council finally agreed in October 1996 that the subvention would be drastically cut from $15 million to $4 million in the 1996–97 financial year. The University would support only the School's 'core staff', which was defined as comprising the Director, the School Secretary and their personal secretary.[52] SPACE had no alternative but to accept this reduction in the University's subvention.[53]

The financial relationship between SPACE and the University therefore underwent a revolutionary change in the four years after 1992. In 1996, SPACE not only became virtually financially independent of the University, but it also became a major non-government contributor to the University's finances. In subsequent years, the School made huge direct contributions to the University, and continued to make substantial payments to HKU departments, as well as full compensation for the use of University facilities. In the nine years from 1996, the average annual net payment from the School to the University was approximately $64.5 million, with massive payments of $89.3 million in 2001–02 and $102.3 million in 2002–03 (see Table 7.1). From being financially dependent on the University, the continuing and professional education activities of SPACE were now helping to fund the University. After 1999–2000, the University ceased to make any contribution to SPACE and the School became fully self-financing (see Appendix 3). By 2007, the annual income of HKU SPACE was in excess of $800 million and the SPACE reserve fund had grown to $553.6 million.[54]

Departure of Lee Ngok and the Tricker Review, 1995

Disputes over academic developments within SPACE and the cutback in the University's subvention revealed an urgent need to redefine the relationship between SPACE and the University. Reviews were therefore conducted during the mid-1990s to seek ways to strengthen links between SPACE and the University. The reviews identified several problems and suggested solutions, but the School and the University seemed unenthusiastic about taking any substantial action immediately. Such unwillingness was particularly apparent in the School after July 1995 when the departure of Lee Ngok left SPACE without any strong leadership for a period of more than two years.

The initial request for a formal review came from the academic staff of SPACE. In September 1994 the Board of Studies received a protest from staff against a possible reduction in the University's subvention. The academic staff believed that 'a drastic reduction in central funding to SPACE has profound implications for academic policy', and might affect the University's overall policy on continuing education. They demanded, among other things, that 'a review of academic policy should be undertaken . . . before any major change in SPACE funding is contemplated'.[55] The Board of Studies endorsed this view and the Director made an official request to the Vice-Chancellor on behalf of the Board on 5 October 1994.[56]

This was, in fact, a convenient time to launch a full review of the School because Lee Ngok had just decided to resign from the directorship to take up the post of Pro-Vice-Chancellor at the University of Southern Queensland in Australia, with effect from 1 July 1995.[57] As in the case of Roger Williams's retirement a decade earlier, a change of leadership provided an opportunity for the University and the School to readjust their relationship with each other. Third-party observations also contributed to the University's decision to start a formal review to strengthen its relationship with SPACE. Since 1993 the UPGC had been undertaking a wide-ranging review of higher education. Despite the UPGC's reluctance to finance continuing and professional education programmes, it did not completely reject the idea that 'there may still be a need for a Government input, particularly in providing for development into new areas'.[58] Professor Richard Taylor, Head of the Department of Adult Continuing Education at the University of Leeds and an External Adviser of SPACE, visited Hong Kong in October 1994

Table 7.1 SPACE Finances, 1991–2005

Year	Income	Expenditure	Surplus / (Deficit)	Received from HKU	Payment to HKU	Net receipt from / (payment to) HKU	SPACE Fund Balance	Accumulated fund Balance
1991–1992	72.46	70.62	1.84	19.75	3.60	16.15	2.48	
1992–1993	91.34	83.17	8.17	21.73	5.12	16.61	9.13	
1993–1994	131.81	140.60	(8.79)	25.25	3.60	21.65	0.34	
1994–1995	171.02	150.75	20.27	28.53	3.60	24.93	20.61	
1995–1996	218.59	217.84	0.75	24.09	3.82	20.27	20.38	
1996–1997	264.71	226.40	38.31	2.85	15.70	(12.85)	54.08	
1997–1998	295.39	257.23	38.16	4.98	49.84	(44.86)	88.07	
1998–1999	382.01	316.97	65.04	5.79	61.02	(55.23)	43.28	237.31
1999–2000	451.52	388.19	63.32	5.90	66.63	(60.73)		283.48
2000–2001*	523.72	472.70	51.02	0	77.08	(77.08)		314.49
2001–2002	646.37	598.50	47.87	0	89.31	(89.31)		338.36
2002–2003	704.84	694.48	10.36	0	102.29	(102.29)		332.72
2003–2004	720.65	682.91	37.74	0	62.33	(62.33)		355.17
2004–2005	787.62	687.92	99.70	0	75.80	(75.80)		460.80

(Amounts are expressed in millions of dollars)

* After incorporation in 2000–2001, a new accounting practice was adopted. The Accumulated Fund Balance refers to the net assets owned by HKU SPACE.

to make suggestions on strategic issues which the School needed to confront and resolve. He argued against the University's proposal to cut subsidies to the School, claiming that 'any diminution in this element of support would seriously undermine SPACE's high reputation, and thus ultimately its effectiveness'. Instead, he claimed that 'the development, at a variety of levels, of SPACE/University integration should be a major strategic objective for the University and the School over the next five years'. Such integration might be achieved through formal accreditation of the SPACE courses by HKU, inclusion of the School's finances within the UPGC's framework, and enhancing SPACE representation on appropriate faculty boards and the Senate.[59] These observations encouraged the University to take steps to strengthen its relationship with SPACE.

The Vice-Chancellor, Professor Wang Gungwu, decided in November 1994 to initiate a full review of SPACE.[60] The review panel was chaired by Professor R. I. Tricker of the School of Business, one of the School's most outspoken adversaries in the 1987 battle over degree programmes offered jointly by SPACE and overseas partner universities. The seven-member review panel was 'to provide the School with an opportunity for self-evaluation and self-improvement', and its main tasks were to assess the validity of the School's objectives in the context of the University's mission, the extent to which those objectives were being achieved, the appropriateness of the means by which the school was trying to achieve those objectives, and the adequacy of the resources available for achieving its objectives. It was also given the task of advising the Senate and Council on any measures necessary to remedy defects and to assist the School in its future development.[61] The panel reported in May 1995. While appreciating that 'by almost any criterion SPACE has been highly successful', it was concerned about the relationship between the School and the University. The University was advised of the necessity of 'a shift in the strategic focus of SPACE', but this shift would have serious implications for both SPACE and the University.[62] The panel advised the University to 'identify the SPACE mission more clearly within the mission of the University as a whole'. SPACE should develop 'strategic alliances' with the subject departments as well as with overseas universities. The participation of departments in SPACE programmes should not rely solely on involvement by individual teachers, but also through a 'mutually beneficial partnership' between the two parties under an agreed mechanism. SPACE could contribute its expertise on adult education and distance learning, its networks with overseas institutions, administrative support, as well as facilities and accommodation in this partnership. The subject departments would be responsible for subject expertise, academic quality assurance and teaching resources for the programmes.[63]

The Tricker review panel also recommended that SPACE, with the assistance of HKU's internal departments, should localise the existing overseas degree programmes as quickly as possible. This should again be achieved through institutional co-operation rather than just via the participation of individual teachers. Furthermore, subject specialists at SPACE should be 'more closely associated with their cognate subject departments and faculties'. They could be designated as members of the cognate departments and faculties so as to be involved in formal or informal departmental discussions, research activities and student supervision. In the long term, the University would need to reconsider the external degree programmes for which SPACE and the relevant departments could jointly develop courses.[64] The Tricker proposal for an alliance with faculties did not mean that SPACE's activities would be subordinated to the University's teaching departments. On the contrary, the relationship was aimed at maintaining and strengthening the identity of SPACE as a unique academic unit within the University with the special role of providing professional and continuing education. The Tricker panel believed that 'the mind-set, which sees the University's mainstream activities as those funded by the Government, with continuing education as a mere adjunct to this . . . will have to change'.[65] The panel was optimistic that when more departments benefited from co-operation with SPACE, this mentality would change.

The Panel's proposal for closer collaboration with academic departments received supportive responses from the Management Board and the staff of SPACE. The Management Board noted at its meeting on 6 June 1995 that 'it was recognised by both the School and Departments/Faculties that there was a need for a change of direction'.[66] A staff meeting of SPACE on 9 June 1995 also endorsed the ideas of closer association with subject departments, course localisation and external degree programmes.[67] The Tricker Report was finally endorsed by the Senate in October 1995.[68] Unfortunately, the 1995 review had its own serious shortcomings. As the Management Board of the School observed, the review panel 'did not address issues of implementation should the recommendations be accepted by the School and the University'.[69] The Senate also failed to take any substantial steps to implement the Tricker proposals except for asking the School's Board of Studies and Management Board, and other relevant committees to take follow-up action.[70] Therefore, there was no concrete working plan to implement the recommendations of the Tricker Report once it had received Senate's endorsement.

Implementation of the Review Panel's recommendations and other substantial changes in the relationship between SPACE and the University were even less likely to take place because of the absence of stable leadership in SPACE between 1995 and 1998. The selection process for a new director started three months before Lee Ngok's departure in July 1995, but it failed to find a suitable candidate and the University had to re-advertise the vacancy in early 1996.[71] Before Lee's departure, the SPACE staff and the University had been concerned about the possibility that the delay in appointing a new director would affect the administration and strategic development of SPACE.[72] To make the situation even more critical, Bill Howarth, the Deputy Director who had been Acting Director of SPACE for over fifteen months, resigned and left the School suddenly for personal reasons in mid-November 1996. John Cribbin, the School Secretary, remarked that the position was 'somewhat critical at present in terms of coping with the senior management workload'.[73] The senior management of the School was so understaffed that the University appointed Professor S. L. Wong, and later Professor S. T. H. Chan, for short terms as acting directors until August 1997.[74] Although the two professors were both members of the School's Management Board, they had little working knowledge of day-to-day business at SPACE and their appointments were transitory. Most of the higher level administrative and management work fell on the shoulders of John Cribbin as School Secretary during this difficult period. Instability within the senior management, therefore, prevented most of the Tricker recommendations from being implemented, and also led to a freeze of any major changes in the role of SPACE within the University.

A New Director and a New Corporate Identity

Important strategic developments within SPACE were much delayed until Professor Enoch C. M. Young was appointed in June 1997 as the new Director of SPACE with effect from February 1998.[75] Young was a distinguished physicist who received his undergraduate education at HKU and doctoral training at Bristol University in the United Kingdom. He returned to HKU in 1967 and gained a great deal of administrative experience in his twenty years in the Physics Department, rising to the post of Sub-Dean of the Faculty of Science in 1987. He then moved to the City University of Hong Kong where he was the founding head of the department of Applied Science, and later Dean. In the 1990s he undertook the more senior roles of Dean of the Graduate School, Vice-President (Academic), and finally Vice President for Institutional Advancement.[76] His connection with SPACE dated back to the 1970s, when he was a part-time tutor of the DEMS. As Director-Designate he was attached to the School as a consultant between September 1997 and February 1998, allowing him to begin in advance a review of 'the School's current activities, an appraisal of its strengths and weaknesses and significant reforms to its organisational structure and forward planning'.[77]

Enoch Young quickly managed to inject a new vision and new managerial concepts into a School which was celebrating its fortieth anniversary in 1997–98. In January 1998 he completed a preliminary policy review, in which he reinforced the traditional role of School as 'the extension arm of the University'.[78] In order to achieve his development goals, Young was determined to establish the School's autonomous status within the University. The internal management structure of the School was reformed significantly so as to build SPACE into a more efficient enterprise. Seven academic divisions, each of which was co-ordinated by a head, were set up in late 1997 to 'streamline internal administration' and 'promote links with Faculties and departments'.[79] The senior administration of the School was strengthened with the appointment of two deputy directors in mid-1998, and the creation of associate directorships in 2001.[80] The new deputy directors were Dr Michael Luk, formerly of HKU's Department of History and more recently from the Hong Kong Institute of Education, and Dr S. M. Shen, who was finishing her term as Dean of Social Sciences at HKU. Administrative and auxiliary units were created for quality assurance, research and development, human resources, finance, and public relations.[81] Not surprisingly, the re-organisation and expansion of internal structures led to a significant rise of the number of full-time staff. In November 2005, the School had 790 full-time employees, four times the number of staff in 1997.[82] SPACE had therefore become an even larger unit within HKU in terms of staff members, and this provided even more reason for it becoming administratively independent of the University.

The most important step towards greater autonomy was the incorporation of the School. The School's almost completely self-financing nature and the need to respond to the changes in continuing and professional education markets called for a more independent structure for SPACE, and this was best achieved through the incorporation of the School. Incorporation was not an entirely new concept for SPACE. The 1991 review had mentioned the possibility of incorporation as a long-term development strategy for the School, but such a view now received strong support during the vice-chancellorship of Professor Patrick Y. C. Cheng (1996–2000). Soon after Enoch Young took office in February 1998, he met with the Vice-Chancellor and both of them agreed in principle to re-organise SPACE 'into a limited company, with its own staff structure, salary scales, and conditions of service'.[83] In November 1998 the Management Board agreed in principle to establish a corporate structure for the School.[84] Six months later the School submitted a proposal for incorporation to the University Council, listing its reasons for pursuing incorporation:

> One advantage is that such a structure clearly differentiates the activities from public funding . . . A corporate structure will allow the University to provide for the more flexible approach necessary for the SPACE operations as the Company can develop appropriate rules and procedures not open to the University as a public funded institution.[85]

Professor Young further explained the rationale for the proposed incorporation at the Council meeting on 7 May 1999:

> In view of the increasing demand for continuing education and the need to respond promptly to these community needs, the incorporation of SPACE would allow a

> greater degree of flexibility which SPACE required in order to operate in an increasingly competitive environment.[86]

The Council had no objection to this proposal, subject to the School supplying further details of incorporation and company ownership. These details were quickly confirmed by the University administration and the Council formally approved the incorporation of the School of Professional and Continuing Education at its meeting on 24 June 1999.[87] The incorporation process was finally completed on 6 October 1999, and at the same time SPACE was transformed into a new legal entity with the name 'HKU School of Professional and Continuing Education', more commonly to be known as 'HKU SPACE'.[88]

As the School was a non-profit organisation for educational purposes, the normal status of a 'limited company' (a business engaged in making profits and therefore subject to profits tax) was not appropriate for the new entity. HKU SPACE was therefore formed as a 'company limited by guarantee'. It had neither share capital nor shareholders, but there was a provision that each of the five Company Members would undertake a 'guarantee' of up to $100 to indicate their responsibility for the affairs of the Company.[89] The old SPACE Management Board would be replaced by the new 'HKU SPACE Management Board' made up of all existing members. One of the most crucial provisions in the constitution of HKU SPACE was that, being a legal entity, the new Company had full control over its own financial affairs. HKU SPACE, with the approval of its Management Board, could sell and deal with all or any part of its assets, and it could also borrow or raise money for the purposes of the School.[90] Although the School had always exercised such financial powers on advice from the University, the new corporate identity did allow HKU SPACE to release itself from rigid University procedures and deal with its financial resources more flexibly and efficiently.

Although HKU SPACE is now a legally and financially independent entity, its work is still scrutinised by the University as well as the community in various ways. HKU had always overseen the academic development of the School since 1992 through the Board of Studies which was a committee of Senate. Incorporation of SPACE in 1999 did not change this academic supervision, but it coincided with a University-wide review aiming at streamlining the academic committee structure of the University.[91] The School proposed that the existing Board of Studies be replaced by a smaller and more authoritative board which would direct the academic affairs of the School and advise the University on continuing and professional education and lifelong learning policy.[92] The Senate resolved in December 1999 to set up a new 'Board for Continuing and Professional Education and Lifelong Learning' to replace the existing Board of Studies. Chaired by the Vice-Chancellor, the new Board would 'provide a wider advisory role on CPE/Lifelong Learning policy in the University and will undertake specific academic responsibility for the

School' and engage the University's senior management in the School's academic affairs.[93] The membership was reduced from sixty to about nineteen in order to increase efficiency.[94] The new Board received course validation and monitoring reports from the School's Quality Assurance Committee to ensure the quality and standard of the courses offered by the School. In 2000, HKU SPACE further formed a School Advisory Board comprising external members from the community. It was responsible for advising HKU SPACE at a strategic level and marked a return to previous policies of community engagement. The School Advisory Board was initially chaired by Dr Cheng Hon-kwan and consisted of four ex-officio members and fourteen appointed members.[95] The Advisory Board served as an important bridge between the School and the community and assisted the School in setting long-term development strategies.

Lifelong Learning and the Links with HKU Faculties

While the School worked for greater autonomy and developed a new corporate identity, it did not overlook the importance of strong links between itself and the academic units of the University. The School had long recognised that it relied heavily on the University for its all-important brand name, its guarantee of academic quality, and many of its physical facilities, but it had not yet established firm working relationships with other parts of HKU. Enoch Young therefore tried to identify ways in which the School and the University could be drawn more closely together. In the preliminary policy review of January 1998, he suggested that 'lifelong learning can be the bridge for the School to work more closely with the University', and he wanted to include this concept, which had been widely used in the West but was quite novel in Hong Kong, in the School's mission statement.[96]

The idea of 'lifelong learning' can be traced back to the ancient Greek philosophers who considered lifelong learning to be the key to a healthy mind, body and soul. Modern interpretations of the concept developed in the early twentieth century in the United Kingdom. The 1919 Report of the Ministry of Reconstruction's Adult Education Committee emphasised the 'lifelong' element in adult education. It suggested that adult education should be a 'permanent national necessity' which should be both universal and lifelong. In the next few decades, this phrase was frequently used in academic discussion and policy debates in Europe and America, but it was so poorly defined that to many people the term 'lifelong learning' seemed to be 'a little bit folksy' and not very felicitous.[97] In general, 'lifelong learning' has more recently been defined as 'the act of learning throughout one's lifetime' and can be applied to 'the underlying function of lifelong education although not limited by it, since one can learn without subjecting oneself to the external ritual of the educational process'.[98] In many ways lifelong learning is complementary to other similar concepts such as 'adult education', 'recurrent education', 'continuing education' or 'continuing and professional education'.

In Hong Kong, the phrase 'lifelong learning' was seldom used by either government agencies or educational institutions until the late 1990s.[99] The term was first adopted officially by the government in the 1998 Policy Address, in which the Chief Executive, Tung Chee-hwa, acknowledged that lifelong learning 'plays an important part in helping us to make progress in society'.[100] In the context of this government policy statement, the 'progress' being referred to involved 'providing the working population with further opportunities for life-long continuing and professional education' and creating a 'knowledge economy' for China by increasing the number of post-secondary students who could gain access to higher education in Hong Kong.[101] This has been seen by at least one commentator as an essentially political move by the government aimed at establishing a 'depoliticised economic discourse of lifelong learning' which has proven particularly useful to a government lacking democratic legitimacy.[102] There can be no denying, however, that this new policy had an almost immediate impact on the CPE sector in Hong Kong. The government later proposed that the percentage of students engaged in higher education should be increased to 60 per cent of school-leavers, providing the basis for a boom in lifelong learning opportunities in the years after 2000.[103] In 1999, the Education Commission established the cultivation of 'lifelong learning interest and abilities' of students as one of the directions of educational reforms which had been initiated by the Chief Executive in 1997.[104] The Education Commission further elaborated the necessity of promoting a culture of lifelong learning in the final report of its review of education in Hong Kong:

> In a knowledge-based society, new knowledge emerges while existing knowledge becomes obsolete quickly. The problems that we encounter in our daily lives and at work have become increasingly complicated and diverse, while social contact has become more frequent and enriched. To cope with these challenges, people must break away from their old selves. They must seek more knowledge and be ready to venture into new domains of knowledge. They need to make more efficient use of knowledge and devise novel means to solve problems. They must also continue and enrich themselves through their lives. Our education system must therefore lay a solid foundation and provide extensive opportunities for life-long learning.[105]

SPACE was one of the institutions which quickly incorporated 'lifelong learning' into its core values. Even before the 1998 Policy Address, the new SPACE Director had already made use of this concept to explain his ambition of further developing the School as the 'extension arm' of HKU. It was clear that Young did not intend to meddle with academic argument over the definition of 'lifelong learning'. Instead, he tried to relate this new concept to previous notions which the School had adopted. At a public reception in late 2000, Young made special reference to 'lifelong learning', affirming that:

> Education does not end with the schools or even universities. Continuing upgrading of knowledge, skills and concepts implies continuous learning or, to use the proper term, the pursuit of 'continuing and professional education' (CPE), the underlying philosophy of which is 'Lifelong Learning' and 'Lifewide Learning'.[106]

Both the School and the University recognised the growing importance of the concept of 'lifelong learning' in modern educational discourse and tried to pursue a common mission to promote lifelong learning in society. In its Annual Report for 1997–98, SPACE proposed as one of its strategic aims a more effective collaboration with the University's faculties 'through mutually beneficial joint projects to deliver self funding programmes of lifelong education'.[107] Lifelong learning elements were inserted into the School's revised mission statement in 1998 and the University also showed its support for lifelong learning by including a mention of it in HKU's Vision and Mission Statement. In June 1999, the Senate started revising the University's Vision and Mission Statement, which had been in use since 1993. Enoch Young proposed adding a lifelong learning element into the Statement 'to acknowledge the commitment of the University to the provision of life-long learning in the University'.[108] In October 1999, the Senate endorsed this addition to the University's Vision and Mission Statement, part of which now reads:

> The University of Hong Kong will endeavour:
>
> . . .
>
> To provide a comprehensive education, developing fully the intellectual and personal strengths of its students while developing and extending lifelong learning opportunities for the community.[109]

The inclusion of a lifelong learning section in the Statement signified HKU's official acknowledgement of lifelong learning as one of its core activities. As the School was responsible for the majority of the University's work in continuing education, the new Statement implied that the HKU SPACE would play a more crucial role in the development of the University.[110] In more recent years the UGC has approved a role statement for the University of Hong Kong which specifically mentions lifelong learning as a goal of the University. HKU is the only university in Hong Kong to include such a goal in its role statement, further reinforcing and accentuating HKU SPACE's leadership in the area of lifelong learning.

However, the mere inclusion of 'lifelong learning' as one element of the mission statements of the School and the University did not help to strengthen the relationship between the School and HKU's faculties at an operational level. In a report submitted to the Management Board in February 2001, the School listed three potential barriers to further collaboration with the faculties:

> (a) [HKU] departments tend to take for granted the full [financial] support provided by the University for their activities. Some may assume that . . . self-funding programmes [can be organised] without extra cost and hence perceive collaboration with SPACE as potentially expensive since these costs have to be included as programmes expenses.
> (b) SPACE senior management is not sufficiently integrated with University senior management to ensure maximum efficiency . . .
> (c) SPACE activities may not be sufficiently visible within the University (e.g. in publications, the web-page) given the scale of its activity.[111]

HKU SPACE was very aware of the first barrier which acted as a financial disincentive preventing the University's faculties from co-operating with the School. HKU SPACE programmes were operated in a completely self-financing mode by the end of the 1990s and the University recovered from SPACE the full cost of University facilities used by the School. Faculties, however, were only required to pay the University 15 per cent of the income generated from self-financing courses, which was usually insufficient to cover the cost incurred by the use of University resources. Such a difference in costing prevented the faculties from collaborating with HKU SPACE because the faculties' share of surplus income would inevitably be diminished by the requirement to pay full costs to the University for the HKU SPACE programmes.[112] In 2001, the University sharply reduced overhead charges for faculty-based programmes to 3.75 per cent of fee income, which further encouraged the faculties to organise self-financing courses of their own. The School remarked that 'HKU presents itself both as a Partner in some cases and a Competitor in others', a situation which was clearly 'undesirable' from SPACE's point of view.[113]

In order to foster a closer association between the University and HKU SPACE, the Vice-Chancellor commissioned one of his pro-vice-chancellors, Professor John Malpas, to undertake a new review of HKU SPACE in August 2001. The six-member Review Panel was asked to 'appraise the position and capacity of HKU SPACE in realising the University's commitment to continuing and lifelong education; and to look at the governance, management and quality assurance systems of HKU SPACE, so as to satisfy the University that the relationship between HKU SPACE and other parts of the University are in accord'.[114] Among various issues examined by the panel, the relationship between the University and the School was the real focus of this review.

The Malpas panel submitted its report in January 2002. In the very first part of the Report, the panel highlighted the vital role played by HKU SPACE in the University:

> The HKU–School of Professional and Continuing Education ('the School') has long been regarded as an integral part of the University of Hong Kong, that both embodies and implements the latter's vision and mission in satisfying Hong Kong society's needs for lifelong learning.[115]

Five years after the Tricker Report, the Malpas Report admitted that the understanding of the School's role among many members of the University still needed to be improved. The observation of the Tricker Report on the relationship between the School and the University was in general still valid in 2002: HKU SPACE was often 'on the periphery in the University's mainstream thinking', and 'some mental adjustments' towards HKU SPACE were still needed within the University.[116] The Malpas panel identified several specific problems underpinning the weak relationship between the School and the rest of the University. First, HKU SPACE appeared to be 'competing with Faculties in offering similar programmes'. This situation was caused by a lack of communication between HKU SPACE and the faculties. The School was not obliged to consult the relevant faculties before introducing new courses and most HKU SPACE faculty contacts remained informal and personal. It was even alleged that HKU SPACE was in the habit of presenting proposals to its Board 'with *fait accompli* rather than to seek programme approval in consultation'.[117] Second, it was perceived that HKU SPACE programmes were of a lower standard than those of the University.[118] More seriously, the Review Panel pointed out the paradoxical relationship between HKU SPACE and the University:

> On the one hand, the School has become the acknowledged leader in the enterprise of lifelong learning. On the other hand, its corporate status and quasi-independence seem to distance the School gradually from the University . . . It is as if the School has taken on an academic identity of its own . . . The Review Panel detected a sense of non-interference between some University staff and the School. One historical and logical explanation for such feelings is that academic colleagues appear only vaguely aware of the School's acts and are only individually engaged in some of its academic work.[119]

The Review Panel made a number of recommendations to remedy these problems. At the governance level, the composition and function of the Board of Continuing and Professional Education and Lifelong Learning needed to be reformed. The restructured Board would comprise a chairman, six members from the University and six members from HKU SPACE in order to reflect in a more balanced way the views of both the University and the School. The new Board would also be more proactive in the realm of policy development for continuing education. Furthermore, it was proposed that HKU SPACE should have more seats on the Senate in order to enhance its participation in academic decision-making. These new seats were to be given to the deputy directors of HKU SPACE and two academic staff members elected by the staff of the School.[120] At departmental level, HKU SPACE and the faculties were to set up a mechanism to 'maintain regular contact and communicate with each other'. The review panel recommended that each faculty should assign an associate dean to liaise with HKU SPACE and deal with continuing education work related to the faculty. It was felt that the division heads of HKU SPACE should also sit on the Boards of relevant faculties. The School was advised to consult the relevant faculties before introducing new programmes, and the University was asked to encourage faculty members to participate in HKU SPACE programmes.[121] The Malpas Report also suggested that 'the University should insist on the widespread use of the full name of the HKU–School of Professional Continuing Education, which gives the School a strong visual identity as well as a public message that the School is a part of the University'.[122] This ostensibly minor recommendation had potential to make a major impact, and has proven to be an effective means of strengthening the formal identification of SPACE as an integral part of the University.

The Malpas Report was enthusiastically supported by HKU SPACE, although with some minor counter-proposals. For example, the School suggested that its restructured Board should include two lay Council members in order to reflect the views of the community.[123] It also recommended that apart from the expansion of the SPACE membership in the Senate, the Director should enjoy membership of the Council, the General Purposes Committee and the Academic Development Committee in order to secure the comprehensive participation of SPACE in University affairs.[124] Dr Michael Luk, the Acting Director of HKU SPACE, expressed his conviction when the Senate discussed the Malpas Report that 'any perception that HKU SPACE was too autonomous could be removed with improved communication between HKU SPACE and other parts of the University'.[125] The Senate and the Council agreed with this view and supported the recommendations of the Malpas Report in principle. The Senate this time took a more pro-active approach than after the Tricker review in implementing reforms in the relationship between HKU SPACE and the faculties. At its meeting on 5 November 2002, the Senate decided to review the structure of the Board of Continuing and Professional Education and Lifelong Learning, and appointed Professor John Malpas to lead a working group to 'consider and oversee the implementation of recommendations of the review panel'.[126]

Before the Implementation Working Party submitted its proposals, HKU SPACE and the University had already taken some measures to indicate their enthusiasm for a closer relationship between each other. HKU SPACE launched a new logo in November 2002 prominently displaying the School's full name so that the public would recognise a clear link between the School and the University.[127] The Council later agreed to 'amend the University Statutes by listing therein the diplomas, certificates and other sub-degree qualifications awarded to students to make it clear to the outside world that HKU SPACE awards were conferred by the University.[128] The Council also approved in June 2003 a new policy paper, 'Strategic Development 2003–2008', in which the 'lifelong learning' concept was further incorporated into the University's core philosophy. In this document, the University proclaimed its vision to 'produce well-rounded graduates with lifelong abilities'.[129] It also identified 'partnership with society and serving the community' as one of its four strategic goals, and in this area it was HKU SPACE which was seen as an important participant.[130]

The Senate finally adopted the proposals of the Implementation Working Party in December 2003. There were two key measures regarding the improvement of the relationship between the School and the rest of the University. First, the Board was to be reconstituted into a committee whose role was to advise the Senate, through the Academic Development Committee as appropriate, 'on the strategic direction of development of as well as policy issues and all other matters relating to continuing and professional education and lifelong learning'.[131] The Board's jurisdiction was extended from HKU SPACE to all lifelong learning activities outside the faculties, such as those carried out by the Poon Kam Kai Institute of Management. The maximum membership was suggested as fifteen, including the Vice-Chancellor as chairman, six Senate-appointed members, six HKU SPACE-nominated members, and not more than two co-opted members.[132] The second measure was to set up a number of Joint Consultative Committees (JCCs) as communication channels between HKU SPACE and the faculties. Each JCC was to be co-chaired by a divisional head of HKU SPACE and an associate dean who was responsible for lifelong learning in the particular faculty. The Joint Consultative Committees would discuss proposals for new programmes and the academic planning and development which might affect both sides.[133]

Despite all these efforts, HKU SPACE and the University have continued to experience difficulties in establishing a firm partnership with each other. The University has not yet amended its Statutes to include HKU SPACE qualifications, and recently it tried to evict the School from its on-campus headquarters in the T. T. Tsui Building. The University still appears reluctant to accord HKU SPACE equal status with the faculties and has avoided enhancing the School's representation in the senior management of the University. From August 2002, discussion about increasing the School's participation in the University's governance was integrated into the overall review of governance and management of the University launched by the Council in response to the Sutherland Report published by the government in March 2002.[134] The University submitted its *Fit for Purpose* report to the Council in February 2003. The report proposed a significant reduction in the size of both Senate and Council and thus thwarted any idea of providing additional representation for HKU SPACE on the two bodies.[135] HKU SPACE nevertheless continued to voice its eagerness to be more closely involved in the University's new policy-making structures. For example, Professor Young, a Senate-elected member of Council at the time, told the Council that HKU SPACE should play a more active and prominent part in the proposed Vice-Chancellor's Advisory Group, which aimed to 'enhance communications between the executive and members of the faculties'.[136] The School also submitted a written response to the Council, asking that the Director of HKU SPACE be a member of the Council and the Vice-Chancellor's Advisory Group, and that teachers of HKU SPACE should be eligible to be elected and act as electors for the Senate.[137] The Vice-Chancellor, however, responded to the School's requests in the same way that he replied to complaints from other quarters of the University, including the faculties:

> The Director of HKU SPACE should be regarded as equivalent to a Dean of a Faculty, called upon as a resource person at Council meetings if the Council so wished, and can perhaps be considered a member of the Vice-Chancellor's Advisory Group.[138]

HKU SPACE was not satisfied with this answer. At its meeting in June 2003, the Council heard a suggestion that academic staff of HKU SPACE should be 'eligible for electing, and being elected to be, academic members of the Council and the Senate'.[139] Despite the ardent desire of HKU SPACE to participate more fully in the higher decision-making bodies of the University, the proposal for more School representatives in the Senate was finally turned down by the Implementation Working Group in November 2003. It argued that the size of the Senate had been restricted by the recommendations of the *Fit for Purpose* report and further expansion was not desirable.[140] The University also refused to grant the Director of HKU SPACE ex-officio membership of Council in the same way that deans were also excluded from Council membership. It is true that the relationship between HKU SPACE and the senior management of the University is still maintained in many ways, such as the Director's participation in the Senate, occasional briefings for Council members by HKU SPACE, and other non-constitutional channels.[141] These channels include attendance of the Director by invitation at the Vice-Chancellor's Advisory Group. Nevertheless, the Director is not a member of all University committees on which the deans have ex-officio seats, so the assertion that there is still a strong link between the University and HKU SPACE is less plausible now than it was before the management reforms implemented in 2003.

As well as these structural barriers to full participation by the School in University governance, the faculties still appear to remain unenthusiastic about strengthening their links with HKU SPACE. The response of faculties to the proposal for Joint Consultative Committees was extremely negative and no faculty-based JCCs were established. The University produced a compromise proposal in September 2004 to form a single University-wide JCC, which finally held its first meeting in April 2005.[142] This single JCC is at present co-chaired by the Deputy Vice-Chancellor or a Pro-Vice-Chancellor and the Deputy Director (Quality Assurance) of HKU SPACE, and its members include associate deans of faculties, the Principal of the Community College and division heads of HKU SPACE. All new programme proposals from the faculties and HKU SPACE are required to be circulated among the members of the Joint Consultative Committee. If any JCC member wishes to discuss a particular proposal, the JCC is supposed to convene a small working group which reports to the JCC the results of its discussions within two weeks.[143] While the performance of the reformed Joint Consultative Committee system is yet to be evaluated, the initial lukewarm response to the proposal for JCCs indicates that the faculties are still not very keen to increase co-operation with HKU SPACE.

A third area of concern is the lack of any substantial University-wide policy on the development of lifelong learning. Although HKU has repeatedly declared its commitment to the 'lifelong learning' concept in its policy papers, the University has not provided a concrete development plan in this field. Most of the academic decisions and long-term planning for lifelong learning are dealt with by HKU SPACE alone. The University administration, on the other hand, seems not to be very eager to take part in these developments. The lack of any agreed working plan in this area means that HKU tends to respond to proposals from HKU SPACE passively, weakening the potential impact of developments in lifelong learning proposed by the School. In this sense it appears that some of the scholarly criticisms of the 'lifelong learning' policies adopted in Hong Kong at the behest of the government are well-founded. The University sometimes appears to pay lip service to the concept of lifelong learning without giving due recognition to the entity within the University which provides the majority of lifelong learning opportunities. This is, however, a difficult area to evaluate because very few HKU academics appear to have a clear idea of what the University means by 'lifelong learning'. This problem may be addressed more fully as the University moves closer towards reforming its curriculum in preparation for the four-year undergraduate degree in 2012.

Statistics therefore show a disappointing trend in collaboration between the School and other parts of the University. Years of effort have not resulted in any appreciable increase in the number of programmes jointly organised by the School and HKU's faculties. The number of such joint degree (either undergraduate or postgraduate) programmes dropped from twenty in 2000–01 to seven in 2003–04, and the FTE enrolments fell from 1,325 in 2001–02 to 1,105 in 2003–04. Most collaboration between the School and other parts of the University still remains on an ad hoc basis, with individual HKU teachers participating in teaching, assessment, or quality assurance exercises, but very few faculty-level initiatives.[144] Institutional collaboration exists in such areas as the Cyberport Institute of Hong Kong and the Hong Kong Putonghua Education and Assessment Centre, but the scale of such collaboration is either limited or experimental. It seems that despite the measures adopted in the past decade, HKU SPACE and most of the faculties of the University have not yet succeeded in establishing strong partnerships with each other.

Academic Developments

The School has always responded to continuing and professional education demands in the community quickly by devising new programmes for part-time learners. Traditional subjects like Business Management, Housing Management, Languages, and Law are still flourishing, but the School continues to diversify the subjects it offers. HKU SPACE now offers courses in a wide range of fields at all levels, from Fine Arts to Science, and from doctoral degrees to single public lectures. These courses are provided through its ten divisions, the Community Colleges, five academic centres, and several ventures in China. It is not possible to examine all the developments which have taken place in the last ten years, but the introduction of Chinese Medicine programmes and the establishment of the Cyberport Institute will perhaps suffice as typical examples of the School's attempts to respond to new demands, one very successfully and the other less so.[145] Moreover, the School's Quality Assurance system, which is an essential tool for maintaining high standards in the School's programmes, was established in the past decade and has become a key factor in sustaining the academic development of HKU SPACE. This aspect of the School's recent history will also be considered below to demonstrate both the ways in which the School has responded to doubts about the quality of its programmes and some of the problems associated with such developments.

Chinese Medicine Programmes

Before the 1990s, there was no systematic training for practitioners of Chinese Medicine in Hong Kong. Recognition of Chinese Medicine was not a government priority until a Working Party on Chinese Medicine was appointed in 1989.[146] Likewise, the Department of Extra-Mural Studies paid no attention to Chinese Medicine education before the 1990s. In autumn 1991, however, the DEMS, in association with academics in the University's Faculty of Medicine, started an extra-mural certificate course for existing Chinese Medicine practitioners.[147] This was followed by the introduction of another Traditional Chinese Medicine (TCM) certificate course and an interest class in 1992. In October 1992, the University received a donation of $2 million from a local businessman to support Chinese Medicine teaching at SPACE.[148] In the 'Ten Year Strategy' for SPACE published in 1993, it was noted that Chinese Medicine was an area which had great potential if collaboration with institutions in South China could be secured.[149] By 1996, the TCM courses had graduated some 944 students but this still remained a relatively insignificant subject area for SPACE.[150] At that time the School offered no programme leading to a qualification as a Chinese Medicine practitioner. Rather, the courses mainly aimed at 'introducing aspects of Chinese Medicine to western qualified practitioners' or providing continuing education to current Chinese Medicine practitioners, most of whom had received formal training on the Chinese Mainland.[151] Furthermore, HKU still had no intention of including Chinese Medicine programmes into its undergraduate curriculum. The Medical Faculty told SPACE in April 1996 that although it supported the upgrading of SPACE Chinese Medicine programmes to diploma or even higher levels, the Medical Faculty was prepared to play no more than 'a contributory role only' in Chinese Medicine education in the foreseeable future.[152]

The development of Traditional Chinese Medicine teaching at SPACE and the University was gradual in the following years. In 1994, the government-appointed Working Party on Chinese Medicine published a report encouraging local tertiary institutions to 'look into the possibility of offering training courses' in Chinese Medicine.[153] In response to the government proposals, HKU approved the establishment of a Centre for Traditional Chinese Medicine under SPACE, with the Vice-Chancellor as Acting Director. This Centre would serve as 'a focus for the development of TCM education; satisfying current needs and amenable to future expansion'.[154] In September 1997, SPACE started a four-year Diploma in Traditional Chinese Medicine programme in collaboration with Shanghai University of Traditional Chinese Medicine and nominally under the auspices of HKU's Faculty of Medicine. Lectures and laboratory practicals would be held in Hong Kong, but clinical practicums were conducted at Mainland Chinese Medicine hospitals.[155] During the 1997–98 academic year, there were also three other Chinese Medicine diploma or certificate programmes in different subjects and with different lengths of study offered by SPACE.[156]

The really rapid growth of Chinese Medicine programmes offered by SPACE did not begin, however, until the new Chief Executive declared in his 1997 Policy Address his ambition to develop Hong Kong as 'an international centre for the manufacture and trading of Chinese medicine, for research, information and training in the use of Chinese medicine'.[157] Local universities reacted promptly by initiating undergraduate programmes in Chinese Medicine from 1998. As the demand for a Chinese Medicine programme at tertiary level became more pressing, the University decided in June 1998 to establish the School of Traditional Chinese Medicine (STCM) under the auspices of the Faculty of Medicine. The Senate approved a proposal from the new School and SPACE to introduce a six-and-a-half-year part-time Bachelor of Traditional Chinese Medicine programme in collaboration with the Shanghai University of Traditional Chinese Medicine.[158] SPACE was heavily involved in this programme both academically and administratively. All seven initial full-time teachers of the programme were placed under the aegis of SPACE, while the teachers from the Medical Faculty were only involved in some of the courses.[159] In mid-1999, the University extended the scope of Chinese Medicine education by introducing a Master of Traditional Chinese Medicine, a Bachelor of Pharmacy in Chinese Medicine, and a Diploma in Tui-na. SPACE played an important role in all of these developments.[160]

Apart from its heavy involvement in Chinese Medicine courses, the School has also run Chinese Medicine clinics since 1998. The first SPACE Traditional Chinese Medicine clinic started operation in the Admiralty Learning Centre in February 1998 and aimed at providing clinical traineeships for its students as well as generalist and specialist consultation for the community.[161] The clinic was well received by the public, with about forty consultations on average per day in the first nine months. The clinic's services were expanded in November 1998 by adding a specialist section for Acupuncture and TCM Orthopaedics and Traumatology.[162] In the following years Chinese Medicine clinics and pharmacies were opened in learning centres in Admiralty and Tsim Sha Tsui.[163] Moreover, large areas of floor space in the School's premises, especially those at Austin Tower, Tsim Sha Tsui, were allocated to the Chinese Medicine Division for teaching and clinical services.

Rapid development in the past ten years has made Chinese Medicine an important subject area for HKU SPACE. The emphasis in the School's Chinese Medicine education strategy is nowadays placed on postgraduate education and professional training.[164] In 2004–05, over 5,500 students enrolled in Chinese Medicine courses, ranging from a short course conducted in Japanese to master's programmes. In 2006, there were twenty-eight full-time academic staff, four technicians and sixteen supporting staff working in the Chinese Medicine Division, forming one of the largest teams in HKU SPACE.[165] These developments in Chinese Medicine programmes are a good example of how SPACE continues to respond quickly to new opportunities and demands, especially those proposed by the government, but are also indicative of the diversification in learning areas which has taken place at SPACE in the last ten years.

The Cyperport Institute

Similar to the Chinese Medicine programmes, the establishment of the Cyberport Institute, in which HKU SPACE has played a significant role, was in response to a government initiative. The government announced in the 1999–2000 Budget Speech that it planned to develop a Cyberport at Telegraph Bay in Pokfulam as one of its major measures to develop an information services industry in Hong Kong.[166] The Cyberport project included an academic plan aiming to 'help groom talents to support the many IT developments and related business in Hong Kong'.[167] In March 2001, the government issued an open invitation for such an academic plan. HKU wanted to take advantage of this major development on its doorstep and submitted its proposal for a Cyberport Institute in May 2001. The government eventually selected the University to establish the Institute once the Cyberport project was completed.

The new Cyberport Institute, which was established in March 2002, was expected to be active in three areas: academic programmes, internship and placement, and research and development.[168] HKU SPACE was invited by the University to be the 'lead manager' of the Institute and became responsible for the overall management of the Institute.[169] Following the official inauguration of the Institute on 25 June 2002, HKU SPACE started the first academic programme, a Postgraduate Diploma in Information Technology, in November 2002.[170] The Institute is equipped with state-of-the-art computer laboratories, network workshop and lecture rooms, and has offered a number of postgraduate or post-experience courses on a full-time or part-time basis over the last few years. The Institute has also contacted leading information technology companies to provide technical support, placement opportunities and scholarship funding, and to collaborate with the Institute in its academic activities. In particular, the Institute established close co-operation with Cisco, Hewlett Packard, IBM, Microsoft and Oracle as its five 'Founding Industrial Partners', and PCCW as its 'Principal Corporate Partner'.[171] Initial progress therefore indicated that the Cyberport Institute had great potential for future growth.

Unfortunately, more recent statistics indicate that the Institute has not achieved the success which had originally been anticipated. In the 2002–3 academic year, the Institute admitted twenty-six students and expected that enrolments would rise to 170 in the next year, but the actual enrolment in 2003–4 was a disappointing twenty-three, far below expectations.[172] Alerted by the poor enrolment, the Institute sought ways to improve the situation. The advisors to the Institute, for example, suggested in March 2004 that the course content be reviewed and that further collaboration with external professional bodies be encouraged.[173] It is perhaps too soon to conclude that the Cyberport Institute has failed to achieve its objectives. It is still a young institution with only four years of operational experience from 2003, and a longer period is needed before any final judgement can be made about the performance of the Institute. The project does, however, demonstrate the dangers involved in responding to new opportunities, especially when they are driven by government policies which are badly timed or fail to gain the support of the public at large. The Cyberport development was very badly timed and only came into full operation after the bursting of the IT bubble, so it is generally considered to be one of the most embarrassing failures of the Tung Chee-hwa government. What should have been another success story for HKU SPACE in a new field of endeavour has instead turned into a failing enterprise.

Quality Assurance

The academic development of SPACE has been expressed not only in the diversity of subject areas or the number of courses offered each year, but also by continuous efforts to improve course quality and the introduction of a robust mechanism to assure and improve course quality. Before the mid-1990s, there was no unified system within either the Department of Extra-Mural Studies or the School of Professional and Continuing Education to control the quality of its programmes. The Senate, through the Committee on Extra-Mural Studies and later the SPACE Board of Studies, oversaw the general academic quality of continuing and professional education within the University. The standard of programmes at degree level was supervised by HKU or the awarding institutions through academic committees or similar bodies. In other courses the quality was largely monitored and maintained by the teachers themselves, who had great autonomy in curriculum development, teaching methods and modes of assessment. For decades, the quality of extra-mural courses was kept at a satisfactory level under this system, but by the mid-1990s such an inconsistent traditional approach was no longer felt to be sufficiently objective in dealing with the massive number of courses and the complex curricula offered by the School. The expansion of overseas degree programmes offered through adult education providers in Hong Kong also created problems for SPACE. Some of the programmes offered by other institutions in Hong Kong were sub-standard, and SPACE realised that it needed to adopt strict measures to maintain public confidence in its own programmes. The concept of 'quality assurance' in the education sector, which first appeared in the West in the 1980s and became increasingly popular in Hong Kong from the 1990s, was therefore a convenient way to achieve this objective.[174]

The desirability of a quality assurance system for SPACE was first mooted by Lee Ngok in 1992, and was later included in the 'Ten Year Strategy' document in 1993.[175] The School anticipated that the proposed Federation of Continuing Education would 'offer a means of assurance of quality which will help to ensure [that] . . . what it is offered is coherent and, where it is offered in conjunction with an overseas institution, it is done so in a planned and effective way'.[176] The School even considered adopting ISO 9000 standards as part of its quality assurance mechanism, but this was later found to be too difficult to implement.[177] In October 1994, Richard Taylor, an external adviser to SPACE, conducted a strategic review and advised the School to prepare a policy document for the appointment, monitoring and evaluation of part-time tutors. The School was also advised to set up quality assurance procedures for external examining, internal moderation of assessment and student feedback.[178] The University was by this time aware of the quality assurance issue at SPACE. The Tricker Report remarked in 1995 that 'even programmes that do not carry HKU awards benefit from the association with HKU's good name' and the University should therefore be 'in control of the academic standards of all programmes offered by SPACE'. Tricker recommended that an Academic Quality Assurance Committee be created in each broad subject area (such as Law, Humanities and Business Studies) which would review curricula and report on the quality of course proposals.[179] SPACE responded to the Tricker Report's recommendations by proposing in April 1996 that a School Committee on Quality Assurance be established and a Quality Officer appointed. The proposal for a single quality assurance committee did little, however, to improve the existing mechanism, and the benefits of a quality assurance system were greatly impaired by excluding certificate and short courses from scrutiny.[180]

A comprehensive quality assurance system was finally established in the School under the new Director. Enoch Young gave quality assurance very high priority among a number of tasks that needed to be dealt with after he joined SPACE in September 1997.[181] He invited Mrs Alma Craft, the Assistant Registrar in the Quality Assurance Office of the University of Greenwich, to visit SPACE in December 1997 as an external adviser for the School's quality assurance practices. She recommended that the School should codify the quality assurance policies and procedures in a more systematic way.[182] SPACE adopted Mrs Craft's recommendations and worked to implement a School-wide quality assurance system from 1998.[183] During that year Dr S. M. Shen, Deputy Director of SPACE, was asked by the Director to 'steer the development work and [oversee] the EQW [Education Quality Work]'.[184] In August 1999, a Senior Quality Assurance Officer was appointed to lead a team in the implementation of the Quality Assurance system, and this was followed by the creation of a Quality Assurance Committee in November of the same year.[185] Responsible to the new Board of Continuing and Professional Education and Lifelong Learning, the Quality Assurance Committee was asked 'to oversee and monitor the implementation of quality assurance policies and mechanisms, including programme validation, modification, monitoring and review'.[186]

The central part of this Quality Assurance system was a codified quality assurance handbook which each academic or administrative staff member of the School could consult and follow. After a year of preparation, HKU SPACE published the full and abridged editions of the *Quality Assurance Manual* in October 2000 and May 2001 respectively.[187] The *Manual* details the procedures for setting up partnerships with other institutions, designing programmes, obtaining the School's approval for offering programmes, as well as the monitoring and evaluation of programmes. The requirements and procedures vary among courses at different levels, but normally a proposed programme has to be carefully scrutinised to consider whether the objectives, admission requirements, curriculum, modes of delivery and assessment, and other administrative features of the programme meet the standard of the academic award which the graduates will receive upon the completion of their studies. With the exception of short and introductory certificate courses, which can be approved at division level, all courses have to be examined by an ad hoc Internal Validation Panel, which is formed by academics from HKU SPACE, the University and external specialists. In cases where the proposed programme involves a new external partner, a Collaborations Approval Panel will also be formed to consider whether such collaboration is up to the desired standard. The Quality Assurance Committee oversees the implementation of the entire quality assurance system, endorses programme proposals and receives annual monitoring reports on the quality of courses from Academic Committees or divisions.[188]

There was never any doubt that numerous problems would occur during the implementation of a new quality assurance system which involved such detailed documentation and complex procedures. Mrs Craft observed that 'there was roughly a 50/50 split between positive and negative comments' given by staff members at the beginning of the implementation process. Some staff members complained about the additional work involved, while others questioned whether all programmes needed to go through such a long approval process.[189] There was also lack of consistency in format and content among the first batch of Annual Monitoring Reports submitted by different divisions in early 2001, making it difficult for the School to evaluate the overall effectiveness of the quality assurance system.[190]

In spite of these teething difficulties, the Quality Assurance system of HKU SPACE has been highly praised by external bodies. In January 2002, a panel of local and overseas experts undertaking a 'University Review of Governance, Management and Quality Assurance System' gave very favourable comments on the School's Quality Assurance system. An independent research firm also ranked the School top in all quality-related factors in a 2003 survey, concluding that HKU SPACE was the premium provider of continuing and professional education services in Hong Kong.[191] In the 'Second Round Teaching and Learning Quality Process Reviews Report' published in January 2003, the UGC also praised the Quality Assurance system and other developments at HKU SPACE. In particular, the UGC felt that the *Quality Assurance Manual* published by the School 'deserves special mention and is highly recommended to other institutions as a reference for quality assurance process'. The UGC suggested that the University itself should consider whether the quality assurance system of HKU SPACE could be extended to other parts of the University.[192] Such recognition from these bodies indicates that HKU SPACE is today playing a leading role in Hong Kong in quality assurance. The UGC's recommendation that the use of SPACE's *Quality Assurance Manual* be extended to the University proper has, however, fallen on deaf ears. The University has instead adopted a less intrusive and more flexible system which continues to give teachers greater autonomy. This is perhaps due to the rather bureaucratic and time-consuming nature of SPACE's quality assurance mechanism which is seen by many in the University as appropriate for SPACE programmes but not for their own. In 2003–04, the School's Quality Assurance Committee received 229 Annual Monitoring Reports covering 291 courses.[193] During the period between 1999 and 2005, a total of 224 new programmes were approved under the Quality Assurance system involving untold man-hours of administrative work.[194] The Quality Assurance system has therefore been successfully implemented and operates relatively smoothly, but it remains a very time-consuming instrument of control and therefore a source of complaint from some staff in the School.[195]

Teaching Accommodation

Apart from the diversity and quality of programmes, teaching accommodation is another crucial factor affecting the ongoing development of the School. Most of the part-time learners who have daytime jobs need to rush to class after work, and therefore well-located teaching venues are essential to their studies. The University's main campus at the junction of Bonham and Pokfulam Roads has been considered for decades as an inconvenient venue for part-time learners, and has never been able to accommodate all of the School's courses. This problem was initially relieved in the 1960s by borrowing rooms from schools and voluntary associations, and later by setting up a Town Centre which migrated to several locations in Central (see Chapter 4). By the end of the 1980s, the Town Centre was permanently located at the Shun Tak Centre, supported by the on-campus head office, and temporary teaching accommodation both on the HKU main campus and across the city were used heavily during evenings and weekends. As the number of courses and the student population grew, however, it became necessary to seek additional teaching and office space close to the work places of the School's part-time learners.

In the early 1990s, SPACE continued to look for new teaching accommodation, especially premises which could be managed by the School on a permanent basis. After several years of operation, the Town Centre on the ninth floor of the Shun Tak Centre became insufficient to house any more programmes or students. In 1989 and 1991, additional units at Shun Tak Centre were purchased by the University to extend the space available but this was still not enough to satisfy all the demands.[196] In 1992, the School secured a long lease of two floors in a former school building at Shek Kip Mei. This Regional Centre was the School's first permanent teaching venue in Kowloon, providing eleven classrooms for part-time classes.[197] The School gradually expanded the Shek Kip Mei Regional Centre over the next few years and finally occupied the whole four-storey building.[198] The third teaching centre was opened on the fourteenth floor of Fortress Tower, North Point, in November 1994. Purchased by the School for $79 million, the premises had a floor area of about 14,600 square feet and housed lecture rooms and a computer laboratory.[199] There was also a proposal in 1995 for SPACE to invest $5 million in the construction of a residential wing at St John's College in Pokfulam, which would have enabled the School to accommodate its overseas exchange students, but this project was never realised because of financial disagreements between the University, the School and St John's College.[200]

There were also various changes to the on-campus facilities of the School in the early 1990s. The head office of the Department of Extra-Mural Studies on the ground floor of the Main Building was removed to the seventh floor of the Knowles Building in early 1991.[201] Even though 32 per cent of the extra-mural courses were being conducted on campus in 1989–90, the DEMS did not occupy any permanent on-campus teaching facilities at this time.[202] Lack of on-campus teaching facilities was finally remedied when T. T. Tsui, a well-known businessman and art collector, offered the University a donation of $13 million in 1991 to build a University Art Gallery at the 'Woodside' site on Bonham Road.[203] Lee Ngok immediately saw an opportunity to make use of the 'airspace' above the proposed low-rise building and suggested to the Vice-Chancellor, Wang Gungwu, that the DEMS be allowed to participate in the building project.[204] The Department of Extra-Mural Studies therefore became a partner in this building project in May 1991.[205] The overall cost of the project was about $70 million, which was met partly by the Tsui donation, but also by the sale of part of the Extra-Mural Town Centre; the rest was from the HKU Endowment Fund. SPACE was required to pay an annual rent to the University for the use of the new building.[206] Construction began in 1993 and was completed in early 1996.[207] The twelve-storey T. T. Tsui Building, the top seven floors of which were occupied by SPACE, came into operation in May 1996 and was officially opened on 8 November 1996. The building became the new headquarters of SPACE and at that time housed the majority of the School's full-time academic staff.[208]

The past decade has witnessed a significant expansion and improvement in the School's teaching accommodation in response to persistent demands for additional teaching space. Keen competition among continuing and professional education providers in Hong Kong also compelled the School to improve the physical environment of its teaching facilities. The slogan 'bringing the University to the students' adopted by the School has driven the rapid expansion of its learning centres throughout Hong Kong.[209] In present-day Hong Kong it is no longer so difficult for people to cross Victoria Harbour or to travel to the different districts in the city, but sometimes the additional half-hour journey can be a crucial factor for potential adult learners in choosing whether they take up part-time studies. The School wanted to ensure that its learning centres were conveniently located so that no student wishing to enrol in a HKU SPACE course would be put off by travel problems. The School also believed that the acquisition of additional learning centres would allow it finally to phase out the use of secondary schools as teaching venues, leading to an improvement in course quality in terms of the physical learning environment.[210]

As the School was gaining financial autonomy during the mid-1990s, it became more determined to enhance the quantity and quality of its teaching facilities.

The first major attempt to expand its teaching accommodation during this period was the relocation of the Town Centre. After having operated in the Shun Tak Centre for ten years, the SPACE Town Centre was no longer in excellent condition by 1996 and needed to undergo internal renovation at a cost of more than $10 million. Faced with such a huge renovation bill, SPACE decided in December 1996 to look into alternative locations for the teaching centre.[211] It was soon found that the third floor of Admiralty Centre, with a gross floor area of over 50,000 square feet and directly accessible from the Admiralty MTR station, was suitable for SPACE to set up a new teaching centre. The University agreed in April 1997 to purchase the premises for approximately $400 million using its own funds and a bank mortgage. The new premises would be divided into two parts, with SPACE occupying 30,000 square feet of floor area.[212] The new Admiralty Learning Centre was quickly refurbished and came into operation on 27 October 1997.[213] It housed twenty-one high-quality teaching rooms, a computer laboratory, a meeting room, a part-time tutors' room and Traditional Chinese Medicine clinics.[214] The Admiralty Learning Centre continued expanding over the next few years, housing more classrooms, offices, and an expanded Chinese Medicine clinic. This well-equipped and centrally-located learning centre, together with the School's other office and learning facilities in adjoining commercial buildings in Admiralty, has now become the principal off-campus teaching space used by HKU SPACE.

Apart from the relocation of the flagship Town Centre to Admiralty, the School purchased or leased other premises in Admiralty, Causeway Bay, North Point, Tsim Sha Tsui, and most recently Kowloon Bay for setting up learning centres.[215] Each of these learning centres is close to an MTR station and is therefore convenient for commuters. Learning centres designed for different purposes allow the School to offer courses which require specific facilities, such as Art and Design, Information Technology, and Chinese Medicine. The Island East Campus and the new Kowloon East Campus, opened in November 2002 and February 2007 respectively, are entirely occupied by the School's Community College and therefore it has been possible to utilise internal space more efficiently. In September 2005, HKU SPACE occupied 357,580 square feet of permanent teaching space, which was more than ten times the space occupied in 1991. The combined learning centres provided 178 lecture rooms and 34 computer laboratories and studios with a seating capacity of 15,360.[216] The new Kowloon East campus adds a further fifty classrooms, several laboratories, studios and a library, bringing the total floor area of all the School's premises to 644,265 square feet in January 2007.[217] These figures show the astonishing pace of expansion in the teaching accommodation of HKU SPACE in recent years, an expansion which has been necessary to keep pace with soaring enrolments and the introduction of many new programmes.

China Development

The link between HKU SPACE and China can be traced back to surprisingly early years. In 1966, Roger Williams, at that time Deputy Director of Extra-Mural Studies, organised the first and only study tour to Beijing.[218] This early development was curtailed because of retrenchment in the Department of Extra-Mural Studies in the mid-1960s and continuing political turmoil in China. Professor Lee Ngok recognised the potential of the 'colossal education market' in China in the 1980s and hoped that joint ventures would flourish between Hong Kong institutions and Chinese partners. But he was also cautious about exploiting this market and felt that 'providers will need to make shrewd strategic choices before they see the fruition of their efforts'.[219] Since the mid-1980s, therefore, the DEMS has established a number of important contacts with the Chinese Mainland. The earliest attempt came in mid-1987 when the International Institute of Technology and Business Management, a local organisation with very good contacts in China, invited the Department of Extra-Mural Studies to organise a certificate programme in Management for executives from China in Hong Kong.[220] Later, the first course offered jointly with a mainland university was introduced in 1988, when the DEMS started a Certificate in Social Studies programme for employees of Xinhua News Agency in collaboration with Jinan University in Guangzhou. Students who successfully completed the course were recognised as Diploma graduates of the Jinan University.[221]

By 1993, SPACE was convinced that 'provision of courses in China may become a significant part of the School's operation' in the future, and included provision of continuing and professional education services to China as part of its first mission statement.[222] The University also endorsed the role of SPACE in promoting such programmes for China and the surrounding region, and further suggested that the School should consider trying to conduct these programmes outside Hong Kong.[223] By early 1998, the School was offering three courses in China in partnership with Jinan University, and five other courses were offered in Hong Kong in collaboration with mainland institutions such as Fudan University and the Shanghai University of Traditional Chinese Medicine. All these programmes were at diploma or sub-diploma level, covering various subjects in Accounting, Business Studies, Social Studies or Chinese Medicine.[224] However, for political and regulatory reasons there was still little substantial development of the School's ventures in relation to the Chinese Mainland before Enoch Young assumed the directorship of SPACE in 1997–98. In the last ten years, Dr Michael Luk has been closely involved with the Director in overseeing the development of SPACE's programmes in China.

The huge demand for continuing and professional education services generated by rapid economic development in China during the 1990s provided incredible opportunities for SPACE to expand its activities in the Mainland. After the handover of Hong Kong to China in 1997, HKU and SPACE were increasingly aware that links with China provided a new opportunity to assist in the modernisation of China in a way which was gratifyingly consistent with the original aims of Lord Lugard and the founders of the University. Provision of educational opportunities to China therefore became more central to the University's mission, and SPACE, with the active encouragement of Vice-Chancellor Patrick Y. C. Cheng, was eager to bring its educational expertise into the Chinese continuing and professional education market.[225]

The School's new ventures in China can be divided into four categories. The first area consists of the many short courses, seminars and exchange activities which are conducted either in Hong Kong or China for Mainland officials, executives and professionals. In most cases participants are not awarded any formal academic qualification, and the format of these activities varies enormously. For example, since mid-2000 HKU SPACE has offered a number of customised short courses for executives and senior officials, which usually last for one to three weeks, through the Centre for Executive Development (CED). Between July 2003 and June 2004, thirty-five senior executive courses were held.[226] The CED also organises a number of mainland study programmes for Hong Kong professionals and executives in order to facilitate mutual understanding between Hong Kong and China.[227] Recently, there have been increased demands for executive training, and an Executive Certificate in Anti-Corruption Studies has been offered to more than 160 government officials of the Beijing Municipal Economic Reform Commission and the Commission for Discipline Inspection.[228]

The second area of collaboration is similar to the School's partnerships with other overseas universities. SPACE and mainland universities offer joint programmes in Hong Kong, and students are awarded academic qualifications by the mainland universities upon the completion of their programmes. The mainland institutions are responsible for the curriculum, maintaining academic standards and assessment, while SPACE provides local support and contributes to the teaching of the programmes. The School started its first mainland degree programme leading to a Second Degree in Chinese Law awarded by Tsinghua University in 1999.[229] This was followed by the two-year part-time Bachelor and Master programmes in Accounting in collaboration with Dongbei University of Finance and Economics in 2001.[230] In recent years, there have also been attempts to offer other undergraduate and postgraduate programmes in Chinese Medicine and Sports Education.

The third area of School co-operation with mainland institutions has been in offering programmes which were conducted on the Chinese Mainland. The first examples of such collaboration were the courses jointly organised by SPACE and Jinan University from the late 1980s. This type of venture was later extended to courses for higher degrees and in September 1998 a two-year part-time International Master of Business Administration (IMBA) programme was jointly organised in

Shanghai by the HKU School of Business, HKU SPACE and Fudan University. This was the first HKU degree programme which was taught mainly outside Hong Kong. While all three participating institutions contributed to teaching this self-funded programme, Fudan University played an essential role by providing the teaching facilities, while SPACE was specifically responsible for operational arrangements.[231] This scheme laid a strong foundation for subsequent joint ventures between HKU SPACE and other mainland institutions.

The fourth type of collaboration between the School and Chinese institutions has required a greater input of resources and a higher level of commitment. Since 1999 HKU SPACE has established teaching centres in various mainland cities to act as School 'outposts' in developing continuing and professional educational services in China. During 1998–99 the School invested $5 million on behalf of HKU in an experimental attempt to develop the Tsinghua University–University of Hong Kong Shenzhen Research and Development Centre.[232] This Centre was opened on 7 October 1999 in the Research Institute of Tsinghua University in Shenzhen with the objective of promoting academic collaboration between the two universities.[233]

The first formal teaching centre of HKU SPACE in China was established in Shanghai in partnership with 'Forward', a publicly listed subsidiary of Fudan University, at Shanghai Central Plaza on 8 September 2000.[234] This development resulted from the close ties established between HKU and Professor Yang Fujia, President of Fudan University, who was impressed by the work of SPACE when he visited Hong Kong in 1997–98.[235] The Shanghai Learning Centre, providing seven teaching rooms, a computer laboratory and an office suite, was the first teaching centre operated by a Hong Kong higher education institution in the Chinese Mainland.[236] HKU SPACE made an initial investment of US$1 million in the venture and took up financial and legal liability as well as responsibility for academic administration, while the Forward company was responsible for the daily operation of the Learning Centre.[237] In the first two semesters the School and other HKU faculties offered at least ten courses at postgraduate or diploma level in HKU SPACE Shanghai, and the range of programmes was extended to Master-level courses in September 2001.[238] In the following years, a number of HKU SPACE learning centres on a smaller scale were opened in Beijing, Shanghai, Hangzhou, Guangzhou and Zhuhai in partnership with different institutions.[239] It is now generally recognised that there is a huge potential market for continuing and professional education courses in China, and HKU SPACE has ambitions to take a lead among Hong Kong providers in the years to come.

The School's activities in China are still in their initial stages and have certainly had their fair share of setbacks. Since the very beginning of its China activities, HKU SPACE realised that there were bound to be lengthy and exhausting negotiations before the School would be able to secure approval from mainland authorities to start new projects in China.[240] The School must comply with numerous regulations controlling partnership arrangements, taxation, admission of students and academic qualifications. These regulations are complex, vary considerably across the country and change frequently.[241] The School has had to take on a larger-than-usual level of risk because of managerial difficulties, heavy capital commitment and the high financial risk involved in every project in China.[242] The Shanghai Learning Centre, for example, was once regarded by HKU SPACE as its 'flagship' in China, but the venture was discontinued in 2005. There were many reasons for this failure. The learning centre in Shanghai incurred much higher operational costs than were expected and there were difficulties working with a commercial partner when the number of courses and enrolments in these courses failed to meet the original targets.[243] New legislation which took effect in China in September 2003 was fatal to the project since it banned any partnerships with non-educational institutions, including the School's Fudan partner, the 'Forward' company.[244] There was also some criticism in Hong Kong that the School's activities in China appeared to be too scattered and lacked any clear direction.[245]

These sorts of problems are bound to continue in the Chinese continuing and professional education market for some years to come, but SPACE's 'painful episode' in Shanghai and other problems with its China operations have not weakened the School's confidence in the future development opportunities in China.[246] The School's various projects in China admitted over 1,000 students and generated 10 million yuan of revenue for HKU SPACE in 2003–04, and by 2006 the total student enrolment in China increased by one-third.[247] While the School has decided to go back to its traditional policy of starting programme-based projects rather than establishing more learning centres in China, it is still enthusiastic about the Global College project in Suzhou, which involves a campus of fifteen hectares and enrolments of more than 300 students in 2005–06 (see Chapter 8).[248] This project, on a scale never before contemplated by HKU SPACE, has been recognised by the Jiangsu government as one of the 'Ten Best Privately Run Colleges' in the province, and is indicative of the School's determination to explore further opportunities in the continuing and professional education market in China. As economic growth accelerates in China, it seems likely that the demand for high-quality adult education programmes will continue to grow, and HKU SPACE is undoubtedly in a very strong position to make a significant impact in this field in the next ten years.

Conclusion

Despite difficulties and setbacks in the last fifteen years, there can be no doubt that HKU's School of Professional and Continuing Education has made an impressive contribution in its provision of adult education and lifelong learning opportunities in Hong Kong and the surrounding region. The keen competition in the local continuing and professional education market has not affected the status of HKU SPACE as the leading provider in Hong Kong.[249] High academic standards have been maintained by teaching staff and a comprehensive quality assurance system has been introduced to much acclaim. A close working relationship with the University of Hong Kong and reputable overseas universities, together with a wide diversity of programmes and improving teaching facilities, have continued to attract students from all walks of life, especially professionals and executives.[250] In 2005–06, the School offered 1,077 programmes with 4,022 part-time courses or modules and a local enrolment of 111,708 (18,962 FTE).[251] The new programmes being offered in China and the pre-degree opportunities provided by the Community College, which will be discussed in the next chapter, have been impressive bearing in mind that these initiatives are at an early stage of development. HKU SPACE has grown into a huge enterprise providing quality educational services for students who cannot or who prefer not to pursue their studies at a university in the conventional way. In this sense the School continues to honour the primary objectives of adult education adopted by the University half a century ago.

CHAPTER EIGHT

The Community Colleges, 2000–2007

THROUGHOUT ITS FIRST FIFTY YEARS, HKU's School of Professional and Continuing Education has aimed at providing a wide range of opportunities for part-time adult higher education to the Hong Kong community. Most of its programmes were conducted in the evenings and on weekends, and a large proportion of its students were adults who were occupied with their families or jobs while studying at SPACE. From 2000, however, the School started to be involved in an even broader range of educational services to the community through full-time sub-degree programmes offered by a new HKU SPACE Community College. The Community College today offers Associate Degree (AD) and Higher Diploma (HD) programmes to young secondary-school-leavers who want to acquire further generic skills and professional expertise for articulation into higher education or employment. Although the new full-time sub-degree programmes are significantly different from the School's traditional activities in terms of the composition of the student population, administration, and the modes of course delivery and assessment, they nevertheless conform to the School's fundamental objective of providing lifelong learning opportunities to members of the community. Faced with various challenges and constraints as its sub-degree programmes have developed since 2000, HKU SPACE has managed to extend its services in this area by offering top-up degree programmes for Associate Degree and Higher Diploma graduates and opening more community colleges in Hong Kong and the Chinese Mainland. Despite its short history, the Community College has become an integral and distinctive branch of present-day HKU SPACE, and an important part of an attempt by the Hong Kong government to extend the benefits of higher education to a larger portion of the post-secondary population.

HKU SPACE Community College: Establishment and Administration

The establishment of HKU SPACE Community College was closely connected with the government's post-1997 education reforms. In the second consultation paper on the framework for education reform published in September 1999, the Education Commission outlined the necessity to 'encourage the establishment of various types of post-secondary colleges' offering full-time courses as one of the paths for secondary-school-leavers to pursue their studies.[1] SPACE immediately recognised that it could play an active role in this major government policy initiative:

> (a) SPACE has a philosophy of access to a ladder of educational opportunity which in principle can be extended to reach this demand [for post-secondary colleges];
> (b) A number of courses may already be able to meet this need or may be adapted to do so;
> (c) There is significant under-utilised day time capacity in the SPACE learning centres which could be taken up to meet this demand. Moreover, these centres are at convenient downtown locations.[2]

The School commissioned a consultant to advise on how it could best respond to the government's call, and in October 1999 the American 'community college' concept was adopted for the development of HKU SPACE's full-time post-secondary programmes.[3]

Community colleges in the United States aim to offer a 'low-cost, flexible post-secondary education that allows students to equip themselves for the work environment as well as to seek progression to complete a university degree'.[4] Most American community colleges offer two-year programmes leading to the Associate Degree qualification, which is equivalent to completing studies at the second-year undergraduate level. The composition fees of community colleges are often lower than those of universities so that more students can afford to further their studies after high school. The community college system has a long history in America, which can be traced back to the 1890s when the newly established University of Chicago started to offer a two-year junior undergraduate programme. This was followed by the establishment of the first public community college in Joliet, Illinois in 1901.[5] The twentieth century saw the evolution of this mode of higher education into a national network, with more than 1,100 community colleges teaching 44 per cent of the whole undergraduate student population in the United States by 2003.[6] The success of the community college system in the United States provided a well-tested and workable model for HKU SPACE to develop full-time post-secondary education in Hong Kong.

The School's 'community college' approach was adopted by the Education Commission as a crucial part of the wider educational reform in Hong Kong.[7] In the final proposal for educational reform in September 2000, the Commission outlined clearly its proposal for creating a community college network in Hong Kong. It defined community colleges in Hong Kong as being those parts of the higher education system which perform one or more of the following functions:

(a) providing learners with an alternative route to higher education which, to a certain extent, articulates with university programmes;
(b) providing a second opportunity to learners who have yet to attain qualifications at secondary level through formal education; and
(c) providing a variety of learning opportunities to assist individual learners to acquire skills and qualifications to enhance their employability.[8]

In order to differentiate community colleges from the more conventional matriculation studies with their rigid curricula and examination-oriented teaching modes, the Education Commission laid down some basic operational principles for community colleges in Hong Kong. Community colleges were to have more lenient entry requirements than universities, but the quality of the exit qualification would be stringently monitored. Colleges were to provide flexible modes of learning, including lectures, group discussions and projects, online learning and correspondence courses. The course duration would also be flexible enough to allow students to learn at their own pace. Most importantly, the community colleges would not be publicly funded. They would therefore need to secure financial support from student fees, the private sector and non-governmental organisations, and the government would only help the community colleges through policies and start-up assistance such as the provision of premises and land.[9] The Commission's proposals were echoed by the Chief Executive in his 2000 Policy Address, in which he promised to create 28,000 additional places for higher education so that 60 per cent of senior secondary-school-leavers would be able to receive tertiary education.[10]

Before the government declared its final policy on the post-secondary education system, HKU SPACE had already begun planning in early 2000 for the first community college in Hong Kong. The scheme for a HKU SPACE Community College was quickly drafted. The School envisaged that its Associate Degree programmes would equip students with critical skills for further studies or employment, as well as general education for civil citizenship.[11] The programmes as originally planned would consist of three levels, each of which required one year of full-time studies. The first two levels, leading to the Certificate in General Studies (CGS) and the Advanced Certificate in General Studies (ACGS), would teach both generic and specific skills. The third-level students would choose an Associate Degree programme specialising in Arts, Applied Science, Business Studies, General Studies, or Professional Studies, and there would be a high degree of flexibility enabling the students to enter and exit the Associate Degree system.[12] Secondary Five and Seven graduates could be admitted to different levels according to their previous academic achievements, and all students who completed each level would be entitled to a qualification, without the need to complete all three levels for the final Associate Degree qualification.[13] It was envisaged that the AD programmes would be taught 'through a more flexible, holistic and student-centered approach', which would include traditional lectures, seminars and workshops, but also project-based learning and continuous assessment. This academic programme would be supported by counselling services and the SPACE Online Universal Learning system (SOUL).[14]

Approval of the plan in February 2000 by the HKU SPACE Board of Directors and the Board of Continuing and Professional Education and Lifelong Learning allowed the Vice-Chancellor, Professor Patrick Y. C. Cheng, to announce the establishment of the HKU SPACE Community College on 14 March 2000.[15] The first task of the new College was to build a core group of staff to prepare the college for its first student intake in the autumn of 2000. Ms Jennifer Ng, Head of the Division of Finance and Business at HKU SPACE, was appointed to be Acting College Principal and was directly responsible to the Director of HKU SPACE. Ms Currie Tsang, who had been Assistant Registrar at the London Institute, became the College Academic Secretary in July 2000.[16] The College also managed to appoint an educational counsellor, twenty full-time teachers, and a small executive and clerical staff within a very short time.[17] In the first six months, this core team prepared and executed the whole action plan for Hong Kong's first associate degree programme. This included devising course syllabuses, drafting regulations, seeking suitable accommodation and beginning to recruit high-quality students.[18] The School's foresight was repaid in the summer and autumn of 2000, when the College successfully attracted 6,600 applications, nearly nine times the number of places available for the first intake. An inauguration ceremony for the College was held in Loke Yew Hall on 27 September 2000, with 494 Certificate and 199 Advanced Certificate students commencing their courses in the General Studies programme in October 2000.[19]

The management of the College in the first couple of years took some time to mature. A significant number of the leading officers were seconded from HKU SPACE and were required to perform duties concurrently in both the School and the Community College. The administration was strengthened when Professor K. F. Cheng, a former Dean of Science at HKU, assumed the post of College Principal in October 2001.[20] The College management was restructured in September 2002, with a College Management Committee consisting of the principal officers of the School and the College being formed to advise the School Director on the management of the College.[21] The College Council, which was later renamed as the Advisory Council, was also established at this time, consisting largely of external members and aiming at advising the College on matters of strategic development.[22] The College Management Committee reports to the HKU SPACE Board of

Directors through the Director, and receives guidance from the Advisory Council. There is also an academic governance mechanism, which will be mentioned below, to ensure the academic quality of the College. The Community College has developed a strong administrative structure over the last seven years, in which the College Principal oversees the operation of the College with support from a Deputy Principal (Professor K. W. Ng), two Vice Principals (Dr F. T. Chan and Ms Currie Tsang), as well as domain co-ordinators and other officers.[23]

Challenges and Achievements

Being the first community college to be established in Hong Kong, HKU SPACE Community College has been a trailblazer in delivering full-time sub-degree programmes, and this has meant that the College has had to face many uncertainties and challenges in its formative years. As community colleges and associate degrees were totally new concepts in Hong Kong, the government, the universities, and even HKU SPACE itself did not have much experience in delivering these programmes. Likewise, the general public did not know what to expect and this posed a number of obstacles to the College's development. Rapid changes in public demand for post-secondary education, severely limited resources, weak public confidence in Associate Degree qualifications, the need to improve students' performance and keen competition from other providers have all compelled the College to go to extraordinary efforts in establishing its programmes. Despite these challenges, the College has managed to secure a leading role in the provision of sub-degree programmes in Hong Kong over the last seven years and has now turned its attention to assisting with the development of the HKU SPACE Global College at Suzhou and the HKU SPACE Po Leung Kuk Community College in Causeway Bay.

Programmes

One of the remarkable achievements of the College in the past seven years has been its ability to diversify and improve the range of programmes it offers. The initial three-level programme structure lasted for only a short period because all Associate Degree programmes were ultimately expected to conform to the common descriptors imposed by the government. The Community College's Associate Degree programme was therefore reorganised according to a two-tier structure in the second academic year (2001–02). The Certificate of General Studies programme was retitled as the Pre-Associate Degree (Pre-AD) programme, while the Advanced Certificate of General Studies programme was incorporated into the new two-year Associate Degree programme as the first year of the curriculum (AD-I). In the same year, four

AD programmes were introduced: Associates of Arts, Business Administration, Applied Science in Information Technology, and Applied Science in Life Science. The College has continued to expand the diversity of its Associate Degree curriculum in recent years by providing two additional programmes: the Associate of Applied Science in Physical Science and the Associate of Arts in Legal Studies. The student population in all Associate Degree programmes was 3,101 in February 2006 and had risen slightly to 3,123 by December 2006.[24] All Associate Degree programmes focus on the development of both generic skills and academic knowledge. Students take compulsory courses in English, Chinese and Putonghua at each level, and they are also required to attend various core and elective courses related to their specialist areas. In the second year of the Associate Degree programmes (AD-II), students choose specific themes which allow them to develop a deeper understanding of a particular field. This curricular structure allows students to develop generic skills and specialist academic knowledge in tandem during their studies at the College.

Despite the merits of the Associate Degree curriculum, the School and the College soon found that their programmes did not always satisfy the needs of school-leavers, especially those who wanted to develop vocational or professional skills in order to start their careers earlier. HKU SPACE first tried to meet this demand by taking part in 'Project Springboard' and putting it under the direction of the Community College. Aiming 'to provide additional opportunity for those not succeeding at HKCEE level', the project was initiated by the Education and Manpower Bureau and was implemented by members of the Federation for Continuing Education. The Project Springboard programme was to be taught over one year on a full-time basis, and covered basic generic knowledge as well as some specialised subjects such as Accounting, Insurance and Nutritional Science. The successful students received a certificate comparable to five HKCEE passes for employment purposes.[25] The College started the first course for Project Springboard in October 2000.

The College's participation in Project Springboard was short-lived. HKU SPACE was not very enthusiastic about the Project from the start because the academic level of the programme was much lower than that which the School was hoping to establish for its other programmes. The School participated in the Project because, as a Federation of Continuing Education founding member, it considered it important to lend support to the Federation's scheme.[26] The actual enrolment figures were also not encouraging. The College planned to offer 400 to 450 places in the 2000–01 academic year, but only 276 students were admitted and 176 of them completed the programme.[27] The enrolment for the programme dropped to 168 in the next academic year, and the School therefore ceased to provide courses for the project from the end of the 2001–02 academic year.[28]

The School and the College tried from the start to offer full-time vocationally-oriented programmes which would equip students with both generic skills and, more importantly, specialist skills suitable for particular professions. The College proposed in April 2001 to start three-year Career Development Programmes (CDPs), intending to convert some of the School's existing part-time diploma courses into full-time mode. Following the original structure of the Associate Degree programmes, the Career Development Programmes were based on a three-tier system which allowed students to enrol in and leave programmes according to their needs. Secondary Five graduates could start their studies at the first-year Certificate level, while Secondary Seven graduates could enrol directly in the second-year Diploma course, which was later retitled as the Advanced Certificate. Students would be awarded a Higher Diploma qualification after completing a third year of studies, or the Certificate or Diploma after finishing the corresponding study level. The College proposed that about 30 per cent of the content of the programmes would focus on generic skills training, while the remaining 70 per cent would concentrate on the subject of specialism.[29] The first six Career Development Programmes, specialising in Sales, Marketing and Advertising, Information Technology, Accounting, Librarianship, Interior Design and Architecture, were offered in 2001–02, and the College continued to expand the Higher Diploma programmes in the following years. In February 2006, there were eighteen Higher Diploma programmes offering two-year or three-year curricula for 2,620 students and by December 2006 the number of students enrolled had risen significantly to 3,028.[30]

While the Community College has ploughed significant resources into programme diversification, it has also sought to ensure programme quality. Quality assurance is recognised as being particularity important for the HKU SPACE Community College for three reasons. First, high programme quality builds up public confidence in the community college system. Second, the College needs to compete with other providers in the sector and the best way of doing this is through quality. Third, the performance of the Community College impacts directly on the image of HKU SPACE and the University. The College has therefore maintained a comprehensive quality assurance mechanism since the very beginning of its operation and many of the quality assurance measures adopted are transplanted from systems which have been tried and tested at HKU SPACE or the University. An Academic Board consisting of the principal officers of the School and the College, programme teachers and representatives from the University has been established under the Quality Assurance Committee of HKU SPACE to supervise the College's overall academic standards.[31] As it is required to report to the Senate's Board of Continuing and Professional Education and Lifelong Learning via the School's Quality Assurance Committee, the University indirectly monitors the academic standards of the Community College. Introduction of new Associate Degree or Higher Diploma programmes must also go through the School's Internal

Validation procedure, in which syllabuses are scrutinised by internal and external assessors, and are approved by the University's Board of Continuing and Professional Education and Lifelong Learning. These measures are part of the larger SPACE Quality Assurance system whose purpose is to ensure that all HKU SPACE programmes meet the required standards.

Another key quality assurance measure has been the introduction of an academic assessors system. The College appoints external assessors for each subject area to 'review the course syllabuses and to comment on the delivery approach, course materials and all forms of assessments, including examination papers and standard of the students', a system which resembles HKU's external examiner system.[32] In 2003–04, thirty-eight assessors, mostly working at HKU, were appointed to oversee Pre-AD, AD and HD programmes. The system provides continuous and objective checks on programme quality, and also strengthens academic connections between the College and the University. The Quality Assurance system has been further supplemented by a number of other activities. Even though it does not participate in curriculum development, the College Advisory Council has functioned as a forum for external members to provide the College with suggestions on strategic curriculum development. Staff-Student Consultative Committee meetings (another system borrowed from HKU), student evaluation of teaching, meetings of Boards of Examiners and rigorous supervision of the whole system by the College Principal and domain co-ordinators also facilitate the improvement of academic programmes.

In the past seven years, therefore, the Community College has developed a diverse range of programmes for full-time post-secondary students which are supported by a sound Quality Assurance system. These developments have been appreciated by the Hong Kong community, the government and non-government educational bodies. The UGC's Second Teaching and Learning Quality Process Review (TLQPR) in 2003, for example, found that 'the Community College has adhered very much to the requirements for proper processes and procedures in curriculum design and delivery, the implementation and monitoring of quality in teaching and learning, and the use and application of student assessment'.[33] This commendation indicates that the College has made a sound start in quality assurance and has created a solid foundation upon which a world-class community college can be built.

Students

The Community College is an 'alternative route to higher education' and it was always anticipated that the majority of its students would be those who did not perform well in public examinations and are therefore denied entry into mainstream undergraduate studies via matriculation. In 2005–06, about 60 per cent of the Pre-

AD and HD-I students received only ten points or less in their HKCEE scores, and 52 per cent of the AD-I students achieved no more than four AL points in their HKALE score.[34] Such students are generally considered to possess inferior intellectual qualities and to be far less competent than better performing students in public examinations. One of the main tasks of the College, therefore, is to inspire these students to activate and develop their lifelong learning abilities and equip themselves with generic skills and specific expertise to prepare for further studies or employment. Academic programmes backed up with a sound quality assurance system (mentioned above) are the mainstay of the College's activities, but the mere provision of courses is far from being enough to accomplish the challenging task facing the College's managers and teachers. The Community College has sought to establish other academic and support services to encourage the intellectual and personal development of students. These support services have not in the past been necessary for part-time courses offered by HKU SPACE.

One of the commonest weaknesses among Associate Degree and Higher Diploma students has been that the standard of their English is generally poor when they are first admitted to the College. The College therefore devotes a great deal of time and effort trying to improve proficiency in English. The College offers a specialised Bi-Lingual Studies theme within the Associate of Arts programme, so that students with a particular interest in English can advance their studies through a number of content-based English courses such as Phonetics and Translation. Other students are exposed to as much English as possible. English language courses are compulsory for all students, and most other courses are also taught in English. Students are required to give presentations and conduct in-class discussion in English, and there are many facilities and activities to create an active English-language environment outside of classes. The Multimedia English Learning Centre in the Wanchai Learning Centre was established in 2002–03 to help students to practise speaking in English in their spare time.[35] The College organises speech competitions, essay competitions and student conferences to enhance students' confidence in using the English language in public.[36] Dr Lee Shiu, a member of the Advisory Council, proposed and sponsored a summer immersion programme in English in 2003 to allow one hundred College students to practice English by engaging them in communication with foreign teachers.[37] Students therefore have many opportunities to learn and advance their English at the College and this is, of course, completely in keeping with HKU's status as an English-language university.

Many students are serious about English education at the College because they recognise the importance of good English proficiency in further university studies and the Hong Kong employment market.[38] Diligent students seem to benefit a great deal from the College's activities and try to improve their English to a level comparable with local undergraduates. Some of them have even been benchmarked as good or competent users in the International English Language Testing System

(IELTS).[39] The academic assessors of the English subjects have also observed a fairly good quality of student performance in projects and examinations. The College's efforts in language education therefore help to prepare students for a more active use of English in both study and working environments.

Apart from their poor proficiency in English, many students admitted to the Community College also suffer from the serious failure of the conventional education system to cater for students who do not conform to the traditional expectations of the examiners. The secondary education system in Hong Kong has long been criticised for being too examination-oriented, giving students little room to think and develop independent minds. Public examinations are also known to impose high levels of stress on students, and those youngsters who possess potential for intellectual development do not necessarily perform well under this type of secondary education. They often lose any incentive to learn as a result of unsatisfactory performance in school, so the College must attempt to assist these students in identifying their own abilities and nurture their interest in learning.[40] The mode of learning at the College is similar to that at a university, emphasising analytical and critical thinking, self-motivation to learn, and there is a great deal of discussion with classmates and teachers. Students are assessed not only through examinations, but also according to their performance throughout the course, so that they do not suffer from unnecessary examination pressure. While the students initially find it difficult to adapt themselves to this new mode of learning, many of them soon enjoy learning in the university mode.[41]

There are other factors which give students greater incentives to learn. There is keen competition among AD/HD graduates for the limited number of places available at local universities and this compels them to work hard in order to secure good academic results. There are also scholarships and prizes available in the College which help in a material way to 'encourage students to excel in their studies'.[42] By the 2005–06 academic year, the College was offering six groups of scholarships and three groups of awards and prizes. The most prestigious scholarship is the Chan Tat Chee Scholarship, established in 2001 and awarded to the best Associate Degree student who gains admission to the second year of studies at the University of Birmingham in the United Kingdom. Awardees receive £10,000 annually for two years.[43] Another Chan Tat Chee Scholarship is awarded each year to the best student entering the second year English Studies major in the School of English at HKU. Dr Peter Lee, the trustee of the Scholarship, has praised the high standard of the awardees.[44] Another scholarship scheme, the 'HKU SPACE Community College Scholarships', was initiated in 2005. Seventy-five scholarships, valued at $10,000 each, were awarded in that year to current or newly admitted students on the basis of their academic performance at the College or in their previous secondary schools.[45] The honour and financial rewards from these scholarships encourage students to achieve better academic results at the College, especially those students wishing to articulate to undergraduate studies.

While the traditional part-time student of HKU SPACE is usually busy with both work and study, the full-time student of the Community College spends much of the day at the College. Moreover, the College not only regards itself as a 'provider' of knowledge and skills, but also aims at providing a path for 'whole-person development' of students.[46] Both the College and the students, therefore, organise a number of extra-curricular activities to enrich student life. The College worked with students to establish a student union in December 2002.[47] The Student Union organises activities independently of the College administration and co-ordinates student clubs and societies representing a wide range of sports and interests.[48] The College itself has also maintained a wide range of support services and extra-curricular activities for its students. It maintains counselling services to assist in students' personal and career development choices, and organises a student ambassador scheme, a mentorship scheme and a choir. Each year sees the organisation of an athletics meet, an orientation day and an exchange programme to China in collaboration with HKU. The Community College Alumni Association was established in October 2003 to strengthen the connection between graduates and the College.[49]

The College has therefore invested an enormous amount of effort in the academic and personal development of its students, and this has been appreciated by students, teachers and outside bodies. Unfortunately, all these achievements were hampered until recently by a lack of campus facilities and insufficient recognition of its qualifications by outside bodies. While the accommodation problem has now been largely solved with the opening of the Kowloon East campus, it is likely that it will take some time before the Community College's graduates receive proper recognition for their academic achievements.

Accommodation and Facilities

Lack of accommodation and facilities haunted the College until recently. With little government financial support, the College was unable to undertake the huge capital investment necessary to expand its facilities until a site was found in mid-2003. This serious problem restricted the development of the College, especially in terms of student life on campus. Even with the opening of the Kowloon East campus in February 2007, which has relieved the most pressing problems, the College sees a need to continue the search for more resources to support future expansion.

The accommodation of the College in the first year of operation was far from satisfactory. Most of the teaching was conducted at the Admiralty Learning Centre, while some classes were held on campus at HKU and staff offices were located at the United Centre in Admiralty.[50] Despite the convenient location, the Admiralty Learning Centre was originally designed for part-time courses and was not equipped with discussion areas, refreshment corners or a library suitable for full-time students.[51] It was also too small to accommodate the large number of full-time students who were recruited in the first year.[52] Finding larger and more suitable accommodation was therefore a high priority for the College during the first year of operation.

The School managed to find larger premises relatively quickly, and a new learning centre was opened on 14 September 2001 on the second floor of the Causeway Centre in Wanchai.[53] It was the second-largest learning centre of HKU SPACE at the time, providing 34,000 square feet of floor area for the Community College and the additional accommodation also proved to be a boon for the School's evening and weekend courses. In addition to the twenty classrooms and two computer laboratories, the Wanchai Learning Centre was also furnished with common areas and lockers to make it more comfortable for full-time students.[54] It was further enlarged to 50,000 square feet in September 2002, allowing the College to provide ten more classrooms, a specially designed computer room and the Multimedia English Learning Centre.[55] The Wanchai Learning Centre served as the College's head office and the main teaching venue for its Associate Degree programmes until the opening of the Kowloon East campus in February 2007.

The development of full-time Higher Diploma programmes required the School to search for additional space for the College. In October 2001, HKU SPACE signed an agreement to acquire a 23-storey building on 494 King's Road, North Point. The purchase was financed by a ten-year interest-free loan of $152 million from the government.[56] This building, given the name of Island East Campus, was opened on 11 November 2002. The Island East Campus initially provided 75,000 square feet of space for 1,600 full-time students. Its facilities include twenty-seven classrooms, two lecture theatres, three computer rooms, an architectural workshop and student activity rooms. These are used primarily for the Higher Diploma programmes but also service a few part-time HKU SPACE courses.[57]

These two new learning centres, in spite of their size and impressive facilities, did not entirely solve the problem of insufficient accommodation. Students were not satisfied with the physical environment of the College's two buildings, complaining in evaluation surveys about a lack of genuine campus life and suitable recreational and teaching facilities. They were also discontented with the rather limited access to computer facilities.[58] The Island East Campus in particular was criticised as being so small that students were not able to find resting places during breaks between lessons.[59] Although students of the Community College are allowed to use HKU libraries and sport facilities on the main campus, these facilities are a long way from the learning centres and students are therefore reluctant to use them.[60] While the College emphasises that teaching can still be conducted effectively without a large campus, lack of facilities has hindered self-study opportunities and extra-curricular activities.[61] Staff members shared these opinions of the students. As the College's teaching facilities and staff offices were scattered around the city, teachers often found it difficult to communicate with students.[62] Much time was wasted travelling between different venues for lessons and meetings, staff offices tended to be crowded, and there were few academic or support facilities made available for teachers. All these problems reduced the efficiency of the College's teaching and administration in the first six years of operation.

The main reason for this accommodation problem was the government's reluctance to subsidise community colleges. Since the very beginning of the education reform, the government made it clear that the community college system should be predominantly self-financing and should not rely on public funds. While some community colleges in Hong Kong share campuses with their parent institutions, the HKU SPACE Community College did not have this advantage because of the very limited space available on HKU's main campus, and so has had to spend much of its limited resources on accommodation. Without significant government support, the School and the College were not able to afford an expensive campus in town.

The self-financing policy has nevertheless been somewhat modified in recent years. In 2001–02, the government set up an interest-free loan fund of $5 billion for local community colleges to rent or buy premises.[63] HKU SPACE Community College immediately benefited from this fund and secured a total of $212 million in loans for the refurbishment of the Causeway Centre facility and the purchase and refitting of the Island East Campus. However, the most substantial direct aid from the government has come in the form of a grant of land for the construction of the new College campus in Kowloon Bay. In November 2002, the Government listed five sites for development as possible campuses for community colleges. In May 2003, HKU SPACE Community College was granted a 2,000 square-metre site in Kowloon Bay.[64] The land grant was followed by the government's interest-free ten-year loan of $279 million for the development of the site.[65] Although the Kowloon Bay site is located far away from the College's existing teaching facilities, it is conveniently connected to an MTR station and, most importantly, was large enough to provide a fairly spacious campus specially designed for the needs of the Community College. The construction of the thirteen-storey building started in October 2004 and the complex, with a floor area of over 15,000 square metres, was opened on 8 February 2007 and named after Dr and Mrs Lee Shiu, who donated $20 million towards the construction costs.[66] The new campus is designed to accommodate 3,000 full-time students and is equipped with fifty classrooms, a variety of laboratories and studios, a library, an auditorium, a multi-purpose sports centre and environmentally-friendly green areas on the upper levels. It will provide state-of-the-art facilities to the College's Associate Degree students, and will also accommodate part-time classes for SPACE students in the Kowloon area.[67] The Kowloon East campus has therefore provided the College's full-time Associate Degree students with a world-class learning environment which allows them to experience an all-round student life on a proper campus.

Recognition

The community college, being a very new form of post-secondary education in Hong Kong, has faced problems in gaining public recognition of its sub-degree qualifications, especially the novel associate degree. The role of the community colleges as an 'alternative route' to higher education will be greatly weakened if these new qualifications are not recognised by other educational institutions and employers. Unfortunately, the Hong Kong community initially seemed very reluctant to acknowledge qualifications gained in community colleges, perhaps because of the connection in people's minds between the colleges and students who had failed in public examinations. Despite the successes of the College's sub-degree programmes, there are still many in the community who are suspicious of graduates who hold Associate Degrees and Higher Diplomas. The government has refused to finance additional undergraduate places at the universities to accommodate qualified community college graduates who wish to articulate to full degree programmes, so local universities have been very cautious about admitting Associate Degree and Higher Diploma graduates to existing places at universities. Critics have even claimed that the community colleges produce sub-standard graduates with little hope of pursuing undergraduate studies, so there is currently a crisis in the perception of sub-degree qualifications in Hong Kong. As HKU SPACE Community College was the first community college to be established in Hong Kong, it faced extraordinary difficulties in convincing the public to recognise the academic standing of its qualifications. Although the College has made remarkable progress in educating the public about its qualifications, a negative attitude towards the Associate Degree and Higher Diploma qualifications still remains as one of the College's greatest challenges for the future.

The most important element of public confidence in the community college system is the recognition given to Associate Degree and Higher Diploma qualifications by local and overseas universities. Such recognition directly affects the ability of qualified community college graduates to proceed with their studies at higher levels, often regarded as the *raison d'être* of these sub-degree programmes. It is particularly important for the Associate Degree programmes as many of these students see the community college system as a stepping stone to full-time undergraduate university studies.[68] The initial responses from local and overseas universities were not, however, very encouraging. By December 2000, three months after the first Certificate and Advanced Certificate programmes had commenced at HKU SPACE Community College, only three overseas universities had granted the College's Associate Degree graduates exemption from the first year of undergraduate studies.[69] The number of overseas universities recognising the Associate Degree qualifications rose to thirty-four by the end of 2001–02, but most of them regarded the Associate Degree graduates as fulfilling the admission requirements for entry to the first year of their undergraduate degree programmes, rather than the second year of studies.[70]

More disappointing for the College, however, was the fact that even HKU, the College's parent university, was reluctant to recognise that its Associate Degree graduates had sufficient academic standing for automatic entry into the second-year undergraduate curricula. There was no co-ordination of admission policies at HKU for Associate Degree graduates applying to the different faculties, and by December 2000 only four faculties had indicated that they would regard both Advanced Certificate and Associate Degree graduates as satisfying entry requirements. Two of these four faculties were prepared to grant Associate Degree graduates very limited exemption from junior-level courses.[71] The reluctance of the faculties at this early stage was perhaps reasonable given the need to maintain strict admission criteria to control the quality of their students and the fact that they did not have any past experience of Associate Degree graduates in Hong Kong. However, this refusal to acknowledge that an Associate Degree qualified an applicant for entry to the second year of an undergraduate degree programme had a significant negative impact on public confidence in the sub-degree qualifications awarded by the HKU SPACE Community College and other community colleges.

The College, the School and even the UGC recognised this problem as a serious barrier to the acceptance of the community college concept in Hong Kong. From time to time, the College and the School repeated the worries of their Associate Degree and Higher Diploma students about qualification recognition, but these comments seemed to fall on deaf ears.[72] It was noted that local secondary schools had little interest in information seminars organised by the HKU SPACE Community College.[73] Career masters failed to support the College because there was no guarantee that its Associate Degree programmes would ensure a clear path articulating to further studies.[74] The UGC also noted in its Second TLQPR Report on the University in January 2003 that:

> Within a short period of time, the Community College of SPACE has demonstrated that it is capable of delivering high quality programmes and providing an alternative route for students wishing to progress towards university education . . . The major challenge for the College will be to demonstrate the value-added components of AD programmes, to address any negative perceptions associated with ADs, and to ensure that there are alternative attractive career and professional paths for those who may not choose to enter the university.[75]

The College had long understood that the essential means to improve the public's confidence in its sub-degree qualifications was to ensure the quality of its students and to increase the number of graduates being admitted to universities.[76] In fact, the College's work in articulation with universities has been intensive since the introduction of these programmes. HKU SPACE has organised full-time top-up degree programmes in collaboration with overseas universities for Associate Degree and Higher Diploma graduates of the College since the 2002–03 academic year. These top-up degree programmes were soon placed under the School's Centre for International Degree Programmes (CIDP). In 2006–07 there were fifty-five overseas higher education institutions recognising the College's Associate Degree and Higher Diploma qualifications for the purpose of admission to their undergraduate programmes (see Appendix 7).

A large number of the College's graduates have therefore succeeded in enrolling in local or overseas universities. In 2005, for example, at least 518 of the College's 793 AD graduates (65 per cent) continued their full-time studies at local or overseas universities. Among these, 135 were studying at HKU, 145 were enrolled at the Centre for International Degree Programmes, and thirteen were studying abroad. By the end of 2005 the College had successfully placed at least 2,682 of its graduates in undergraduate programmes at various universities.[77] In 2005–06, approximately 60 per cent of Community College graduates were admitted to degree programmes in Hong Kong and overseas, with 304 of the 1,303 students admitted to UGC-funded places at the University of Hong Kong. This brought the total number of graduates placed in degree programmes since the College's first year of operation to 3,982.[78]

In recent years the College has regularly received positive comments from HKU about the performance of the best of its Associate Degree graduates.[79] A few of these students perform particularly well and are placed on the Deans' Honours Lists, and some have graduated with First Class Honours degrees. The UGC's policy to subsidise 840 additional full-time second and third-year undergraduate places for Associate Degree graduates for the 2005–08 Triennium has further helped the College to increase the admission figures for its graduates articulating into degree programmes at local universities.[80] The forthcoming 3+3+4 education reform, which plans to transform the tertiary education sector from the existing three-year undergraduate curriculum into a four-year curriculum, is also foreseen by the College as a good opportunity to incorporate more fully the community college system into the first two years of the new undergraduate curriculum.[81] All these developments seem likely to improve the prospects of the College's graduates and strengthen public recognition of the Associate Degree and Higher Diploma qualifications.

Despite considerable progress in gaining recognition for AD and HD awards, public confidence in these qualifications should not be overstated as they have still not secured wide acceptance among universities or in society at large. The universities continue to recognise Associate Degree and Higher Diploma qualifications at their own discretion and normally admit the College's graduates on an individual basis. In fact, it has become clear that the UGC is unwilling to allow local universities to have any internal 'through-train' arrangements within their institutions which would allow sub-degree students to progress automatically to degree programmes in the same institution.[82] Moreover, the universities are still very cautious about the academic attainments of Associate Degree and Higher Diploma graduates. The College's Associate of Arts in Legal Studies graduates are not, for example, given advanced standing in admission exercises at any of the local universities offering LLB programmes.[83] In 2005, HKU's Faculty of Arts was concerned about whether students directly admitted into the second year of the Associate Degree programmes (AD-II) were well enough prepared for articulation to undergraduate studies, warning that students of the Community College should not 'develop any expectation that they have a good chance of gaining direct entry to our [Bachelor of Arts] second year'. At that time the Community College's hopes were frustrated by an Arts Faculty regression analysis which had indicated that there was a 'low correlation between GPAs attained by AD students at your [HKU SPACE Community] College and GPAs they attained in the BA curriculum at HKU'.[84] With further experience of admitting the College's graduates, however, HKU's Arts Faculty is now more confident in the ability of these students to undertake undergraduate studies, and in September 2006 the Faculty admitted seventy-seven AD and HD students, of whom eleven were directly admitted to the second year of the undergraduate degree.[85]

It is perhaps premature to make any conclusive statements about the College's full-time post-secondary programmes when so many challenges and difficulties still face a Community College which has existed for only seven years. In fact, at the moment it seems that the College is little affected by these drawbacks and continues to attract large enrolments every year. Indeed, the School's development of the community college concept has been further strengthened in recent years by the initiation of similar projects which are being pursued in both Hong Kong and the Mainland in parallel with HKU SPACE Community College.

Extension of the Community College Concept

The remarkable success of the HKU SPACE Community College despite numerous ongoing challenges and difficulties has convinced the School that the community college concept is sustainable and ready for further expansion. HKU SPACE has therefore initiated several projects associated with the community college system. Some of them are being directed by the HKU SPACE Community College itself while others are run separately from the College but maintain a close connection. Three of these developments will be discussed below: the Centre for International Degree Programmes, new opportunities on the Chinese Mainland and a collaboration with the Po Leung Kuk in Hong Kong.

Full-time Top-up Degree Programmes and the Centre for International Degree Programmes

Top-up degree programmes are designed for those students who want to use their Associate Degree or Higher Diploma qualifications as a foundation for undergraduate studies in another institution which allows them to gain a bachelor's degree within a shorter period of time than the usual candidature. HKU SPACE has for many years organised part-time degree programmes in which students with previous academic or working experience are exempted from some examinations and can therefore finish their studies earlier. This arrangement has its merits in preventing students from re-studying what they have already done and hence maximises the benefit which they receive from their new studies. This arrangement can also be applied to community college graduates, who are considered to have finished the junior part of the undergraduate curriculum and are therefore thought to be capable of starting their university studies at a higher level than other secondary-school graduates.

Unfortunately, many AD and HD graduates wishing to continue their studies face difficulties in finding such advanced places at local universities, and it is often not viable for them to study abroad. HKU SPACE has therefore provided these students and especially those graduating from its own Community College with a faster and less expensive way to complete undergraduate studies and secure a bachelor's degree through full-time, self-financed top-up degree programmes. These programmes recognise the Associate Degree and Higher Diploma graduates as having attained a sufficient level of competence in undergraduate studies to allow them to finish the degree programmes within a shorter period, usually two years. It is also envisaged that involving overseas universities in the programmes helps to develop the international vision of students and broaden their horizons.

Middlesex University in the United Kingdom was the School's first partner in full-time top-up degree programmes, having offered a joint programme leading to the Bachelor of Arts in Media and Cultural Studies since 2002. This is a two-year full-time programme available for the College's Associate of Arts graduates majoring in Media and Cultural Studies, but other Associate Degree graduates can also be considered for admission. Classes are held in Hong Kong and are jointly taught by lecturers from Middlesex University and HKU SPACE. The curriculum is similar to that provided in the United Kingdom at the Middlesex campus, but courses taught in Hong Kong also consider the local context.[86] In 2002–03 HKU SPACE added another full-time top-up degree programme for its Associate Degree graduates which leads to the Bachelor of Science in Business of the University of London, with the London School of Economics as the lead school.[87]

When these full-time top-up degree programmes were first introduced, there was no distinct unit within HKU SPACE to manage them. It was for this reason that in March 2003, the School established the Centre for International Degree Programmes (CIDP) to develop this new area of SPACE's work.[88] Headed by Dr Dorothy Chan, who was concurrently Associate Director of HKU SPACE and Vice-Principal of the Community College, the Centre for International Degree Programmes was set up as a branch of the School but worked closely with the Community College on the development of top-up degrees for the College's graduates. Since July 2004, the CIDP has occupied the sixth floor of the United Centre where its permanent teaching rooms and administrative offices are located.[89]

Although top-up degree programmes provide Associate Degree and Higher Diploma graduates with a feasible and efficient solution to further studies, they were not initially popular among the qualified AD and HD graduates. Enrolments in the first two programmes were lower than expected because many potential students seemed to prefer part-time to full-time top-up programmes.[90] However, later Associate Degree and Higher Diploma graduates seem to have realised the merits of the full-time mode of study and more of them are now choosing to study through the Centre for International Degree Programmes. In 2004–05, there were 716 full-time students studying in fourteen programmes in collaboration with six overseas universities, and by 2007 there were 896 students enrolled in fifteen programmes offered by seven overseas universities.[91] The number of programmes and the students enrolled in them are expected to grow over the next few years. This development is an important means of increasing the number of AD and HD graduates who can articulate their studies into full-time undergraduate programmes, and is a key strategy in gaining wider acceptance for these sub-degree programmes.

Links with the Chinese Mainland

In the past decade, the American community college model was established not only in Hong Kong, but also in the Chinese Mainland. The first community college in China was set up in Jinshan, Shanghai, in 1994 and since then a number of community colleges or similar educational institutions have appeared across China offering sub-degree and non-qualification-bearing programmes.[92] Since the 1990s HKU SPACE has worked to extend its educational services to the Chinese Mainland (see Chapter 7), and after the establishment of the Community College, the School began to make use of its experience in full-time sub-degree programmes to initiate community college projects as a part of the School's expansion in China.

The first pilot project was implemented in Zhuhai, Guangdong province, in October 2002 when HKU SPACE collaborated with Beijing Normal University's Zhuhai campus to offer a '2+2' programme. The students in this programme spent the first two years in Zhuhai to acquire an Associate Degree in Business Administration awarded by HKU SPACE, and the next two years at one of thirty-four overseas universities which recognised the Associate Degree qualification of HKU SPACE. Alternatively, they could proceed with their studies in Zhuhai and receive a degree from the Beijing Normal University after meeting all the usual degree requirements.[93] The School was at first very ambitious about the potential of this pilot project, and in January 2003 it expected that two hundred mainland students and one hundred Hong Kong students would enrol in this scheme annually.[94] The actual numbers were much smaller and the plan to admit Hong Kong students to the Zhuhai programme was soon abandoned.[95] Only twenty-three mainland students graduated two years after the inauguration of the programme, and fifteen of them went on to pursue their studies overseas.[96] Despite these disappointingly small numbers, HKU SPACE still considered the pilot programme to have been a success and was eager to continue the partnership in Zhuhai for a few more years.[97] Beijing Normal University terminated the scheme in August 2005, however, because of 'a change of internal policy'. Some of the students switched to other programmes offered by Beijing Normal University, while others continued their studies either at overseas institutions, the HKU SPACE Community College in Hong Kong, or the community college which was newly established by HKU SPACE in Suzhou, Jiangsu province.[98]

HKU SPACE started an extensive project to develop a community college in Suzhou in March 2003.[99] For this joint venture the School entered into a partnership with the Global EduTech Management Group (GEM), a privately-owned educational investment, holding and management firm with a Malaysian Chinese background, and the University of Science and Technology of Suzhou, a public tertiary institution. After a year of negotiation with the two partners and local and provincial authorities, a contract was signed by the three partners on 10 March 2004.[100] The new community college, later named the HKU SPACE Global College, would be built in the Suzhou Industrial Park and aimed to 'train manpower with a global vision to meet demand following the tremendous economic growth of Suzhou and the Yangtze River Delta', especially after China's entry into the World Trade Organization.[101] Total investment in the project amounted to 20 million yuan, of which 9 million yuan was provided by HKU SPACE.[102]

In view of the School's bitter experience in attempting to maintain control over its previous joint ventures in China, HKU SPACE bargained for stronger administrative and academic power in the Suzhou project. Leading posts in the Global College were held by Hong Kong academics. Professor C. F. Lee, Pro-Vice-Chancellor of HKU, was invited to be the College President and to supervise the overall management of the Global College. Professor C. K. Leung, a former Dean of Arts at HKU who had previously worked in the Department of Extra-Mural Studies (1965–73) as one of its first staff tutors, returned to HKU SPACE as College Executive President to supervise the Global College on site. The daily operation of the Global College was undertaken by a new company of which HKU SPACE and

GEM held equal shares, but HKU SPACE enjoyed 'a casting vote on all academic matters and management decisions related to those academic matters'.[103] The GEM company is mainly responsible for developing the campus which will ultimately occupy fifteen hectares in the Suzhou Industrial Park. Before the new campus is available in 2007, the Global College is being housed in a government composite building in the Industrial Park.

HKU SPACE managed to gain approval from provincial authorities to establish the tripartite partnership in July 2004, but further permission was required which involved even more lengthy and complex negotiations to launch educational programmes in Suzhou. The Global College admitted its first cohort of students to a Zhuhai-model '2+2' Associate Degree programme in October 2004.[104] It was able to start the programme in a relatively short period of time because two-year AD programmes were outside the control of the conventional education system in China and therefore required simpler procedures for approval. After fourteen months of negotiations with the provincial government, in May 2005 the Global College was finally allowed to offer three-year *dazhuan* programmes leading to a qualification which is officially recognised in China as a sub-degree diploma.[105] Apart from the *dazhuan* qualification, the students will also be awarded an Associate Degree from HKU SPACE upon graduation and will therefore be eligible for further studies in Hong Kong or overseas. In September 2005, the first batch of 220 *dazhuan* students, the majority of whom came from Jiangsu province, commenced their studies in four streams in Business Administration, Marketing, Accounting and Logistics.[106] HKU SPACE now wishes to take further steps to obtain degree-granting status for the Global College so that it can provide a platform for HKU and the School's overseas partners to offer degree courses in China.[107]

While HKU SPACE has 'exported' its expertise in post-secondary education to the Chinese mainland, it has also 'imported' mainland students to study in its sub-degree programmes in Hong Kong. Since September 2003, the Community College has been recruiting students from China to study its Associate Degree programmes in Hong Kong. The College initially planned to admit 80 to 100 Shenzhen secondary school graduates to study two-year AD programmes at the College from September 2004. These students would pay tuition fees at a slightly higher level than Hong Kong students which, together with accommodation and living expenses, would put the cost of an Associate degree at about $100,000 for the two years of study.[108]

There were three major problems in implementing this scheme. First, while HKU SPACE was putting a lot of effort into developing its connections in China, the Community College had virtually no reputation or network in the China market. The College had to find an appropriate channel to promote its programmes, and this was a difficult task. The College first collaborated with two Chinese education agencies on publicity and admission exercises in Shenzhen, but it soon preferred to turn to the University's China Affairs Office to supervise its recruitment exercises.[109] Second, although the Hong Kong government supported in principle the admission of Chinese students to local associate degree programmes, these students were not allowed to study in Hong Kong because of strict immigration controls. The delay in changing this policy rendered the scheme unfeasible in the 2004–05 academic year.[110] Third, it was difficult for the College to find a student hostel near the teaching venue which was both large enough to house all the students, and could be easily administered by the College. The College put considerable effort into searching and negotiating for suitable living accommodation, but progress was slow in the first months.

These problems were gradually solved as 2005 wore on. The Hong Kong government announced a relaxation of its immigration policy in May 2005, meaning that the Community College could officially launch its admission exercise in China through the HKU China Affairs Office.[111] The College also succeeded in converting some of the University's staff quarters in Pokfulam into a student hostel.[112] The first group of twenty-eight Chinese mainland students was recruited into two Associate Degree programmes for the 2005–06 academic year.[113] In 2006–07, twenty-five new first-year students were recruited, bringing the number of Mainland students at the Community College to thirty-eight. The greatest obstacle to further expansion remains the lack of suitable residential accommodation. If this problem can be resolved the College hopes to recruit sixty new students from China in 2007–08.

HKU SPACE–Po Leung Kuk Collaboration

The School's most recent project to expand its community college activities is a joint venture with the Po Leung Kuk (PLK) to start a new community college which began operation in September 2006. Established in 1878, the Po Leung Kuk has been one of the best-known charity organisations in Hong Kong for more than a century.[114] Its formal educational services began in 1946 when a primary school was founded in its headquarters in Causeway Bay.[115] These services expanded rapidly in the post-War period and the Po Leung Kuk is now one of the largest sponsoring bodies in the local education system, with 106 schools at different levels under its control in 2003–04.[116] Prior to its partnership with HKU SPACE, they had been operating a small 'Po Leung Kuk Community College of Hong Kong', offering accredited Pre-AD and AD programmes since 2002–03. The collaboration between HKU SPACE and the Po Leung Kuk aims to combine the strengths of the two institutions and provide 'quality education to prepare students for success in life'.[117]

Contacts between the two institutions started in late 2003 when the Po Leung Kuk made two parallel suggestions to HKU SPACE for jointly-offered sub-degree programmes. The less complex project involved a partnership between the HKU SPACE Community College and the Po Leung Kuk Regional College of Continuing Education in the New Territories to offer a one-year Pre-AD programme in evening mode for adult learners. HKU SPACE Community College would have been responsible for the curriculum, quality assurance, and the qualification awarded, while the Po Leung Kuk would provide administration, teaching venues and programme delivery with some assistance from HKU SPACE Community College.[118] An agreement was reached in December 2004 and the programme was scheduled to start in September 2005.[119] However, the project did not get off the ground because of the poor public response. Only fifteen applications were received and the programme had to be cancelled.[120]

The other project involved the joint establishment of a new community college providing full-time Associate Degree and Higher Diploma programmes. The Po Leung Kuk proposed to redevelop the west wing of its headquarters in Causeway Bay as the campus of the new community college. The new building is expected to provide a floor area of 170,000 square feet and will be large enough to accommodate two thousand students. The Po Leung Kuk will also provide the new College with administrative support and will deliver part of the academic programme. HKU SPACE will be responsible for all academic management and support matters including the awarding of qualifications.[121] HKU SPACE welcomed this proposal because the Po Leung Kuk could provide the premises which it desperately needed for expanding its community college services. The project is also beneficial to the Po Leung Kuk because it will strengthen its post-secondary education services with strong academic support from HKU SPACE.

After a year of negotiations, HKU SPACE and the Po Leung Kuk signed a formal twenty-five-year agreement on 15 November 2004. The new community college will be set up as a company limited by guarantee with a name 'HKU SPACE Po Leung Kuk Community College'. The two institutions are equal partners in the project and will have equal representation on the College Council. HKU SPACE will make use of the new Causeway Bay campus for its own evening and weekend courses when the Community College is not using the facilities, and arrangements have been made for the harmonious usage of common facilities.[122] The cost of establishing the new Community College has been large, but a ten-year interest-free government loan of $254 million was acquired in 2005 to finance the construction of the new building, bringing the total loans from government for HKU SPACE–sponsored community colleges in Hong Kong to $745 million.[123]

The new College is not part of the existing HKU SPACE Community College. Being a separate legal entity, the HKU SPACE Po Leung Kuk Community College is not considered to be a branch of HKU SPACE and hence has no official connection with the HKU SPACE Community College. However, the appointment of Professor K. F. Cheng as Principal of the new HKU SPACE Po Leung Kuk Community College establishes a vital link between the two colleges. The adoption of the same Quality Assurance system and the participation of the same staff in the management teams of the two colleges ensure consistency in academic and administrative standards. There is also a consensus that the two Colleges should be complementary rather than competitive in programmes and student admissions.[124] For this reason none of the first four Associate Degree and three Higher Diploma programmes offered by the new HKU SPACE PLK Community College in 2006–07 overlap with those offered by the older HKU SPACE Community College. The two colleges will therefore be able to recruit students with different interests and strengths, rather than compete with each other for the same group of potential students.

The curriculum structure of the new College is similar to that of HKU SPACE Community College. Both generic skills and specialist subjects are emphasised in the programmes. The Associate Degree and Higher Diploma programmes require three years of study, but Secondary Seven graduates can be admitted directly to the second year of studies. This programme structure will likely prove as popular to potential students as HKU SPACE's original Community College curriculum, but much work remains to be done in the years ahead. The University has full academic control over the awards conferred in the new college in the same way that it does for other HKU SPACE programmes, with oversight by the Board for Continuing and Professional Education and Lifelong Learning. The HKU SPACE quality assurance process is used in approving all programmes. The first cohort of students was recruited in the 2006–07 academic year but was rather smaller than expected, probably due to the fact that the new campus in Causeway Bay will not be available until 2008.[125] In the meantime, classes are being held at the School's Admiralty Learning Centre and the full curriculum is being developed. The number of students is expected to reach two thousand in 2009–10 when the College and its new campus will be in full operation.[126]

The development of full-time top-up degrees, sub-degree programme projects in the Chinese Mainland, and collaboration with the Po Leung Kuk have extended and diversified the community college activities of HKU SPACE. Moreover, these projects have contributed to strengthening the community college system in Hong Kong and may eventually assist in the recognition of Associate Degree and Higher Diploma qualifications. It is, of course, too early to judge the success of these programmes in securing better careers for graduates, but the large proportion of students who have been able to articulate their sub-degree studies to undergraduate programmes is a good indication that the college community concept is producing the results that it was originally hoped it would deliver.

'A Bridge to a Brighter Future': The Story of Carol Chum

There have already been many success stories in the short history of the HKU SPACE Community College, but one student's achievements in particular have impressed all who have been monitoring the development of the College. Miss Carol Chum, an Associate of Arts in Media and Cultural Studies graduate from 2003, is a fine example of how the Community College serves as an alternative route to university studies and provides a 'bridge to a brighter future' for many young Hong Kong students. Carol Chum is not entirely typical of the students who have enrolled in the Community College's programmes. At the time of her enrolment in 2001 she was an adult learner who had already been employed for six years, but what she experienced in those six years was essentially the same as her younger classmates. Entry into a university has never been an easy task in Hong Kong, and the very intense competition for undergraduate places in the mid-1990s meant that Miss Chum, like most Secondary Seven students, was not able to secure a university place after finishing her secondary-school education. She decided to start a career in drama production but despite her enthusiasm for her job in the performing arts, she was prevented from further career development because she did not possess an advanced academic qualification. This disadvantage was particularly obvious when she tried to change jobs. Part-time studies might have helped her to improve her situation but when she attempted to read for a degree through part-time studies she found it very difficult to strike a balance between work and study. She therefore decided to terminate her part-time degree studies, but she was convinced that she would perhaps do better in full-time studies.

Carol Chum had many options to consider when returning to study full-time in 2001, ranging from university studies as an undergraduate to the new sub-degree programmes being offered by post-secondary institutions. She finally decided to enrol in an Associate Degree programme at HKU SPACE Community College. The College impressed her in several ways. The teaching mode at the College was similar to that at universities and this allowed her to find out whether she would be able to adapt herself to full-time higher education after having left school for so many years. The reputation of HKU and the high quality of HKU SPACE courses were another crucial factor, while her curiosity about subjects in media and cultural studies also provided her with strong incentives to study at the College. In spite of the limited physical facilities available at the Wanchai Learning Centre at that time, Chum was content with her student life at the Community College. She found the teachers were helpful and inspiring, younger classmates were friendly and more devoted to their studies than she had expected, and she was able to fit in very well. The workload was usually heavy, but as the programme was not examination-oriented she did not feel that she was under too much pressure.

Carol Chum's decision to spend two years at HKU SPACE Community College proved very rewarding. The courses not only enhanced her competitiveness in the workforce, but also nurtured a genuine academic interest in media and cultural studies. The flexible programme structure allowed her to choose courses which were most suitable for her own personal and intellectual development and motivated her to make the most out of her learning opportunities. Chum's brilliant performance in the Associate Degree programme was warmly commended by the College, and she was awarded the Chan Tat Chee Scholarship to help finance her undergraduate studies in Media, Culture and Society at the University of Birmingham. She graduated from Birmingham and returned to Hong Kong in 2005, having experienced an exciting intellectual environment in the United Kingdom, feeling more independent as a lifelong learner, and with broader horizons than she thought possible when she was studying at HKU SPACE Community College. She is now planning to pursue a career in the academic world, having been inspired by her teachers.[127] Carol Chum's story illustrates the determination of many Community College students to advance their personal and career prospects through a 'second chance' at higher education, but it also demonstrates how HKU SPACE can provide 'a bridge to a brighter future' to students like Carol who have great potential in higher education.

Conclusion

Community colleges are one of the major initiatives of HKU SPACE in recent years and have extended the School's provision of lifelong learning opportunities from the traditional pool of largely working adults to a new market of younger school-leavers who are desperate for a second chance at higher education. In the first seven years of operation, the HKU SPACE Community College has encountered a number of challenges, from the difficulty in securing teaching venues to public scepticism about the entire community college concept. The School's latest projects in community college education both in Hong Kong and the Mainland are likewise subject to the same difficulties. The ongoing debate over education reform, including the four-year undergraduate curriculum, has also cast a shadow of uncertainty over the future of community colleges. Perhaps the biggest unsolved problem is the issue of recognition of sub-degree qualifications, a matter which both the government and the universities seem strangely unwilling to confront constructively. Many of these problems therefore remain to be solved, but the current feedback on the development of community colleges by HKU SPACE has been remarkably positive.

In 2004–05, HKU SPACE Community College enrolled 4,903 full-time students in fifty-five programmes and was the largest community college in Hong Kong; in 2005–06, the offerings had expanded to seventy-one programmes with

5,760 students, and a further 1,428 mainland enrolments.[128] In 2005–06, the Community College's full-time student body accounted for 30 per cent of the entire FTEs for HKU SPACE, and a total of 2,317 students graduated from the Pre-AD, Associate Degree and Higher Diploma programmes.[129] The Community College's full-time programmes have therefore become the School's largest area of operation in terms of FTEs, even though part-time bachelor's degrees still enrol the largest number of students by head count.[130] Full-time top-up degree programmes through CIDP, Associate Degree and *dazhuan* programmes in the new teaching centres in China, and the new Community College established in partnership with the Po Leung Kuk have further strengthened the provision of full-time post-secondary education by HKU SPACE. It will still be some time before it becomes clear how much these community colleges will be able to contribute to society, and to what extent their status will be recognised by both government, the public, and the universities which sponsor them. What is clear, however, is that these institutions have already begun to build 'a bridge to a brighter future' for many of their students, and these graduates are more productive members of society as a result of their studies at the community colleges of HKU SPACE.

Conclusion

FROM SMALL BEGINNINGS FIFTY YEARS AGO the University of Hong Kong's Department of Extra-Mural Studies has grown into today's School of Professional and Continuing Education, one of the world's five largest providers of continuing and lifelong learning programmes. From an enrolment of only 330 students in 1957, today's student population has grown to nearly 112,000 per annum, representing a full-time equivalent enrolment of 18,961. These students took 1,085 programmes and courses in 2005–06, of which 939 were part-time and 146 were full-time, and classes took place in twelve learning centres spread across Hong Kong. The School employs 820 full-time staff and approximately 2,000 part-time teachers, making its teaching force larger than that of the University. Collaboration in programme delivery currently takes place with sixty academic institutions based in the United Kingdom, Australia, the United States, Canada and Hong Kong, and SPACE has mainland Chinese partners in the cities of Beijing, Guangzhou, Hangzhou and Suzhou. It has been estimated that approximately 1.7 million students have taken courses in the Department of Extra-Mural Studies or HKU SPACE in the last fifty years.[1] By any standards these figures indicate how incredibly successful HKU SPACE has become at delivering adult education courses to a very large cross-section of the Hong Kong community.

This book has attempted to sketch the main outlines of HKU SPACE's history in order to explain the success of the University's adult education activities over the last fifty years. In doing so we have recounted a story about which the University can be justly proud, for not only has the scale of extra-mural operations expanded enormously, but current operations are much more sophisticated than could ever have been predicted fifty years ago. Beginning with a limited mission to provide mainly 'liberal' courses for adult learners in the best British extra-mural tradition, the Department of Extra-Mural Studies transformed itself from the 1970s into a provider of professional and continuing education to meet the demands of a rapidly expanding modern economy. Already by the mid-1980s more than three-quarters of the courses offered were 'vocational' in nature, and today less than a quarter of the School's courses could be classified as purely 'liberal' in the old sense.[2] The current self-financing policy and the difficulties of implementing cross-subsidisation of courses mean that the original aim of learning purely for pleasure has been replaced by a more pragmatic attitude to lifelong learning. While this may be lamented by some educational purists, it has nevertheless meant that extra-mural study has become more focused and efficient at HKU over the last fifty years. The main educational thrust of HKU SPACE has therefore changed completely since 1957, but this transformation has assisted in no small way the development of the modern Hong Kong economy.

The achievements of the last fifty years have undoubtedly been great, but it is also evident that there were numerous problems along the way, some of which the University and SPACE are still in the process of resolving. Perhaps the most serious of these is the problem of recognition. We have seen how in the early years of the Department of Extra-Mural Studies it took some time before the Director and his staff were recognised as 'Teachers' of the University. Moreover, throughout their history neither the DEMS nor SPACE was ever considered to be a proper 'Teaching Department' because they did not play any part in the undergraduate teaching role of the University. From its earliest years the University considered non-matriculated students to be inferior to full-time undergraduates, so that 'externals' and 'extra-murals' were never fully accepted as 'real' students. In recent times this attitude has manifested itself in various ways. Most tellingly, the University has failed to list HKU SPACE awards in its Statutes. No less worryingly, the Community College's Associate Degree graduates initially found it difficult to have their qualifications recognised for articulation to undergraduate studies.

The lack of recognition given to these students for their pre-degree studies was not restricted to HKU alone, however, for there was a more widespread uneasiness within Hong Kong society about these relatively new qualifications. Most providers of associate degree and higher diploma programmes in Hong Kong were concerned about the slowness of recognition for their awards in the early years of the new millennium, but in the last two years the situation has changed dramatically as more overseas universities have recognised the qualifications gained by students of HKU SPACE and other continuing education providers in Hong Kong. In 2005–06 a total of 1,303 HKU SPACE Community College graduates were admitted to local and overseas degree programmes, with 632 admitted to UGC-funded places in Hong Kong (including 304 at HKU), 622 to self-funded degrees, and 49 went overseas. Typically, 70 per cent of Associate Degree graduates from the Community College now proceed straight to further study, and nearly 4,000 have commenced bachelor's degrees since 2001.[3] While problems of recognition created some serious headaches for the Community College in the past, it seems that Hong Kong is beginning to become more aware of the very real achievements of community college students within the local higher education sector.

It nevertheless seems that despite the enunciation of clear government policies on continuing education in the late 1990s, adult higher education remains an area of relatively low priority in wider education policy in Hong Kong. Some would say that continuing education has been used as a political tool in Hong Kong but has gained very little real support from policy makers, and today garners only minimal financial support from a government which is suddenly flush with surplus income. The University Grants Committee refuses to fund the majority of continuing education programmes at university level now that the self-funding model promoted since the late 1960s is so well established, and universities are restricted in the support which they are allowed to give to continuing education programmes. At HKU, extra-mural studies have long been extremely profitable for the University. The School of Professional and Continuing Education has for the last ten years been a net contributor to the University's finances ($78 million in the 2004–05 financial year alone) and in 2005–06 had a turnover of $842 million. Continuing education is therefore 'big business' in Hong Kong in the early twenty-first century, and consequently the competition among providers of this cultural commodity is keen. HKU SPACE is the largest and, many would argue, the most successful of the many providers of adult educational opportunities in Hong Kong and has certainly shown an extraordinary level of entrepreneurial flair under its last two directors. This has put it in an enviable position to take advantage of market opportunities in the last few years.

It also seems that the market for continuing higher education in Hong Kong is, for the time being at least, assured. The latest market survey in 2005–06 indicated that 28 per cent of adults in Hong Kong are in continuing education programmes compared with 18 per cent in 2003–04. This perhaps reflects the fact that the economy has recovered from the recent downturn but it does not mean that the market for continuing education is anywhere near the point of saturation. In most OECD countries, around 40 per cent of adults are engaged in continuing education so Hong Kong still has a long way to go before it reaches this figure.[4] Moreover, Hong Kong is now in the final stages of transforming itself from an industrial to a 'knowledge-based' economy, so continuing and professional education will be of great importance for some time to come as Hong Kong relies more heavily on service industries in the future. It might also be expected that as this new Hong Kong society evolves, lifelong learning will become a more central feature of the city's culture and demand will continue to grow in a self-sustaining way. In this sense the government's policies on 'lifelong learning' already seem to have been embraced by a society which is thirsty for skills enhancement and improved promotion prospects in the workplace. HKU SPACE is well poised to meet this rising local demand for continuing education in all its manifestations.

HKU SPACE's influence in the Hong Kong continuing education sector has been considerable since it started higher adult education in Hong Kong fifty years ago, but more recently the School has begun to exert some influence in regional developments. After several decades of relatively little engagement with the international continuing education community, the School in 2002 organised the Second Asia-Pacific Conference on Continuing Education and Lifelong Learning, and in 2006 hosted the Fourth Conference with a large international gathering of scholars and practitioners. This recent engagement has to a certain extent returned HKU SPACE to a more prominent role in regional and international developments, a position which was first established by Ieuan Hughes in the 1960s. The opening of China to the outside world has provided a number of new opportunities for SPACE to extend its services and these are being pursued actively despite the obvious problems of doing business in China. SPACE is also exerting a positive influence in other ways. In China, like Hong Kong, continuing adult education has long been considered inferior to conventional higher education, but these notions are beginning to change now that Tsinghua University has embraced continuing education as one of its three fundamental strategic missions. Tsinghua has used the HKU SPACE model in implementing this continuing education mission and the Ministry of Education is now using the Tsinghua school of continuing education as a model for the rest of China. The current Director of HKU SPACE travels to China frequently to speak about the successful model developed by the School over the last fifty years, and plans are now being made for conducting training courses for deans of mainland continuing education schools. In this sense the School has taken on a role which would have been welcomed by the founders of HKU who were so keen for the University to provide leadership in the modernisation of China.

HKU SPACE's role within Hong Kong and the wider region is therefore an increasingly important one, and this is something which the University seems to be recognising more openly. The recent appointment of Professor Lee Chak-fan to be the next Director of the School marks the first occasion on which a Pro-Vice-Chancellor of the University has held this post. The University has included 'lifelong learning' in its mission statement for some years, but this mission has recently been given greater prominence by being included as part of the University's formal role statement endorsed by the UGC. This means that HKU SPACE's special role within HKU is now central to the University's wider role in society, even though in other respects the School differs greatly from more mainstream parts of the University. Research is one area in which the School continues to fall short of the University's primary mission despite numerous attempts over the years to encourage staff to engage in research on continuing education. Early work by Ieuan Hughes and Duncan Macintosh was followed in the 1980s by Lee Ngok and Agnes Lam, and in the 1990s by John Holford, John Cribbin and Peter Kennedy. This work has resulted in numerous articles in books and international journals, and two major books on continuing education in the Hong Kong context published in 1994 and 2002, but research output from SPACE remains disappointing.[5] Former extra-mural staff such as C. K. Leung and Gordon Redding established impressive research reputations in their own fields of specialisation in the 1960s and 1970s, so HKU SPACE may once again make contributions to the University's research culture in the future. There are also now greater opportunities for collaboration between the School and the University departments and research centres, but School staff are not eligible for research grants from the UGC's Research Grants Committee so funding of research is likely to remain problematic. The recent appointment of Dr W. Y. Zhang as Research Consultant under the Director represents an attempt to give greater prominence to research work, but any results from this initiative will take many years to mature and HKU SPACE's principal role within the university will always be one of teaching rather than research.

It is this teaching role which has allowed HKU SPACE to bring the benefits of higher education to the people of Hong Kong. The University of Hong Kong's normal undergraduate and postgraduate programmes have always been limited in the number of students who can be accepted to participate in full-time higher education, and despite the massive expansion of the 1980s and 1990s HKU today remains a relatively small university by international standards. The old Department of Extra-Mural Studies provided a valuable opportunity for its earliest students to taste the benefits of a liberal university education without having to enrol in full-time studies, and in later years the School of Professional and Continuing Education has transformed the lives of many thousands of workers who have been able to upgrade their qualifications and aspire to promotion or even complete career changes. A large percentage of today's students at HKU SPACE are already graduates who are seeking to expand their career opportunities or simply continue learning for life, and this group are extremely efficient and ambitious learners. The School is also giving a valuable second chance to students who do not perform well in the secondary education system in Hong Kong. Its Community College is already a recognised leader in the provision of Associate Degree and Higher Diploma programmes.

In the last fifty years HKU SPACE has produced far more graduates than the University and has therefore had at least as great an impact on the local community and relations between 'gown' and 'town'. These graduates are to be found leading enterprises of every kind across Hong Kong and hundreds of thousands of other graduates work in a huge diversity of fields. This pattern of graduate activity seems likely to continue well into the future as the School engages in finding new ways of responding to the educational aspirations of Hong Kong people. In fact many would say that HKU SPACE is only beginning to hit its stride in delivering high-quality continuing higher education to a broad cross-section of the city's citizens and that many opportunities remain to be fully exploited. It is therefore likely that in its next fifty years HKU SPACE will play an increasingly important role in continuing higher education both in Hong Kong and the wider region, and will be one of the major participants in relations between the University of Hong Kong and the people of Hong Kong.

Epilogue

Lives of great men all remind us
We can make our lives sublime,
And, departing, leave behind us
Footprints on the sands of time.

Henry Wadsworth Longfellow (1807–1882)

AS A 1952 MEDICAL GRADUATE, I witnessed the birth in 1957 of the precursor of HKU SPACE — namely, the HKU Department of Extra-Mural Studies. Despite being a practising physician by profession, I was already deeply involved in social and political activities soon after graduation. By 1954, I was one of the founding members of the Hong Kong Civic Association and was elected its Honorary Secretary. In those days, the only government consultative body which had elected members on its board was the Urban Council. The year 1956 saw Civic Association members (myself included) being actively engaged in political election campaigns for Urban Council seats. It was when the city was in the grip of 'election fever' in 1956 that the University announced its intention to launch a Department of Extra-Mural Studies. As an amateur politician and a staunch HKU-phile, I was highly excited and immediately sensed the immense impact this innovative initiative of the University would have on the community at large. In my opinion, not only did such a move by the University bring 'gown' to 'town', but the emergent Department of Extra-Mural Studies would also throw open the doors of this citadel of higher learning — our beloved HKU — to those people of Hong Kong who wished to better themselves in a variety of ways. These included:

(a) To study for study's sake with no other motive than a desire to enrich oneself and to broaden one's horizons;
(b) To acquire value-added upgrading of knowledge and skills for career advancement;
(c) To earn a tertiary degree for a new profession of one's choice, prospects which were denied to many, or perhaps not even thought of, during secondary school days;

(d) To cater for 'late developers' who did not do well in their youth; or to give a second chance to those who achieved passing grades which were not competitive enough to gain entrance to the University due to insufficient tertiary places;
(e) To provide opportunities in later life to those who were accepted for admission but who, despite generous scholarship and/or bursary grants, could not proceed to further studies on account of being forced to become bread-winners for their families; and
(f) Lastly, we must not forget one factor which I do not tire of repeating, and that is the desirability of the unavailable. To some children, attending school may seem boring, tiring, laborious, and nit-picking. It is only after they leave school and start to earn a living that they discover the joy of learning and realise the value of education.

The above list is by no means exhaustive. There must be many other circumstances whereby HKU SPACE offers adolescents and adults alike, particularly the ever-increasing members of the 'Third Generation', chances to improve and enrich themselves through continuing adult education and lifelong learning. In this way HKU SPACE fosters the intellectual life of the community. Moreover, in recent years, HKU SPACE has also been able to mount programmes in the Chinese Mainland to offer opportunities for post-secondary study and to provide professional education and high-level training courses for government officials.

All these factors, in essence, explain why I have been such a steadfast and loyal champion of this extension arm of the University since its inception and throughout the fifty years of its history. Surprisingly, despite the fact that there must have been more than a million individuals who have registered for HKU SPACE courses over the past fifty years, the clamour for the formation of an alumni association was not apparent until Professor Enoch Young took the initiative to invite several past students to a meeting for this purpose some three years ago. To cut a long story short, the HKU SPACE ALUMNI was eventually established at an impressive 'Inaugural Ceremony' at the University's Loke Yew Hall on 27 June 2004, and I had the honour of being elected the Founder President.

One of the first things I did as ALUMNI President was to bring to the attention of Professor Enoch Young and Dr Michael Luk, the Director and Deputy Director of HKU SPACE respectively, the idea of publishing a history of HKU SPACE. In my opinion, a history of HKU SPACE would be a most relevant and fitting part of the celebrations for our Golden Jubilee Anniversary. Since HKU SPACE ALUMNI was established in 2004, the proposed history would ideally also include the activities and achievements of the more than one million past students. How had each of them benefited by taking SPACE courses? How had some of them, buttressed by value-added adjuncts from SPACE courses, contributed to the community of Hong

Kong, and possibly to China and beyond? These were fascinating questions to me. However, I was told that whilst HKU SPACE would definitely chronicle its past, it had neither the human nor financial resources to publish a special publication incorporating both HKU SPACE and its alumni.

Faced with such a reality, I obtained the tacit approval of Professor Enoch Young to approach the University's Department of History for help. I therefore arranged to meet Dr Peter Cunich in October 2005. Dr Cunich was most supportive and helpful. He agreed to co-ordinate the writing of a jubilee history of HKU SPACE and I was happy to support the appointment of Mr Lawrence M. W. Chiu as the research assistant for the project with a donation of $152,000. The result of their endeavours is this present book, painstakingly researched and beautifully drafted by the authors.

Even though the title of the book is 'HKU SPACE and its Alumni', readers may be surprised to find that information about the alumni in this publication is negligible. This is deliberate, because to do justice to the achievements of our alumni and to recount even selected representative case histories of over one million past students would be a Herculean task. It would take at least two or more years to complete as well as require much more human and financial resources than are presently available. It was therefore decided that we publish the material already on hand as a first volume, and the next volume will be the Journal of the Alumni. I take this opportunity to announce that following the publication of this volume, HKU SPACE ALUMNI will be setting up a special fund-raising committee not only to identify those members of the Alumni whose exploits and contributions to society are worthy of mention, but also to solicit funds for the recruitment of Research Assistants as well as to raise money for travelling expenses necessary for the gathering of material and information. I do hope that a generous response and enthusiastic support from past students will be forthcoming.

The time has now come for me to perform my pleasant duty as the sponsor of this publication to thank the two authors. Mr Lawrence Chiu undertook the bulk of the initial research work and compiled the historical materials into a draft text. Dr Cunich supervised the whole work from start to finish and also wrote large sections of the text. I am also grateful to the HKU Department of History for its administrative and financial support. The credit of publishing the book goes to the Hong Kong University Press and HKU SPACE who have guaranteed the production costs in anticipation of healthy sales income. All of this was possible through the tremendous backing and support given to the project by Professor Albert Chen, the Chairman of the University Press Committee and Dr Colin Day, the University Publisher. To the Director of HKU SPACE, Professor Enoch Young, and the Deputy Director, Dr Michael Luk, a debt of gratitude is due for their continual guidance and encouragement. Particularly, I would like to thank Dr Darwin Chen, whose personal role and contribution made this publication possible.

I took the liberty of quoting a stanza from Longfellow's 'A Psalm of Life' to serve as an 'hors d'oeuvre' to the main body of my epilogue, and to remind fellow Alumni and other readers that it is within the power and capability of each and every individual to make life 'sublime'; 'And, departing', to leave 'footprints on the sands of time', no matter what the size of the footprints. There can be no denying that continuing adult education and lifelong learning do enhance and enrich the quality of life. It goes without saying that attending or participating in HKU SPACE courses or projects can and will make our lives more 'sublime' and will enable us to leave behind us bigger and better 'footprints'. That is why I wish to share with fellow Alumni and other readers the concluding stanza in Longfellow's poem:

> Let us, then, be up and doing,
> With a heart for any fate;
> Still achieving, still pursuing,
> Learn to labor and to wait.

Dr Peter C. Y. Lee, K.St.J., J.P.,
M.B.,B.S., F.H.K.A.M.(FM), LL.D.(HKU),
F.H.K.C.F.P., F.R.C.G.P., M.C.F.P.C.,
F.R.A.C.G.P., LL.D.(Birm.U), FAFPM, FHKAM.

President, HKU SPACE ALUMNI
Founding President, the Hong Kong College of Family Physicians (1976–1988)
Past-President, World Organization of Family Doctors (WONCA) (1992–1995)

Appendices

Appendix 1: Succession Lists, 1956–2007

The Department of Extra-Mural Studies, 1956–1991

- **Directors**

1956 Mr R. L. Marshall (appointed but did not take up post)
1956–1960 Mr Gerald H. Moore
1960–1967 Mr Ieuan W. Hughes
1968–1986 Mr Roger Arthur Williams
1986–1991 Professor Lee Ngok

- **Deputy Directors**

1965–1968 Mr Roger Arthur Williams
1990–1991 Mr Duncan J. H. Macintosh (Continuing Education)
1990–1991 Mr W. B. Howarth (External Studies)

- **(Senior) Assistants to the Director / Senior Assistant Registrar**

1958–1965 Mr T. C. Lai
1965–1986 Mrs Priscilla Tso Mark Yuen-yee
1990–1991 Mr John A. Cribbin

- **Chairmen of the Board of Extra-Mural Studies (Director as the ex-officio Chairman)**

1957–1960 Mr Gerald H. Moore
1960–1967 Mr Ieuan W. Hughes

- **Chairmen of the Committee on Extra-Mural Studies**

1967–1971 Professor J. B. Gibson (Pro-Vice-Chancellor, ex-officio)
1971–1976 Professor C. T. Huang (Pro-Vice-Chancellor, ex-officio)
1976–1979 Professor S. Y. King

1979–1982 Professor P. B. Harris
1982–1986 Professor M. A. Brimer
1986–1990 Professor B. S. Morton
1990–1991 Professor B. Weatherhead

SPACE / HKU SPACE, 1991–Present

- **Directors**

1992–1995 Professor Lee Ngok
1997–1998 Professor Enoch Young (Director-designate)
1998–2007 Professor Enoch Young
2007– Professor C. F. Lee (Director-designate)

- **Deputy Directors**

1992 Mr Duncan J. H. Macintosh (Continuing Education)
1992–1996 Mr W. B. Howarth
1998– Dr Michael Y. L. Luk
1998– Dr S. M. Shen

- **Senior Assistant Registrar / School Secretary**

1992– Mr John A. Cribbin

- **Chairmen of the Board of the School of Professional and Continuing Education**

1992 Professor B. Weatherhead (Interim)
1992–1995 Professor Lee Ngok
1995–1996 Mr W. B. Howarth
1997–2000 Professor S. L. Wong

- **Chairmen of the Board for Continuing and Professional Education and Lifelong Learning (Vice-Chancellor as ex-officio Chairman)**

2000 Professor Cheng Yiu-chung
2000–2002 Professor W. I. R. Davies
2002– Professor Tsui Lap-chee

- **Chairmen of the Management Board for SPACE**

1992–1993 Professor R. T. T. Young
1993–1997 Professor S. T. H. Chan
1997–1999 Professor S. L. Wong

- **Chairmen of the Management Board / Board of Directors of HKU SPACE**

1999–2000 Professor S. L. Wong
2000–2004 Dr Darwin Chen
2004– Mr Linus W. L. Cheung

- **Chairmen of HKU SPACE Advisory Board**

2000–2004 Dr Cheng Hon-kwan
2004– Dr Darwin Chen

Acting appointments are excluded.

Appendix 2: Enrolments, 1957–2006

Year	Number of courses/ Programmes	Enrolments*	Percentage of Effective Enrolments#	Full-Time Equivalents (FTE)	Academic Awards	Lecturing Hours	Teaching venue		
							HKU Campus	Town Centre	Others/ Unspecified
1956–1957	12	330							
1957–1958	24	888	62.5						
1958–1959	44	1,112	68.8						
1959–1960	41	1,114	62.6						
1960–1961	60	2,290	64.8						
1961–1962	94	2,653	74.2				57		37
1962–1963	183	4,130	81.4				85		98
1963–1964	193	5,221	71.0				81		112
1964–1965	281	6,341	75.9				86		195
1965–1966	231	5,734	74.6				80	92	59
1966–1967	218	5,347	79.0			5,417	64	143	11
1967–1968	211	4,727	74.5			6,431	54	114	43
1968–1969	181	4,337	68.7			6,626	44	98	39
1969–1970	180	4,223	68.9			7,836	58	84	38
1970–1971	216	5,547	69.8	399		9,001	92	88	36
1971–1972	217	5,808	72.3			10,779	88	89	40
1972–1973	211	5,630	66.9			10,875	82	95	34
1973–1974	210	6,268	70.0			10,912	78	86	46

(Appendix 2 continued on p. 255)

Year	Number of courses/ Programmes	Enrolments*	Percentage of Effective Enrolments#	Full-Time Equivalents (FTE)	Academic Awards	Lecturing Hours	Teaching venue		
							HKU Campus	Town Centre	Others/ Unspecified
1974–1975	299	9,017	70.0			12,756	120	97	82
1975–1976	366	11,086	70.3	957	828	16,345	164	96	106
1976–1977	452	13,336	72.0		903	16,974	162	123	167
1977–1978	499	14,513	72.4		992	19,048	189	144	166
1978–1979	585	17,032	69.0		1,153	21,466	177	269	139
1979–1980	671	20,032	65.1		1,089	24,052	209	312	150
1980–1981	790	23,292	65.2	1,664	1,143	27,709	269	341	180
1981–1982	777	22,774	66.3		990	27,716	259	355	163
1982–1983	809	23,940	67.5		1,092	31,162	240	376	193
1983–1984	859	26,403	70.4		1,213	33,876	246	402	211
1984–1985	950	28,416	72.0		1,275	36,938	279	441	230
1985–1986	1,026	30,442	72.6	2,462	1,352	39,196	317	462	247
1986–1987	1,052	31,621	72.8		1,323	38,972	319	504	229
1987–1988	1,132	33,826	71.8		1,381	41,675	348	504	280
1988–1989	1,232	36,275	71.4		1,817	45,464	439	515	278
1989–1990	1,277	37,926	72.2		2,298	48,549	416	546	315
1990–1991		38,782		7,559	3,100				
1991–1992		44,361			4,157				
1992–1993		47,084		9,238	4,358				

(*Appendix 2 continued on p. 256*)

Year	Number of courses/ Programmes	Enrolments*	Percentage of Effective Enrolments#	Full-Time Equivalents (FTE)	Academic Awards	Lecturing Hours	Teaching venue		
							HKU Campus	Town Centre	Others/ Unspecified
1993–1994		52,318		10,732					
1994–1995		57,985		10,124					
1995–1996									
1996–1997		67,796		11,287					
1997–1998	1,145	69,031		12,098					
1998–1999		83,083		12,920					
1999–2000	671	90,030		13,492					
2000–2001	789	95,101		14,875					
2001–2002	806	106,672		17,551					
2002–2003	875	107,298		17,608	11,394				
2003–2004	927	105,427		17,414	12,244				
2004–2005	1,014	106,968		17,711	14,050				
2005–2006	1,077	111,708		18,962	15,148				

* The total enrolment in each year is a sum of registered students in all courses. A student might enrol in more than one course/programme in the same year, or might study a course/programme for a period of longer than one year. The number of students in headcount, therefore, will be considerably smaller than the enrolment figure.

Students who attended at least 2/3 of the classes.

Appendix 3: Finances, 1957–2005

Year	EMS / SPACE Activities				University Funding to the EMS / SPACE			EMS/ SPACE Fund Balance	HKU SPACE Accumulated Fund Balance	Total Expenditure of the University
	Course Fee Income	Total Income	DEMS/ SPACE-financed Expenditure	Surplus/ (Deficit)	University-funded Expenditure	HKU's Net Receipt from/ (Contribution to) EMS/ SPACE Activities	Percentage of University Funding to Total EMS/ SPACE Expenditure			
Centrally-Funded										
1957–1958	0.03				0.07					9.51
1958–1959					0.08					9.78
1959–1960					0.10					11.19
1960–1961					0.09					13.50
1961–1962					0.12					15.37
EMS Fund										
1962–1963	0.19	0.34	0.33	0.02	0.15			0.02		16.18
1963–1964	0.20	0.55	0.48	0.07	0.23			0.08		16.93
1964–1965	0.27	0.43	0.37	0.06	0.27			0.15		18.48
1965–1966	0.24	0.64	0.64	0.00	0.39			0.15		22.39
1966–1967	0.31	0.84	0.78	0.06	0.52			0.21		28.53
1967–1968	0.43	0.45	0.49	(0.04)	0.48	(0.52)	50.43	0.17		31.77

(Appendix 3 continued on p. 258)

Year	EMS / SPACE Activities				University Funding to the EMS / SPACE					
	Course Fee Income	Total Income	DEMS/ SPACE-financed Expenditure	Surplus/ (Deficit)	University-funded Expenditure	HKU's Net Receipt from/ (Contribution) to) EMS/ SPACE Activities	Percentage of University Funding to Total EMS/ SPACE Expenditure	EMS/ SPACE Fund Balance	HKU SPACE Accumulated Fund Balance	Total Expenditure of the University
1968–1969	0.42	0.47	0.35	0.12	0.49	(0.37)	59.05	0.29		35.80
1969–1970	0.49	0.53	0.42	0.11	0.59	(0.47)	59.44	0.40		45.36
1970–1971	0.76	0.82	0.72	0.10	0.73	(0.63)	51.12	0.49		45.32
1971–1972	1.00	1.04	0.90	0.13	0.86	(0.72)	49.34	0.63		52.76
1972–1973	0.95	1.00	0.82	0.18	1.00	(0.82)	55.52	0.83		64.12
1973–1974	1.22	1.26	1.11	0.15	1.10	(0.96)	50.37	0.99		80.69
1974–1975	1.57	1.61	1.40	0.21	1.30	(1.09)	48.46	1.16		89.15
1975–1976	1.87	1.93	1.67	0.27	1.42	(1.15)	46.37	1.44		93.67
1976–1977	2.52	2.55	2.13	0.41	1.81	(1.40)	46.26	1.80		114.34
1977–1978	2.70	2.73	2.74	(0.01)	2.22	(2.23)	45.05	1.80		143.70
1978–1979	2.99	3.04	2.64	0.39	2.79	(2.39)	51.55	2.18		151.64
1979–1980	3.59	3.64	3.21	0.43	3.20	(2.77)	50.12	2.63		181.98
1980–1981	4.29	4.36	3.69	0.67	4.31	(3.64)	54.00	3.36		257.39
1981–1982	5.11	5.18	4.33	0.85	5.60	(4.76)	56.51	4.53		320.47
1982–1983	6.57	6.65	5.18	1.47	6.45	(4.97)	55.54	6.05		381.61

(Appendix 3 continued on p. 259)

Year	EMS / SPACE Activities				University Funding to the EMS / SPACE					
	Course Fee Income	Total Income	DEMS/ SPACE-financed Expenditure	Surplus/ (Deficit)	University-funded Expenditure	HKU's Net Receipt from/ (Contribution to) EMS/ SPACE Activities	Percentage of University Funding to Total EMS/ SPACE Expenditure	EMS/ SPACE Fund Balance	HKU SPACE Accumulated Fund Balance	Total Expenditure of the University
1983–1984	8.74	8.89	7.07	1.83	6.84	(5.01)	49.26	8.51		416.12
1984–1985	10.03	10.23	8.00	2.23	9.53	(7.30)	54.43	10.81		466.50
1985–1986	11.76	11.89	13.26	(1.37)	35.82	(37.19)	73.00	9.71		608.55
1986–1987	14.49	14.63	14.16	0.46	9.43	(8.97)	40.03	10.88		671.50
1987–1988	17.76	17.90	15.30	2.61	10.96	(8.35)	41.79	1.00		774.49
1988–1989	21.10	21.30	18.15	3.15	12.03	(8.88)	39.85	1.00		1,101.39
1989–1990	33.60	34.86	33.58	1.27	14.27	(13.00)	29.83	2.27		1,330.34
1990–1991	45.81	48.49	60.89	(12.39)	18.62	(31.01)	23.42	0.64		1,614.85
SPACE Fund										
1991–1992	70.03	72.46	70.62	1.84	19.75	(17.90)	21.85	2.48		1,916.22
1992–1993	89.87	91.34	83.17	8.17	21.73	(13.56)	20.72	9.13		2,283.53
1993–1994	129.92	131.81	140.60	(8.79)	25.25	(34.04)	15.22	0.34		2,684.98
1994–1995	168.13	171.02	150.75	20.27	28.53	(8.26)	15.91	20.61		3,344.38
1995–1996	211.37	218.59	217.84	0.75	24.09	(23.34)	9.96	20.38		3,402.14
1996–1997	255.29	264.71	226.40	38.31	2.85	35.46	1.24	54.08		3,631.27

(*Appendix 3 continued on p. 260*)

Year	EMS / SPACE Activities				University Funding to the EMS / SPACE			EMS/ SPACE Fund Balance	HKU SPACE Accumulated Fund Balance	Total Expenditure of the University
	Course Fee Income	Total Income	DEMS/ SPACE-financed Expenditure	Surplus/ (Deficit)	University-funded Expenditure	HKU's Net Receipt from/ (Contribution to) EMS/ SPACE Activities	Percentage of University Funding to Total EMS/ SPACE Expenditure			
1997–1998	279.79	295.39	257.23	38.16	4.98	33.18	1.90	88.07		4,197.47
1998–1999	360.46	382.01	316.97	65.04	5.79	49.25	1.79	43.28	237.31	4,267.98
1999–2000*	428.77	451.52	388.19	63.32	5.90	39.43	1.50		283.48	4,781.60
2000–2001	495.72	523.72	472.70	51.02	0	31.02			314.49	5,612.24
2001–2002	619.89	646.37	598.50	47.87	0	23.87			338.36	4,923.32
2002–2003	680.25	704.84	694.48	10.36	0	(5.64)			332.72	4,847.77
2003–2004	692.60	720.65	682.91	37.74	0	20.05			355.17	4,817.69
2004–2005	753.51	787.62	687.92	99.70	0	77.70			460.80	4,652.04

(Amounts are in millions of Hong Kong dollars)

* After incorporation in 2000–2001, a new accounting practice was adopted. The Accumulated Fund Balance refers to the net assets owned by HKU SPACE.

Appendix 4: Teaching Accommodation Managed by DEMS/SPACE, 1965–2007

Operation	Name	District	Address	Purchased/ Leased	Initial Gross Floor Area (square feet)	Extension	Remarks
1965–1967	Extra-Mural Law Centre	Central	8/F, Chiao Shang Building, 92–94 Queen's Road Central	Leased	5,024		
1967–1978	Extra-Mural Town Centre	Central	11–12/F, Universal House, 151 Des Voeux Road Central	Leased	9,023		Building renamed in 1977 as Nanyang Commercial Bank Building
1978–1986	Extra-Mural Town Centre	Central	8/F, Wing On Centre, 111 Connaught Road Central	Leased	15,250		
1986–1997	Extra-Mural Town Centre	Sheung Wan	9/F, West Tower, Shun Tak Centre, 200 Connaught Road Central	Purchased	22,464	1989–1996 — 15/F (Purchased, 3,989 sq.ft.) 1991–1997 — 14/F (Purchased, 2,549 sq.ft.) 1994–2000 — 10/F (Leased, 3,980 sq.ft.)	

(*Appendix 4 continued on p. 262*)

Operation	Name	District	Address	Purchased/ Leased	Initial Gross Floor Area (square feet)	Extension	Remarks
1992–2006	Shek Kip Mei Regional Centre	Shek Kip Mei	3/F Ka Chi School, 5 Wai Chi Street	Leased	4,300 (3/F and 4/F)	1999–2006 — Whole building (Leased)	
1994–Present	North Point Study Centre	North Point	14/F, Fortress Tower, 250 King's Road	Purchased	14,647	2001 — 11/F (Purchased, 3,279 sq. ft.) 2003 — 4/F, 7/F 2004 — 13/F	
1997–Present	Admiralty Town Centre	Admiralty	3/F Admiralty Centre, 18 Harcourt Road	Purchased	36,173	1998–1999 — 6/F (Leased, 2,367 sq. ft.) 2000 — 2/F (Purchased, 21,384 sq. ft.) 2006 — Shops 201, 202, 203, 204, 238 (Purchased, 2,448 sq. ft.)	
1999–Present	North Point Learning Centre	North Point	18/F and 8/F, AIA Tower 183 Electric Road	Leased	18,039		8/F has been vacated since late 2004

(Appendix 4 continued on p. 263)

Operation	Name	District	Address	Purchased/ Leased	Initial Gross Floor Area (square feet)	Extension	Remarks
1999–Present	Admiralty Learning Centre	Admiralty	Unit C1, 34/F United Centre, 95 Queensway	Leased	5,730	1999 — Unit B, 12/F (Purchased, 6,725 sq. ft.) 2003 — Unit A, 12/F (Purchased, 5,257 sq.ft.) 2004 — 6/F (Purchased, 29,110 sq. ft.)	
1999–Present	Tsim Sha Tsui Learning Centre	Tsim Sha Tsui	UG01 and 1/F Austin Tower, 22–26A Austin Avenue	Purchased	24,006		
2000–Present	Quarry Bay Learning Centre	Quarry Bay	15–16/F CEF Lend Lease Plaza, 663 King's Road	Leased	15,636		Building renamed in 2002 as MLC Millennia Plaza, and in 2007 as Prosperity Millennia Plaza

(Appendix 4 continued on p. 264)

Operation	Name	District	Address	Purchased/ Leased	Initial Gross Floor Area (square feet)	Extension	Remarks
2000–2006	Tsim Sha Tsui Learning Centre Extension	Tsim Sha Tsui	12/F and 15/F, 238 Nathan Road	Leased	13,756		
2001–Present	Wanchai Learning Centre	Wanchai	2/F Causeway Centre	Leased	34,000	2002 — 3/F (Leased, 15,440 sq. ft.)	
2002–Present	Island East Campus	North Point	494 King's Road	Purchased	74,890		
2003–Present	The Cyperport Institute of Hong Kong	Pokfulam	Level 4 and Level 5, Cyberport 1, 100 Cyberpor Road	Leased	25,000		
2007–Present	Kowloon East Campus	Kowloon Bay	28 Wang Hoi Road	Developed by SPACE	Over 161,500		
From 2008 (expected)	HKU SPACE Po Leung Kuk Community College	Causeway Bay	West Wing of Po Leung Kuk Headquarters, 66 Leighton Road	Developed by HKU SPACE and Po Leung Kuk	170,000		

Note: Temporary teaching accommodation from secondary schools or other organisations is not included in the list. Accommodation solely for administrative, staff or clinical purposes is also excluded.

Appendix 5: HKU SPACE Learning Centres in China

Year	City	Name	Address
2000–2003	Shanghai	SPACE of the University of Hong Kong and Fudan University	38/F Central Plaza, 381 Huaihai Road (Middle)
2000–2003	Beijing	Beijing Hong Kong Centre for Professional Education (in collaboration with Beijing Advanced Financial Management College)	13/F, Prime Tower, 22 Chao Wao Dajie
2002–2004	Shanghai	SPACE of the University of Hong Kong and Fudan University (2nd Learning Centre)	17/F, Xinyibai Building, 800 Nanjing Road (East)
2001–Present	Guangzhou	Sun Yat-sen University – HKU Joint Centre for Professional Education	3/F, School of Continuing Education, Sun Yat-sen University, No.135, Xingang West Road (East Gate Entrance)
2002–Present	Hangzhou	Zhejiang University – The University of Hong Kong Centre for Advanced Business Studies	Room 375, Jiao Xue Zhu Lou, Xixi area, Zhejiang University
2002–2005	Zhuhai	HKU SPACE Zhuhai (in collaboration with Beijing Normal University (Zhuhai campus))	Beijing Normal University (Zhuhai campus), Jingfeng Road, Tanjiawan, Xiangzhou district
2003–Present	Beijing	Tsinghua University School of Continuing Education / HKU SPACE Joint Programme Management Centre	Room 410, 4/F, Section B, Innovation Building, Tsinghua Science Park
2005–Present	Suzhou	HKU SPACE Global College	3/F, Multipurpose Building, Dushu Lake Higher Education Town, Suzhou

Appendix 6: Overseas Partners of DEMS/HKU SPACE

Country	Partner Institution	Academic year of the first joint course in undergraduate or higher level offered	First joint course
UK	University of London	1964–1965	LLB (Preparation course)
UK	University of Bath	1991–1992	Master of Science in Construction Management by Distance Learning
UK	University of Leicester	1992–1993	M.A. in Pubic Order
UK	Napier Polytechnic / Napier University	1993–1994	B.Sc. (Hons) in Life Sciences (Applied Medical Science)
UK	University of Strathclyde	1994–1995	Master of Science in International Marketing
UK	University of Greenwich	1995–1996	MSc in Property Development and Investment by Distance Learning MSc in Construction Management and Economics by Distance Learning
UK	Kingston University	1995–1996	Bachelor of Arts in Music
UK	Manchester Metropolitan University	1996–1997	LLB
UK	Middlesex University	1996–1997	Master of Arts in East-West Theatre Studies
UK	University of Ulster	1996–1997	PgD in Human Nutrition / PgD in Dietetics / MSc in Human Nutrition / MSc in Human Nutrition and Dietetics
UK	Sheffield Hallam University	1999–2000	BA(Hons) Banking, Insurance and Finance

(Appendix 6 continued on p. 267)

Country	Partner Institution	Academic year of the first joint course in undergraduate or higher level offered	First joint course
UK	University of Surrey	1999–2000	MSc in Applied Professional Studies in Lifelong Learning
UK	University of Sunderland	2000–2001	BSc in Pharmaceutical Management
UK	University of Nottingham	2002–2003	Doctor of Education (Lifelong Education)
UK	University of Newcastle upon Tyne	2005–2006	Master of Science in International Shipping and Logistics
UK	University of Wales Institute, Cardiff	2005–2006	MSc in Environmental Risk Management (MSc in Food Safety Management)
UK	University of Hull	2006–2007	BSc (Hons) Accounting
Australia	Charles Sturt University – Riverina	1989–1990	Graduate Diploma of Arts (Library and Information Science)
Australia	Curtin University of Technology	1989–1990	B.Bus in Accounting
Australia	University of New England		Master of Health Administration
Australia	University of New South Wales	1990–1991	Extra-Mural Postgraduate Certificate in Commerce and Economics (Credit exemption for MCom (Finance))
Australia	Monash University	1993–1994	Master of Business in Accounting
Australia	Victoria University of Technology	1994–1995	M.A./Graduate Diploma /Graduate Certificates in Recreation and Sports Management

(Appendix 6 continued on p. 268)

Country	Partner Institution	Academic year of the first joint course in undergraduate or higher level offered	First joint course
Australia	University of Sydney	1996–1997	Graduate Diploma in Museum Studies
Australia	University of Wollongong	1998–1999	Master of Education/ Graduate Certificate in Information Technology
Australia	University of New England	1999–2000	Master of Educational Administration
Australia	Deakin University	2003–2004	Bachelor of Arts (Architecture)
New Zealand	University of Otago	1990–1991	Master of Pharmacy (Pharmacy Practice)
USA	University of California Berkeley Extension	1999–2000	Professional Diploma in Marketing
USA	California State University, Fullerton	2002–2003	Master of Arts in Communications
USA	University of Michigan – Dearborn	2004–2005	Master of Science in Finance
China	Fudan University	1998–1999	Master of Business Administration (International)
China	Tsinghua University	1999–2000	Second Bachelor Degree in Chinese Law
China	Dongbei University of Finance and Economics	2001–2002	Bachelor in Accounting Master in Accounting
China	Beijing University of Chinese Medicine	2006–2007	Master Degree in Chinese Medicine
China	Beijing Sport University	2006–2007	Master in Physical Education and Sport Training
China	Hubei College of Traditional Chinese Medicine	2006–2007	Bachelor of Traditional Chinese Medicine
Japan	Osaka University of Foreign Studies	2006–2007	Master in Japanese Language and Culture

Note: This list includes only the overseas partners who offered part-time undergraduate or postgraduate (including postgraduate diploma or certificate) courses with the DEMS and SPACE.

Appendix 7: Overseas Higher Education Institutions which recognised the AD/HD qualifications of HKU SPACE Community College in 2006–07

Country	Partner Institution	Qualifications Recognised
UK	University of Birmingham	AD
	City University of London	AD
	University of Essex	AD
	University of Huddersfield	HD
	Kingston University	AD/HD
	University of Leicester	AD
	University of Liverpool	AD
	University of London	AD/HD
	Manchester Metropolitan University	AD/HD
	Middlesex University	AD/HD
	Napier University	AD/HD
	Northumbria University	AD/HD
	University of Nottingham	AD
	Oxford Brookes University	AD/HD
	University of Southampton	AD
	University of St. Andrews	AD
	University of Strathclyde	AD/HD
	University of Sunderland	AD
	University of Surrey	AD
	University of Ulster	AD
	University of York	AD
USA	The School of the Art Institute of Chicago	HD
	University of California – Los Angeles	AD
	California State University San Macros	AD
	Fairleigh Dickinson University	AD
	University of Hawaii	AD
	University of Illinois at Chicago	AD
	University of Kansas	AD
	Iowa State University of Science and Technology	AD
	University of Michigan – Dearborn	AD
	Montana State University	AD
	The State University of New York at Buffalo	AD

(Appendix 7 continued on p. 270)

Country	Partner Institution	Qualifications Recognised
Canada	McMaster University	AD
	McGill University	AD
	Simon Fraser University	AD
	University of Toronto	AD
	University of Victoria	AD
Australia	Adelaide University	AD
	Bond University	AD
	Charles Sturt University	AD/HD
	Curtin University of Technology	AD/HD
	Deakin University	AD
	Edith Cowan University	HD
	La Trobe University	HD
	University of Melbourne	AD/HD
	Monash University	AD/HD
	Murdoch University	AD
	University of New England	AD
	Queensland University of Technology	AD
	The University of Queensland	AD
	University of South Australia	AD/HD
	University of Southern Queensland	AD
	University of Technology Sydney	HD
	University of Western Australia	AD/HD
	University of Wollongong	AD

Source: HKU SPACE Community College *Prospectus 2006–2007*, pp. 85–86.

Appendix 8: Mission Statements, 1993 and 2001

SPACE Mission Statement, Objectives and Priorities, March 1993

Mission Statement

- To offer educational opportunity to the community, principally on a part time, evening or weekend basis
- To provide access to career and training opportunities both in the form of continuing education as well as at degree, postgraduate and professional level
- To cooperate with the Faculties of the University, with other institutions in Hong Kong and with an international network of overseas institutions in offering a wide range of courses with appropriate mechanisms to ensure these are of high quality and represent good value for students
- To conduct research into manpower, educational and training needs, into the effectiveness of different teaching media and in the subject mechanisms of academic staff
- To contribute, through the provision of continuing professional education opportunities, to the well being of Hong Kong, and of China, particularly Southern China

Objectives and Priorities

In fulfilling the aims above the School has set the following objectives and priorities:

- To maintain and develop a balanced programme of continuing and professional education which provides access to study for the community and which enables students to obtain qualifications from a basic level to degree, professional and postgraduate level
- To provide the mechanism and expertise for the extension of part time external degree opportunities in the University of Hong Kong and also, where appropriate, part time external degrees of overseas universities
- To carry out applied research to ensure the School's programmes continue to meet community needs
- To develop a range of teaching and learning strategies and materials through the work of the Distance Learning Unit, using new technologies where appropriate; and to continue collaboration with the Open Learning Institute
- To further develop the concept of an international network of credit transfer and recognition and to ensure the levels of the School's programmes are well understood in this context
- To promote the establishment of a Federation of Continuing Education in Hong Kong
- To provide an appropriate framework for the School to offer courses in China and collaboration with educational institutions in China
- To keep the School's structure under review to ensure it continues to serve the University and the community in the most effective ways; in particular, to explore the idea of establishing a limited company through which the University's links with the community and with industry could be mediated and promoted to best advantage
- To develop the courses offered in the six major academic clusters covered by the School to ensure that they remain relevant and are continually updated

- To maintain and extend the facilities for teaching in the community through the operation of further regional study centres.

Source: HKUSPACEMBM 29 May 1993, 8, Appendix F, document SPACE/7/493, 10 March 1993.

HKU SPACE Statement of Vision, Mission and Values, 2001

Vision

As the Extension Arm of the University of Hong Kong in extending lifelong learning opportunities for the community, HKU SPACE seeks to become a world-class centre of excellence for the provision of professional and continuing education serving Hong Kong, mainland China and the region.

Mission

HKU SPACE strives for excellence in:

- Delivering high quality programmes to meet the needs of learners and employers
- Collaborating with other parts of The University of Hong Kong and other institutions in expanding lifelong learning opportunities
- Enhancing access to education for career advancement and personal development
- Conducting research in adult and continuing education, as well as in subject specialisms
- Promoting lifelong learning for the development of a learning society and the community's pursuit of quality of life

Values

HKU SPACE places particular value on:

- Service to learners
- Partnership to maximize lifelong learning opportunities
- Accountability to stakeholders
- Creativity in teaching and learning
- Excellence in quality

Source: BCPE&LLM 19 April 2004, Appendix A, Annex B, HKU SPACE Strategic Plan, April 2002.

Appendix 9: Major Bachelor or Higher Degree Programmes Jointly Organised by SPACE and HKU, 1992–2006

Faculty	Title	Award	Years offered
Architecture	Postgraduate Diploma in Construction Management	Joint	1993–1999
	Postgraduate Diploma in Surveying (Real Estate) (Quantity Surveying)	Joint	1996–2001
	Professional Diploma in Architectural Studies	HKU SPACE	2004–
	Postgraduate Diploma in Cultural Heritage Management	HKU SPACE	2005–
Business and Economics	Bachelor of Management Studies	HKU	1998–
	Bachelor of Accounting	HKU	1998–
Education	Bachelor of Science (Sports Science and Leisure Management)	HKU	1998–2002
	Bachelor of Education (IT Education/ Library and Information Studies)	HKU	2000–2002
Engineering	Postgraduate Certificate in E-commerce and Internet Technology (in Shanghai)		
Law	Postgraduate Certificate in Laws	HKU	1990–2001 (full-time)
			1992–2001 (part-time)
	Hong Kong Common Professional Examination Certificate	Joint	1992–1997
Medicine	Bachelor of Science (Hons) in Nursing	HKU	1994–1998
	Bachelor of Chinese Medicine	HKU	1998–2002 (part-time)
			2000–2005 (full-time)
	Bachelor of Pharmacy in Chinese Medicine	HKU	1999–
	Bachelor of Science (Hons) in Applied Medical Sciences	HKU	1999–2005
	Master of Chinese Medicine in Acupuncture and Moxibustion	HKU	2002–2005

(Appendix 9 continued on p. 274)

Faculty	Title	Award	Years offered
Medicine	Postgraduate Diploma in Sport and Exercise Medicine	University of Bath	2004–
	Postgraduate Diploma in Principles of Sex Counselling and Therapy	HKU SPACE	2004–
Social Sciences	Master of Housing Management	HKU	1992–
	Bachelor of Housing Management	HKU	1998–
	Master of Housing Management (Professional Stream / Academic Stream)	HKU	1999–
	Postgraduate Certificate / Diploma / Master in Social Work and Social Service Management (in Shanghai)		2001–
	Bachelor of Criminal Justice	HKU	2001–2003

Appendix 10: Terms of Reference for the Board for Continuing and Professional Education and Lifelong Learning (Committee of the Senate), December 2000

Power and Duties

Subject to the provisions of the Statutes, the Board shall:

1. advise the Senate on policy issues relating to CPE and Lifelong Learning.
2. be responsible to the Senate for the academic programmes, teaching and research in the School of Professional and Continuing Education (SPACE) as the Extension arm of the University.
3. in respect of degrees awarded by the University of Hong Kong and administered by SPACE:
   a. recommend, on the advice of the Director, proposed degree programmes to the Senate;
   b. resolve, on the recommendation of the Board of Examiners that successful candidates be presented to the Chancellor for the conferment of degrees;
   c. approve amendments to syllabuses;
   d. approve waivers of regulations (other than those for M.Phil. and Ph.D., and those governing eligibility for honours) in cases of individual students;
   e. approve suspension of curricula;
   f. appoint internal examiners.
4. in respect of diplomas and certificates:
   a. approve, on the recommendation of the Director, the introduction of new diploma and certificate programmes;
   b. approve amendments to syllabuses and regulations;
   c. resolve, on the recommendation of Boards of Examiners, that successful candidates be awarded diplomas and certificates.
   d. appoint internal examiners.
5. in respect of partnerships with other universities or institutions:
   a. approve, on the recommendation of the Director, the introduction of new partnership programmes with other universities or institutions where the award is of the partner body;
   b. approve (or recommend) amendments to syllabuses and regulations;
   c. receive, from the Boards of Examiners, reports on the examinations.
6. To receive reports and recommendations from the Director, on the advice of the Quality Assurance Committee which shall operate the School's quality assurance policy and procedures and:
   a. recommend new programmes to the Board;
   b. report annually to the Board on quality assurance matters.
7. To receive reports and recommendations from the Director, on the advice of the Research and Development Committee which shall advise on:
   a. regulations for research funds wholly based in the School;

   b. regulations for conference grants and other awards for staff which are wholly based in the School;
   c. research in lifelong learning issues;
   d. research and development projects carried out by staff in the School;
   e. market research and future community needs in lifelong learning.

8. approve Honorary and Visiting appointments in the School of Professional and Continuing Education, except those at professorial level which shall be recommended to Senate.

9. submit an annual report to the Senate and such other reports as the Senate may require from time to time.

10. exercise any other power which the Senate may delegate to it.

11. do all such other acts and things as are requisite to exercise any power and to perform any duty which Senate may delegate to it.

Membership

1. The Vice-Chancellor (Chairman) Professor Y. C. Cheng

2. Pro-Vice-Chancellor (Academic) (Vice-Chairman) Professor S. L. Wong

3. Two members of the Management Board, appointed by the Senate
   Professor R. C. C. Ko
   Professor Nelson Chow

4. Two additional Senate members, appointed by the Vice-Chancellor
   Professor Francis Chin
   Professor David Tse

5. Two lay members appointed by the Vice-Chancellor from the SPACE Advisory Board
   Mr Philip Wong
   Dr Peter C. Y. Lee

6. Director of SPACE (ex-officio)
   Professor E. C. M. Young

7. Two Deputy Directors of SPACE (ex-officio)
   Dr M. Luk
   Dr S. M. Shen

8. One representative from each of the eight SPACE divisions

Accounting and Commerce	Mr D. Lam
Applied Science and Information Technology	Dr F. T. Chan
Arts and Humanities	Mr R. Booker
Finance and Business	Ms J. Ng
Housing and Built Environment	Dr T. M. Kwong
Law	Mr M. Fisher
Social Sciences and Education	Mrs Y. L. Cheng
Traditional Chinese Medicine	Prof Sarah Hui

Source: BCPE&LLM 22 February 2000, 1, Appendix A, document 44/200, 20 December 1999.

Appendix 11: HKU SPACE Organisation Chart, January 2006

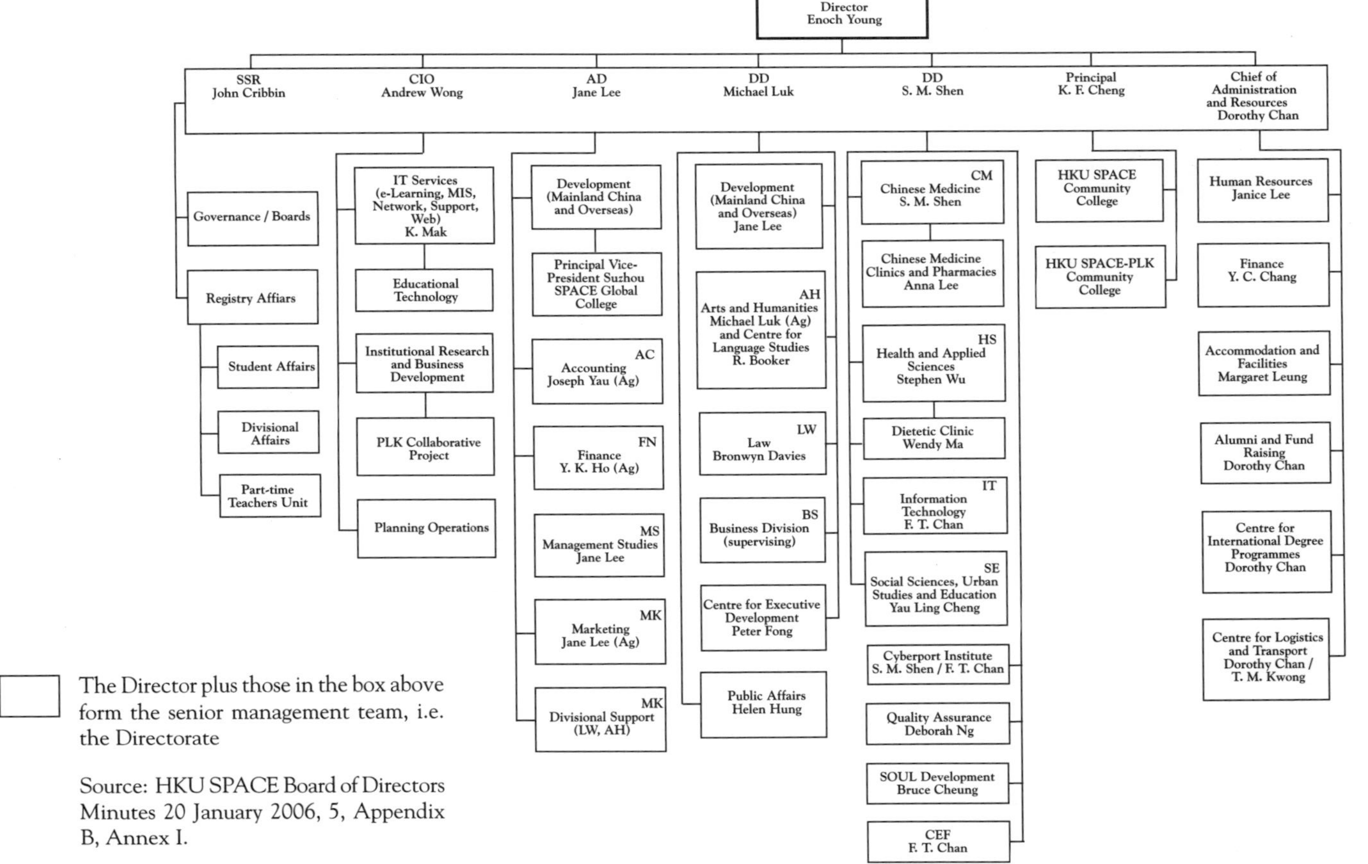

Source: HKU SPACE Board of Directors Minutes 20 January 2006, 5, Appendix B, Annex I.

Notes

INTRODUCTION

1. The University's 'Vision and Mission Statement' may be found in the *University of Hong Kong Calendar 2005–2006*, back of title page.
2. Problems of definition are discussed at greater length by John Cribbin, 'Growth and Development of Lifelong Learning in Hong Kong', in John Cribbin and Peter Kennedy (eds.), *Lifelong Learning in Action: Hong Kong Practitioners' Perspectives* (Hong Kong: Hong Kong University Press, 2002), pp. 15–19. See also Christopher K. Knapper and Arthur J. Cropley, *Lifelong Learning in Higher Education*, 3rd ed. (London: Kogan Page, 2000), pp. 1–21 for a discussion of the basic concepts of lifelong learning.
3. The levels of academic courses offered by HKU SPACE are listed on the School's website and include: short courses for personal development, continuing professional development (CPD) courses, professional programmes, diploma and certificate programmes, associate degree and higher diploma programmes, bachelor's degrees, master's degrees and postgraduate diplomas and certificates, and doctorates; see 'Academic Level of Courses', http://hkuspace.hku.hk/about/about.php (2003), accessed on 23 March 2007.
4. Education Commission Report No. 1, October 1984, p. 71.
5. For an arresting discussion of the political use of the term 'lifelong learning' in the Hong Kong higher education context see Peter Kennedy, 'The politics of "lifelong learning" in post-1997 Hong Kong', *International Journal of Lifelong Education*, vol. 25 (2004), pp. 589–624.
6. See especially Robert Peers, *Adult Education: A Comparative Study* (London: Routledge, 1958), and the views expressed by Ieuan Hughes in his university lecture delivered at HKU on 1 December 1960: 'The University and Adult Education', in the *Supplement to the University of Hong Kong Gazette*, vol. 9, no. 5 (1962), pp. 1–6.
7. Colonial Office, *Report of the Commission on University Education in Malaya* (Kuala Lumpur: Government Press, 1948), pp. 65–66.

CHAPTER ONE

1. The requirement to pass the Matriculation Examination as a condition of entry to HKU is to be found in the rules governing admission in the early *University Calendars*; see, for example, *Calendar* for 1913–14, p. 26.
2. University of Hong Kong Ordinance (The University Ordinance, 1911; No. 10 of 1912, amended) in University of Hong Kong, *Calendar 1913–1914* (Hong Kong: Noronha & Co., 1913), p. 67.
3. Frederick Lugard, 'The problem of Universities in the East in regard to their influence on character and moral ideals', read at the Congress of the Universities of the British Empire, London, 3 July 1912, reproduced in Bernard Mellor, *Lugard in Hong Kong: Empires, Education and a Governor at Work, 1907–1912* (Hong Kong: Hong Kong University Press, 1992), pp. 171–177.
4. *Ibid.*, p. 173.
5. Robert Peers, *Adult Education: A Comparative Study* (London: Routledge, 1958; reprinted 1998), Part 1, 'The Background of English Adult Education', pp. 3–100.
6. *Ibid.*, pp. 49–60.
7. Negley Harte, *The University of London, 1836–1986: An Illustrated History* (London: Athlone Press, 1986), p. 149. See also O. R. McGregor, 'The Social Sciences', pp. 218–221, and W. L. Twining, 'Laws', pp. 102–105, in F. M. L. Thompson (ed.), *The University of London and the World of Learning, 1836–1986* (London: Hambledon Press, 1990).
8. Peers, *Adult Education*, p. 69.
9. *Ibid.*, p. 76.
10. Anthony Sweeting, *Education in Hong Kong, Pre-1841 to 1941: Fact and Opinion: Materials for a History of Education in Hong Kong* (Hong Kong: Hong Kong University Press, 1990), pp. 195–203.
11. *Ibid.*, pp. 213–219.
12. *Ibid.*, pp. 196–198.
13. HKUFA, Minutes of the Board of the Faculty of Arts, 13 January 1919.
14. *Ibid.*, 24 November 1919.
15. *Ibid.*, 20 September 1921, 14, and 24 September 1921, 2.
16. *Ibid.*, 25 October 1921, 7, and 7 February 1922, 11.
17. *Ibid.*, 2 February 1923, 8.
18. *University Calendar*, 1930, p. 36. This regulation refers to the Senate resolution of 31 January 1928 allowing 'Apprentices in Engineering indentured to approved firms' to be admitted 'to the 1st year lectures in engineering at the University as external students, provided that they pass an entrance examination in English and Mathematics of matriculation standard'. External fees for 1931 are given in *University Calendar*, 1931, p. 38.
19. HKUA, University Memoranda, vol. 1, no. 2, 8 February 1928; 'Note on Chinese Studies in the University'.
20. University of Hong Kong, *Report of the Special Committee appointed to advise on the Teaching of Chinese* (Hong Kong: Newspaper Enterprise Ltd., 1932), pp. 7–8.
21. Senate Minutes [hereafter HKUSM] 31 January 1928, 26.
22. *University Calendar*, 1930, p. 36.

23. These figures have been reconstructed from the early student records of the Faculty of Arts.
24. *Report of the University (1937) Committee* (Report No. 8/1937) (Hong Kong: Government Printer, 1937), p. 11; *Report of a Committee on the Development of the University* (*University Development Report*) (Hong Kong: Government Printer, 1939), p. 29.
25. HKU, annual *Report*, 1934–1938, p. 75.
26. HKUFA, Early Student Records, 1929.
27. Betty Draper's diary for 1929 is still in the hands of her son, Mr Dan Quail, but a copy has been placed in the Hong Kong University Archives. We are grateful to Mr Quail for allowing us to use his mother's diary.
28. Council Minutes [hereafter HKUCM] 12 August 1912, 14; 22 August 1930, 17 and 18.
29. HKUSM 31 January 1928, 26.
30. Peers, *Adult Education*, pp. 83–91.
31. The general findings of this committee and the controversy they generated are summarised in Anthony Sweeting, 'The University by Report', in Chan Lau Kit-ching and Peter Cunich (eds.), *An Impossible Dream: Hong Kong University from Foundation to Re-establishment, 1910–1950* (Hong Kong: Oxford University Press, 2002), pp. 224–30.
32. *Report of the University (1937) Committee*, pp. 4–5, 6, 9, 11, 13.
33. *University Development Report*, p. 2.
34. HKUA, University Memoranda, vol. 2, 1935–1939, no. 131 (10 May 1938).
35. HKUA, Registry Old Files, folder no. 39; Minutes of Meetings of University Bodies and other relevant papers during Internment, Jan. 1942–Aug.1945; Lancelot Forster's note of 10 July 1942.
36. Anthony Sweeting, 'Training Teachers: Processes, Products, and Purposes', in Chan and Cunich (eds.), *An Impossible Dream*, pp. 80–81, 83–84.
37. *University Development Report*, pp. 18, 32, 33, 34. See also University Memoranda, vol. 2, no. 142 (27 January 1939).
38. HKUA, Registry Old Files, folder no. 39; Lancelot Forster's note of 10 July 1942.
39. *Ibid.*
40. Anthony Sweeting, 'Controversy over the Re-opening of the University of Hong Kong, 1942–48', in Clifford Matthews and Oswald Cheung (eds.), *Dispersal and Renewal: Hong Kong University During the War Years* (Hong Kong: Hong Kong University Press, 1998), p. 399.
41. For the poetry lectures see Norman H. Mackenzie, 'An Academic Odyssey: A Professor in Five Continents (Part 2)', in Matthews and Cheung (eds.), *Dispersal and Renewal*, pp. 180–181. For the Shamshuipo orchestra, see Solomon Bard, 'Mount Davis and Sham Shui Po: A Medical Officer with the Volunteers', in *Dispersal and Renewal*, pp. 200–201. For Clifford Matthews's experience of 'continuing professional education' in Shamshuipo camp, see Clifford Matthews, 'Life Experiences from Star Ferry to Stardust', also in *Dispersal and Renewal*, p. 234.
42. HKUA, Registry Old Files, folder no. 39; Minutes of informal meeting of 25 May 1943.
43. *Ibid.*; HKUSM 8 February 1944, 1 and 14 November 1944, 3.
44. *Ibid.*, 30 November 1944; the whole of this Senate meeting was devoted to discussion of post-War development.
45. HKUA, Interim Period Minutes, Registrar's collection, vol. 7; Minutes of the Provisional Powers Committee, 4 March 1947, 2, and Appendix 1.8(a).

46. *Ibid.*, Minutes of Interim Committee, 7 January 1947, 3.
47. HKUA, Registry Dead Files; Interim Committee Miscellaneous, file 25/3, letter dated 14 July 1947.
48. HKUA, Interim Period Minutes; Minutes of the Interim Committee, 10 September 1947, 32.
49. Asquith Committee Report quoted in Sweeting, 'Controversy over the Re-opening of the University', p. 414.
50. Colonial Office, *Report of the Commission on Higher Education in the Colonies* (London: HMSO, 1945), pp. 18–19.
51. Peers, *Adult Education*, p. 117.
52. *Ibid.*, p. 109.
53. HKU *Vice-Chancellor's Report*, 1963–64, p. 79; and 1964–65, p. 89.
54. HKU *Calendar*, 1951–52, pp. 67 and 68, General Regulations G7 and G8.
55. HKU *Calendar*, 1952–53, pp. 63–64.
56. HKU *Calendar*, 1952–53, pp. 63–64.
57. Peers, *Adult Education*, pp. 83–86, 95–99.
58. See Peter Cunich, 'University Finances', in Chan and Cunich (eds.), *An Impossible Dream*, pp. 193–212.

CHAPTER TWO

1. Chan Lau Kit-ching, 'The Post-War Re-establishment of the University of Hong Kong, 1945–1950', in Chan Lau Kit-ching and Peter Cunich (eds.), *An Impossible Dream: Hong Kong University from Foundation to Re-establishment, 1910–1950* (Hong Kong: Oxford University Press, 2002), pp. 241–264; Anthony Sweeting, 'Controversy over the Re-opening of the University of Hong Kong, 1942–48', in Clifford Matthews and Oswald Cheung (eds.), *Dispersal and Renewal: Hong Kong University during the War Years* (Hong Kong: Hong Kong University Press, 1998), pp. 397–424.
2. Anthony Sweeting, *Education in Hong Kong, 1941–2001: Visions and Revisions* (Hong Kong: Hong Kong University Press, 2004), p. 142.
3. *Ibid.*, pp. 141–144.
4. N. G. Fisher, A *Report on Government Expenditure on Education in Hong Kong* (Hong Kong: Government Printers and Publishers, 1950), p. 26.
5. John Keswick *et al*, *Report of the Hong Kong Government Committee on Higher Education* (Hong Kong: Government Printer, 1952) [hereafter Keswick Report], pp. 9–11.
6. Director of Education, *Annual Departmental Report by the Director of Education for the Financial Year 1951–2* (Hong Kong, 1952), p. 19.
7. Keswick Report, para. 72, p. 17.
8. The Evening Institute was first created in 1907 but its activities were suspended during the Second World War. It was restored soon after the War; see Director of Education, *Annual Departmental Report for 1950–1* (Hong Kong, 1951), p. 29.
9. The Hong Kong Technical College was formed in 1947 from the Government Trade School, which had itself been established in 1938 but closed during the War; see Director of Education, *Annual Departmental Report for 1947/8* (Hong Kong, 1948), pp. 17–19.
10. Director of Education, *Annual Departmental Report for 1951–2*, pp. 106–109.
11. *Ibid.*, p. 124.

12. Jiulü, 'Guanli Wenshang Zhuanke Xuexiao jianshi' (A brief history of the Evening School of Higher Chinese Studies), *Adult Education Bulletin*, vol. 44, 1973, p. 16.
13. Technical Education Investigating Committee, A *Report on Technical Education and Vocational Training in Hong Kong* (Hong Kong, 1953), p. 29.
14. Keswick Report, para. 64, p. 15.
15. *Ibid.*, Appendix 16, pp. 61–63.
16. *Ibid.*, p. 61.
17. *Ibid.*, para. 62, p.14.
18. *Ibid.*, Appendix 16, pp. 61–63.
19. *Ibid.*, para. 62, p. 14.
20. *Ibid.*, para. 69, p. 16.
21. Colonial Office, *Report of the Commission on Higher Education in the Colonies* (London: HMSO, 1945), p. 3.
22. *Ibid.*, p. 18.
23. *Ibid.*, pp. 18–19.
24. *Ibid.*, p. 19.
25. *Ibid.*, p. 19.
26. Colonial Office, *Report of the West Indies Committee of the Commission on Higher Education in the Colonies* (London: HMSO, 1945), paras. 139–148, pp. 39–41; Colonial Office, *Report of the Commission on Higher Education in West Africa* (London: HMSO, 1945), paras. 41–44, pp. 58–59.
27. Colonial Office, *Report of the Commission on Higher Education for Africans in Central Africa* (London: King and Jarrett, 1953), p. 38.
28. HKUA, Registry Old Files, 13/7, p. 3. (Memorandum No. 3 by B. Mellor)
29. Colonial Office, *Report of the Commission on University Education in Malaya* (Kuala Lumpur: Government Press, 1948), p. 65.
30. *Ibid.*, pp. 65–66.
31. Singapore Council for Adult Education, *The Singapore Council for Adult Education: What It Is and What It Does* (Singapore: Singapore Council for Adult Education, n.d.), p. 1. The formal commencement of a department of extra-mural studies in Singapore did not, however, materialise until the appointment of a Director of Extramural Studies at the University of Singapore, which split from the University of Malaya in 1963. See J. F. Conceicao, 'The University and Adult Education', in *Proceedings of the National Conference on Adult Education, 23–25 September 1971* (Singapore: Adult Education Board, 1972), p. 38.
32. Robert Blake, *Jardine Matheson: Traders of the Far East* (London: Weidenfeld and Nicholson, 1999), pp. 238–253.
33. Keswick Report, p. vii. The other members were Mr Fung Ping-fan, Mr Lam Chi-fung, Mr Richard Charles Lee, O.B.E., Mr Leonard Geoffrey Morgan, Professor Kenneth Ewart Priestley, and Mr David McLellan (Secretary). Mr Christopher Paul D'Almada e Castro, Mr Bernard Mellor and Mr Arnaldo de Oliveira Sales served on the Committee at different times, but were not in Hong Kong to sign the Report in 1952. (Keswick Report, p. iii.) Professor K. E. Priestley and Bernard Mellor would later be associated with the development of extra-mural studies at HKU over many years.
34. *South China Morning Post*, 11 December 1951 (HKUA, Registry Old Files, 13/9).

35. HKUA, Registry Old Files 13/7; letter from A. W. Cassian, Hongkong Teachers' Association, to the Secretary of the Committee on Higher Education, 11 January 1952.
36. *Ibid.*, 13/8; Minutes of the 13th Meeting of the Committee on Higher Education, 21 February 1952.
37. *Ibid.*, 13/7; Memorandum No. 3 by B. Mellor, p. 4.
38. *Ibid.*, p. 4.
39. *Ibid.*, 13/8; Minutes of the 14th Meeting of the Committee on Higher Education, 27 February 1952.
40. Keswick Report, para. 16, p. 4.
41. *Ibid.*, para. 17, p. 5.
42. *Ibid.*, paras. 17–18, p. 5.
43. *Ibid.*, paras. 28–29, pp. 7–8.
44. *Ibid.*, para. 34, p. 8.
45. *Ibid.*, para. 78, p. 17.
46. *Ibid.*, para. 78, p. 18.
47. *Ibid.*, para. 79, p. 18.
48. *Ibid.*, para. 80, p.18.
49. *Ibid.*, para. 143, p. 32.
50. *Ibid.*, para. 144, p. 32.
51. *Ibid.*, para. 143, p. 32.
52. *Report of the Commission on Higher Education in the Colonies*, p. 19.
53. Keswick Report, para. 145, p. 32.
54. *Ibid.*
55. For example, the annual expenses of a proposed Institute of Education were $98,000; the annual cost of establishing a Research Department in the Institute of Far Eastern Studies was $48,000; and the cost of establishing an Institute of English was $62,380 per annum. The $95,080 subsidy proposed for the Department of Extra-Mural Studies represented nearly 4 per cent of the University's budget for salaries and wages in 1951–52 (total $2,406,654), but a much smaller 2.2 per cent of the salaries and wages budget for 1952–53 (total $4,335,818).
56. Keswick Report, para. 146, p. 32.
57. *Hong Kong Hansard*, 18 March 1953, pp. 65–66.
58. Senate Minutes [hereafter HKUSM] 20 October 1954, 1(e); 'Report of the Working Party' (the 1953 Report), Appendix A, para. 17, p. 5. HKUSM 1 February 1955, 19; a report by Professor Gordon King dated 27 January 1955, Appendix C.
59. HKUSM 20 October 1954, 1(e); 'Report of the Working Party' (the 1953 Report), Appendix A, para. 17, p. 5.
60. HKUA, Registry Old Files, 13/12; 'Report of the Hong Kong Government Committee on Higher Education: Third Memorandum of the Vice-Chancellor's Working Party', 28 June 1953, p. 3.
61. Keswick Report, para. 80, p. 18.
62. These courses included, in Architecture: 'Theory and Practice of Architectural Design'; in Economics and Politics, courses in 'Accounting, Commercial Law, and Secretarial Practice', trade unionism, and a Certificate course in Social Study; in Education, courses in Chinese educational philosophy, 'Greek and Roman architecture for secondary school teachers', 'history of the overseas Chinese with special reference to Hong Kong', mental

health in education, teaching English as a foreign language, and 'Social and Cultural History of the Western World from the Renaissance to the Present Day'; and in Languages: Ancient Literary Chinese, Modern Literary Chinese, a beginner's course in Cantonese, 'Colloquial Chinese', Chinese characters and character-writing, spoken Mandarin, French, French literature and language, Japanese, German, Italian, Latin, Sanskrit and Spanish. See HKU Senate and Council Minutes, 1953–56, *passim*.

63. HKUSM 15 August 1953, 4(a).
64. In 1954–55, for example, most of the government evening courses except the Evening School of Higher Chinese Studies required students to pay less than $25 per term; see Director of Education, *Annual Departmental Report for 1954–55*, p. 13.
65. Council Minutes [hereafter HKUCM] 17 December 1953 and 29 September 1955.
66. HKUSM 1 February 1955, 19, Appendix C; letter from E.S. Kirby to the Registrar, 21 January 1955.
67. *Ibid.*
68. HKUCM 19 May 1955, 3(i).
69. Minutes of the Board of the Faculty of Arts 4 September 1953, 'Memorandum upon Development Policy over the next five years'.
70. 'Report on Visit to University of Hong Kong, April 1953, by Sir Alexander M. Carr-Saunders and Professor D. G. James', paragraph II (c), reprinted in Anthony Sweeting, 'The Reconstruction of Education in Post-War Hong Kong, 1945–54: Variations in the Process of Education Policy Making' (unpublished Ph.D. dissertation, University of Hong Kong, 1989), vol. 4, p. 1192. See also Sweeting, *Education in Hong Kong*, p. 165. We are grateful to Professor Sweeting for alerting us to the existence of this copy of the Carr-Saunders James Report.
71. Sweeting, 'The Reconstruction of Education in Post-War Hong Kong', vol. 4, p. 1195.
72. Ivor Jennings and D. W. Logan, *A Report on the University of Hong Kong* (Hong Kong: The University of Hong Kong, 1954), para.1, p.1.
73. *Ibid.*, para. 295, p. 113.
74. Court Minutes [hereafter HKUCourt] 2 December 1953; 'Treasurer's Speech on Budget Estimates for 1952–53'. See also HKUA, Registrar's Office Dead File: Carr-Saunders/ James Visitation 1953.
75. HKUCM 17 March 1955, 5(f).
76. HKUSM 5 April 1955, 5(b).
77. The working party consisted of two members of the Senate not sitting on the Council from each of the Faculties of Arts, Science and Medicine. They were Professors D. Barker (Chairman), Hao Pao-chang, Wong Yung-chow, F. S. Drake, L. G. Kilborn and B. Harrison; see HKUSM 2 March 1954, 13(d).
78. HKUSM 20 October 1954, 1(e); 'Report of the Working Party' (the 1953 Report), Appendix A, document 98/74, para. 10, p. 4, and para. 17, p. 5.
79. They were Professor K. E. Priestley (Chairman), Professor D. Barker, Mr J. H. Gransden, and the Registrar, Mr B. Mellor as secretary.
80. The original report of the Committee on Extra-Mural Studies is missing from the Registry archive. These recommendations were quoted in a Draft Memorandum written by G. H. Moore; see HKUCourt 21 May 1957, 6; Appendix C, document 84/17, 25 January 1957, para. 2, p.1.
81. HKUSM 7 June 1955, 4; HKUCM 23 June 1955, 5.

82. HKUSM 4 January 1955, 5, Appendix A; Joint Establishments Committee Report, 3 December 1954, para. 22, p. 4.
83. HKUCourt 29 June 1955, 11.
84. HKUCM 24 January 1956, 15.
85. Mr Moore was not an applicant when the University initially advertised for a Director of Extra-Mural Studies, but he was appointed under the original terms of the advertisement; see HKUSM 5 May 1959, 6, Appendix E; letter from Vice-Chancellor to G. H. Moore, 12 February 1959; G. H. Moore to the Vice-Chancellor, 4 April 1959.
86. Spencer Wong, 'Development of Adult Education in Hong Kong since World War II' (unpublished Ph.D. dissertation, University of Edinburgh, 1975), p. 100.
87. University of Hong Kong, *Departmental Reports, 1956–1957* (Hong Kong: University of Hong Kong, 1957), p. 25.
88. HKUSM 3 May 1955, Appendix E; letter from J. H. Gransden to the Registrar, 24 March 1955.
89. Wong, 'Development of Adult Education in Hong Kong', p. 100.
90. HKUSA 6 November 1956, 8, Appendix E; letter from F. S. Drake to the Registrar, 31 October 1956.
91. *Ibid.*
92. *Ibid.*
93. HKUSM 6 November 1956, 8.
94. HKUCM 21 February 1957, 4(f), Appendix C; memorandum by A. Rowe-Evans, 28 January 1957.
95. HKUCourt 21 May 1957, 6, Appendix C; 'Draft Memorandum: Extra-Mural Studies', document 84/17, 25 January 1957, para. 1, p. 1.
96. *Ibid.*, para. 2(a), p. 1.
97. *Ibid.*, para. 2(c)(vii), p. 3.
98. *Ibid.*, para. 2(c)(viii), p. 3.
99. *Ibid.*, para. 2(c)(viii), p. 4.
100. *Ibid.*, para. 2(c)(ix), p. 4.
101. *Ibid.*, paras. 2(c)(iii) and (iv), p. 2.
102. *Ibid.*, para. 2(c)(ii), p. 2.
103. *Ibid.*, para. 2(c)(v), p. 2.
104. *Ibid.*, para. 3(a), p. 4.
105. *Ibid.*, para. 3(d), p. 5.
106. *Ibid.*, para. 3(b), p.4.
107. *Ibid.*, para. 3(d), p. 6.
108. *Ibid.*, para. 3(d), p. 5.
109. *Ibid.*, para. 3(d), p. 6.
110. *Ibid.*, para 4(i), p. 7.
111. *Ibid.*, para. 4(ii), p. 7.
112. *Ibid.*, para. 4(iii), p. 7.
113. HKUSM 5 February 1957, 18.
114. HKUCM 21 February 1957, 8(d).
115. *Ibid.*
116. HKUSM 5 March 1957, 4.
117. *Ibid.*; HKUSM 7 May 1957, 8; and BEMSM 22 May 1957.

118. HKUCourt 21 May 1957, 6.
119. *Departmental Reports*, 1956–57 p. 25.
120. Board of Extra-Mural Studies Minutes 22 May 1957, 1(c), Appendix A; letter from the Vice-Chancellor to the Director of Extra-Mural Studies, 22 May 1957.

CHAPTER THREE

1. HKPRO, HKRS 457–3–6; letter from the Vice-Chancellor to the Colonial Secretary, 26 March 1957. There had originally been three sections in the Evening School: General Arts, Journalism, and Commerce. The Journalism section was closed in July 1956 because of low enrolments; see Director of Education, *Education Department Annual Summary, 1955–56* (Hong Kong: Government Printer, 1956), p. 14.
2. Board of Extra-Mural Studies Minutes [hereafter BEMSM] 22 May 1957, 3.
3. *Ibid.*, 29 November 1957, 3; Appendix B, document 24/117; 'Amended Report of the Committee appointed by the Board of Extra-Mural Studies on the School of Higher Chinese Studies'.
4. BEMSM 29 November 1957, 3.
5. Senate Minutes [hereafter HKUSM] 4 February 1958, 9, Appendix D; 'Director's Recommendations concerning the Evening School of Higher Chinese Studies', 2 December 1957.
6. HKUSM 4 February 1958, 9; Council minutes [hereafter HKUCM] 27 February 1958. 6(f).
7. *Wah Kiu Yat Po*, 19 June 1957 (see HKPRO, HKRS457–3–6).
8. HKPRO, HKRS457–3–6; letter from the Deputy Colonial Secretary to the Acting Registrar, 1 May 1958.
9. HKUCM 20 March 1958, 7.
10. HKPRO, HKRS458–3–6; letter from the Acting Registrar to the Deputy Colonial Secretary, 3 May 1958.
11. HKPRO, HKRS457–3–6; memo from W. J. Dyer to Colonial Secretary, 20 May 1958.
12. *Ibid.*, memo from AS2 to ACS, 23 May 1958.
13. *Ibid.*, letter from the Deputy Colonial Secretary to the Acting Registrar, 21 June 1958.
14. These phenomena were commented upon by Moore in May 1959; see BEMSM 10 December 1959, 11, Appendix E; 'A recommendation on the Evening School of Higher Chinese Studies by the Director of Extra-Mural Studies', 14 May 1959.
15. 247 candidates were offered first-year places in September 1958, 136 of them actually enrolled in the School, and only 62 students were still studying at the Evening School in June 1959. The attrition rate was therefore 74 per cent; see BEMSM 10 December 1959, 11, Appendix E, Annex I; letter from the Director of Education to the Director of Extra-Mural Studies, 29 April 1959.
16. HKPRO, HKRS457–3–6; memo from the Director of Education to the Colonial Secretary, 13 May 1952.
17. BEMSM 10 December 1959, 11, Appendix E; 'A recommendation on the Evening School of Higher Chinese Studies', 14 May 1959.
18. BEMSM 10 December 1959, 11.
19. HKPRO, HKRS457–3–6; letter from Alastair Todd to Bernard Mellor, 22 January 1965. The Evening School continued to function but under the Education Department's

auspices in the following decades. It was reorganised into the Institute of Languages in Education in 1982, and merged with three other teacher training colleges to form the Hong Kong Institute of Education in 1994.

20. HKUSM 5 May 1959, 6, Appendix E, document 84/49; letter from Mr G. H. Moore to Professor F. E. Stock, 7 October 1958.
21. *Ibid.*
22. *Ibid.*
23. *Ibid.*, document 84/49; letter from the Vice-Chancellor to Mr G. H. Moore, 25 February 1959.
24. *Ibid.*, document 84/49; letter from Mr G. H. Moore to the Vice-Chancellor, 4 April 1959.
25. HKUVC 225/60; memo from Gerald Moore to the Vice-Chancellor, 25 May 1959.
26. HKUSM 5 May 1959, 6, Appendix E, document 85/49; 'Extra-Mural Studies (Confidential)', 29 April 1959.
27. *Ibid.*
28. HKUSM 2 June 1959, 10(b).
29. BEMSM 10 December 1959, 2(a). *Departmental Reports*, 1959–60, p. 68.
30. Interview with Mr T. C. Lai, 29 June 2006.
31. HKUSM 15 December 1959, 14; Court Minutes [hereafter HKUCourt] 5 January 1960, 5(d).
32. Development and General Purposes Committee Minutes [hereafter DGPCM] 2 June 1969, 12.
33. Ieuan Hughes, 'Hong Kong: An Extra-Mural Profile', *University of Hong Kong Gazette*, vol. 10, no. 4 (16 April 1963), p. 37.
34. BEMSM 20 April 1959, 8; and HKUSM 2 June 1959, 10.
35. BEMSM 10 March 1961, 5; and HKUSM 4 April 1961, 9.
36. *Departmental Reports*, 1958–59, p. 25. HKUSM 4 June 1964, 9(a), Appendix F; letter from H. A. Rydings, Librarian, to Mrs E. L. Alleyne, Secretary of Library Committee, 3 May 1963.
37. *Departmental Reports*, 1958–59, p. 25.
38. HKUCM 20 March 1958, 8, Appendix D, revised document 30/28; 'Observations on the Colonial Secretary's letter of April 13, 1957', 13 March 1958.
39. HKPRO, HKRS457–3–10; memo from AS2 to DCS, 6 May 1959.
40. *Departmental Reports*, 1959–60, p. 68.
41. *University of Hong Kong Gazette*, vol. 15, no. 3 (1 March 1968), p. 39.
42. Ieuan Hughes, 'The University and Adult Education: A University Lecture', *Supplement to the University of Hong Kong Gazette*, vol. 9, no. 5 (1 June 1962), p. 1.
43. *Ibid.*, p. 3.
44. *Ibid.*, p. 4.
45. *Ibid.*, p. 6.
46. HKU Department of Extra-Mural Studies, *Extra-Mural Courses*, 1965–66, inside cover, quoting 'Design for Democracy', a reprint of the 1919 Final Report of the Ministry of Reconstruction Adult Education Committee.
47. HKUSM 4 April 1961, 9, Appendix E, documents 7/41 and 8/41; 'Draft Survey of Staff' and 'Scheme of Development'.
48. Hughes, 'The University and Adult Education', p. 6.

49. *Ibid.*
50. BEMSM 10 March 1961, 11.
51. HKUSM 4 April 1961, 9; HKUCM 25 April 1961, 4.
52. HKUSM 2 October 1962, 10, Appendix E, Annex A, document 9/765; 'Modifications already made to the Staffing Structure of the Plan', 24 September 1962.
53. Priscilla Mark graduated with a B.A. in History and a Diploma in Education from HKU. Before becoming a full-time staff tutor, she was a part-time tutor for extra-mural English courses; see HKUSM 16 July 1965, 22, Appendix P, document 9/765; and *Departmental Reports*, 1962–63, p. 55.
54. HKPRO, HKRS457–3–10; letter from W. Mallory-Browne to L. T. Ride, 18 October 1961.
55. *Ibid.*, memo from Director of Education to Colonial Secretary, 12 July 1961.
56. The Education Department suggested that the proposed secondment, which would cost about $31,500 for one year, should be funded by a special ear-marked grant from the government. See letter from F. E. Stock to Colonial Secretary, 14 June 1961; letter from A. J. M. Prata to the Bursar, HKU, 15 June 1961; and memo from Director of Education to Colonial Secretary, 12 July 1961 (all are in HKRS457–3–10).
57. HKPRO, HKRS457–3–10; letter from E. B. Teedsale to L. T. Ride, 20 November 1961.
58. *Ibid.*, memo from DCS to CS, 13 January 1962.
59. *Ibid.*, personal letter from C. B. Burgess to Lindsay Ride, 6 January 1962; and memo from the Colonial Secretary, 15 January 1962.
60. *Ibid.*, letter from L. T. Ride to the Colonial Secretary, 2 May 1961.
61. Mr Fung Ping-fan, for instance, appealed for an extension of the DEMS during a budgetary debate in the Legislative Council in March 1962 (*Hong Kong Hansard*, 19 March 1962, p. 85). See also the memo from Director of Education to Colonial Secretary, 1 May 1962; and letter from G. C. Hamilton to L. T. Ride, 21 June 1962 (HKRS457–3–10).
62. HKUVC 225/60; Ieuan Hughes, 'Address to Hong Kong Rotary, 13/2/62: Adult Education and Opportunity'.
63. *China Mail*, 13 February 1962. An article expressing similar sentiments was written by Hughes for the *South China Morning Post*, 14 February 1962 (HKUVC 225/60).
64. *China Mail*, 14 February 1962, 'Education Puzzle' (HKUVC 225/60).
65. HKUVC 225/60; memo from Ieuan Hughes to Lindsay Ride, 29 March 1963.
66. *China Mail*, 19 February 1962, 'Adults at School' (HKUVC 225/60).
67. HKUVC 225/60; Vice-Chancellor's address at Extra-Mural Rally, 30 March 1963. The BEMS was 'deeply shocked at the situation' at its meeting on 27 March 1963 and remarked that lack of government support would force it to reduce the number of extra-mural classes to 40–60 classes, meaning 'the death of Extra-Mural Studies' (HKUVC 225/60, 'The Immediate Situation', 27 March 1963).
68. *Ibid.*
69. *South China Morning Post–Herald*, 31 March 1963 (HKUVC 225/60).
70. HKUSM 2 October 1962.
71. The two additional staff tutorships were to be created as a result of a review and recommendations by the BEMS at the end of the 1964–65 academic year; see HKPRO, HKRS457–3–10; letter from E. B. Teesdale to Sir Lindsay Ride, 10 May 1963.

72. Priscilla Mark took her unpaid study leave during 1963–64 and resumed her established post in 1964–65 (BEMSM 17 June 1964, 7). As no local candidates with previous extra-mural experience were available, four half-time staff tutors were appointed in lieu of the two full-time staff tutors provided in the revised Seven Year Plan. All of them were young HKU Arts graduates, except for Perry Siu, who was a graduate of the University of Sydney (HKUSM 3 September 1963, 2).
73. HKUVC 225/66; letter from Sir Lindsay Ride to Sir Charles Wilson, 11 November 1966. *Vice-Chancellor's Report*, 1964–65, p. 60.
74. HKUCM 18 March 1965, 15.
75. Ina Kwok left the Department in October 1964 to join the HKU Department of Economics and Social Science. Y. C. Jao left for the Hong Kong and Shanghai Bank in April 1965. Perry Siu also left in April on appointment as a staff tutor in the new Extra-Mural Department at the Chinese University; see *Vice-Chancellor's Report*, 1964–65, p. 61.
76. HKUVC 225/66; letter from Sir Lindsay Ride to Sir Charles Wilson, 11 November 1966. Lai was replaced by Priscilla Mark. The DEMS succeeded in recruiting three full-time tutors in 1965–66 and all were graduates of HKU. Laurence C. T. Pang, an Economics graduate and formerly a teacher, joined the Department in November 1965 and was responsible for Economics and Commerce subjects. C. K. Leung was a Geography and Geology graduate and had been an executive officer in the government. He was appointed in September 1965 and specialised in the subjects of Geography, Sociology, Education, Psychology, Philosophy and Languages. John Chan was an M.A. graduate in History and joined the Department in November 1965. He took charge of the LLB (London) scheme, which will be mentioned in the next chapter.
77. HKUSM 5 May 1959, 5.
78. Styler's trip was arranged under the sponsorship of the British Council Committee for Commonwealth Exchange (*Departmental Reports*, 1961–62, p. 75).
79. *Departmental Reports*, 1961–62, p. 76.
80. *Ibid.*
81. HKUSM 5 June 1962, 17, Appendix F, document 31/42; the Styler Report. Styler also gave suggestions on course structure and other arrangements.
82. *Ibid.*, p. 5.
83. It was expected that external visitors were to be invited in the same way that external examiners were appointed in teaching departments (HKUSM 8 January 1963, 4; and HKUCM 21 February 1963, 7).
84. Styler attended the Leverhulme Conference organised by the DEMS in October 1964 as Conference Vice-Chairman. He visited the Department in the 1965–66 academic year and submitted a report to the Vice-Chancellor in March 1966 (HKUVC 225/60; 'Memo for V.C. re. Extra-Mural U.G.C. proposals', March 1966).
85. Interview with Mrs Priscilla Tso, 29 March 2006.
86. *Departmental Reports*, 1961–62, p. 73.
87. *Vice-Chancellor's Report*, 1963–64, p. 56.
88. *Departmental Reports*, 1960–61; *Vice-Chancellor's Reports*, 1961–67.
89. Ieuan Hughes and Priscilla Tso (eds.), *Universities and Adult Education in South East Asia: Report on the Leverhulme Conference on Extra-Mural Studies, October 26–31, 1964, Hong Kong* (Hong Kong: Department of Extra-Mural Studies, University of Hong Kong, 1964), p. 3.

90. HKUVC, Adult Education file; letter from Sir Lindsay Ride to Sir Miles Clifford, 20. July 1964.
91. Hughes and Tso, *Universities and Adult Education in South East Asia*, p. 3.
92. *Ibid.*, pp. 5–8.
93. *Vice-Chancellor's Report*, 1964–65, p. 64.
94. W. E. Styler, 'Conference Report and Conclusions', in Hughes and Tso, *Universities and Adult Education in South East Asia*, p. 95.
95. HKUVC 225/2/66; 'Draft Notes re. South East Asian Institute of Adult Education', October 1966.
96. *Ibid.*, 'South East Asian Institute of Adult Education, University of Hong Kong', October 1966.
97. HKUVC, Adult Education file; letter from Arnold S. M. Hely to the Vice-Chancellor, 26 October 1965.
98. HKUVC 225/2/66; 'South East Asian Institute of Adult Education', October 1966.
99. Spencer Wong, 'Development of Adult Education in Hong Kong since World War II' (unpublished Ph.D. dissertation, University of Edinburgh, 1975), p. 114.
100. HKUSM 8 January 1957, 19, Appendices H, I and J.
101. *Departmental Reports*, 1956–57, p. 25.
102. BEMSM 3 October 1957, 2, Appendix A, document 61/97; 'Report of the Extra-Mural Programme 1956/57', 26 September 1957.
103. *University of Hong Kong Calendar 1957–58* (Hong Kong: Cathay Press, 1957), p. 6.
104. BEMSM 22 May 1957, 4.
105. *Departmental Reports*, 1956–57, p. 26.
106. *Vice-Chancellor's Report*, 1964–65, p. 90.
107. HKUSM 5 June 1962, 17, Appendix F, document 31/42; the Styler Report, p. 1.
108. *Vice-Chancellor's Report*, 1962–63, p. 59.
109. G. H. Moore, 'How Extra-Mural Can You Get?', *Journal of Adult Education*, vol. 2, no. 2 (April 1954), pp. 5–6.
110. *Ibid.*, p. 7.
111. BEMSM 10 December 1959, 7, Appendix C, document 18/129a; letter from the Director of Extra-Mural Studies to the Secretary of the Board of Extra-Mural Studies, 6 November 1959. There was no further follow-up action after Moore's departure shortly afterwards.
112. Interview with Mr T. C. Lai, 29 June 2006.
113. HKUSM 4 January 1961, 9, Appendix E, document 8/41; 'The Field of Adult Education'.
114. Hughes, 'The University and Adult Education', p. 3.
115. Hughes, 'Hong Kong: An Extra-Mural Profile', p. 37.
116. *Vice-Chancellor's Report*, 1964–65, p. 96.
117. BEMSM 17 June 1964, 9.
118. In the 1964–65 academic year there were 46 courses with up to six meetings each, 118 courses with seven to twelve meetings, 85 courses with thirteen to thirty meetings, and 21 courses with over thirty meetings (*Vice-Chancellor's Report*, 1964–65, p. 97).
119. HKUSM 5 June 1962, 17, Appendix F, document 31/42; the Styler Report, pp. 4–5.
120. Gerald Moore, *Tsuen-Wan Township: Study Group Report on Its Development* (Hong Kong: Hong Kong University Press, 1959), p. 1.
121. *Departmental Reports*, 1958–59, pp. 24–25.
122. Moore, *Tsuen-Wan Township*, p. 4.

123. *Vice-Chancellor's Report*, 1962–63, p. 58.
124. *Vice-Chancellor's Report*, 1966–67, p. 93.
125. *Wah Kiu Yat Po*, 4 September 1958.
126. BEMSM 22 November 1961, 7 Appendix B, document 80/111; 'Report for 1960–61'.
127. *Departmental Reports*, 1961–62, p. 73.
128. *Vice-Chancellor's Report*, 1964–65, p. 63. HKUVC 622/1/A/67/8; 'Dept. of Extra-mural Studies, H.K.U: A brief account of its historical development', in Minutes of the Joint Committee on Extra-Mural Studies, 24 November 1967, 2, Appendix A.
129. HKUSM 5 June 1962, 17, Appendix F, document 31/42; the Styler Report, p.2.
130. HKPRO, HKRS457–3–10; letter from D. H. Jordan to Director of Extra-Mural Studies, 7 May 1959.
131. *Departmental Reports*, 1961–62, p. 75.
132. Hughes, 'Hong Kong: An Extra-Mural Profile', p. 41.
133. *Departmental Reports*, 1961–62, p. 75; *Vice-Chancellor's Report*, 1964–65, p. 63.
134. *Departmental Reports*, 1962–63, p. 58. HKUVC 225/60; letter from Ieuan Hughes to the Vice-Chancellor, 8 June 1963.
135. *Vice-Chancellor's Report*, 1964–65, p. 67.
136. HKUSM 5 June 1962, 17, Appendix F, document 31/42; the Styler Report, p. 2.
137. Hughes, 'Hong Kong: An Extra-Mural Profile', p. 40.
138. See *Vice-Chancellor's Report*, 1964–65, p. 98. Hughes explained that 'students' included 'some undergraduates ... but most are part-time students at some evening or post-secondary college, and to a certain extent the term is a euphemism for "unemployed"; they are found mainly in the vocationally-biased courses' (Hughes, 'Hong Kong: An Extra-Mural Profile', p. 42).
139. Among 6,431extra-mural students in the 1964–65 academic year, 3,003 were aged between 20 and 29 and 1,366 were aged between 30 and 39. 62.1 per cent of the total enrolment was under 30 years of age; see *Vice-Chancellor's Report*, 1964–65, p. 101.
140. *Departmental Reports* 1959–60, p. 68.
141. Hughes, 'Hong Kong: An Extra-Mural Profile', pp. 38–39.
142. *Ibid.*, p. 43.
143. *Ibid.*
144. *Ibid.*
145. *Departmental Reports*, 1961–62, p. 74.
146. BEMSM 22 November 1961, 7, Appendix B, document 80/111; 'Report for 1960–61'.
147. *Departmental Reports*, 1961–62, pp. 71–72.
148. BEMSM 10 March 1961, 10, Appendix D; 'Jubilee Rally'.
149. *Ibid.*
150. This area is currently (2007) occupied by the Arts Faculty Office.
151. *Departmental Reports*, 1961–62, p. 74.
152. Department of Extra-Mural Studies, *Prospectus 1957–1958*.
153. Hughes, 'Hong Kong: An Extra-Mural Profile', p. 38.
154. HKUSM 5 June 1962, 17, Appendix F, document 31/42; the Styler Report, p. 5.
155. Hughes, 'Hong Kong: An Extra-Mural Profile', p. 38.
156. HKUVC 225/60; letter from G. H. Moore to the Vice-Chancellor, 29 January 1959.
157. *Ibid.*, confidential notes from Hughes to the Vice-Chancellor, 30 March 1963.
158. HKUVC 225/64; personal letter from Lindsay Ride to D. Benson, 6 July 1964.

159. Department of Extra-Mural Studies, *Prospectus 1964–1965*, p. 1.
160. HKUVC 225/60; letter from the Director of Extra-Mural Studies to the Vice-Chancellor, 23 April 1959.
161. HKUSM 3 December 1963, 6(a).
162. HKUCM 26 October 1967, 6(c), Appendix G, document 95/967; 'Financial Arrangements — Extra-Mural Studies', 14 September 1967.
163. Robert Peers, *Adult Education: A Comparative Study* (London: Routledge, 1958; reprinted 1998), pp. 348–351.
164. HKUSM 3 June 1958, 5(a). The new arrangement generally lowered or kept the course fees at the same level as in 1957 because in most cases the increase of course fees was compensated by the cancellation of the registration fee.
165. Committee on Extra-Mural Studies Minutes 31 March 1971, 3, Appendix A, document 263/371; 'Fees of Part-time Extra-Mural Tutors', 24 March 1971, p. 1.
166. *Ibid.*, pp. 1–2.
167. *Ibid.*, p. 1.
168. HKUCourt 21 May 1957, 6, Appendix C, document 84/17; 'Draft Memorandum: Extra-Mural Studies', pp. 5–6.
169. HKUSM 5 June 1962, 17, Appendix F, document 31/42; the Styler Report, p. 4.
170. Hughes, 'Hong Kong: An Extra-Mural Profile', p. 38.
171. *Ibid.*
172. *Departmental Reports*, 1956–57, pp. 26–27.
173. Peers, *Adult Education*, pp. 350–351.
174. *Ibid.*, p. 351.

CHAPTER FOUR

1. Michael Luk, Deputy Director of HKU SPACE, suggested this phrase to describe the achievements of the Department of Extra-Mural Studies from the 1960s to the 1980s; see HKU SPACE's 50th Anniversary commemorative brochure (2006).
2. Department of Extra-Mural Studies, *Prospectus 1965–1966*, p. 1.
3. HKUVC 225/67; 'Individual Staff Duties'. The situation in 1964–65 was even worse: T. C. Lai and five staff tutors had to co-ordinate 281 courses, each of them co-ordinating forty-six courses on average.
4. HKUVC 225/60; memo for VC re. Extra-Mural UGC proposals, March 1966.
5. HKUVC 225/68; letter from R. A. Williams to the Vice-Chancellor, 9 October 1968.
6. Development and General Purposes Committee Minutes [hereafter DGPCM] 27 June 1968 and 2 July 1968, 3, Appendix B, document 171/568 re-amended; 'Submission from the Department of Extra-Mural Studies for the Remainder of the 1967–70 Triennium', 21 May 1968, p. 1. Council Minutes [hereafter HKUCM] 23 January 1969, 5, Appendix B, document 8/169 re-amended; 'Statement of Development Policy 1970–74', p. 18.
7. HKUVC 225/68; letter from S. F. Bailey to the Vice-Chancellor, 8 October 1968.
8. HKUCM 26 October 1967, 6(c), Appendix G; 'Financial Arrangements — Extra-Mural Studies', 14 September 1967.
9. HKUCM 23 January 1969, 5, document 121/1268 re-amended; 'Department of Extra-mural Studies: Proposals for the Quadrennium 1970–1974,' p. 11. HKUCM 26 June

1969, 12, Appendix M, document 221/569 re-amended ; 'Quadrennial Priorities', p. 11.

10. Senate minutes [hereafter HKUSM] 4 January 1977 and 17 January 1977, 20, Appendix R, document 162/177; 'Senate Memorandum for Discussion at the UPGC Visitation in March/April 1977', p. 15.
11. *University of Hong Kong Gazette*, vol. 15, no. 5, pp. 35–36.
12. *Vice-Chancellor's Report*, 1965–66, p. .
13. The Vice-Chancellor asked the University of Glasgow in November 1966 to allow Williams to stay at HKU for another year, but this proposal was rejected by Glasgow (HKUVC 225/66; letter from Charles H. Wilson to K. E. Robinson, 23 November 1966).
14. HKUVC 225/66; letter from Ieuan Hughes to the Vice-Chancellor, 25 January 1967.
15. HKUCM 26 October 1967, 4(ii). *Vice-Chancellor's Report*, 1967–68, p. 45. HKUSM 5 March 1968, 20, Appendix S, document 231/268; 'Post of Director of Extra-mural Studies'.
16. Interview with Dr Darwin Chen, 7 July 2006.
17. HKUCM 23 January 1969, 5, document 121/1268 re-amended; 'Department of Extra-mural Studies: Proposals for the Quadrennium 1970–1974', p. 3.
18. The DEMS admitted 4,223 students to 180 courses. These figures are similar to those of 1962–63, when there were 4,130 students in 183 extra-mural courses.
19. Department of Extra-Mural Studies, *Prospectus 1967–1968*.
20. The study tours were led by Priscilla Tso (Southeast Asia), T. C. Lai (Japan), and Roger Williams (China). Some tours took place more than once during this period.
21. HKUCM 23 January 1969, 5, document 121/1268 re-amended; 'Department of Extra-mural Studies: Proposals for the Quadrennium 1970–1974', p. 3. The DEMS organised a summer school for the Florida Presbyterian College in 1966. From July 1970, it offered summer schools for the American Institute for Foreign Study in alternate years; see Committee on Extra-Mural Studies Minutes [hereafter CEMSM] 19 January 1970, 5, Appendix B, document 114/1169; 'Proposed Visit of a Summer School', 10 November 1969.
22. CEMSM 10 June 1969, 2, Appendix B, document 1/669.
23. The Department's total teaching hours in 1969–70 amounted to 7,836 hours, compared with 5,417 in 1966–67.
24. *Vice-Chancellor's Report*, 1968–69, p. 102.
25. For the historical development of the extra-mural department at CUHK, see Spencer Wong, 'Development of Adult Education in Hong Kong since World War II' (unpublished Ph.D. dissertation, University of Edinburgh, 1975), pp. 151–186.
26. HKUSM 5 June 1962, Appendix F; the Styler Report, 6 April 1962, p. 5.
27. Wong, 'Development of Adult Education in Hong Kong', p. 124.
28. HKUVC 622/1/A/678; Minutes of the JCEMS 21 September 1967, 4.
29. *UGC Report*, October 1965–July 1968, p. 14.
30. HKUCM 4 April 1966, 2, Appendix A, document 23/466; 'Address by the Chairman, University Grants Committee, Mr M. A. R. Herries, to the Council of Hong Kong University', 4 April 1965.
31. DGPCM 27 June 1968 and 2 July 1968, 3, Appendix B, document 171/568 re-amended; 'Submission from the Department of Extra-Mural Studies for the Remainder of the 1967–70 Triennium', 21 May 1968, p. 1.

32. The HKU representatives were Ieuan Hughes and Roger Williams, and the CUHK representatives were T. C. Lai and Perry Siu. It is interesting to note that all four of them were either working or had worked in the DEMS at HKU; see HKUVC 225/66; extract of a memo from Ieuan Hughes to the Vice-Chancellor, 12 May 1967.
33. HKUVC 622/1/A/67/8; Minutes of the JCEMS 21 February 1967; and a memo from Sandy Liveright to Ieuan Hughes and T. C. Lai, 5 April 1967.
34. HKUVC 225/66; extract of a memo from Ieuan Hughes to the Vice-Chancellor, 12 May 1967.
35. *Ibid.*
36. *Ibid.*, extract from note of a discussion between Mr Hughes and Mr Mellor, 26 May 1967.
37. Professor Gibson was at that time Chairman of the Senate Committee on Extra-Mural Studies (CEMS), the function of which will be discussed later in this chapter (*Vice-Chancellor's Report*, 1967–68, p. 45).
38. HKUVC 622/1/A/67/8; Minutes of the JCEMS 21 September 1967, 2.
39. *Ibid.*, Minutes of JCEMS 27 October 1967, 4.
40. *Ibid.*, Minutes of JCEMS 24 November 1967, 4, Appendix E; 'Certificate and Examinable Courses'.
41. *Ibid.*
42. *Ibid.*, Minutes of JCEMS 27 October 1967, 4.
43. *Vice-Chancellor's Report*, 1967–68, p. 45.
44. The original version of the report has not been found. The contents of the report used here are extracted from a 'Submission from the Department of Extra-Mural Studies for the Remainder of the 1967–70 Triennium', dated 21 May 1968, p. 2; see DGPCM 27 June 1968 and 2 July 1968, 3, Appendix B, document 171/568 re-amended.
45. HKUSM 4 February 1969, 13, Appendix N, document 103/1168; letter from M. A. R. Herries, UGC Chairman, to the Vice-Chancellor, 2 October 1968.
46. HKUVC 225/68; letter from S. F. Bailey to the Vice-Chancellor, 8 October 1968.
47. *Ibid.*, letter from R. A. Williams to the Vice-Chancellor, 9 October 1968.
48. *Ibid.*, letter from J. B. Gibson to the Vice-Chancellor, 9 October 1968.
49. HKUSM 4 February 1969, 12, Appendix N, document 104/1168; letter from the Vice-Chancellor to the UGC Chairman, 15 October 1968.
50. HKUCM 23 January 1969, 5, Appendix B, document 8/169 re-amended; 'Statement of Development Policy 1970–74', p. 35.
51. HKUSM 4 February 1969, 13, Appendix N, document 105/1160; letter from Li Choh-ming, Vice-Chancellor of the Chinese University of Hong Kong, to M .A. R. Herries, Chairman of the UGC, 23 October 1968.
52. HKUVC 225/69; 'Report of Meeting of E.M.S. Delegation to U.G.C., March 20th, 1969'.
53. HKUCM 27 March 1969, Appendix A, document 218/369; 'Address by the [UGC] Chairman to the Council of the University of Hong Kong on Thursday 27 March 1969'.
54. Spencer Wong, a staff tutor in the CUHK Department of Extra-Mural Studies and later Director of that Department, made this point in his unpublished doctoral dissertation (see Wong, 'Development of Adult Education in Hong Kong', p. 123).

55. No evidence has been found to suggest how and when the activities of the JCEMS ended. It was noted in February 1973 that a 'Joint Universities Committee' discussed the duplication of extra-mural courses and the possibilities of co-operation with the new Polytechnic, but it is not known whether this Joint Universities Committee was the existing JCEMS or a new body which took over its functions; see Registry Files: Quadrennium 1974–1978, document 200/273, Annex XI; 'Notes on the meeting of representatives of the Extra-Mural Committee with the U.P.G.C. — February 16, 1973', to be found in 'Draft Notes of Discussions Held between Representatives of University Bodies and the Grants Committee at Its Visitation of February 1973, Taken for the Use of the Vice-Chancellor and the Development and General Purposes Committee'.
56. CEMSM 10 June 1969, 3, Appendix C, document 3/669 ; 'Apparent Duplication in E.M.S. Programmes 1968–1970'.
57. Interview with Mr T. C. Lai, 29 June 2006.
58. Even this collaboration was carried out in an indirect way involving little direct co-operation between the two universities.
59. HKUSM 4 February 1969, 13, Appendix N, document 103/1168; letter from M. A. R. Herries, UGC Chairman, to the Vice-Chancellor, 2 October 1968.
60. HKUVC 225/68; letter from S. F. Bailey to the Vice-Chancellor, 8 October 1968.
61. HKUSM 4 February 1969, 13, Appendix N, document 104/1168; letter from the Vice-Chancellor to the UGC Chairman, 15 October 1968.
62. HKUCM 23 January 1969, 5, Appendix B, document 8/169 re-amended; 'Statement of Development Policy 1970–74', p. 35.
63. HKUCM 27 March 1969, Appendix A, document 218/369; 'Address by the Chairman [of the UGC] to the Council of the University of Hong Kong on Thursday 27 March 1969', p. 7.
64. HKUVC 225/69; confidential letter from J. B. Gibson to the Vice-Chancellor, 22 April 1969.
65. HKUVC 622/1/A/69; Minutes of JCEMS 9 May 1969, 3(a).
66. *Ibid.*, Minutes of JCEMS 28 May 1969, 2.
67. HKUSM 4 January 1977 and 17 January 1977, 20, Appendix R, document 162/177; 'Senate Memorandum for Discussion at the UPGC Visitation in March/April 1977', January 1977, p. 15. The UGC was renamed the University and Polytechnic Grants Committee (UPGC) in 1972 when the Hong Kong Polytechnic was included within its purview.
68. HKUCM 18 April 1977, 7, Appendix E attachment, document 167/477; 'Address by the Chairman U.P.G.C. to the Council of the University of Hong Kong on Monday 18 April 1977', p. 17.
69. HKUSM 2 June 1970 and 11 June 1970, 4, Appendix B, document 42/370 amended; 'Staff Tutors on Faculty Boards'. CEMSM 29 March 1977, 4(b)(iii), Appendix E, document 264/377; 'The Role and Teaching Load of Extra-Mural Staff Tutors', 19 March 1977.
70. DGPCM 2 June 1969, 12.
71. HKUVC 225/67; 'Individual Staff Duties'.
72. *Ibid.*, 'Staff Duties: Hong Kong University'.
73. *Vice-Chancellor's Report*, 1966–67, p. 92.
74. CEMSM 29 March 1977, 4(b)(iii), Appendix E, document 264/377; 'The Role and Teaching Load of Extra-Mural Staff Tutors', 19 March 1977.

75. Department of Extra-Mural Studies, *Prospectus 1965–1966*.
76. Minutes of the Committees Review Committee [hereafter CRCM] 18 July 1967, 4, Appendix D, document 60/767, 17 July 1967. The last BEMS meeting was held on 30 December 1964.
77. HKUVC 225/66; confidential letter from the Vice-Chancellor to Mr I. W. Hughes, 19 June 1967. CRCM 18 July 1967, 4, Appendix D, document 60/767, 17 July 1967.
78. HKUSM 3 October 1967, 6.
79. The chairmanship provision was soon relaxed so that the Senate could appoint one of its own members to the post. The CEMS was later allowed to admit co-opted members to the Committee. The first two co-opted members, Dr Peter C. Y. Lee and Professor Y. C. Wong, were appointed to the CEMS in August 1976; see CEMSM 31 August 1976, 2.
80. HKUSM 4 January 1969, 13, Appendix N, document 103/1168; letter from M. A. R. Herries, UGC Chairman, to the Vice-Chancellor, 2 October 1968.
81. HKUVC 225/68; letter from R. A. Williams to the Vice-Chancellor, 9 October 1968.
82. *Ibid.*, Letter from J. B. Gibson to the Vice-Chancellor, 9 October 1968.
83. HKUSM 4 February 1969, 13, Appendix N, document 104/1168; letter from the Vice-Chancellor to the Chairman of the UGC, 15 October 1968.
84. HKUVC 225/69; 'Report of Meeting of E.M.S. Delegation to U.G.C. March 20th, 1969'.
85. CEMSM 27 November 1967, 4, Appendix C; 'A Report on Recent Developments', 23 November 1967.
86. HKUVC 225/67; 'University Adult Education Provision and Aims in Britain', 2 January 1968. Williams quoted from the Report of the Academic Advisory Committee on Birkbeck College of May 1967 that 'it is becoming more and more apparent that in Britain, as in the United States, universities have a function in developing certain types of vocational and professional courses for students not enrolled in the university'. He also suggested that there were at least twenty-six extra-mural courses of a vocational nature which were taught by the University of Bristol in 1967–68; see CEMSM 10 June 1969, 2, Appendix B, p. 5.
87. *Ibid.*
88. HKUCM 23 January 1969, 5. See also Registry file: Proposals for the Quadrennium 1970–1974, document 121/1268 re-amended; 'Department of Extra-mural Studies', p.1.
89. HKUVC 225/68; letter from J. B. Gibson to the Vice-Chancellor, 9 October 1968.
90. *Hong Kong Hansard*, 13 March 1968, p. 99.
91. HKUCM 27 March 1969, Appendix A, document 218/369; 'Address by the [UGC] Chairman to the Council of the University of Hong Kong on Thursday 27 March 1969', pp. 6–7.
92. *Ibid.*, p. 6.
93. HKUVC 225/68; letter from J. B. Gibson to the Vice-Chancellor, 9 October 1968.
94. HKUVC 622/1/A/69; Minutes of JCEMS 9 May 1969, 3(c).
95. One of the reasons for the absence of such figures is that the DEMS adopted different categorisations at different times. A considerable number of courses which were categorised as 'Liberal Studies' courses in the earlier years were regarded as vocational and professional courses in later years.

96. HKU Registry Files: Quadrennium 1974–1978, Annex XI, document 200/273; 'Notes on the meeting of representatives of the Extra-Mural Committee with the U.P.G.C. — February 16, 1973'.
97. The subject area 'mainly for vocational purposes' may, however, include some non-vocational courses.
98. HKUSM 14 January 1986, 12(b), Appendix S, document 232/1185–B; 'Annual Report of the Committee on Extra Mural Studies, 1984–85'.
99. HKUCM 23 January 1969, 5 document 121/1268 re-amended; 'Department of Extra-mural Studies: Proposals for the Quadrennium 1970–1974', p. 6.
100. Triennium Estimates, 1985–88.
101. *Vice-Chancellor's Report*, 1965–66, p. 77. The DEMS scheduled at least thirteen day-time courses during 1966–67; see *Prospectus 1966–1967*, pp. 53–57.
102. *Vice-Chancellor's Report*, 1965–66, p. 79.
103. In fact, there was speculation to this effect in the press at that time; see *Hong Kong Standard*, 6 October 1967; see HKPRO, HKRS70–6–464–1.
104. CEMSM 27 November 1967, 4, Appendix C; 'A Report on Recent Developments', 23 November 1967.
105. Department of Extra-Mural Studies, *Prospectus 1967–1968*.
106. In the first two years of operation the Town Centre was funded by government sponsorship under the London University LLB scheme. In 1970 it was funded by the Extra-Mural Studies Fund. As the annual rent climbed to about $500,000 in the following years, the University started to pay half of the rent from 1974; see CEMSM 20 January 1971, 9, Appendix D; 'Memorandum re. E.M.S. Fund'. See also HKUCM 27 January 1977, 18, Appendix I, document 62/177; 'Extra-Mural Town Centre', 5 January 1977.
107. HKU Registrar's file 9/2/2, document 32/670 amended; 'Extra-Mural Studies, Town Centre'. See also HKUSM 5 December 1978, 17, Appendix V; 'Annual Report 1977–1978', p. 2.
108. DGPCM 27 June 1968 and 2 July 1968, 3, Appendix B, document 171/568 re-amended; 'Submission from the Department of Extra-Mural Studies for the Remainder of the 1967–70 Triennium', 21 May 1968, p. 1.
109. *Ibid.*
110. *Ibid.*
111. HKUSM 2 June 1970 and 11 June 1970, 21(a).
112. HKU Registrar's file 9/2/2, document 120/770; letter from the Vice-Chancellor to the UGC Chairman, 17 July 1970, p. 3.
113. HKUSM 4 February 1969, 13, Appendix N, document 103/1168; letter from M. A. R. Herries, UGC Chairman, to the Vice-Chancellor, 2 October 1968. HKUCM 23 February 1973, 9, Appendix E (Visitation), document 211/273; 'Address by the Chairman to the Council of The University of Hong Kong on Friday 23 February 1973', p. 6.
114. HKU Council Circular 12 October 1973, III, 4, Annex XV, document 77/873; letter from Jimmy Chan Wing-cheung, Clerk of Convocation, to Secretary to the Council of the University of Hong Kong, 11 July 1973.
115. HKU Registry files: Quadrennuim 1974–1978, Annex XI, document 200/273; 'Notes on the meeting of representatives of the Extra-Mural Committee with the U.P.G.C. — February 16, 1973'. HKU Council Circular 12 October 1973 III, 3, Annex XIV, document 151/773; 'Provisional Capital Building Programme for the period ending June 30, 1978'.

116. HKUCM 28 October 1976, 43, Appendix HH, document 278/1076; 'New Town Centre for the Department of Extra-Mural Studies', 21 October 1976.
117. The severe shortage of accommodation for extra-mural courses was evident in the Department's continual borrowing of premises for lessons. In the 1976–77 academic year, the Department had to borrow thirteen teaching venues on Hong Kong Island and five in Kowloon; see HKUSM 3 January 1978, 6 (c), Appendix G, document 130/1177 amended; 'Annual Report 1976–1977', p. 3.
118. Department of Extra-Mural Studies, *Prospectus 1978 Spring*, p. 3.
119. HKUCM 27 January 1977, 18, Appendix I, document 62/177; 'Extra-Mural Town Centre', 5 January 1977.
120. HKUCM 28 April 1982, 31, Appendix Z, document 60/1179; 'Extra Mural Town Centre', 10 April 1979.
121. *Ibid.*
122. HKUCM 25 February 1982, 25, Appendix V, document 325/282; 'Town Centre premises for the Department of Extra-Mural Studies', 19 February 1982.
123. HKUCM 28 April 1982, 31, Appendix Z, document 202/482; letter from C. G. Large, Finance Officer, to R. A. Williams, 19 April 1982.
124. HKUCM 25 February 1982, 25, Appendix V, document 325/282; 'Town Centre premises for the Department of Extra-Mural Studies', 19 February 1982.
125. HKUCM 25 February 1982, 25, Appendix V, document 325/282–A amended; 'Town Centre premises for the Department of Extra-Mural Studies: purchase proposal: comparative cost study', p. 3.
126. HKUCM 25 February 1982, 25.
127. HKUCM 28 April 1982, 31, Appendix Z, document 202/482; letter from C. G. Large, Finance Officer, to R. A. Williams, 19 April 1982.
128. *Ibid.*, document 202/482–A; 'The Location of the Extra Mural Town Centre', 22 April 1982.
129. HKUCM 28 April 1982, 31.
130. At the end of 1984 the University's total 'internal' enrolment (including 1,053 higher degree students) was 7,805; see *University Gazette*, vol. 32, no. 5 (30 June 1985), p. 147.

CHAPTER FIVE

1. For further discussion on early development in legal education in Hong Kong, see Dafydd M. E. Evans, 'The University and Legal Education in Hong Kong', in Dafydd M. E. Evans, *Legal Education in Hong Kong* (Hong Kong: Hong Kong University Press, 1974), pp.1–30.
2. John Keswick *et al.*, *Report of the Hong Kong Government Committee on Higher Education* (Hong Kong, 1952), p. 35.
3. HKU Senate minutes [hereafter HKUSM] 1 June 1971, 10, Appendix I, Annex A, document 135/571–A; 'First Report on Legal Education by Sir Ivo Rigby', June 1967, p. 1.
4. Law was one of the subjects in Higher Commercial Studies, which was offered by the DEMS from 1957. From 1960–61 the Department offered various introductory courses in law, such as Public International Law and Law in Hong Kong; see Board of Extra-Mural Studies Minutes [hereafter BEMSM] 22 November 1961, 7, Appendix B, document 80/111; 'Report for 1960–61'.

5. HKUSM 7 April 1964, 11, Appendix I, document 86/364; 'Law Studies at the University', 1 April 1964.
6. Minutes of the Joint Committee on Extra-Mural Studies [hereafter JCEMS] 24 November 1967, 2, Appendix B (in HKUVC622/1/A/67/8 3.2); 'Dept. of Extra-mural Studies, H.K.U.: A brief account of its historical development'.
7. According to his figures, the solicitor-population ratio in England was about 1:2,300, but the ratio in Hong Kong was only 1:22,700; see HKPRO, HKRS457–3–19; 'Memo from Registrar General to Deputy Colonial Secretary', 4 May 1963.
8. HKRS457–3–19; letter from the Registrar to G. T. Rowe, 3 December 1963.
9. HKUSM 7 April 1964, 11, Appendix I, document 86/364; 'Law Studies at the University', 1 April 1964.
10. HKRS457–3–19; letter from L. E. Ball to B. Mellor, 14 April 1964. HKUSM 1 June 1971, 10, Appendix I, Annex A, document 135/571–A; 'First Report on Legal Education by Sir Ivo Rigby, June 1967, p. 1.
11. HKRS457–3–19; letter from the Registrar to Alastair Todd, 12 June 1964.
12. *Ibid.*, letter from D. T. E. Roberts to B. Mellor, 17 June 1964.
13. HKU Council Minutes [hereafter HKUCM] 18 June 1964, 16.
14. HKRS457–3–19; letter from Alastair Todd to B. Mellor, 13 July 1964. The recurrent and capital expenditures in the first three years were estimated at $1,360,000 and $121,500 respectively. The government would finance the balance after deducting fee income, which was expected to be $75,000 for three years (*ibid.*, letter from the Registrar to Alastair Todd, 30 June 1964). This was an enormous figure for the DEMS because the average annual subsidy granted by the government for this programme (approximately $460,000) was nearly equal to the total expenditure of the DEMS in 1963–64.
15. HKUSM 7 April 1964, 1, Appendix I, document 86/363; 'Law Studies at the University', 1 April 1964.
16. HKPRO, HKRS457–3–19, document 24/564; 'Law and Extra-Mural Studies', 11 May 1964.
17. Members of the Finance Committee of the Legislative Council expressed a concern that the proposed Extra-Mural Law Centre was too expensive and believed that it was not necessary to locate it in Central (HKPRO, HKRS457–3–19; letter from Alastair Todd to B. Mellor, 13 July 1964). The University insisted that the Extra-Mural Law Centre be located in Central (*ibid.*, letter from the Registrar to the Principal Assistant Colonial Secretary, 15 July 1964).
18. *Ibid.*, letter from the Bursar to the Principal Assistant Colonial Secretary (Universities), 14 October 1964.
19. *Vice-Chancellor's Report* 1964–65, p. 65.
20. The Committee was chaired by Ieuan Hughes (Director of the Extra-Mural Studies) and included the Registrar (Bernard Mellor), Mr G. H. H. Golby (Vice-Chairman of Hong Kong Law Society) and Mr J. McRobert (Senior Crown Counsel, Government Legal Department); see *Vice-Chancellor's Report* 1964–65, p. 65.
21. The part-time tutors were Mr G. H. H. Golby, Mr M. S. Cockram, Mr F. G. Cooke, and Mr N. I. Billingham. At least three of them were practising solicitors. Pannam stayed in Hong Kong from December 1964 to March 1965 and passed the tutorial work to local tutors during his absence; see *Vice-Chancellor's Report* 1964–65, p. 65.

22. *Vice-Chancellor's Report* 1965–66, pp. 76–77. Rear and Shepherd were appointed in September and October 1966 respectively; see *Vice-Chancellor's Report* 1966–67, p. 92.
23. *Vice-Chancellor's Report*, 1965–66, p. 77.
24. HKRS457–3–19; 'Report of the Advisers on Law Studies', 19 February 1965. This Committee was comprised of Professor Zelman Cowen (Dean of the Faculty of Law, University of Melbourne), Dr A. G. Guest (External examiner for the Law Faculty at Singapore University) and Dr Clifford Pannam (Senior Lecturer in Law at Melbourne University).
25. HKPRO, HKRS457–3–19; letter from W. C. G. Knowles to the Colonial Secretary, 11 May 1965.
26. *Ibid.*, letter from G. C. Hamilton to K. E. Robinson, 4 July 1966.
27. In September 1966, the Chief Justice appointed a working party on Legal Education chaired by Sir Ivo Rigby and composed of representatives of the Judiciary, the legal profession and the two universities. This Working Party submitted a report in June 1967 titled 'First Report on Legal Education' (HKUSM 1 June 1971, 10, Appendix I Annex A, document 135/571–A). In April 1967, Mr L. C. B. Gower, Inter-University Council Visitor, and Professor Zelman Cowen of the University of Melbourne also submitted a report advising the development of law education in Hong Kong, in particular at HKU; see HKUSM 6 June 1967, 12, Appendix Q, document 34/467 amended; 'Report on Legal Training in Hong Kong'.
28. *Vice-Chancellor's Report* 1966–67, p. 93.
29. *Vice-Chancellor's Report* 1968–69, p. 42.
30. This view had already been expressed by the Special Committee in February 1965; see HKPRO, HKRS457–3–19; 'Report of the Advisers on Law Studies', 19 February 1965, pp. 4–5.
31. HKUSM 6 June 1967, 12, Appendix Q, document 34/467 amended; 'Report on Legal Training in Hong Kong', 5 April 1967.
32. HKUCM 2 March 1968, 6, Appendix F, document 16/568; letter from M. A. R. Herries to K. E. Robinson, 26 April 1968.
33. Minutes of the Development and General Purposes Committee [hereafter DGPCM] 7 March 1969, 2(b), Appendix B, document 73/369; 'Department of Law', 11 March 1969.
34. HKUSSM 4 January 1977 and 17 January 1977, 20, Appendix R, document 162/177; 'Senate Memorandum for Discussion at the UPGC Visitation in March/April 1977', pp. 1–2.
35. The DEMS did not offer courses in all the subjects necessary for the London University law degree. Courses in advanced law subjects were seldom organised until the mid-1980s.
36. CEMSM 23 November 1990, 10, Appendix H, document EMS/6/1190; 'Some Recent Developments in University Adult Education and Staff Development in Great Britain: Report of a Study Visit to Great Britain', October 1990.
37. HKUSM 3 January 1984, 12(b), Appendix K, document 229/1183; 'Annual Report of the Committee on Extra Mural Studies, 1982–83', p. 3.
38. CEMSM 25 November 1988, 8, Appendix E, Annex B; 'Developments for the Future'.
39. The pass rate of students reading the University of London LLB external degree in Hong Kong was, in fact, considerably better than in other parts of the world. In 1984,

for example, at least twenty-eight out of forty-three Hong Kong candidates completed the London University's Final Part I Examination in Law. All twenty-eight successful students came from the DEMS. The worldwide pass rate for this examination was only around 10 per cent; see HKUSM 5 February 1985, 3, Appendix B(C)(c), document 108/1184; 'Annual Report of the Committee on Extra Mural Studies, 1983–84', p. 3. In 1987–88, 402 out of the 848 candidates for the London University LLB external examinations in Hong Kong were DEMS students; see CEMSM 7 April 1988, 5, Appendix C, Annex VII, document 467/388–G; 'External Degree Programme in Law', p. 1.

40. Interview with Dr Patrick Wong Lung-tak, 29 June 2006. Dr Wong is now a Chartered Accountant and an Adjunct Professor of the Hong Kong Polytechnic University. He is also a member of various committees of the government, public bodies and professional organisations.
41. HKUCM 21 March 1968, 3.1, Appendix B, Annex I, document 36/1267 amended; 'Proposed Diploma Course in Management Studies', 3 December 1967.
42. DEMS *Prospectus*, 1964–65.
43. DEMS Annual Report 1964–65, p. 65.
44. HKUCM 21 March 1968, 3.1, Appendix B, Annex I, document 36/1267 amended; 'Proposed Diploma Course in Management Studies', 3 December 1967.
45. CEMSM 27 November 1967, 3.
46. HKUCM 21 March 1968, 3.1, Appendix B, Annex I, document 36/1267 amended; 'Proposed Diploma Course in Management Studies', 3 December 1967.
47. *Ibid.* This 'Committee for the Diploma in Management Studies' had approved the Diplomas in Management Studies of over fifty British universities and technical colleges.
48. HKUSM 2 January 1968, 8; HKUCM 21 March 1968, 3(a); Minutes of the HKU Court [hereafter HKUCourt] 15 May 1968, 5(a).
49. *Vice-Chancellor's Report* 1968–69, p. 42.
50. HKUVC225/68; 'Diploma in Management Studies', 23 August 1968.
51. HKUSM 7 April 1970, 8.
52. *University Gazette*, vol. 30, no. 2 (31 December 1982), p. 54
53. HKUSM 4 February 1969, 20, Appendix T, document 305/169 amended; 'Report of the Working Party on the Development of Management Studies', p. 1
54. HKUSM 4 February 1969, 20.
55. *Ibid.*, Appendix T, document 305/169 amended; 'Report of the Working Party on the Development of Management Studies', p. 2
56. HKUSM 7 April 1970, 11, Appendix L; 'Report to the Vice-Chancellor of the University of Hong Kong on Management Studies and Related Matters by Professor Tom Lupton', 15 December 1969, p. 1.
57. *Ibid.*, p. 6.
58. *Ibid.*, p. 8.
59. *Ibid.*, pp. 9–10.
60. *Ibid.*, p. 13.
61. *Ibid.*, p. 14.
62. Tutors in the period 1970–72, for example, included Dr Edward K. Y. Chen and Dr Y. C. Yao (HKU faculty members), and Mr T. W. Casey and Mr J. W. England (staff tutors of the DEMS). Interview with Dr Darwin Chen, 7 July 2006.

63. These positive comments were, however, moderated by criticisms that some DipMS students were not very intellectual and sometimes simply recalled lecture notes during examinations; see HKUSM 7 December 1982, 14, Appendix Q, and HKUSM 1 November 1983, 12, Appendix N; 'Confidential External Examiners' Reports'.
64. HKUSM 2 November 1976, 11, Appendix D, Annex I, document 227/976; 'Regulations for the Degree of Master of Business Administration (M.B.A.)', p. 1.
65. CEMSM 30 March 1982, 4.
66. HKUSM 1 March 1983, 10, Appendix K, document 247/283; 'Regulations and Syllabuses for the Degree of Master of Business Administration', 16 February 1983.
67. CEMSM 24 November 1983, 8, Appendix G, document 222/1183; 'Report on the Development of the M.B.A. Programme at the University of Hong Kong', April 1983, p. 4.
68. HKUSM 3 January 1984, 14(a), Appendix M, document 224/1183; letter from R. A. Williams to Mr J. A. Cribbin, Secretary to the Committee on Extra Mural Studies, 2 November 1983.
69. HKUSM 3 January 1984, 14; and HKUSM 5 February 1985, 16(a).
70. Interview with Dr Darwin Chen, 7 July 2006.
71. Apart from the DipMS, he has an Honorary Doctoral Degree in Business Administration from Napier University and other postgraduate qualifications in Logistics, Marketing, Accounting, and Business Management. He is a member of various professional organisations in logistics, transport, accounting, management, and marketing. Professor Ho teaches professional subjects at HKU SPACE as an Adjunct Professor, and takes part in external evaluations of professional training courses in Hong Kong. Interview with Professor Stephen Ho Wing-chiu, 7 July 2006.
72. *University of Hong Kong Gazette*, vol. 30, no. 2 (31 December 1982), p. 54.
73. Ieuan Hughes, 'Hong Kong, An Extra-Mural Profile', *University of Hong Kong Gazette*, vol. 10, no. 4 (16 April 1963), p. 40.
74. Kan Lai-bing, 'Training in Librarianship in Hong Kong, 1960–1969', *Journal of the Hong Kong Library Association*, no. 1, 1969, p. 13.
75. Hughes, 'Hong Kong, An Extra-Mural Profile', p. 41.
76. HKUCM 28 April 1983, 37 Appendix CC, Annex I. *Vice-Chancellor's Report*, 1964–65, p. 63.
77. Kan, 'Training in Librarianship in Hong Kong, 1960–1969', p. 13.
78. *Ibid.*, pp. 17–18.
79. *Ibid.*, p. 17.
80. Priscilla Tso and Kan Lai-bing, 'Education and Training in Librarianship in Hong Kong: Twenty Years On', *Journal of the Hong Kong Library Association*, no. 5 (1980), p. 18.
81. *Ibid.*, p. 14.
82. HKUSM 21 January 1982, 1(b)(iii), Appendix B, document 231/1181; 'Annual Report of the Committee on Extra Mural Studies, 1980–81', p. 4.
83. JCEMSM 13 January 1969, 3, Appendix B, Annex I; 'Quadrennium Plans (July 1970 to June 1974)'.
84. JCEMSM 24 January 1967, 4, Appendix E (in HKUVC622/1/A/67/8); 'Certificate and Examinable Courses'.
85. Tso and Kan, 'Education and Training in Librarianship in Hong Kong: Twenty Years On', p. 12.

86. HKUSM 5 February 1985, 3, Appendix B(C)(c), document 108/1184; 'Annual Report of the Committee on Extra Mural Studies, 1983–84', p. 3
87. Mr Ng is also an examiner for various diploma courses in Library Studies (correspondence with Mr Frederick Ng Yip-lap, July 2006).
88. Joe Leung, *Building for Excellence Together: The 50th Anniversary of Social Work Education in the University of Hong Kong* (Hong Kong: Department of Social Work HKU, 2000), pp. 4–9.
89. HKUSM 7 January 1976, 11, Appendix M, document 198/1176; 'Annual Report of the Committee on Extra-Mural Studies for the year 1975–76', pp. 3–4.
90. *Ibid.*, p. 4.
91. *Ibid.*, pp. 4–5.
92. *Ibid.*, p. 5.
93. Interview with Professor Joe Leung, 18 April 2007.
94. Duncan Macintosh, 'English as a "function tool": An extra-mural programme in Hong Kong', *Adult Education*, vol. 44, no. 6 (March 1972), p. 380.
95. *Vice-Chancellor's Report*, 1964–65, p. 96. Among the ten 'English Language and Literature' courses listed in the *Prospectus* for 1964–65, only one was apparently a course in English Literature (DEMS *Prospectus*, 1964–65, pp. 38–41).
96. CEMSM 6 May 1970, 3, Appendix B, document 189/270; 'Language Teaching in the Department of Extra-Mural Studies', 17 February 1970, p. 1.
97. *Ibid.*, p. 2.
98. Macintosh, 'English as a "function tool"', p. 382.
99. CEMSM 17 November 1971, 4, Appendix B, document 65/1171; 'Use of English Courses, 1970/71'. In 1973–74, the Commercial Practice stream was restructured into an independent one-year certificate course called 'English for Business'.
100. CEMSM 17 November 1971, 4, Appendix B, document 65/1171; 'Use of English Courses, 1970/71'.
101. Macintosh, 'English as a "function tool"', pp. 383–384.
102. CEMSM 17 November 1971, 4, Appendix B, Annex A; 'Sponsoring Companies'.
103. In 1973–74, the DEMS started four additional certificate courses: 'English for Business', 'Spoken English', 'Translation Techniques', and 'Teaching English as a Second Language'. These or similar courses continued in subsequent years, but the TESL course was discontinued after the 1980–81 academic year.
104. HKUSM 14 January 1986, 12(b), Appendix S, document 232/1185; 'Annual Report of the Committee on Extra Mural Studies, 1984–85'.
105. Interview with Mr Kenneth Yim Chi-keung, 26 June 2006.
106. CEMSM 6 May 1970, 3, Appendix B, document 189/270; 'Language Teaching in the Department of Extra-Mural Studies', 17 February 1970, pp. 6–7.
107. *Ibid.*, p. 6.
108. DEMS *Prospectus*, 1974–75, p. 71.
109. HKU Senate Circular 21 January 1982, 1(b)(iii), Appendix B, document 231/1181; 'Annual Report of the Committee on Extra Mural Studies, 1980–81', p. 2.
110. There were 2,618 students taking 112 Oriental Language courses, with a total of 7,877 lecturing hours; see HKUSM 3 January 1984, 12(b), Appendix K, document 229/1183; 'Annual Report of the Committee on Extra Mural Studies, 1982–83', p. 3.

111. In 1976–77, in-house courses were organised for the American Women's Association, Banque Nationale de Paris, Cable and Wireless, Continental Banks, Far East Bank, Hong Kong and Shanghai Bank, Hong Kong Electric Company, the Housing Authority, IBM, the Immigration Department, the Prisons Department, Royal Hong Kong Police, United Christian Hospital, United Dockyards, and the Urban Services Department. Organisations which collaborated with the DEMS in mounting courses included the Education Department, the Engineering Alumni Association, the Hong Kong Archaeological Society, Hong Kong Association of Career Masters, Hong Kong Library Association, the Labour Department, Radio Television Hong Kong, and the Recreation and Sports Service; see HKUSM 3 January 1978, 6(c), Appendix G, document 130/1177, CEMS Annual Report for 1976–77, p.1
112. HKUSM 14 January 1986, 12(b), Appendix S, document 232/1185; 'Annual Report of the Committee on Extra Mural Studies, 1984–85'.
113. From 1962, the Housing Division of the Urban Services Department managed low-cost housing for the Housing Authority. In 1973, this Housing Division merged with the Resettlement Department to form a new organisation with the same name and was absorbed into the new Housing Authority.
114. Interview with Mr Simon Li, 22 June 2006.
115. The Resettlement Department was mainly responsible for management of the resettlement estates and squatter control. It sent twelve officers to the programme in the first year; see HKRS156–3–53; memo from the Commissioner for Resettlement to the Principal Government Training Officer, 26 August 1969.
116. Interview with Mr Joseph Lee King-chi, 30 June 2006.
117. DEMS *Prospectus*, 1968–69, p. 10.
118. DEMS *Prospectus*, 1970–71, p. 50.
119, Interview with Mr Joseph Lee King-chi, 30 June 2006.
120. Interview with Mr Michael Fok Po-choi, 28 June 2006.
121. Mok was at that time a Resettlement Officer, a rank equivalent to a senior supervisor of housing assistants; interview with Mr Mok Yiu-kwong, 30 June 2006.
122. Interview with Mr Joseph Lee King-chi, 30 June 2006.
123. HKUSM 7 December 1976, 11, Appendix M, document 198/1176; 'The Annual Report of the Committee on Extra-Mural Studies for the year 1975–76', p. 6.
124. Interview with Mr Simon Li, 22 June 2006.
125. Interview with Mr Mok Yiu-kwong, 30 June 2006.
126. The Certificate course was upgraded to a Diploma course in 1989. The DEMS collaborated with the Centre of Urban Planning and Environmental Management of HKU to offer a part-time master's programme in Housing Management from 1992, and a bachelor's degree conversion programme for holders of the Diploma in Housing Management from 1998.

CHAPTER SIX

1. Anthony Sweeting, *Education in Hong Kong, 1941–2001: Visions and Revisions* (Hong Kong: Hong Kong University Press, 2004), p. 335.
2. *Ibid.*, pp. 335–336.
3. *Ibid.*, p. 337.

4. Interview with Professor Anthony Sweeting, 19 April 2007.
5. Development and General Purposes Committee Minutes [hereafter DGPCM] 18 January 1985, 4.
6. Professor Brimer left the Working Group on 30 June 1986 and Professor Brian Morton replaced him as chairman of the CEMS from 1 July 1986.
7. Since the Director of Extra-Mural Studies, Roger Williams, and the CEMS Chairman, Professor M. A. Brimer, both left office in June 1986, the CEMS was ignorant of the Evans Working Party for about nine months. When Professor Lee Ngok, the new Director of Extra-Mural Studies made his first report to the CEMS in March 1987, the CEMS members were surprised and dismayed at the existence of the Working Party without any formal consultation with the CEMS; see Committee on Extra-Mural Studies Minutes [hereafter CEMS] 27 March 1987, 2. The disgruntlement of the CEMS was solved when the Working Party invited the new Director of Extra-Mural Studies and CEMS Chairman to join the Working Party in April; see CEMSM 25 May 1987, 4, Appendix A, document 212/587(ii); letter from N. J. Gillanders (Registrar) to Professor B. S. Morton (CEMS Chairman), 1 May 1987. There was no representative from the DEMS or the CEMS in the Evans Working Party.
8. DGPCM 25 September 1987, 5, Appendix D, document 52/787 amended; 'Working Party of Extra-Mural Studies: First Report', August 1987.
9. *Ibid.*, p. 2.
10. HKUCM 24 April 1986, 9.
11. *University of Hong Kong Gazette*, vol. 32, no. 1 (30 September 1984), pp. 21–22.
12. HKU Senate Minutes [hereafter HKUSM] 1 April 1986, Appendix N, document 341/386, 21 March 1986.
13. Lee Ngok, 'Opportunity Knocks: Continuing Higher Education in Hong Kong', in the *Supplement to the University of Hong Kong Gazette*, vol. 39, no. 2 (14 December 1992), pp. 33–34.
14. *Ibid.*, pp. 35–37.
15. *Ibid.*, p. 39.
16. DGPCM 25 September 1987, 5, Appendix D, document 52/787 amended; 'Working Party of Extra-Mural Studies: First Report', August 1987, p. 2.
17. *Ibid.*
18. *Ibid.*, pp. 3–4.
19. Education Commission Report No. 1 [hereafter ECR1], October 1984, p. 71.
20. Education Commission Report No. 2 [hereafter ECR2], August 1986, p. 143.
21. For the highly successful University of New England 'model' in external studies see Matthew Jordan, *A Spirit of True Learning: The Jubilee History of the University of New England* (Sydney: University of New South Wales Press, 2004), pp. 165–79.
22. John Llewellyn *et al*, *A Perspective on Education in Hong Kong: Report by a Visiting Panel* (Hong Kong: Government Printer, November 1982), p.76.
23. ECR1, Annex 3, 'UPGC's Report on an Open University in Hong Kong', p. 113.
24. ECR2, p. 173, para. VIII.7.1.e.
25. ECR2, pp. 173–74, paras. VIII.7.1.f, VIII.7.1.j.
26. ECR2, p. 174, para. VIII.7.1.l.
27. The five post-secondary or tertiary institutions were the University of Hong Kong, the Chinese University of Hong Kong, Hong Kong Polytechnic, City Polytechnic of Hong Kong and Hong Kong Baptist University.

28. HKUSM 14 November 1986, 3, Appendix D, document 362/1086; 'Education Commission Report No. 2 — Open Education', 29 October 1986, p. 3.
29. *Ibid.*, p. 1
30. DGPCM 27 June 1968 and 2 July 1968, 3, Appendix B, document 171/568 re-amended; 'Submission from the Department of Extra-Mural Studies, Hong Kong University, for the Remainder of the 1967–70 Triennium', 21 May 1968, p. 2. However, it was decided that the DEMS would not play a significant role in part-time or external degree programmes; see DGPCM 27 June 1968 and 2 July 1968, 3.
31. The Convocation resolved in October 1972 to suggest that the University organise a part-time Bachelor of Arts programme; see DGPCM 6 November 1972, 4, Appendix B, document 23/1172; letter from Laurence C. T. Pang to the Secretary to the Council, 11 October 1972. The UPGC Chairman asked the University to consider offering undergraduate courses by part-time study 'as a matter of urgency' in its Visitation to HKU in February 1973; see HKUCM 23 February 1973, 9, Appendix E, document 211/273; 'Address by the Chairman to the Council of The University of Hong Kong on Friday 23 February 1973', p. 7. In April 1975, Mr P. F. Vowles, Academic Registrar of the University of London, visited the two universities in Hong Kong to advise on 'the possible introduction of external degrees by the two Universities in Hong Kong', and recommended several options for such a system; see HKUSM 2 June 1979, 16, Appendix K, Annex II, document 145/279; 'Summary of Deliberations since 1969 on the possible Introduction of Part-time Degree Courses', 13 February 1979, p. 4.
32. HKUSM 2 June 1981, 6, Appendix N; 'External Studies', April 1981.
33. HKUSM 13 October 1981, 23; and HKUCM 29 October 1981, 35.
34. HKUSM 14 November 1986, 3, Appendix D, document 362/1086; 'Education Commission Report No.2 — Open Education', 29 October 1986, p. 1.
35. *Ibid.*
36. HKUSM 6 October 1987, 33.
37. HKUSM 14 November 1986, 3, Appendix D, document 362/1086; 'Education Commission Report No. 2 — Open Education', 29 October 1986, p. 2.
38. HKUSM 13 January 1987, 42.
39. CEMSM 27 March 1987, 8.
40. DGPCM 25 September 1987, 5, Appendix D, document 52/787 amended; 'First Report', p. 1.
41. HKUSM 5 March 1991, 11, Appendix G, document 563/191; 'Annual Report to the Senate', 31 January 1991, p. 2.
42. The other members were Professors Brian Weatherhead and Tim Moore and Dr F. Y. L. Chin (appointed by the Senate), Drs Michael Martin, S. C. Fan and John Hodgkiss (representing the three faculties which would be involved in the provision of open and distance education courses), Professor Lee Ngok, and the Vice-Chancellor, Professor Wang Gungwu. For the Terms of Reference of the COE, see HKUSM 6 October 1987, 33, Appendix I, Annex III, document 193/987.
43. *Ibid.*
44. CEMSM 7 April 1988, 5, Appendix C, Annexes IV, VII, VIII, and IX.
45. HKUSM 10 February 1989, 31, Appendix T, Annex I.A, document 467/388 amended; 'Proposals for Development in Open, Distance and Continuing Education, 1988–1994', p. 16.

46. *Ibid.*, pp. 17–18.
47. CEMSM 7 April 1988, 5. HKUSM 10 February 1989, 31, Appendix T, document 433/189; 'Extra-Mural Studies Development Plans', 31 January 1989, p.1.
48. HKUSM 10 February 1989, 31, Appendix T, document 433/189; 'Extra-Mural Studies Development Plans', 31 January 1989, p. 2.
49. HKUSM 6 June 1989, 32, Appendix Q, Annex 1, document 215/1288; 'Faculty consultative exercise on Developments in Open and Distance Education', 13 December 1988.
50. *Ibid.*, Appendix Q, Annex 1(iv), document 215/1288 (iv)(a); 'Developments in Open and Distance Education', 28 November 1988.
51. *Ibid.*, document 215/1288 (iv)(c); letter from Paul Morris (Dean, Faculty of Education) to Mr J. A. Cribbin, 9 December 1988.
52. *Ibid.*, Appendix Q, Annex 1(viii), document 215/1288 (viii)(a); letter from Professor C. K. Poon (Dean, Faculty of Science) to Professor Young, 30 November 1988.
53. *Ibid.*, Appendix Q, Annex 1(ix), document 215/1288 (ix)(b); letter from S. G. Redding (Professor of Management Studies) to Secretary, Faculty of Social Sciences, 22 November 1988.
54. *Ibid.*, letter from R. Hoosain (Acting Head, Department of Psychology) to Mr M. Lee (Secretary, Faculty of Social Sciences), 29 November 1988.
55. HKUSM 10 February 1989, 31, Appendix T, Annex I, document 82/189 amended; 'Amended EMS Proposals for Development in Open, Distance and Continuing Education, 1989–1994', p. 6.
56. HKUSM 4 April 1989, 4, Appendix B, document 116/289; 'Annual Report of the Committee on Extra-Mural Studies 1987–88', p. 11.
57. HKUSM 6 June 1989, 32, Appendix Q, document 498/589; 'Interim Report to the Senate', 29 May 1989, p. 4.
58. *Ibid.*
59. HKUSM 5 February 1991, 34, Appendix V, document 449/191; 'Director's Annual Report 1989/90', 18 December 1990, p. 12. For the administrative structure of extra-mural studies and open education at HKU, see Figure 6.1.
60. HKUSM 6 March 1990, 21, Appendix P, document 151/290 amended; 'Annual Report of the Committee on Extra-Mural Studies 1988/89', p. 13.
61. HKUCM 20 December 1991, 17, Appendix K, Annex I.V.B, document 57/1190; 'Distance Learning Unit'.
62. HKUSM 9 January 1992, 43.
63. HKUSM 6 March 1990, 21, Appendix P, document 151/290 amended; 'Annual Report of the Committee on Extra-Mural Studies 1988/89', p. 3.
64. HKUCM 20 December 1991, 17, Appendix K, Annex I.V.B, document 57/1190; 'Distance Learning Unit'.
65. The actual usage of the Chinese Studies Foundation Course package was significantly less than had been expected, and SPACE found the situation 'disappointing' with respect to cost recovery. By January 1996, the number of course material sets purchased by the OLI was only about 45 per cent of the original OLI estimate; see SPACE Management Board Minutes [hereafter SPACEMBM] 25 September 1996, 3, Appendix B, Annex I.I; letter from J. A. Cribbin to Dr K. S. Yuen, 17 February 1996.
66. HKUCM 29 June 1989, 17.

67. See Fr Cyril Joseph Barrett's address at the Honorary Degrees Congregation of 29 March 1983 reproduced in *University of Hong Kong Gazette*, vol. 30, no. 5 (31 May 1983), pp. 111–119.
68. HKUSM 6 March 1990, 21, Appendix P, document 151/290 amended; 'Annual Report of the Committee on Extra-Mural Studies 1988/89', p. 8.
69. ECR2, p. 165.
70. *Ibid.*, pp. 165–168.
71. HKUSM 4 April 1989, 4, Appendix B, document 116/289; 'Annual Report of the Committee on Extra-Mural Studies 1987–88', p. 10.
72. HKUSM 6 March 1990, 21, Appendix P, document 151/290 amended; 'Annual Report of the Committee on Extra-Mural Studies 1988/89', p. 11.
73. HKUSM 10 February 1989, 31, Appendix T, Annex I, document 82/189 amended; 'Amended EMS Proposals for Development in Open, Distance and Continuing Education, 1989–1994', p. 3.
74. Interview with Mr Mick Fisher, 20 May 2007.
75. HKUSM 6 March 1990, 21, Appendix P, document 151/290 amended; 'Annual Report of the Committee on Extra-Mural Studies 1988/89', pp. 11–12.
76. *Ibid.*, p. 10.
77. *Ibid.*, pp. 10–11.
78. CEMSM 26 April 1989, 7, Appendix E, Annex; 'London University Proposal'.
79. HKUSM 6 March 1990, 21, Appendix P, document 151/290 amended; 'Annual Report of the Committee on Extra-Mural Studies 1988/89', p.4.
80. Interview with Mrs Teresa Bradley, 13 April 2007.
81. HKUSM 6 March 1990, 21, Appendix P, document 151/290 amended; 'Annual Report of the Committee on Extra-Mural Studies 1988/89', p. 12.
82. CEMSM 26 April 1989, 7, Appendix E, Annex; 'London University Proposal'.
83. CEMSM 26 April 1989, 7.
84. HKUSM 15 March 1988, 35, Appendix U, document 388/188; 'Annual Report of the Committee on Extra-Mural Studies, 1986–87', p. 3.
85. HKUSM 6 March 1990, 21, Appendix P, document 151/290 amended; 'Annual Report of the Committee on Extra-Mural Studies 1988/89', p. 12. The Town Centre was on the ninth floor of the Shun Tak Centre.
86. CEMSM 24 November 1989, 4, Appendix C, document 172/1189; 'University of London: Administration of External Degree Enrolment — Interim Report'.
87. HKUSM 6 March 1990, 21, Appendix P, document 151/290 amended; 'Annual Report of the Committee on Extra-Mural Studies 1988/89', p. 12.
88. HKUSM 5 February 1991, 34, Appendix V, document 449/191; 'Director's Annual Report 1989/90', p. 11.
89. CEMSM 24 May 1987, 7, Appendix E, Annex I(i), document 243/587; letter from D. W. Watts to Professor Lee Ngok, 27 February 1987.
90. HKUSM 2 June 1987, 29, Appendix K Annex I, document 369/587; 'Position Paper: Curtin/EMS Part-time B.Bus. Degree Programme', p. 2.
91. *Ibid.*, p. 4.
92. CEMSM 25 May 1987, 7.
93. *Ibid.* In June 1987, Duncan Macintosh, a staff tutor of the DEMS, submitted a long paper to the Director and the CEMS to express his reservations about the DEMS–

Curtin joint venture. He was not content with the fact that there was no prior consultation with the DEMS staff and the Faculty of Social Sciences, and remarked that the DEMS should not 'change for change's sake' when considering the introduction of a new mode of operation in meeting society's needs. See CEMSM 16 September 1987, 6, Appendix D, Annex II, document 102/987; 'The Role of the Department of Extra Mural Studies in Relation to Distance Learning and Part-time/External Degree Courses, with Particular Reference to the Proposed Curtin/EMS B.Bus. Programme', 10 June 1987.

94. CEMSM 25 May 1987, 7.
95. HKUSM 2 June 1987, 29.
96. HKUSM 6 October 1987, 34, Appendix J, document 293/987; 'Proposed Curtin/EMS B.Bus Programme', 30 September 1987, pp. 2–3.
97. *Ibid.*, Appendix J, Annex III, document 187/987; letter from R. I. Tricker, Acting Head, Department of Management Studies, and Professor of Finance and Accounting, to Professor Lee Ngok, Director of Extra-Mural Studies, 15 September 1987.
98. *Ibid.*, Appendix J, Annex IV, document 276/987; letter from Professor Lee Ngok to Professor R. I. Tricker, 24 September 1987.
99. HKUSM 6 October 1987, 34.
100. HKUSM 6 October 1992, 23, Appendix H, document SPACE/24/692; 'Review of the Agreement between Curtin University and the University of Hong Kong concerning the B.Bus. Degree Programme', p. 2.
101. HKUSM 5 December 1989, 1, Appendix A; 'Academic Development Proposals, 1991–1994', November 1989, p. 11. For a full list of overseas partners of the DEMS from 1989, see Appendix 6.
102. HKUSM 1 May 1990, 26.
103. *Ibid.*
104. Interview with Professor Ronald D. Hill, 25 April 2007.
105. For a diagram of the School's proposed organisational structure, see HKUSM 27 June 1989, 1, Appendix A, Annex XVI(B), document 350/1188; 'Academic Development Proposals to 1996–97', p. 35.
106. *Ibid.*, p. 31.
107. *Ibid.*
108. *Ibid.*, p. 32.
109. *Ibid.*, p. 29.
110. HKUSM 27 June 1989, 1.
111. HKUSM 6 June 1989, 32, Appendix T, Annex 2, document 316/489; 'External Studies and Distance Education at the University of Hong Kong', 4 February 1989, p. 1.
112. The University tended towards options B and F, but also option D.
113. HKUSM 6 June 1989, 32, Appendix T, Annex 2, document 316/489; 'External Studies and Distance Education at the University of Hong Kong', 4 February 1989, pp. 8–9, 13.
114. *Ibid.*, p. 9.
115. HKUSM 6 June 1989, 32, Appendix Q, document 498/589; 'Interim Report to the Senate', 29 May 1989, p. 5.
116. *Ibid.*, p. 7.
117. HKUSM 6 June 1989, 32.
118. HKUSM 6 June 1989, 32, Appendix Q, document 498/589; 'Interim Report to the Senate', 29 May 1989, p. 6.

119. HKUCM 22 February 1990, 21, Appendix P, Annex I, document 236/1189; 'Proposals for the establishment of two Deputy Directors in the Department of Extra-Mural Studies in 1990–92 and the School of Extension Studies (tentative title) in 1992', pp. 1–2.
120. *Ibid.*, p. 2.
121. *Ibid.*, pp. 5–6.
122. *Ibid.*, p. 9.
123. *Ibid.*, Appendix P, Annex I.I, document 467/1189; John Cribbin, 'Joint Working Party: Committee on Open Education and Extra Mural Studies', 23 November 1989.
124. *Ibid.*
125. *Ibid.*
126. CEMSM 24 November 1989, 7; and HKUCM 22 February 1990, 21, Appendix P, Annex I.I, document 467/1189–A; John Cribbin, 'Joint Working Party: Committee on Open Education and Extra Mural Studies', 23 November 1989.
127. HKUSM 5 February 1991, 34, Appendix V, document 449/191; 'Director's Annual Report 1989/90', p. 1.
128. General Purposes Committee Minutes [hereafter GPCM] 12 January 1990, 8.
129. GPCM 6 April 1990, 3, Appendix C, document 500/390; 'Academic Policy Formulation: External Degree-level Courses', 30 March 1990. The GPC Working Party was asked to examine the development of non-traditional degree-level programmes and the role of the University and faculties in such developments, and to advise on the mechanism to ensure the continuation of such developments.
130. *Ibid.*
131. CEMSM 21 March 1990, 3.
132. GPCM 11 May 1990, 5.
133. For the terms of reference and membership, see HKUCM 20 December 1991, 17, Appendix K, Annex I.I, document 273/391; 'Joint Working Party of the Committees on Open Education and on Extra-Mural Studies', p. 1. The members were Professor Ian Davies (chairman), Professor Rosie Young (Chairman of the Committee on Open Education), Professor Brian Weatherhead (Chairman of the Committeee on Extra-Mural Studies), Professor Lee Ngok (Director, DEMS), Dr L. K. C. Chan (Arts), Professor R. I. Tricker (Social Sciences), Professor E. L. G. Tyler (Law) and Dr M. D. Linton (Education).
134. The CEMS and the COE held a joint meeting on 27 February 1991 to finalise the Davies Report before submission to the University; see CEMSM 27 February 1991, 1, Appendix A.
135. HKUCM 20 December 1991, 17, Appendix K, Annex I.I, document 273/391; 'Joint Working Party of the Committees on Open Education and on Extra-Mural Studies', p. 10.
136. *Ibid.*, p. 11.
137. *Ibid.*
138. *Ibid.*, p. 12.
139. *Ibid.*, pp. 11–12. The DEMS later explained to the GPC that it included 'Professional' in the name because many of the courses provided by DEMS/SPACE aimed at professional people to update skills and knowledge; see HKUCM 20 December 1991, 17, Appendix K, Annex I, document 212/991; 'Proposed School of Professional and Continuing Education', 10 October 1991, p. 6.

140. HKUCM 20 December 1991, 17, Appendix K, Annex I.I, document 273/391; 'Joint Working Party of the Committees on Open Education and on Extra-Mural Studies', p. 4.
141. *Ibid.*, p. 5.
142. Under the External Studies Division there were to be fourteen areas: Legal Education, Business Studies, Economics, Geography, Pharmacy, Computer Science, Librarianship, Housing Management, Medical Science, Social Work, Psychology, Engineering, Education, and Translation. Under the Continuing Education Division there were to be seventeen areas: Art and Design, Biomedical and Health Science, Business, Computer Science and Engineering, Economics Banking and Statistics, Education (including Adult Education), English and European Studies, Geography and Urban Studies, Journalism Communication and Music, Law, Librarianship, Management and Sports Science, Medical Laboratory Science, Oriental Languages and Studies, Philosophy and Translation, Psychology, and Social Work and Sociology; see HKUCM 20 December 1991, 17, Appendix K, Annex I(V), document 208/1190 (annexes Ai and Aii).
143. *Ibid.*, Appendix K, Annex I.I, document 273/391; 'Joint Working Party of the Committees on Open Education and on Extra-Mural Studies', p. 9.
144. GPCM 10 May 1991, 9, Appendix I; GPCM 23 May 1991, 3.
145. HKUSM 5 November 1991, 41.
146. HKUCM 20 December 1991, 17.

CHAPTER SEVEN

1. It is necessary to clarify the use of the abbreviated name 'SPACE' at the beginning of this chapter to avoid confusion. The 'School of Professional and Continuing Education', established in 1992, usually had its name abbreviated to 'SPACE'. Since the School became a company limited by guarantee with the name 'HKU–School of Professional and Continuing Education' in October 1999, the abbreviation 'HKU SPACE' has been customarily used, although 'SPACE' is still common. This chapter will use 'SPACE' to refer to the School before the incorporation and 'HKU SPACE' after its incorporation. When there is a need to refer to the School throughout the whole period 1992–2007, 'the School' or the abbreviation 'SPACE' will be used.
2. Minutes of the Board for Continuing and Professional Education and Lifelong Learning [hereafter BCPE&LLM] 22 February 2000, 8, Appendix H, Annex II, document SPACE/53/200; 'The University and Lifelong Learning', 14 February 2000.
3. For the 1993 Mission Statement, see Appendix 8.
4. FCETI was established in 1994 by six higher institutions in Hong Kong: Caritas, City Polytechnic of Hong Kong, Hong Kong Baptist College, Lingnan College, the Open Learning Institute, and HKU; see Minutes of the SPACE Board of Studies [hereafter BSSPACEM] 27 June 1994, 13, Appendix H, Annex I, document SPACE/8/694; 'The Federation For Continuing Education In Tertiary Education', 16 June 1994.
5. The six clusters were Humanities/Languages, Social Sciences, Biomedical/Life Sciences, Computer Science, Accountancy/Business Studies, and Law; see SPACE Management Board Minutes [hereafter SPACEMBM] 18 May 1992, 7, Appendix G; 'Future Issues for the School of Professional and Continuing Education', 11 May 1992. The concept of 'full-time student equivalent' (FTE) was adopted by the UGC as a means to standardise

the calculation of student numbers in different programmes. One FTE refers to one student in a full-time programme. It should be noted that the UGC did not apply the concept of FTEs to the continuing education sector at that time and the above figure was calculated by SPACE (SPACEMBM 3 July 1998, 4, Appendix C, Annex I.I).

6. University Grants Committee (Hong Kong), *Higher Education in Hong Kong: A Report by the University Grants Committee* (Hong Kong: Government Printer, 1996), p. 80.
7. For the terms of reference of the first Board of Studies and Management Board, see Senate minutes [hereafter HKUSM] 3 March 1992,3, Appendix B, document 460/192, Annex I, document 260/1091 re-amended, January 1992; SPACEMBM 18 May 1992, 1, Appendix A, document 109/191–B; and Council Minutes [hereafter HKUCM] 25 June 1992, 28.
8. HKUCM 20 December 1991, 17, Appendix K, Annex II, document 273/391; 'Joint Working Party of the Committees on Open Education and on Extra-Mural Studies', pp. 2–6.
9. For details see Committee on Extra-Mural Studies minutes [hereafter CEMSM] 1968–91.
10. BCPE&LLM 18 April 2005, 10, Appendix G, Annex I; 'Collaboration with HKU Faculties/Department/Centres'. For details of the Ordinary/Higher Technical Certificate in Medical Laboratory Science, see Dr K. J. Anderson's report submitted in 1984 (CEMSM 30 November 1984, 10, Appendix H, document 336/1184–A).
11. HKUSM 4 December 1990, 44, Appendix BB, Annex I. II; 'Draft Proposal to Establish a P.C.L.L. Course in the University of Hong Kong's E.M.S. Department', October 1990, p. 6. See also Michael Fisher, 'Continuing Legal education in Hong Kong', in *Lifelong Learning in Action: Hong Kong Practitioners' Perspectives*, ed. John Cribbin and Peter Kennedy (Hong Kong: Hong Kong University Press, 2002), pp. 209–218.
12. HKUSM 3 March 1992, 34 and 35.
13. BSSPACEM 30 March 1992, 8, Appendix F, Annex III, document SS11/392; 'Proposed Master of Housing Management'.
14. BSSPACEM 8 January 1996, 7, Appendix F, document SPACE/1/196; 'Annual Report, B.Sc. (Nursing Studies)', 2 January 1996.
15. HKUSM 8 June 2000, 30, Appendix N, document SPACE/47/200 amended; SPACE Annual Report 1998/1999, p. 2.
16. For details, see Appendix 9.
17. HKUCM 28 October 1993, 5, Appendix D, document SPACE/38/693 amended; 'Proposed Bachelor's Degree in Nursing Studies (B.Sc. (Nursing Studies))', 22 July 1993, p. 2.
18. BSSPACEM 22 June 1992, 14, Appendix J, Annex I.I, document 331/392–A; letter from J. A. Cribbin to Registrar, 15 January 1992. *Ibid.*, Appendix K, document SPACE/25/692; 'Higher Degrees in the School of Professional and Continuing Education', 18 June 1992. Dr John Holford, for seven years a member of the DEMS and SPACE academic staff (Staff Tutor, Senior Staff Tutor, Senior Lecturer 1988–95), commented in his report in 1996 that 'progress [in research on continuing education] was made [in SPACE] during the early 1990s, but this remained relatively narrowly-based, resting on contributions from a small number of School staff'; see SPACEMBM 17 April 1996, 7, Appendix F, document SPACE/26/496; 'Developing Research in Continuing Education and Lifelong Learning'.

19. Extract from the minutes of the Board of the Faculty of Social Sciences, 21 January 21 1992; see BSSPACEM 30 March 1992, 8, Appendix F, Annex I, document SS9/392.
20. HKUSM 1 March 1994, 23, Appendix L, Annex I; letter from Mrs Betty Tsui, Secretary of the Faculty of Social Sciences, to Mr J. A. Cribbin, 22 February 1994.
21. *Ibid.*, document 380/294; letter from S. G. Redding, Director of the Business School to the Registrar, 25 February 1994.
22. *Ibid.*, document 474/294; letter from Professor Lee Ngok to the Registrar, 28 February 1994.
23. HKUSM 1 March 1994, 23.
24. *Ibid.*; and HKUSM 6 June 1995, 14.
25. In November 1980, the University Finance Committee decided that after the Town Centre at Shun Tak Centre went into operation, the DEMS would be allowed to keep $1 million in the EMS Fund as a 'buffer' for its development and any balance exceeding this amount should be returned to the University; see HKUCM 27 April 1989, 24, Appendix Q, document 84/489–A. This policy was implemented in 1987–88 by transferring $5 million from the EMS Fund to a new reserve for open education and $4.8 million to the University recurrent budget; see HKUSM 15 March 1988, 35, Appendix U, document 388/188; 'Annual Report of the Committee on Extra-Mural Studies, 1986–87', p. 3.
26. This figure excluded the financial contribution from SPACE to the University for the year, which amounted to about $5 million. There were also indirect costs for the School's use of University's teaching facilities which did not appear in the annual accounts. For details, see Figure 7.1 and Appendix 3.
27. John Cribbin, 'Financial Aspects of the Operation of the School of Professional and Continuing Education at the University of Hong Kong', in G. Dhanarajan *et al.* (eds.), *Economics of Distance Education: Recent Experience* (Hong Kong: Open Learning Institute Press, 1994), pp. 189–191.
28. SPACEMBM 29 May 1993, 12, Appendix J, document SPACE/19/593; 'Adequacy of the SPACE Fund', 24 May 1993, p. 3.
29. HKUCM 25 June 1992, 28; HKUCM 17 June 1993, 7. In practice, SPACE observed the 10 per cent buffer rule and retained $9.13 million in the SPACE Fund by the end of the 1992–93 financial year.
30. HKUCM 30 December 1993, 14, Appendix K, Annex I, document SPACE/21/1193 amended; 'Additional Teaching Accommodation', 8 December 1993.
31. *Ibid.* The final purchase price of the North Point teaching centre was $79 million, $55 million of which was financed by a bank mortgage; see HKUCM 28 April 1994, 1.
32. HKUCM 30 June 1994, 28, Appendix X, document 72/694, Annex III; 'SPACE — Five Years Forecast 1993/94 to 1997/98'.
33. These indirect contributions consisted of (i) interest earned on the SPACE Fund, over $1m in 1993–94; (ii) contribution to the Town Centre, $1.56m per annum; (iii) contribution to the Town Centre 15/F extension costs, $2.034m per annum; (iv) posts supported in the Finance Office and Computer Centre; (v) seconded post from the Registry; (vi) contributions for library use by SPACE students, about $1m per annum; (vii) contribution to indirect costs for SPACE students on University (Statute III) courses, over $2m per annum; (viii) facilities and other fees payable to departments; (ix) provision of computer equipment in joint arrangements with certain departments;

(x) provision of services to the University, e.g. the Distance Learning Unit and, prospectively, videoconferencing; see HKUCM 30 June 1994, 28, Appendix X, Annex IV; letter from J. A. Cribbin to Mr P. B. L. Lam, Director of Finance, 11 May 1994.

34. *Ibid.*
35. *Ibid.*, letter from P. B. L. Lam to J. A. Cribbin, 20 May 1994.
36. *Ibid.*, letter from J. A. Cribbin to Mr P. B. L. Lam, 20 May 1994.
37. *Ibid.*, letter from P. B. L. Lam to J. A. Cribbin, 25 May 1994.
38. SPACEMBM 27 May 1994, 6.
39. HKUCM 30 June 1994, 28, Appendix X, document 72/694; 'Adequacy of SPACE Fund', 8 June 1994.
40. HKUCM 30 June 1994, 28.
41. BSSPACEM 26 September 1994, 12, Appendix I, document SPACE/18/994–b; 'The University and the Future of Continuing Education', 21 September 1994.
42. The other four tertiary institutions were City University Hong Kong, the Chinese University of Hong Kong, Hong Kong Baptist University, and the Hong Kong Polytechnic University; see HKUCM 27 June 1996, 29, Appendix V, document 307/596, Annex II, 19 April 1996.
43. Interview with Professor Lee Ngok, 9 May 2007.
44. HKUCM 29 June 1995, 33, Appendix AA, document 443/695; 'Adequacy of SPACE "buffer" Fund and Student Housing in the St. John's College Third Wing Development', 21 June 1995, pp. 2–3.
45. This FTE figure was probably understated because it was later reported that the School had more than 10,000 FTEs in 1994–95 academic year. For details of the school's FTE load in the last decade, see Appendix 2.
46. HKUCM 29 June 1995, 33, Appendix AA, document 601/695; letter from Prof Lee Ngok to Mr M. G. Spooner, Secretary of Council, 27 June 1995.
47. *Ibid.*, document 614/695; letter from P. B. L. Lam to Mrs C. Cheng, Senior Assistant Registrar, 28 June 1995.
48. HKUCM 29 June 1995, 33.
49. HKUCM 27 June 1996, 29.
50. *South China Morning Post*, 15 February 1996.
51. HKUCM 31 October 1996, 23, Appendix T, document 378/1096; 'Block Grant Subsidy to the School of Professional and Continuing Education', 17 October 1996.
52. HKUCM 31 October 1996, 23.
53. *Ibid.*, Appendix T, document 378/1096; 'Block Grant Subsidy to the School of Professional and Continuing Education', 17 October 1996. The residual subsidies from HKU to SPACE were phased out in 2000–01 after the School was incorporated; see SPACEMBM 27 October 1999, 7.
54. Interview with Professor Enoch C. M. Young, 7 May 2007.
55. BSSPACEM 26 September 1994, 12, Appendix I, document SPACE/18/994–b; 'The University and the Future of Continuing Education', 21 September 1994.
56. BSSPACEM 26 September 1994, 12. SPACEMBM 30 November 1994, 5, Appendix E, document 5/1194, Annex I; letter from Lee Ngok to the Vice-Chancellor, 5 October 1994.
57. Lee Ngok announced his resignation on 7 October 1994; see SPACEMBM 30 November 1994, 5, Appendix E, document 5/1194, Annex II; letter from Director to all SPACE

colleagues, 7 October 1994. Lee Ngok continued at USQ until March 1997 when he returned to Hong Kong to become Executive Director of the Vocational Training Council (1997–March 2003). He is currently Senior Consultant to the President of the Polytechnic University and the Co-ordinator of the Public Policy Research Institute. He still plays competition hockey as captain of the HKU Hockey Team.

58. University and Polytechnic Grants Committee of Hong Kong, *Higher Education, 1991–2001: An Interim Report* (Hong Kong: University and Polytechnic Grants Committee of Hong Kong, 1993), para. 24.
59. SPACEMBM 30 November 1994, 5, Appendix E, document SPACE/5/1194, Annex III; 'Report on the Visit of Professor Richard Taylor, External Policy Adviser, to the School of Professional and Continuing Education (SPACE), Hong Kong University, October 1994', November 1994.
60. *Ibid.*, Appendix E, Annex II; letter from C. G. Smyth to Prof Lee Ngok, 16 November 1994.
61. Apart from Professor Tricker as chairman, the other members of the review panel were Dr John Bacon-Shone from the Faculty of Social Sciences; Professor D. K. O. Chan, appointed by the Senate; Mr J. C. C. Chan, a lay member of the Council; Professor S. T. H. Chan, chairman of the SPACE Management Board; Mr Darwin Chen, Executive Director of the Hong Kong Community Chest; and Professor Richard Taylor, Director of Adult Education at the University of Leeds; see HKUSM 3 October 1995, 23, Appendix S, document 555/595; 'Review Panel for the School of Professional and Continuing Education'.
62. *Ibid.*, pp. 2–3.
63. *Ibid.*, p. 3.
64. *Ibid.*, pp. 4–5.
65. *Ibid.*, p. 5.
66. SPACEMBM 6 June 1995, 6.
67. HKUSM 3 October 1995, 23, Appendix S, document SPACE/30/695; 'SPACE Staff Comments on the Review Panel Report (555/595) discussed at a Staff Meeting on 9 June 1995', 26 June 1995.
68. HKUSM 3 October 1995, 23.
69. SPACEMBM 6 June 1995, 6.
70. HKUSM 3 October 1995, 23.
71. BSSPACEM 10 April 1995, 6; and 8 January 1996, 13.
72. SPACEMBM 29 January 1996; and 7 February 1996, 13, Appendix O, document SPACE/31/595, 5 June 1995.
73. SPACEMBM 6 December 1996, Appendix C, document SPACE/48/1196; 'Senior Management and Administration Issues'.
74. Professor S. L. Wong was Acting Director of SPACE from 1 December 1996 to 30 June 1997, and Professor S. T. H. Chan from 1 July 1997 to February 1998; BSSPACEM 16 April 1997, 4, Appendix B, document SPACE/3/497, 2 April 1997; and 23 June 1997, 2, Appendix A, document SPACE/11/697, 16 June 1997.
75. HKUCM 26 June 1997, 3, Appendix B–2(c); 'SPACE Annual Report 1997/1998'. HKU Senate Circular 14 April 1999, 20, Annex IX, document SPACE/11/299 amended, p. 1.
76. *Ibid.*, 'SPACE Annual Report 1997/1998', p. 1.

77. SPACEMBM 3 July 1998, 2, Appendix A, document SPACE/2/798; 'Report of Activities for 1997/98', 26 June 1998.
78. *Ibid.*, 4, Appendix C, Annex I; 'Policy Review by Professor E. C. M. Young, Director-designate', January 1998, p. 1.
79. SPACEMBM 28 November 1997, 7. The seven divisions were for Applied Science, Arts and Humanities, Business Studies, Law, Social Sciences and Education, Traditional Chinese Medicine, and Urban Studies and Real Estate.
80. HKUSM 19 June 1998, 3, Appendix B–8. HKU SPACE Board of Directors minutes [hereafter HKUSPACEBDM] 5 November 2001, 6(a), Appendix E, document SPACE/96/1001; 'Staffing Issues', 29 October 2001.
81. HKU SPACE Annual Report 1999–2000, p. 2; Annual Report 2001–02, p. 3.
82. BCPE&LLM 28 November 2005, 5. In March 1997, there were 173 full-time employees in the School; see SPACEMBM 17 March 1997, 6, Appendix D, document SPACE/10/397; 'Staff Matters', 12 March 1997.
83. SPACEMBM 3 July 1998, 4, Appendix C; letter from H. W. K. Wai, Registrar, to Professor E. C. M. Young, 13 February 1998.
84. SPACEMBM 25 November 1998, 8.
85. HKUCM 7 May 1999, 15, Appendix L, document 448/499; 'Incorporation of the School of Professional and Continuing Education', 30 April 1999.
86. HKUCM 7 May 1999, 15.
87. HKUCM 24 June 1999, 17.
88. HKU Council Circular 22 December 1999, 9, Annex VIII, document 364/1199, 15 November 1999. The name 'HKU SPACE' had to be used because the company name 'SPACE' was already being used. The School of Professional and Continuing Education as a sub-division of studies of the University was not, however, disestablished at this time and existed legally without any activity until the Council's resolution on 22 December 2004; see HKU Council Circular 16 December 2004, 1.
89. The five Company Members were designated by the University: the Vice-Chancellor, the Pro-Vice-Chancellor (Academic), the Director of Finance, and later the Director of SPACE; see HKU SPACE Annual Report 2000–01, p. 4.
90. HKU SPACE Memorandum of Association, Articles 3.10, 3.11.
91. BCPE&LLM 19 April 2004, 4, Appendix B, document SPACE/15/404; 'Academic Approval of HKU SPACE Awards: A Background Paper', 13 April 2004.
92. SPACEMBM 9 July 1999, 4, Appendix B attachment; 'SPACE Committee Structure', 17 May 1999.
93. HKU Senate Circular 6 December 1999, 20, Annex IX, document 513/1199; 'Board for Continuing and Professional Education (CPE) and Lifelong Learning', 22 November 1999.
94. For the terms of reference of the BCPE&LL, see Appendix 10.
95. HKU SPACE Prospectus, Autumn 2000, p. vi.
96. SPACEMBM 3 July 1998, 4, Appendix C, Annex I; 'Policy Review by Professor E. C. M. Young, Director-designate', January 1998, p. 1.
97. F. W. Jessup, 'The Idea of Lifelong Learning' in F. W. Jessup (ed.), *Lifelong Learning: A Symposium on Continuing Education* (Oxford: Pergamon Press, 1969), p. 25. For further discussion, see Therese W. H. Shak, 'Lifelong Education: Definition, Agreement and Prediction' (unpublished Doctor of Education thesis, University of British Columbia,

1989), pp. 2–5; and Albert Tuijnman, 'Lifelong Learning: Evolution of a Conceptual Map and Some Implications', in John Cribbin and Peter Kennedy (eds.), *Lifelong Learning in Action: Hong Kong Practitioners' Perspectives* (Hong Kong: Hong Kong University Press, 2002), pp. 9–12.

98. Shak, 'Lifelong Education', p. 9.
99. In the Ten Year Plan of 1988, the CEMS mentioned that the proposed Division of Continuing Education would address the new concept of 'lifelong education' which was now being used in Commonwealth universities. There was not, however, any further elaboration of the meaning of 'lifelong education' at that time; see HKUSM 27 June 1989, 1, Appendix A, Annex XVI.B, document 350/1188; 'Academic Development Proposals to 1996–97', p. 31.
100. Tung Chee Hwa, 1998 Policy Address by the Chief Executive (Hong Kong: Government Printer, 1998), para. 104. See also Hong Kong Government, *Policy Objectives: The 1998 Policy Address* (Hong Kong: Government Printer, 1998), p. 123.
101. Peter Kennedy, 'The politics of "lifelong learning" in post-1997 Hong Kong', *International Journal of Lifelong Education*, vol. 23 (2004), pp. 592–595, 602–603.
102. *Ibid.*, p. 596.
103. *Ibid.*, p. 603.
104. Education Commission, *Education Blueprint for the 21st Century: Review of Academic System: Aims of Education* (Hong Kong: Education Commission, 1999), p. 11.
105. Education Commission, *Review of Education System: Reform Proposals: Excel and Grow* (Hong Kong: Education Commission, 2000), p.1.
106. Enoch C. M. Young, 'Towards a Learning Society — HKU SPACE and Lifelong Learning in Hong Kong' (A talk given at the Annual General Meeting of the Hong Kong Library Association on 7 December 2000), in SPACE Board of Studies files.
107. HKU Senate Circular 14 April 1999, 20, Annex IX, document SPACE/11/299 amended; 'SPACE Annual Report 1997/1998', p. 2.
108. HKUSM 1 June 1999, 18.
109. HKUSM 26 October 1999, 15, Appendix N, Annex I, document 217/1099.
110. The Senate's agreement to Professor Young's proposal was hardly enthusiastic; however, the feeling among many members was that the addition was necessary simply to satisfy the demands of HKU SPACE so that the whole statement could be adopted without any further debate.
111. HKUSPACEBDM 19 February 2001, 7, Appendix F, document SPACE/6/201; 'Director's Report', 15 February 2001.
112. BCPE&LLM 22 February 2000, 8, Appendix H, Annex II, document SPACE/53/200; 'The University and Lifelong Learning', 14 February 2000, p. 7.
113. BCPE&LLM 19 April 2004, 3, Appendix A, Annex B; 'HKU SPACE Strategic Plan' (Abridged version), April 2002, p. 13.
114. HKUCM 26 November 2002, 13, Appendix M, document 284/1102; 'Report on the Review of the HKU School of Professional and Continuing Education', 19 November 2002, p. 1. This report includes the terms of reference of the Malpas Review Panel.
115. *Ibid.*, Appendix M, Annex II, document 454/102 amended; 'Report on the Review of the HKU–School of Professional and Continuing Education', 17 January 2002, p. 1.
116. *Ibid.*, p. 2.
117. *Ibid.*

118. *Ibid.*, pp. 2–3.
119. *Ibid.*, p. 5.
120. *Ibid.*, pp. 4–5.
121. *Ibid.*, p. 6.
122. *Ibid.*, p. 5.
123. *Ibid.*, Appendix M, Annex III, document 557/1002; 'Response to the Review of HKU SPACE', 18 April 2002, p. 2.
124. *Ibid.*, p. 3.
125. HKUSM 5 November 2002, 24.
126. *Ibid.*
127. *HKU SPACE News*, no. 14 (Autumn 2002).
128. HKUCM 26 November 2002, 13(f)(v).
129. HKU Council Circular 28 May 2003, 3, Annex III, document 405/403 amended; 'Strategic Planning 2003–2008', p. 1.
130. *Ibid.*, pp. 6, 13.
131. HKUSM 9 December 2003, 33, Appendix V, Annex I, document 590/1103; 'Terms of Reference of the Board of Continuing and Professional Education and Lifelong Learning'.
132. *Ibid.*; HKUCM 27 January 2004, 9, Appendix J, document 590/1103 amended; 'Terms of Reference of the Board of Continuing and Professional Education and Lifelong Learning'.
133. HKUSM 9 December 2003, 33, Appendix V, document 589/1103; 'Report on the Review of HKU School of Professional and Continuing Education (HKU–SPACE)', 30 November 2003, p. 3.
134. HKU Council Circular 20 August 2002; 'Review of Governance and Management', 20 August 2002.
135. University of Hong Kong, *Fit for Purpose: A Review of Governance and Management Structures at The University of Hong Kong* (Hong Kong: University of Hong Kong, 2003), pp. 12, 17.
136. HKUCM 14 February 2003, 5. The *Fit for Purpose* report proposed that a new Vice-Chancellor's Advisory Group be established consisting of the Senior Management Team and the deans of the faculties to advise the Vice-Chancellor on management issues; see *Fit for Purpose*, p. 22.
137. HKUSPACEBDM 30 June 2003, 9, Appendix K, Annex I.A; 'Fit for Purpose: HKU SPACE Response', 14 April 2003.
138. HKUCM 24 June 2003, 9, Appendix J, document 266/603; 'Reform of University Governance and Management', 17 June 2003, p. 3.
139. HKUCM 24 June 2003, 9.
140. HKUSM 9 December 2003, 33, Appendix V, document 589/1103; 'Report on the Review of HKU School of Professional and Continuing Education (HKU–SPACE)', 30 November 2003, p. 2.
141. HKUCM 27 July 2004, 12; HKUCM 27 September 2005, 11.
142. HKU Senate Circular 9 September 2004, 7, Annex II, document 47/804 amended; 'Joint Consultative Committees — Proposed Changes', 1 September 2004. BCPE&LLM 20 June 2005, 8, Appendix F, document SPACE/136/605; 'Joint Consultative Committee', 14 June 2005.
143. BCPE&LLM 20 June 2005, 8, Appendix F, document SPACE/136/605; 'Joint Consultative Committee', 14 June 2005.

144. BCPE&LLM 18 April 2005, 10 Appendix G, document 497/305; 'HKU and HKU SPACE, Moving Forward Together: Fulfilling the University's Lifelong Learning Mission', 7 April 2005.
145. For a detailed discussion of various issues in the recent academic development of HKU SPACE, see John Cribbin and Peter Kennedy (eds.), *Lifelong Learning in Action: Hong Kong Practitioners' Perspectives* (Hong Kong: Hong Kong University Press, 2002).
146. BSSPACEM 24 June 1996, 8, Appendix D, document SPACE/21/596; 'Course Development in Traditional Chinese Medicine: Diploma in Clinical Acupuncture, Diploma in Acupuncture and Moxibustion'.
147. SPACE Prospectus, Autumn 1991, p. 26.
148. HKUCM 29 October 1992, 26, Appendix S, Annex I, document 360/1092, 30 June 1992.
149. SPACEMBM 29 May 1993, 8, Appendix F, document SPACE/22/493; 'Ten Year Strategy', p. 7.
150. SPACEMBM 17 April 1996, 11, Appendix J, Annex II, document SPACE/49/396; 'Proposal for the Establishment of a "Centre of Traditional Chinese Medicine" in the School of Professional and Continuing Education, The University of Hong Kong'.
151. BSSPACEM 24 June 1996, 8, Appendix D, document SPACE/21/596; 'Course Development in Traditional Chinese Medicine: Diploma in Clinical Acupuncture, Diploma in Acupuncture and Moxibustion'.
152. *Ibid.*, Appendix D, Annex IX; letter from Professor S. P. Chow to Mr J. A. Cribbin, 9 April 1996.
153. Hong Kong Government, *Report of the Working Party on Chinese Medicine* (Hong Kong: Government Printer, 1994), p. 20. HKUSM 3 December 1996, 20; and HKUSM 19 June 1998, 2, Appendix A–7, Annex IV.II, document 556/1096; 'Centre for Traditional Chinese Medicine', 12 November 1996.
154. HKUSM 19 June 1998, 2, Appendix A–7, Annex IV.II, document 556/1096; 'Centre for Traditional Chinese Medicine', 12 November 1996.
155. BSSPACEM 23 June 1997, 7, Appendix G, document SPACE/51/397; 'Diploma in Traditional Chinese Medicine: Course Proposal'.
156. HKUSM 19 June 1998, 2, Appendix A–7, Annex IV.I; 'Course Proposal for a Bachelor of Traditional Chinese Medicine (B.TCM)', pp. 2–3.
157. Tung Chee Hwa, *Building Hong Kong for a New Era* (1997 Policy Address by the Chief Executive) (Hong Kong: Government Printer, 1998), para. 132.
158. HKUSM 19 June 1998, 2, Appendix A–7, Annex IV.I; 'Course Proposal for a Bachelor of Traditional Chinese Medicine (B.TCM)', p. 2. HKU Council Circular 26 June 1998, 3.
159. HKUSM 19 June 1998, 2, Appendix A–7, Annex IV.I.D; 'Bachelor of Traditional Chinese Medicine (B.TCM): Teaching staff titles, affiliations and academic qualifications'.
160. HKUSM 8 June 2000, 30, Appendix W, document SPACE/47/200 amended; 'SPACE Annual Report 1998–1999', 27 April 2000, p. 13. HKU SPACE later withdrew from the Bachelor of TCM and Master of TCM programmes in 2003.
161. HKU Council Circular 6 November 1998, 16, Annex XII, document SPACE/18/998; 'Traditional Chinese Medicine'.
162. SPACEMBM 25 November 1998, 9(b)(ii).

163. For example, a Chinese Medicine Mingyi Guan (Master of Chinese Medicine Clinic) was opened in April 2005 to train Chinese Medicine practitioners and to provide a consultation service to the community; see *SPACE News*, no. 24 (Summer 2005).
164. BCPE&LLM 19 April 2004, 3, Appendix A; 'HKU SPACE Development Plan', November 2003, p. 25.
165. HKUSPACEBD 20 January 2006, 8, Appendix E, document SPACE/81/106, January 2006.
166. 1999–2000 Budget Speech, para. 59.
167. HKU Council Circular 21 March 2002, 3, Annex III, document 138/302–A; 'Invitation for Proposals for "Academic Plan" for Hong Kong's Cyberport', p. 3.
168. *Ibid.*, Annex III, document 137/302; 'A Proposal for the Establishment of a Cyberport Institute of Hong Kong, The University of Hong Kong', 8 March 2002, pp. 4–5. *HKU SPACE News*, no.13 (Autumn 2002).
169. HKU SPACE Annual Report 2001–02, p. 2. HKU Council Circular 21 March 2002, 3, Annex III, document 137/302; 'A Proposal for the Establishment of a Cyberport Institute of Hong Kong, The University of Hong Kong', 8 March 2002, p. 5.
170. HKU SPACE *Prospectus* (Autumn 2003), p. 385.
171. HKUSM 3 February 2004, 14, Appendix P, document SPACE/108/1103 amended; 'Cyberport Institute of Hong Kong: Annual Report', 13 November 2003, pp. 1–2.
172. HKUSM 7 December 2004, 13, Appendix N, Annex I, document SPACE/130/304; 'Cyberport Institute of Hong Kong — Development Plan'.
173. *Ibid.*, Appendix N, Annex 2, document SPACE/29/504.
174. For further discussion, see John Cribbin, 'Quality Assurance in Lifelong Learning', in Cribbin and Kennedy (eds.), *Lifelong Learning in Action*, pp. 143–145.
175. Lee Ngok, 'Opportunity Knocks: Continuing Higher Education in Hong Kong', in a Supplement to the *University of Hong Kong Gazette*, vol. 39, no. 2 (14 December 1992), p. 42.
176. SPACEMBM 29 May 1993, 8, Appendix F, document SPACE/22/493; 'Ten Year Strategy', p. 3.
177. BSSPACEM 27 June 1994, 15, Appendix J, document SPACE/31/694; 'Quality Assurance Issues', 23 June 1994.
178. SPACEMBM 30 November 1994, 5, Appendix E, document SPACE/5/1194, Annex III; 'Report on the visit of Professor Richard Taylor, External Policy Adviser, to the School of Professional and Continuing Education (SPACE), Hong Kong University, October 1994', November 1994.
179. HKUSM 3 October 1995, 23, Appendix S, document 555/595; 'Review Panel for the School of Professional and Continuing Education', p. 6.
180. BSSPACEM 24 June 1996, 12, Appendix H, document SPACE/16/696; 'Quality Assurance: SPACE', April 1996.
181. SPACEMBM 28 November 1997, 6, Appendix F, document SPACE/13/1197; 'Report from the Director-designate'.
182. HKU Senate Circular 14 April 1999, 20, Annex IX, document SPACE/11/299; 'SPACE Annual Report 1997/98'. Mrs Craft was later appointed by the University as External Adviser until 30 June 2002; see BCPE&LL Circular 23 August 2001, 3.
183. HKUSM 4 March 2003, 15, Annex N.1; 'Second Round Teaching and Learning Quality Process Reviews: Report on The University of Hong Kong', p. 17.

184. *Ibid.*, p. 17. HKUSM 8 June 2000, 30, Appendix W, document SPACE/47/2000 amended; 'Annual Report 1998/99', p. 5. Education Quality Work [EQW] was a term that had become popular at that time as part of the UGC's Teaching and Learning Quality Process Review [TLQPR] of universities in Hong Kong.
185. BCPE&LL Circular 23 November 2000, 2, Appendix B, document SPACE/79/1100; 'Quality Assurance at HKU SPACE: External Adviser's Report', 9 August 2000. *SPACE News*, no.7, (Spring 2001).
186. HKU SPACE, *Quality Assurance Manual* (Hong Kong: HKU School of Professional and Continuing Education, 2000), chapter 2, p. 2.
187. HKU SPACE Annual Report 2000–01, p. 7. HKUSM 4 March 2003, 15, Annex N.1; 'Second Round Teaching and Learning Quality Process Reviews: Report on The University of Hong Kong', p. 17.
188. For the authorisation routes in the programme approval process, see *Quality Assurance manual*, chapter 4, p. 7. This manual contains full details of the quality assurance system used by HKU SPACE.
189. HKUSPACEBDM 19 February 2001, 7, Appendix F, Annex II; 'Report of QA Development at HKU SPACE', January 2001.
190. BCPE&LLM 9 April 2001, 7, Appendix F, document SPACE/19/401; 'Annual Monitoring Reports for 1999–2000', 3 April 2001.
191. HKUSM 4 March 2003, 15, Appendix N, Annex I.1; 'Second Round Teaching and Learning Quality Process Reviews: Report on The University of Hong Kong', pp. 17–18.
192. *Ibid.*, pp. 18, 20.
193. BCPE&LLM 18 July 2005, 4, Appendix B, document 98/705; 'Annual Monitoring Reports for 2003–2004', 6 July 2005.
194. BCPE&LLM 9 January 2006, 5, Appendix D, document 349/1205; 'Report on Quality Assurance Activities in HKU SPACE 2004–05', 5 October 2005.
195. In 2005, for example, the School started a review of the Quality Assurance system, and made amendments to the *Quality Assurance Manual*; see BCPE&LLM 9 January 2006, 6, Appendix E, document 350/1205; 'Review of the HKU SPACE Quality Assurance System', 9 December 2005.
196. HKUCM 27 April 1989, 24, Appendix Q, document 305/489; letter from C. G. Large, Finance Officer, to the Registrar, 19 April 1989. HKUCM 23 April 1991, 3, Appendix B, document 51/491; 'Department of Extra-Mural Studies: Purchase of Additional Property', 2 April 1991.
197. SPACEMBM 24 June 1997, 4, Appendix C, Annex I; 'Shek Kip Mei: Ka Chi School'.
198. Shek Kip Mei Regional Centre closed when the lease expired in 2006.
199. HKUCM 28 April 1994, 1.
200. SPACEMBM 6 June 1995, 5. HKUCM 28 May 1985, 2, Appendix A, document 320/1095 (Annex XVIII, document 423/995); letter from Rev Paul Tong, Master of St John's College, to Mr P. B. L. Lam, Director of Finance, 18 September 1995.
201. HKUSM 5 February 1991, 34, Appendix V, document 449/191; 'Director's Annual Report 1989/90', pp. 15–16. HKUCM 27 June 1991, 30, Appendix BB, Annex I.1; 'Proposed Redevelopment of Woodside Art Gallery plus Tower Block for EMS', 2 May 1991.
202. HKUSM 5 February 1991, 34, Appendix V, Annex I.

203. HKUCM 23 April 1991, 27.
204. Interview with Professor Lee Ngok, 9 May 2007.
205. HKUCM 27 June 1991, 30, Appendix BB, Annex I.II; letter from Prof Lee Ngok to Mr N. J. Gillanders, Registrar, 29 May 1991.
206. The rent was calculated so as to recover interest on the capital from the Endowment Fund used for the development of the building; see HKUCM 25 June 1992, 33, Appendix U, document 283/692; 'Capital Projects Submission 1992', 18 June 1992, p. 25. SPACEMBM 29 January 1996 and 7 February 1996, 13, Appendix M; 'SPACE Teaching Centres Owned by the University'.
207. HKUCM 27 April 1995, 20, Appendix O, document 511/1195 re-amended; 'Capital Projects Submission 1996', para.6.1.
208. BSSPACEM 15 April 1996, 7. SPACEMBM 25 September 1996, 15.
209. *SPACE News*, no.1 (Autumn 1999).
210. SPACEMBM 25 November 1998, 6', Appendix C, document SPACE/22/1198; 'Accommodation', 19 November 1998.
211. SPACEMBM 6 December 1996, 9.
212. HKUCM 26 June 1997, 1, Appendix A, Annex I, document 77/697; 'School of Professional and Continuing Education (SPACE): Swap of Properties at Shun Tak Centre with Admiralty Centre', 27 May 1997.
213. SPACEMBM 28 November 1997, 5, Appendix E, document SPACE/12/1197; 'Admiralty Centre/T.T. Tsui Building', 25 November 1997. The Admiralty Centre was officially opened on 13 January 1998; see *SPACE News*, no.1, Autumn 1999.
214. HKU Senate Circular, 14 April 1999, 20, Annex IX, document SPACE/11/299 amended; 'Annual Report 1997/98', p. 5.
215. For details of the fifteen current learning centres, see HKU SPACE, 'Learning Centres', www.hkuspace.hku.hk/centre_facility/, 2003, accessed 26 April 2007. See also Appendix 4.
216. HKUSPACEBDM 14 October 2005, 7, Appendix D, Annex I.
217. The authors are grateful to Professor Enoch Young for providing this figure.
218. HKUVC 225/66; letter from Lindsay Ride to Sir Charles H. Wilson, 11 November 1966.
219. Lee, 'Opportunity Knocks', p. 43.
220. HKU Registry Archive, 8/2/1; 'E.M.S. Certificate in Management: Position Paper'.
221. HKUSM 6 March 1990, 21, Appendix P, Annex IV; 'Examinable Courses 1988/89', p. viii. *SPACE News*, no.5, (Autumn 2000).
222. SPACEMBM 29 May 1993, 8, Appendix F, document SPACE/22/493; 'Ten Year Strategy', p. 24.
223. SPACEMBM 25 September 1996, 7, Appendix G, document SPACE/43/996; 'New Courses for 1996/97', 18 September 1996.
224. SPACEMBM 3 July 1998, 4, Appendix C, Annex V.
225. SPACEMBM 25 November 1998, 14.
226. HKUSPACEBDM 19 October 2004, 4, Appendix A, Annex I.A; 'Senior Executives Courses (Mainland China and Overseas)'.
227. *Ibid.*, Appendix A, Annex I, document SPACE/14/2004; 'Development in China Mainland (October 2004)', 25 September 2004.

228. HKU SPACE, Annual Report 2005/2006 (draft), p. 13. The authors are grateful to John Cribbin for providing them with a copy of this draft report before final publication.
229. HKUSPACEMBM 27 October 1999, 12, Appendix K, document SPACE/39/1099; 'New Developments', 20 October 1999.
230. BCPE&LL Circular 23 November 2000, 1, Appendix A, document SPACE/74/1000; 'Proposal for Master of Art (Accounting) and Bachelor of Accounting Programmes: Collaboration with Dongbei University of Finance and Economics'.
231. HKUSM 7 April 1998, 12, Appendix L, Annex, document 596/398; 'Joint Master of Business Administration (International) Programme with Fudan University', 20 January 1998.
232. HKUSM 8 June 2000, 30 Appendix N, Document SPACE/47/200 amended; 'Annual Report 1998/99', p. 6.
233. *SPACE News*, no. 2 (Winter 1999).
234. *Ibid.*, no. 6 (Winter 2000).
235. Interview with Professor Enoch C. M. Young, 7 May 2007. Professor Yang Fujia is now Chancellor of the University of Nottingham (UK) and a prime mover in establishing Nottingham's Ningbo campus in China.
236. *Ibid.* HKUSPACEBDM 19 September 2000, 8.1, Appendix Q, document SPACE/30/900; 'China Development', 15 September 2000.
237. *Ibid.* HKUSM 6 March 2001, 9, Appendix G, Annex I, document E135/600 re-amended; 'MSc in E-commerce and Internet Technology (with SPACE and Fudan University in Shanghai, China)', pp. 1, 3.
238. HKUSPACEBDM 19 February 2001, 8, Appendix G, Annex I; 'SPACE Shanghai: Progress Report', February 2001.
239. For details of the School's learning centres in China, see Appendix 5.
240. HKUSPACEBDM 19 September 2000, 8.1.
241. HKUSPACEBDM 5 November 2001, 7, Appendix F, Annex III, document SPACE/8/1101; 'China Development'.
242. HKUSPACEBDM 14 July 2003, 11, Appendix M, Annex II; 'HKU SPACE in China'.
243. HKUSPACEBDM 5 March 2002, 3. BCPE&LLM 19 April 2004, 3, Appendix A; 'HKU SPACE Development Plan', November 2003, p. 30.
244. HKUSPACEBDM 8 October 2003, 2.
245. HKUSPACEBDM 2 March 2004, 5, Appendix D, document SPACE/203/204; 'Report of a meeting of the Advisory Board of the HKU School of Professional Continuing Education held at 9.30 a.m. on Tuesday, 3rd February 2004 in the Senate Room, 10/F Knowles Building, University of Hong Kong, Pokfulam Road', para. 7.1.
246. HKUSPACEBDM 19 October 2004, 7(c)(x).
247. HKUSPACEBDM 3 March 2004, 9, Attachment; 'HKU SPACE Annual Report 2003/2004', p. 20. HKU SPACE Annual Report 2005/2006 (draft), pp. 12–13.
248. BCPE&LLM 19 April 2004, 3, Appendix A; 'HKU SPACE Development Plan', November 2003, p. 31. For details of the Global College, see Chapter 8.
249. In 2002–03, HKU SPACE provided courses to 17,537 FTEs, which was nearly double the School of Continuing Education of HKBU, the second largest CPE unit of a local university in terms of FTE; see Federation of Continuing Education in Tertiary Institutions figures as provided at www.fce.org.hk/~fceorg/facts_table02-03.htm.

250. In a survey of the background of students enrolled in HKU SPACE courses in 2004–05, over 40 per cent of the respondents declared themselves as owners of companies, executive or professionals; see HKU SPACE Annual Report 2004/2005, p. 38.
251. HKU SPACE Annual Report 2005/2006 (draft), 'Student Statistics'.

CHAPTER EIGHT

1. Education Commission, *Review of Education System: Framework for Education Reform: Learning for Life* (Hong Kong: Education Commission, 1999), p. 22.
2. HKU SPACE Management Board Minutes [hereafter HKUSPACEMBM] 27 October 1999, 12, Appendix K, document SPACE/39/1099; 'New Developments', 20 October 1999, p. 2.
3. *Ibid.*, 12(b)(iv).
4. Community College Advisory Council Minutes [hereafter CCACM] 29 May 2003, 10, Appendix E; 'Development of Associate Degree Programmes in the US', p. 2.
5. *Ibid.*, p. 1. Professor William Rainey Harper, first President of the University of Chicago, 'was widely recognized as the founder of the junior college movement'; see Willard J. Pugh, 'A "Curious Working of Cross Purposes" in the Founding of the University of Chicago', in Roger Geiger (ed.), *The American College in the Nineteenth Century* (Nashville, Vanderbilt University Press, 2000), p. 262.
6. CCACM 29 May 2003, 10, Appendix E; 'Development of Associate Degree Programmes in the US', p. 1.
7. Board for Continuing and Professional Education and Lifelong Learning Minutes [hereafter BCPE&LLM] 22 February 2000, 6, Appendix F, Annex I; 'Responses to the Education Commission *Review of the Education System: Framework for Education Reform: Learning for Life*', 16 December 1999, p. 3.
8. Education Commission, *Learning for Life, Learning through Life: Reform Proposals for the Education System in Hong Kong* (Hong Kong: Education Commission, 2000), p. 126.
9. *Ibid.*, pp. 127–128.
10. Tung Chee Hwa, *Serving the Community, Sharing Common Goals* (2000 Policy Address by the Chief Executive) (Hong Kong: Government Printer, 2000), para. 66.
11. HKU SPACE Board of Directors Minutes [hereafter HKUSPACEBDM] 16 February 2000, 8, Appendix J, document 131/200A; 'Proposal on the Establishment of a Community College of the School of Professional and Continuing Education, The University of Hong Kong', p. 5.
12. The Associate in General Studies and the Associate in Professional Studies programmes were not ultimately introduced.
13. The AD qualification is awarded by HKU SPACE as a HKU award, but despite a Council resolution on 26 November 2002 to the effect that all SPACE awards should be listed in the University Statutes, neither AD nor HD qualifications are currently included in the list of degrees and academic distinctions conferred by HKU in the University Statutes; see *Calendar 2005–2006*, pp. 33–36.
14. HKUSPACEBDM 16 February 2000, 8, Appendix J, document 131/200; 'A Proposal on the Establishment of a Community College of the School of Professional and Continuing Education, The University of Hong Kong', pp. 2, 6. For the mission statement of HKU SPACE Community College, see 'A Report on the Establishment of the HKU–SPACE Community College', 12 October 2000, p. 4.

15. *SPACE News*, no. 4 (Summer 2000).
16. HKU SPACE Board of Directors Circular 13 June 2000, Annex I, document SPACE/30/600; 'The Community College Programme', 13 June 2000, p. 1.
17. 'A Report on the Establishment of the HKU–SPACE Community College', p. 12. For the staff profile of the College, see *SPACE News*, no. 5 (Autumn 2000).
18. Interview with Ms Currie Tsang, 19 April 2006.
19. 'A Report on the Establishment of the HKU–SPACE Community College', p. 12.
20. HKU SPACE Annual Report 2001–02, p. 1
21. HKU SPACE Community College Management Committee Minutes [hereafter CCMCM] 2 September 2002, 2, Annex I to the minutes.
22. The first chairman of the College Council was Mr Linus Cheung. The College Council decided to change its name to 'Advisory Council' in order to emphasise its advisory role; see CCACM 29 May 2003, 2.
23. CCMCM 6 December 2005, 9, Appendix F.
24. BCPE&LLM 23 July 2002, 3.5, Appendix B, Annex V. *Ibid.*, 21 September 2003, 5.4, Appendix C. This figure includes the students of both Pre-AD and AD programmes; see CCMCM 28 February 2006, 9, Appendix G, Annex I; 'Development Plan for 2006–07', 25 February 2006. We are grateful to Ms Currie Tsang who supplied the figures for December 2006. Between December 2005 and December 2006, Pre-AD enrolments dropped from 397 to 317, but AD numbers rose from 2,744 to 2,806.
25. HKUSPACEBDM 19 September 2000, 7.2, Appendix M, document SPACE/26/900; 'Project Springboard', 18 September 2000.
26. *Ibid.*
27. *Ibid.* HKU SPACE Annual Report 2000–01. p. 10.
28. HKU SPACE Annual Report, 2001–02.
29. BCPE&LLM 9 April 2001, 6, Appendix E, document SPACE/14/401; 'SPACE Career Development Programmes (CDPs) — A Proposal on the Development of Vocationally-Oriented, Full-time Programmes for Post-Secondary Students', 6 April 2001.
30. CCMCM 28 February 2006, 9, Appendix G, Annex I; 'Development Plan for 2006–07', 25 February 2006. We are grateful to Ms Currie Tsang who supplied the figures for December 2006.
31. 'A Report on the Establishment of the HKU–SPACE Community College', Appendix C. The Academic Committee was restructured into the Academic Board with an enlarged membership in 2003; see HKU SPACE Community College Academic Board Minutes [hereafter CCABM] 2 June 2003, 1, Appendix A.
32. 'A Report on the Establishment of the HKU–SPACE Community College', Appendix C.
33. HKU Senate Minutes [hereafter HKUSM] 4 March 2003, 15, Appendix N, Annex I (Appendix 1); 'Second Round Teaching and Learning Quality Process Reviews: Report on The University of Hong Kong', 25 February 2003, p. 21.
34. These points are calculated on the basis of grades received in the best subjects in the public examination. Students receive one point for Grade E, two points for Grade D, three points for Grade C and so on. The minimum requirement for matriculation is eight points in the best six subjects in the HKCEE. There is no unified admission requirement for the universities, but it is virtually impossible for a student who receives less than five AL points to be admitted to a local university.

35. CCABM 10 June 2004, 6, Appendix F; 'Annual Monitoring Reports 2002–03 for Pre-Associate/Associate Degree Programmes', 17 March 2004.
36. Interview with Professor Mimi Chan, 20 April 2006.
37. CCACM 3 February 2005, 4, Appendix C; 'Community College Annual Report 2003–04', 23 January 2005, p. 5.
38. Interview with Mr Andric Chan, Mr Stephen Choi and Miss Vivian Chan, 22 April 2006.
39. Interview with Professor Mimi Chan, 20 April 2006.
40. Interview with Professor K. F. Cheng, 19 April 2006.
41. Interview with Mr Andric Chan, Mr Stephen Choi and Miss Vivian Chan, 22 April 2006.
42. HKU SPACE Community College Annual Report 2004–05, p. 10.
43. CCABM 2 June 2003, 7, Appendix F; 'Annual Monitoring Report 2001–2002', p. 16.
44. Interview with Dr Peter Lee, 27 July 2006.
45. CCMCM 4 October 2005, 2.1, Attachment; 'College Principal's Report for the Meeting on 4 October 2005', p. 13.
46. HKU SPACE Community College Annual Report 2004–05, p. 1.
47. CCMCM 15 July 2003, 6, Appendix D; 'Community College Students Union (CCSU)'.
48. HKU SPACE Community College, *Prospectus 2005–2006*, p. 86.
49. CCACM 3 February 2005, 4, Appendix C; 'HKU SPACE Community College Annual Report 2003–04', 23 January 2005, p. 8.
50. HKUSPACEBDM 19 September 2000, 7.1, Appendix L, document SPACE/25/900; 'Community College Development', 15 September 2000.
51. Interview with Ms Currie Tsang, 19 April 2006.
52. 'A Report on the Establishment of the HKU–SPACE Community College', p. 13.
53. HKU SPACE Annual Report 2001–02, p. 1.
54. HKUSPACEBDM 23 July 2002, 8, Appendix G, document SPACE/94/702; 'Community College Campus Development Strategy', 17 July 2002. *SPACE News*, no. 9 (Autumn 2001).
55. *SPACE News*, no. 14 (Autumn 2002).
56. HKU Council Minutes [hereafter HKUCM] 27 November 2001, 15, Appendix K, document 218/1001; 'Purchase of 494 King's Road by HKU SPACE and Application for Short and Medium Term Loans with the Education and Manpower Bureau', 19 October 2001.
57. *SPACE News*, no. 14 (Autumn 2002).
58. CCABM 2 June 2003, 7, Appendix F; 'Annual Monitoring Report 2001–2002', p. 8.
59. Interview with Mr Andric Chan, Mr Stephen Choi and Miss Vivian Chan, 22 April 2006.
60. CCABM 10 June 2004, 6, Appendix F; 'Annual Monitoring Reports 2002–2003 for Pre-Associate Degree/Associate Degree Programmes', p. 8.
61. Interview with Professor K. F. Cheng, 19 April 2006.
62. Interview with Professor Mimi Chan, 20 April 2006.
63. HKUSPACEBDM 20 July 2001, 1, Annex A, document SPACE/84/701; 'Community College Development'.
64. HKUSPACEBDM 14 July 2003, 12, Appendix N, document SPACE/50/603; 'Community College Campus', 23 June 2003.

65. HKUCM 28 October 2003, 1, Appendix A, Annex I, document 347/903; 'Land Grant and Interest-free Loan awarded by the Education and Manpower Bureau ("EMB") to HKU School of Professional and Continuing Education ("HKU SPACE" or the "School")', 8 October 2003.
66. *HKU SPACE News*, no. 22 (Winter 2004); *HKU SPACE News*, no. 31 (Spring 2007).
67. CCACM 28 March 2006, 5, Appendix D; 'College Principal's Report', 3 February 2005.
68. In fact, 92.8 per cent of new AD students in the 2004–05 academic year put studying at local universities as their first priority after graduation, in comparison with 68.6 per cent of new HD students who gave the same answer; see CCMCM 22 February 2005, Attachment in Annex B. Professor Enoch Young also declared that AD and HD degrees should not be regarded as 'terminal awards'; see CCMCM 24 April 2004, 1.4, Attachment; 'Proposal for Launch of HKU Self-financed Degree Programmes'.
69. These were the University of Leicester in Britain, Queensland University of Technology in Australia, and the University of Michigan (Dearborn) in the United States; see HKUSPACEBDM 19 February 2001, 9, Appendix H, document SPACE/8/201; 'Progress Report December 2000', 15 February 2001.
70. HKU SPACE Community College Council Minutes [hereafter CCCM] 20 November 2002, 3, Appendix B; 'College Principal's Report', 31 October 2002.
71. They were the faculties of Science, Social Sciences, Dentistry and Law. Science and Social Sciences granted some exemptions from junior courses; see HKUSPACEBDM 19 February 2001, 9, Appendix H, document SPACE/8/201; 'Progress Report December 2000', 15 February 2001.
72. HKUSPACEBDM 5 March 2002, 4, Appendix D, document SPACE/82/202; 'Community College Development', 2 March 2002.
73. CCCM 20 November 2002, 4.3, Appendix E; 'Linkage with Secondary Schools and Industry'.
74. Interview with Ms Currie Tsang, 19 April 2006.
75. HKUSM 4 March 2002, 15, Appendix N, Annex I (Appendix 1); 'Second Round Teaching and Learning Quality Process Reviews: Report on The University of Hong Kong', p. 22.
76. Interview with Ms Currie Tsang, 19 April 2006.
77. HKSPACEBDM 20 January 2006, 7, Attachment; 'College Principal's Report'.
78. HKU SPACE Community College, *Annual Report 2005–06*, pp. 5, 9–10.
79. Interview with Professor Mimi Chan, 20 April 2006.
80. CCMCM 24 February 2004, 1.4, Attachment; 'Proposal for Launch of HKU Self-financed Degree Programmes'.
81. Interview with Professor K. F. Cheng, 19 April 2006.
82. CCMCM 24 February 2004, 1.4.
83. BCPE&LLM 21 July 2003, 5.4. While the Law departments of HKU and the City University of Hong Kong have long refused to grant any advanced standing to the Associate of Arts in Legal Studies graduates from HKU SPACE Community College, it is likely that CUHK, which commenced its own LLB programme in 2006–07, will also follow the same practice.
84. CCMCM 14 June 2005, 4, Appendix D; letter from Dr. T. A. Stanley (Chairman, Faculty Admissions Committee, Faculty of Arts, The University of Hong Kong) to Professor K. F. Cheng, 9 May 2005.

85. Sixty-two AD students were admitted to the first year and ten directly to the second year, while four HD students were admitted to the first year and one directly to the second year. We are grateful to HKU's Faculty of Arts for providing this information.
86. BCPE&LLM 17 June 2002, 3.4, Appendix C Annex IV, document 45/502; 'Proposal for BA in Media and Cultural Studies Programme (in collaboration with School of Arts, Middlesex University)', 8 June 2002.
87. BCPE&LLM 21 October 2002, 5 Appendix D, Annex XII.
88. HKU SPACE Annual Report 2003–04, p. 7.
89. *Ibid.*
90. It was expected that there would be twenty-five students in the Middlesex University programme, but the actual figure was twenty-three. The University of London programme was even less popular. Only twenty-three out of the fifty places were filled; see CCMCM 2 September 2002, 1. We are grateful to Dr Eddy Lee for providing figures for 2006–07 enrolments.
91. HKU SPACE Annual Report 2004–05, p. 36.
92. For further information, see Gerard Postiglione, 'Community College Development in China', *International Higher Education*, no. 2003 (Spring 2001), pp. 17–18; Zhang Jianqiu, 'Woguo shequ xueyuan de fazhan ji qi xianzhuang fenxi' (An analysis of development and current situation of community colleges in China), *Yunnan Education Research*, no. 82 (2002), pp. 23–26.
93. *HKU SPACE News*, no. 14 (Autumn 2002). The category of 'associate degree' was not recognised within the education system in China and hence the AD qualification awarded by HKU SPACE in Zhuhai was not officially recognised in China.
94. CCMCM 16 January 2003, 4.
95. CCMCM 21 March 2003, 7.
96. *HKU SPACE News*, no. 22 (Winter 2004).
97. HKUSPACEBDM 2 March 2004, 9.
98. HKUSPACEBDM 14 October 2005, 8, Appendix E, Annex I; 'China Mainland Development'.
99. HKUSPACEBDM 2 March 2004, 9, Attachment.
100. HKUSPAECBDM 13 July 2004, 11, Appendix H, document SPACE/16/704; 'The Suzhou Project', 12 July 2004.
101. *HKU SPACE News*, no.19 (Spring 2004). The new community college's name is rendered differently in the English and Chinese versions. The official Chinese name can be translated as 'Suzhou HKU SPACE Vocational Institute of Technology', but in order to highlight the new community college's difference from the typical local institutions in Suzhou, the provincial government allowed the new community college to use the English name 'HKU SPACE Global College' and an abbreviated Chinese name of 'HKU SPACE College' for non-official occasions; see HKUSPACEBDM 15 July 2005, 7, Appendix G; 'China Mainland Development', 7 July 2005.
102. HKU SPACE invested 2 million yuan directly to the Global College, and 7 million yuan into a new company which was responsible for the management of the Global College. The School holds 50 per cent of shares of this company; see HKUSPACE Board of Directors Circular 5 March 2005, document SPACE/24/305, 5 March 2005.
103. HKUSPAECBDM 13 July 2004, 11, Appendix H, document SPACE/16/704; 'The Suzhou Project', 12 July 2004.

104. *HKU SPACE News*, no. 22 (Winter 2004).
105. HKUSPACEBDM 15 July 2005, 7, Appendix G, document SPACE/90/705; 'China Mainland Development', 7 July 2005.
106. HKUSPACEBDM 14 October 2005, 8, Appendix E, Annex I; 'China Mainland Development'.
107. HKUSPACEBDM 15 July 2005, 7, Appendix G, document SPACE/90/705; 'China Mainland Development', 7 July 2005.
108. CCMCM 27 January 2004, 7, Appendix G; 'Admission of Students from China'; and CCMCM 24 February 2004, 2.
109. CCMCM 27 January 2004, 7, Appendix G; 'Admission of Students from China'; and CCMCM 23 November 2004, 2.
110. CCMCM 28 May 2004, 7.
111. CCMCM 14 June 2005, 3, Appendix B; 'Mainland Student Admission: Progress Report III (June 2005)'.
112. CCMCM 28 February 2006, 9, Appendix G; 'Development Plan for 2006–07', 25 February 2006, p. 8.
113. CCMCM 6 December 2005, 11, Appendix G; 'Proposal on Mainland Student Promotion and Admission Exercise 2006/07', 3 December 2005. The predicted number of new students for 2006–07 was sixty.
114. For the early history of Po Leung Kuk, see The Po Leung Kuk Board of Directors for 1977/1978, *Centenary History of the Po Leung Kuk, Hong Kong, 1878–1978* (Hong Kong: The Board of Directors, Po Leung Kuk, 1978).
115. Li Chen Xiujuan, *Xianggang Baoliangju jiaoyu fuwu wushinian* (The fifty years of Hong Kong Po Leung Kuk education services) (Hong Kong: Po Leung Kuk, 1997), p. 26.
116. Po Leung Kuk, *Baoliangju 125 zhounian tekan* (A special issue for the Po Leung Kuk 125th anniversary) (Hong Kong: Po Leung Kuk, 2004), p. 91.
117. HKU SPACE Po Leung Kuk Community College, *Prospectus* (2006).
118. CCMCM 9 December 2003, 7, Attachment; 'Launch of Pre-AD Programme in Evening Mode in collaboration with PLK', 5 December 2003.
119. CCACM 3 February 2005, 5, Appendix D; 'College Principal's Report', 3 February 2005.
120. CCMCM 20 September 2005, 3, Appendix C.
121. HKUSPACEBDM 2 March 2004, 7, Appendix H, document SPACE/207/204; 'Progress Report on HKU SPACE — Po Leung Kuk Community College Project', 25 February 2004.
122. For details of the agreement, see HKUSPACE Board of Directors Circular 25 November 2004, 1.
123. HKUSPACEBDM 18 March 2005, 7, Appendix D, document SPACE/69/305; 'HKU SPACE — Po Leung Kuk Community College'.
124. Interview with Professor K. F. Cheng, 19 April 2006.
125. The projected enrolment for the first cohort was 320 students but the application response was very disappointing in 2006–07.
126. CCMCM 25 January 2006.
127. Interview with Miss Carol Chum, 22 April 2006.
128. HKU SPACE Annual Report 2004–05, p. 39.
129. HKU SPACE (Draft) Annual Report for 2005–06, p. 14.

130. *Ibid.*; in 2005–06 there were 31,632 part-time students enrolled in bachelor's programmes (4,034 FTE, or 21 per cent of total SPACE FTEs), while the 5,760 full-time students accounted for 5,760 FTE (30 per cent of total SPACE FTEs).

CONCLUSION

1. HKU SPACE, 'Facts and Figures', <hkuspace.hku.hk/about/about.php?action=facts_enrolment>, 2003 (updated January 2007), accessed on 26 April 2007.
2. Senate Minutes 4 January 1986, 12(b), Appendix S, Annex III, document 232/1185–C; 'Annual report of the Committee on Extra-Mural Studies, 1984–85'.
3. HKU SPACE Community College, *Annual Report 2005–06*, pp. 9–10.
4. I am grateful to Professor Enoch C. M. Young for providing these figures.
5. The two books are Lee Ngok and Agnes Lam (eds.), *Professional and Continuing Education in Hong Kong* (Hong Kong: Hong Kong University Press, 1994), and John Cribbin and Peter Kennedy (eds.), *Lifelong Learning in Action: Hong Kong Practitioners' Perspectives*, (Hong Kong: Hong Kong University Press, 2002).

Bibliography

Primary Sources

Manuscript

- **Hong Kong Public Record Office**

HKRS457–3–10

- **University of Hong Kong, Faculty of Arts**

Early Student Records, 1912–1966
Minutes of the Board of the Faculty of Arts

- **University of Hong Kong, Registry**

Minutes of the Board for Continuing and Professional Education and Lifelong Learning
Minutes of the Board of Extra-Mural Studies (1957–67)
Minutes of the General Purposes Committee
Minutes of the Finance Committee [of Council]

- **University of Hong Kong, School of Professional and Continuing Education**

Minutes of the Board of Directors of HKU SPACE
Minutes of the Board of Studies of SPACE (1992–1999)
Minutes of the HKU SPACE Community College Academic Board
Minutes of the HKU SPACE Community College Advisory Council
Minutes of the HKU SPACE Community College Council
Minutes of the HKU SPACE Community College Management Committee
Minutes of the Management Board for HKU SPACE

- **University of Hong Kong, University Archives**

Interim Period Minutes, 1946–48
Minutes of the Board of the Faculty of Arts, 1919–23

Minutes of the Committee on Extra-Mural Studies (1967–91)
Minutes of the Committee on Open Education
Minutes of Council meetings, 1911–2006
Minutes of Court meetings, 1911–2005
Minutes of the Development and General Purposes Committee
Minutes of the Provisional Powers Committee, 1946–48
Minutes of Senate meetings, 1912–2006
Registry Dead Files
Registry Old Files
University Memoranda, vol. 1

- **University of Hong Kong, Vice-Chancellor's Office**

Files 225/60 and 225/64

- **Private Collection, Los Angeles, USA**

Diary of Betty Draper, 1929

Printed Sources

Barrett, Cyril Joseph. Address at the Honorary Degrees Congregation of 29 March 1983, reproduced in *University of Hong Kong Gazette*, vol. 30, no. 5 (31 May 1983), pp. 111–119.

Carr-Saunders, Alexander M. and D. G. James. 'Report on Visit to University of Hong Kong, April 1953 by Sir Alexander M. Carr-Saunders and Professor D. G. James', reprinted in Anthony Sweeting, 'The Reconstruction of Education in Post-War Hong Kong, 1945–54: Variations in the Process of Education Policy Making' (unpublished Ph.D. dissertation, University of Hong Kong, 1989), vol. 4, pp. 1188–1207.

Colonial Office. *Report of the Commission on Higher Education in the Colonies* (London: HMSO, 1945).

Colonial Office. *Report of the West Indies Committee of the Commission on Higher Education in the Colonies* (London: HMSO, 1945).

Colonial Office. *Report of the Commission on Higher Education in West Africa* (London: HMSO, 1945).

Colonial Office. *Report of the Commission on University Education in Malaya* (Kuala Lumpur: Government Press, 1948).

Colonial Office. *Report of the Commission on Higher Education for Africans in Central Africa* (London: King and Jarrett, 1953).

Dept of Extra-Mural Studies (HKU). Annual Reports (1985–91).

Dept of Extra-Mural Studies (HKU). *Prospectus* (1957–91).

Director of Education. *Annual Departmental Report by the Director of Education* (Hong Kong: Government Printer, 1946–55).

Education Commission (HK). Education Commission Report No. 1, October 1984.

Education Commission (HK). Education Commission Report No. 2, August 1986.

Education Commission (HK). *Review of Education System: Framework for Education Reform: Learning for Life* (Hong Kong: Education Commission, 1999).

Education Commission (HK). *Education Blueprint for the 21st Century: Review of Academic System: Aims of Education* (Hong Kong: Education Commission, 1999).

Education Commission (HK). *Learning for Life, Learning through Life: Reform Proposals for the Education System in Hong Kong* (Hong Kong: Education Commission, 2000).

Education Commission (HK). *Review of Education System: Reform Proposals: Excel and Grow* (Hong Kong: Education Commission, 2000).

Fisher, N. G. *A Report on Government Expenditure on Education in Hong Kong* (Hong Kong: Government Printers and Publishers, 1950).

Hong Kong Government. *Hong Kong Hansard.*

Hong Kong Government. *Report of the University (1937) Committee* (Report No. 8/1937) (Hong Kong: Government Printer, 1937).

Hong Kong Government. *Report of a Committee on the Development of the University* (*University Development Report*) (Hong Kong: Government Printer, 1939).

Hong Kong Government. *Report of the Working Party on Chinese Medicine* (Hong Kong: Government Printer, 1994).

Hong Kong Government. *Policy Objectives: The 1998 Policy Address* (Hong Kong: Government Printer, 1998).

Hong Kong Government. *1999–2000 Budget Speech* (Hong Kong: Government Printer, 1999).

HKU SPACE. 'A Report on the Establishment of the HKU–SPACE Community College' (Hong Kong: HKU SPACE, 12 October 2000).

HKU SPACE. Annual Reports (2000–2006).

HKU SPACE. *HKU SPACE News* (1999–2006).

HKU SPACE. *Quality Assurance in SPACE* (Hong Kong: HKU School of Professional and Continuing Education, 2001).

HKU SPACE. 'A Report on the Establishment of the HKU–SPACE Community College' (Hong Kong: HKU SPACE, 2000).

HKU SPACE Community College. Annual Reports (2001–06).

Hughes, Ieuan. 'The University and Adult education: A University Lecture', *Supplement to the University of Hong Kong Gazette*, vol. 9, no. 5 (1 June 1962), pp. 1–8.

Hughes, Ieuan. 'Hong Kong: An Extra-Mural Profile', *University of Hong Kong Gazette*, vol. 10, no. 4 (16 April 1963), pp. 00.

Hughes, Ieuan and Priscilla Tso (eds.) *Universities and Adult Education in South East Asia: Report on the Leverhulme Conference on Extra-Mural Studies, October 26–31, 1964, Hong Kong* (Hong Kong: Department of Extra-Mural Studies, University of Hong Kong, 1964).

Jennings, I. and D. W. Logan. *A Report on the University of Hong Kong* (Hong Kong: University of Hong Kong, 1954).

Keswick, John, *et al. Report of the Hong Kong Government Committee on Higher Education* (Hong Kong: Government Printer, 1952).

Llewellyn, John, *et al.* A *Perspective on Education in Hong Kong: Report by a Visiting Panel* (Hong Kong: Government Printer, 1982).

Lugard, Frederick. 'The problem of Universities in the East in regard to their influence on character and moral ideals', read at the Congress of the Universities of the British Empire, London, 3 July 1912, reproduced in Bernard Mellor, *Lugard in Hong Kong: Empires, Education and a Governor at Work, 1907–1912* (Hong Kong: Hong Kong University Press, 1992), pp. 171–177.

Moore, Gerald. *Tsuen-Wan Township: Study Group Report on Its Development* (Hong Kong: Hong Kong University Press, 1959).

SPACE. Annual Reports (1991–99).

Singapore Council for Adult Education. *The Singapore Council for Adult Education: What It Is and What It Does* (Singapore: Singapore Council for Adult Education, n.d.).

Technical Education Investigating Committee. *A Report on Technical Education and Vocational Training in Hong Kong* (Hong Kong, 1953).

Tung Chee Hwa. *Building Hong Kong for a New Era* (1997 Policy Address by the Chief Executive) (Hong Kong: Government Printer, 1998).

Tung Chee Hwa. 1998 Policy Address by the Chief Executive (Hong Kong: Government Printer, 1998).

Tung Chee Hwa. *Quality People, Quality Home* (1999 Policy Address by the Chief Executive, 6 October 1999), (Hong Kong: Government Printer, 1999).

Tung Chee Hwa. *Serving the Community, Sharing Common Goals* (2000 Policy Address by the Chief Executive, 11 October 2000), (Hong Kong: Government Printer, 2000).

Tung Chee Hwa. *Building on Our Strengths, Investing in Our Future* (2001 Policy Address by the Chief Executive, 10 October 2001), (Hong Kong: Government Printer, 2001).

University and Polytechnic Grants Committee. (Hong Kong) *Higher Education, 1991–2001: An Interim Report* (Hong Kong: University and Polytechnic Grants Committee of Hong Kong, 1993).

University Grants Committee (Hong Kong). *Higher Education in Hong Kong: A Report by the University Grants Committee* (Hong Kong: 1996).

University of Hong Kong. *Calendars* (1913–2007).

University of Hong Kong. *Departmental Reports* (Hong Kong: University of Hong Kong, 1957–62).

University of Hong Kong. *Report of the Special Committee appointed to advise on the Teaching of Chinese* (Hong Kong: Newspaper Enterprise Ltd., 1932).

University of Hong Kong. *Vice-Chancellors' Reports* (Hong Kong: University of Hong Kong, 1963–91).

University of Hong Kong. *Fit for purpose: a review of governance and management structures at The University of Hong Kong* (Hong Kong: University of Hong Kong, 2002).

Young, Enoch C. M. 'Towards a Learning Society — HKU SPACE and Lifelong Learning in Hong Kong' (A talk given at the Annual General Meeting of the Hong Kong Library Association on 7 December 2000), (Hong Kong: HKU SPACE, 2000).

Newspapers

China Mail
Hong Kong Standard
South China Morning Post
South China Morning Post–Herald
Wah Kiu Yat Po

Oral Evidence

Mr Geoffrey Bonsall, 4 April 2007
Mrs Teresa Bradley, 13 April 2007
Mr Andric Chan Tsz-fung, 22 April 2006
Dr Dorothy Chan, 22 May 2006
Professor Mimi Chan, 20 April 2006
Miss Veronica Chan Ho-ting, 20 April 2006
Miss Vivian Chan Yee-ting, 22 April 2006
Dr Darwin Chen, 7 July 2006
Professor K. F. Cheng, 19 April 2006
Mr Stephen Choi Tsz-ping, 22 April 2006
Miss Carol Chum, 22 April 2006
Mr Michael Fisher, 20 May 2007
Mr Fok Po-choi, 28 June 2006
Mr Tommy Fung Ching-yin, 20 April 2006
Professor Ronald D. Hill, 25 April 2007
Dr Stephen Ho Wing-chiu, 7 July 2006
Dr Peter Kennedy, 18 April 2007
Mr T. C. Lai, 29 June 2006
Dr Peter C. Y. Lee, 27 July 2006
Mr Joseph Lee King-chi, 30 June 2006
Professor Lee Ngok, 9 May 2007
Professor Joe Leung, 18 April 2007
Mr Simon Li, 22 June 2006
Mr Mok Yiu-kwong, 30 June 2006
Mr Frederick Ng Yip-lap, 7 July 2006
Mr Adrian Rowe-Evans, 17 May 2005
Professor Anthony Sweeting, 19 April 2006
Ms Currie Tsang, 19 April 2006
Mrs Priscilla Tso Mark Yuen-yee, 29 March 2006
Dr Patrick Wong Lung-tak, 29 June 2006
Mr Kenneth Yim Chi-keung, 26 June 2006
Professor Enoch C. M. Young, 7 May 2007

Secondary Sources

Bard, Solomon. 'Mount Davis and Sham Shui Po: A Medical Officer with the Volunteers', in Clifford Matthews and Oswald Cheung (eds.), *Dispersal and Renewal: Hong Kong University During the War Years* (Hong Kong: Hong Kong University Press, 1998), pp. 193–202.

Blake, Robert. *Jardine Matheson: Traders of the Far East* (London: Weidenfeld and Nicholson, 1999).

Chan Lau Kit-ching. 'The Post-War Re-establishment of the University of Hong Kong, 1945–1950', in Chan Lau Kit-ching and Peter Cunich (eds.), *An Impossible Dream: Hong Kong University from Foundation to Re-establishment, 1910–1950* (Hong Kong: Oxford University Press, 2002).

Chan Lau Kit-ching and Peter Cunich (eds.) *An Impossible Dream: Hong Kong University from Foundation to Re-establishment, 1910–1950* (Hong Kong: Oxford University Press, 2002).

Conceicao, J. F. 'The University and Adult Education', in *Proceedings of the National Conference on Adult Education, 23–25 September 1971* (Singapore: Adult Education Board, 1972).

Cribbin, John. 'Financial Aspects of the Operation of the School of Professional and Continuing Education at the University of Hong Kong', in G. Dhanarajan *et al.* (eds.), *Economics of Distance Education: Recent Experience* (Hong Kong: Open Learning Institute Press, 1994), pp. 184–198.

Cribbin, John. 'Growth and Development of Lifelong Learning in Hong Kong', in John Cribbin and Peter Kennedy (eds.), *Lifelong Learning in Action: Hong Kong Practitioners' Perspectives* (Hong Kong: Hong Kong University Press, 2002), pp. 15–34.

Cribbin, John. 'Quality Assurance in Lifelong Learning', in John Cribbin and Peter Kennedy (eds.), *Lifelong Learning in Action: Hong Kong Practitioners' Perspectives* (Hong Kong: Hong Kong University Press, 2002), pp. 143–163.

Cribbin, John and Peter Kennedy (eds.) *Lifelong Learning in Action: Hong Kong Practitioners' Perspectives*, (Hong Kong: Hong Kong University Press, 2002).

Cunich, Peter. 'University Finances', in Chan Lau Kit-ching and Peter Cunich (eds.), *An Impossible Dream: Hong Kong University from Foundation to Re-establishment, 1910–1950* (Hong Kong: Oxford University Press, 2002), pp. 193–212.

Dhanarajan, G. *et al.* (eds.) *Economics of Distance Education: Recent Experience* (Hong Kong: Open Learning Institute Press, 1994).

Evans, Dafydd M. E. 'The University and Legal Education in Hong Kong', in Dafydd M. E. Evans, *Legal Education in Hong Kong* (Hong Kong: Hong Kong University Press, 1974), pp. 1–30.

Fisher, Michael. 'Continuing Legal Education in Hong Kong', in John Cribbin and Peter Kennedy (eds.), *Lifelong Learning in Action: Hong Kong Practitioners' Perspectives* (Hong Kong: Hong Kong University Press, 2002), pp. 209–218.

Geiger, Roger (ed.) *The American College in the Nineteenth Century* (Nashville: Vanderbilt University Press, 2000).

Harrison, Brian (ed.) *University of Hong Kong: The First 50 Years, 1911–1961* (Hong Kong: Hong Kong University Press, 1962).

Harte, Negley. *The University of London, 1836–1986: An Illustrated History* (London: Athlone Press, 1986).

Jarvis, Peter and Colin Griffin (eds.) *Adult and Continuing Education: Major Themes in Education*, 3 vols. (London: Routledge, 2003).

Jessup, F. W. (ed.) *Lifelong Learning: A Symposium on Continuing Education* (Oxford: Pergamon Press, 1969).

Jessup, F. W. 'The Idea of Lifelong Learning' in F. W. Jessup (ed.), *Lifelong Learning: A Symposium on Continuing Education* (Oxford: Pergamon Press, 1969), pp. 14–31.

Jiulü. 'Guanli Wenshang Zhuanke Xuexiao jianshi' (A brief history of the Evening School of Higher Chinese Studies), *Adult Education Bulletin*, vol. 44, 1973.

Jordan, Matthew. *A Spirit of True Learning: The Jubilee History of the University of New England* (Sydney: University of New South Wales Press, 2004).

Kan Lai-bing. 'Training in Librarianship in Hong Kong, 1960–1969', *Journal of the Hong Kong Library Association*, no. 1 (1969), pp. 13–19.

Kennedy, Peter. 'Continuing Education in Hong Kong: Policy Rhetoric and Policy Reform', in John Cribbin and Peter Kennedy (eds.), *Lifelong Learning in Action: Hong Kong Practitioners' Perspectives* (Hong Kong: Hong Kong University Press, 2002), pp. 103–135.

Kennedy, Peter. 'The politics of "lifelong learning" in post-1997 Hong Kong', *International Journal of Lifelong Education*, vol. 23 (2004), pp. 589–624.

Knapper, Christopher K. and Arthur J. Cropley. *Lifelong Learning in Higher Education*, 3rd ed. (London: Kogan Page, 2000).

Lee Ngok. 'Opportunity Knocks: Continuing Higher Education in Hong Kong', in the *Supplement to the University of Hong Kong Gazette*, vol. 39, no. 2 (14 December 1992), pp. 33–45.

Lee Ngok and Agnes Lam (eds.) *Professional and Continuing Education in Hong Kong* (Hong Kong: Hong Kong University Press, 1994).

Leung, Joe. *Building for Excellence Together: The 50th Anniversary of Social Work Education in the University of Hong Kong* (Hong Kong: Department of Social Work HKU, 2000).

Li Chen Xiujuan. *Xianggang Baoliangju jiaoyu fuwu wushinian* (The fifty years of Hong Kong Po Leung Kuk education services), (Hong Kong: Po Leung Kuk, 1997).

Macintosh, Duncan. 'English as a "function tool": An extra-mural programme in Hong Kong', *Adult Education*, vol. 44, no. 6 (March 1972), pp. 380–384.

Mackenzie, Norman H. 'An Academic Odyssey: A Professor in Five Continents (Part 2)', in Clifford Matthews and Oswald Cheung (eds.), *Dispersal and Renewal: Hong Kong University During the War Years* (Hong Kong: Hong Kong University Press, 1998), pp. 179–191.

Matthews, Clifford and Oswald Cheung (eds.) *Dispersal and Renewal: Hong Kong University During the War Years* (Hong Kong: Hong Kong University Press, 1998).

Matthews, Clifford. 'Life Experiences from Star Ferry to Stardust', in Clifford Matthews and Oswald Cheung (eds.), *Dispersal and Renewal: Hong Kong University During the War Years* (Hong Kong: Hong Kong University Press, 1998), pp. 227–246.

McGregor, O. R. 'The Social Sciences', in F. M. L. Thompson (ed.), *The University of London and the World of Learning, 1836–1986* (London: Hambledon Press, 1990), pp. 207–224.

Mellor, Bernard. *Lugard in Hong Kong: Empires, Education and a Governor at Work, 1907–1912* (Hong Kong: Hong Kong University Press, 1992).

Moore, G. H. 'How Extra-Mural Can You Get?', *Journal of Adult Education*, vol. 2, no. 2 (April 1954), pp.

Peers, Robert. *Adult Education: A Comparative Study* (London: Routledge, 1958; reprinted 1998).

Po Leung Kuk. *Centenary History of the Po Leung Kuk, Hong Kong, 1878–1978* (Hong Kong: The Board of Directors, Po Leung Kuk, 1978).

Po Leung Kuk. *Baoliangju 125 zhounian tekan* (A special issue for the Po Leung Kuk 125th anniversary), (Hong Kong: Po Leung Kuk, 2004).

Postiglione, Gerard. 'Community College Development in China', *International Higher Education*, no. 2003 (Spring 2001), pp. 17–18.

Pugh, Willard J. 'A "Curious Working of Cross Purposes" in the Founding of the University of Chicago', in Roger Geiger (ed.), *The American College in the Nineteenth Century*, (Nashville: Vanderbilt University Press, 2000), pp. 242–263.

Styler, W. E. 'Conference Report and Conclusions', in Ieuan Hughes and Priscilla Tso (eds.), *Universities and Adult Education in South East Asia: Report on the Leverhulme Conference on Extra-Mural Studies, October 26–31, 1964, Hong Kong* (Hong Kong: Department of Extra-Mural Studies, University of Hong Kong, 1964), pp. 89–95.

Sweeting, Anthony. *Education in Hong Kong, Pre-1841 to 1941: Fact and Opinion: Materials for a History of Education in Hong Kong* (Hong Kong: Hong Kong University Press, 1990).

Sweeting, Anthony. 'Controversy over the Re-opening of the University of Hong Kong, 1942–48', in Clifford Matthews and Oswald Cheung (eds.), *Dispersal and Renewal: Hong Kong University during the War Years* (Hong Kong: Hong Kong University Press, 1998), pp. 397–424.

Sweeting, Anthony. 'The University by Report', in Chan Lau Kit-ching and Peter Cunich (eds.), *An Impossible Dream: Hong Kong University from Foundation to Re-establishment, 1910–1950* (Hong Kong: Oxford University Press, 2002), pp. 213–240.

Sweeting, Anthony. *Education in Hong Kong, 1941 to 2001: Visions and Revisions* (Hong Kong: Hong Kong University Press, 2004).

Thompson, F. M. L. (ed.) *The University of London and the World of Learning, 1836–1986* (London: Hambledon Press, 1990).

Tso, Priscilla and Kan Lai-bing. 'Education and Training in Librarianship in Hong Kong: Twenty Years On', *Journal of the Hong Kong Library Association*, no. 5 (1980), pp. 11–20.

Tuijnman, Albert. 'Lifelong Learning: Evolution of a Conceptual Map and Some Implications', in John Cribbin and Peter Kennedy (eds.), *Lifelong Learning in Action: Hong Kong Practitioners' Perspectives* (Hong Kong: Hong Kong University Press, 2002), pp. 3–14.

Twining, W. L. 'Laws', in F. M. L. Thompson (ed.), *The University of London and the World of Learning, 1836–1986* (London: Hambledon Press, 1990), pp. 81–114.

Zhang Jianqiu. 'Woguo shequ xueyuan de fazhan ji qi xianzhuang fenxi' (An analysis of development and current situation of community colleges in China), *Yunnan Education Research*, no. 82 (2002), pp. 23–26.

Unpublished Dissertations

Shak, Therese W. H. 'Lifelong Education: Definition, Agreement and Prediction' (unpublished Doctor of Education thesis, University of British Columbia, 1989).

Sweeting, Anthony. 'The Reconstruction of Education in Post-War Hong Kong, 1945–54: Variations in the Process of Education Policy Making' (unpublished Ph.D. dissertation, University of Hong Kong, 1989).

Wong, Spencer. 'Development of Adult Education in Hong Kong since World War II' (unpublished Ph.D. dissertation, University of Edinburgh, 1975).

Index

1937 Report (HKU) 18, 20–21

A

accountancy courses(photo 23), 32–33, 41, 43–44, 46, 50, 71, 112, 117, 119, 132, 133, 154, 208, 209, 218, 219
Adams, Walter 26, 45
Adelaide University 270
Admiralty Learning Centre (photo 25), 200, 207, 262, 263
Admiralty Town Centre 262
adult education 2–5, 30–34, 62–66, 100–101
 accessibility of 143
 in Africa 35, 63, 64
 in Asia-Pacific region 69, 70
 in Australia 26
 in British colonies 25, 33–34, 54, 73
 conferences on 69–70
 definition of 4–5, 62–63, 100–101, 159, 189–190
 demand for 20, 28, 32, 38, 39–40, 45, 55, 72, 92, 113, 116, 217, 243
 at HKU 20, 21, 54, 62–64
  See also extra-mural studies, Hong Kong Government
 in Hong Kong 2–3, 10, 25–26, 28, 30–32, 36–40, 50, 54, 62–64, 65, 66, 70, 142–143, 159, 213–214, 243
 international perspective 3, 6, 7, 11, 19, 25–26, 34–37, 54, 62–63, 84, 102, 241
 market in 4, 11
 non-vocational 20, 26, 28, 38–39, 72
 proposed regional institute in Hong Kong 70
 as a social obligation 64
 in the United Kingdom 4–5, 9–10, 11, 20, 26, 54, 189
Adult Education Committee (UK) 20
Adult Education Regulations (UK) 28
advertising courses 219
Africa 35, 47, 63, 64
Allen, Sir George 37
American Institute of Foreign Study 294 (n21)
Angkor Wat 77
apprentices 15, 16, 280 (n18)
architecture courses 72, 99, 219
Argyle Street (HK) 82
art courses (photo 13), 45, 50, 72, 99, 126, 135, 198, 207
arts courses 49, 50, 56, 72, 84
Asia Foundation 64–65, 85
Asian House 108
Asian-Pacific Bureau of Adult Education 69, 70

Asquith, Cyril 33
Asquith Report (1945) 3, 25–26, 33–35, 39, 40, 41
associate degrees 11, 213, 214, 215–216, 217–218, 219, 226, 233, 235, 245
Association of Certified and Corporate Accountants 43, 112, 118
Association of South East Asian Institutes of Higher Learning 69, 70
Austin Tower 200, 263
Australia 69, 153, 241

B
baby boom 30
Bailey, S. F. 97, 98
Banque Nationale de Paris 305 (n111)
Bard, Solomon 23
Barrett, Fr Cyril 309 (n67)
Baptist University (HK) 125
Bath University 265
Beijing 209, 210, 241, 265
Beijing Municipal Economic Reform Commission 209
Beijing Normal University 213–214, 265
Beijing Sports University 268
Beijing University of Chinese Medicine 268
Benson, Stella 19
Berry, A. J. 121
Birch, G. B. 18
Birkbeck College 297 (n86)
Birmingham University 26, 222, 238
Black, Sir Robert 66
Board of Education (UK) 28
Bond University 270
book-keeping courses 43
Boston University 93
Bradley, Teresa 152
Bradshaw, Peter 148
Brimer, Prof M. A. 138, 252, 306 (n6)(n7)
Bristol University 26, 186
Britain
See United Kingdom
British Council 142, 290 (n78)
British Empire (& Commonwealth) 3, 7–8, 9, 25, 29, 33–36, 40, 141–142, 159
British Institute of Management 118
British West Africa 47
British West Indies 35
Browne, Edith 151
building courses 133
Burgess, Claude 65
business, Chinese 18
business courses 118, 119, 157, 198, 208, 209, 218
Byrne, Prof G. T. 18

C
Cable and Wireless 305 (n111)
Caldecott, Sir Andrew 20
California State University 268, 269
Cambridge University 9
Canada 69, 118, 241
Canton Evening College 32
Cantonese language 77, 92, 130
Caritas (HK) 76
Carnegie Foundation 85, 118
Carr-Saunders, Sir Alexander 25, 35–36, 44–45
Carr-Saunders James Report (1953) 44–45
Causeway Bay 207, 224, 234, 235, 264
Causeway Centre 224, 264
Central (HK) 81, 104, 105, 107, 108–109, 114, 205
Central African Council 35
Centre for the Study of Liberal Education (Boston) 93
Challis, Christine (photo 16)
Chan, Dorothy 231
Chan, F. T. 217
Chan, John 290 (n76)
Chan, Prof L. K. C. 311 (n133)
Chan, Prof S. T. H. 186, 252, 316 (n61) (n74)
Chan Sau Ung-loo 19
Chan Tat Chee Scholarship 222, 238
Charles Sturt University 267, 270
Chartered Bank 131
Chartered Institute of Logistics and Transport (HK) 122
Chartered Institute of Secretaries 44, 112, 118
Chau, K. K. 65

Chau Sik Nin 42
Chen, Darwin 122, 249, 253, 316 (n61)
Cheng Hon-kwan 189, 253
Cheng, Prof K. F. 216, 236
Cheng, Patrick Y. C. 187, 209, 216, 252
Cheng, T. C. 91
Cheong-Leen, Hilton (photo 9)
Cheung, Linus W. L. 253, 326 (n22)
Cheung, Sir Oswald 112
Chiao Shang Building (photo 8), 105, 114
Chicago University 214, 325 (n5)
Chin, F. Y. L. 307 (n42)
China 4, 8, 10, 21, 40, 122, 128, 150, 190, 209, 231–234, 244
  civil war, disastrous impact of 40
  HKU's influence on 21, 22, 24, 190, 209, 231–234, 244
  joint ventures in 208–211, 232, 244, 265
  refugees from 38, 40, 126, 135
China Mail 66
Chinese art & architecture courses 50, 71
Chinese Communist Party 40, 105
Chinese language courses 50, 84, 145, 218
Chinese literature courses 71, 79
Chinese medicine courses 198–200
Chinese as a medium of instruction 31, 38, 49–50, 51, 52, 71, 75, 77–78, 92, 123, 125, 130
Chinese studies courses 15–16, 38, 148, 158
Chinese University of Hong Kong 3, 67, 68, 70, 87, 91–97, 100, 109, 124, 125, 143–144
Chow, T. A. 124
Chu Hoi Evening College 32
Chum, Carol 237–238
Chung Chi College 32, 126
Chung Ip Night School 32
Cisco 201
City Hall 75, 106, 122, 123
City University of Hong Kong 186
City University of London 269
civic university concept 9
Clementi, Sir Cecil 15
Club Lusitano 81
Coleg Harlech 89
Colonial Office (UK) 24, 33–34, 36, 115
colonial universities 33–36
commerce courses 14, 15, 17–18, 46, 49, 50, 56, 57, 71, 72, 73, 117, 126
Commission for Discipline Inspection (China) 209
Commission on Higher Education for Africans in Central Africa 35
Commission on Higher Education in the Colonies (UK) 25, 33–35
Commission on University Education in Malaya 25, 35–36
Committee for International Co-operation in Higher Education 160
communism (in China) 40
community college concept 214–215, 217, 227, 229, 231, 238
company secretarial practice courses 43–44, 46, 50, 71
computer science courses 104
Continental Banks 305 (n111)
continuation classes 10
continuing education 190
continuing and professional education 1, 5, 21, 40, 86, 101–104, 126, 135, 139, 140, 166, 180, 190, 243, 244
  demand for 179
  self-financing policy of HK government 177, 180, 243
  See also extra-mural studies
correspondence courses 33, 113, 138, 141
Council for Adult Education (Singapore) 35, 37
Cowan, Sir Zelman 115, 116, 301 (n24) (n27)
Craft, Alma 203, 204
Cribbin, John (photo 18), 167–168, 178–179, 186, 244, 251, 252
Cultural Revolution (in China) 208
cultural studies 41
Curtin University of Technology (photo 19), 153–157, 176, 267, 270, 309–310 (n93)
Cyberport Institute 197, 200–201, 264

D

D'Almada e Castro, Christopher Paul 283 (n33)
D'Almada e Castro, Leo 112
Davies, Bronwyn 151
Davies, Prof W. I. R. (Ian) 165, 192, 252, 311 (n133)
Davies Report (1991) 164–168, 169
Davies Working Party 164–168, 311 (n133)
dazhuan programmes 233, 239
Deakin University 268, 270
democracy 86
Denmark 69
design courses 126, 207
distance learning 5, 137, 138, 141–143, 150, 160
Dongbei University of Finance and Economics 209, 268
Donohue, Peter 65
Drake, Prof F. S. 28, 48, 53, 56, 71, 285 (n77)
drama courses 41, 45
Draper, Betty 15, 18–19
Dyer, W. J. 53

E

economic geography courses 50
economics courses 41, 43, 71, 72, 76, 119, 152
Edith Cowan University 270
Education Act (UK) (1870) 10
Education Commission (HK) 138, 141, 142–143, 144, 148, 150, 214–215
  First Report (ECR1 1984) 138
  Second Report (ECR2 1986) 142–143, 150
education courses 50, 72, 76, 126
Education Department (HK) (photo 7), 22, 31, 56, 65, 125
Education Quality Work (EQW) 203, 321 (n184)
Eliot Hall, remote fastness of 48, 54, 80
engineering courses 16, 73, 115, 120, 126
England
  See United Kingdom
England, Joseph W. (Joe) 99, 119
English language courses 17, 41, 46, 50, 128–129, 133, 218, 221–222, 304 (n103)
English as medium of instruction 27, 30, 38, 43, 52, 71, 77–78, 92, 123, 125, 221
Essex University 269
Eu, William 19
European Institute of Business Administration (INSEAD) 119
Evans, Dafydd 115, 116, 138
Evans Working Party and Report (1987) 137–141, 144, 165, 166, 306 (n7)
evening courses 37, 43, 75, 81
Evening Institute (HK) 31, 39, 282 (n8)
Evening School of Arts and Commerce 56
Evening School of Higher Chinese Studies (photos 1 & 2), 31–32, 37, 42, 43, 45, 47, 49–50, 51–52, 55–57, 287 (n1) (n15), 287–288 (n19)
Exeter University 142
expatriates 77
extension work 5, 9, 11, 19, 21, 84, 101
external degrees 27, 35, 82, 143–144, 158, 167, 307 (n31)
external studies 2, 4, 7–28, 54, 140, 143–144, 145–149, 157, 167
  See also under University of Hong Kong, external students
extra-mural studies 4, 9–11, 33–35, 40–42, 69–74, 100–101
  accessibility of 143
  benefits to society of 74, 80, 86, 91, 126, 136, 189
  in British colonies 25–26, 33–36, 37, 54, 86
  and career improvement 78–79, 84, 105, 110, 111, 122, 128, 130, 133, 134, 135–136, 243, 245
  and citizenship 73, 86
  definition of 5, 100–101
  demand for in Hong Kong 11, 20, 29, 36, 55, 72, 90, 92, 102, 113, 115, 116, 137, 142, 150, 155, 243
  and democracy 86
  gender issues 39
  humanising potential of 79, 122

life-transforming potential of 73–74, 122, 245
qualifications 40–42, 49
rationale for 33–34, 35, 62–64, 72–74, 102, 139, 159, 212
self-financing policy (in HK) 43, 51, 83, 85, 98, 177, 181, 242–243
as a social service 63, 84
in Southeast Asia 69–70, 86
and technological advances 141
in the United Kingdom 9–10, 11, 20, 26
Extra-Mural Studies, Department of (HKU) 2, 27, 28
academic committees 155, 156, 163
academic standards 58, 88, 116, 118, 121, 125, 129, 133, 150, 155–156, 169, 202
as an academic unit 139
accommodation 3, (photo 10), 41, 48, 79, 80–82, 84, 86, 87, 92, 104–110, 261–264, 299 (n117)
achievements of 86, 136, 169
administrative functions 100–101, 146, 152, 154
administrative structure 145, 157–158, 160–162, 165, 169, 308 (n39) (n59)
awards and qualifications 50, 104, 110, 150, 159
Bachelor of Arts 152
Bachelor of Business 154
Bachelor of Science (Economics) 154
Certificate in Art and Design 94
Certificate in Housing Management 131, 135, 305 (n126)
Certificate in Librarianship 104, 124
Certificate in Social Studies 126, 208
Certificate in Social Work 94
Diploma in Economics (photo 16)
Diploma in Housing Management 174, 305 (n126)
Diploma in Management Studies (photo 9), 117–123
Diploma in Social Studies 126
Master of Arts 158
Master of Law 152
Master of Pharmacy 157
Postgraduate Diploma in Librarianship 125
and Board of Extra-Mural Studies 49, 100
class secretaries 79, 81
classrooms 81, 86, 104, 105, 106, 107–108
collaboration with overseas universities 27, 67–70, 86, 90, 140, 149, 150–158, 169, 202, 309 (n93)
and Committee on Extra-Mural Studies 100
community involvement in 100, 118
competition with Chinese University of HK 87, 91, 125, 143
competition with HKU departments 121, 146–147, 155–156, 157
competition with other institutions in HK 103
conferences 69–70, 76, 244
constitution of 49–52, 58, 85–86, 100
co-operation with Chinese University of HK 68, 87, 89, 91–97, 101, 124, 125, 140, 296 (n58)
co-operation with departments at HKU 50, 100, 140, 145, 154–155, 159
co-operation with other institutions in Hong Kong 118, 140, 143
correspondence courses 141
courses and programmes 71–72, 74, 167, 284–285 (n62)
accountancy 71, 112, 119, 132, 133, 154
architecture 72, 99, 126
art (photo 13), 45, 50, 72, 99, 126, 135
arts 72, 84
building 133
business administration 118
business management 118
Chinese art 71
Chinese language 84, 145
Chinese literature 71, 79
Chinese studies 148, 158
commercial subjects 71, 72, 126

company secretarial practice 71
computer science 104
design 126
economics 71, 72, 76, 119, 152
education 72, 76, 126
engineering 115, 126
English language 128–129, 133, 304 (n103)
fine arts (photo 13), 45, 50, 72, 99, 126, 135
geography 72, 152
higher commercial studies 117
history 72
history education 76
housing management 111, 131–135
industrial relations 119
international affairs 72
Japanese language 128, 130
languages 72, 74, 78, 92, 111, 128–131
law 71, 72, 74, 105, 111, 112–117, 126, 127, 132, 133, 135, 145, 151, 299 (n4)
liberal studies 39, 41, 43, 51, 72, 73, 241–242
librarianship 74, 104, 111, 123–125
management studies 99, 111, 117–123, 127, 135, 208, 302–303 (n63)
Mandarin 131
marketing 120, 154
mathematics 72, 152
medical laboratory science 145
medicine 72, 97, 126
music 41, 45, 50, 72
nursing 174
Oriental languages 131, 304 (n110)
Oriental Studies 72, 78
PCLL 151
perceived inferiority of 50, 61, 244
personnel management 118
pharmacy 157
philosophy 72, 152
phonetics 73
planning 99, 118, 158–159
politics 133
Portuguese language 41, 50
professional 101–104, 111
psychology 72, 127
Putonghua (photo 14), 128, 130–131
quality of 69
quality assurance 202
refresher courses 34, 43, 73, 77, 78, 84, 105, 119, 126, 127, 129
residential courses 76, 118
sales & marketing 120
science 72, 126
secretarial practice 43–44, 46, 50, 71
Shakespeare 71
social sciences 145, 148
social services 133
social studies 208
social work 94, 104, 111, 126–128
sociology 72, 127, 152
Spanish 43
statistics 119, 152
trade unionism 43
translation 145
types of 74–75, 103–104, 129
vocational 72–74, 75, 78, 84, 101–104, 128, 131, 242
as 'cradle of professional studies' in HK 3, 87, 111–112, 136, 293 (n1)
degree courses 94, 150
deputy director 99, 163–164, 251
director 47–48, 55, 58, 60, 64, 86, 99, 139–140, 157, 163–164, 251
see also Hughes, Ieuan
Lee Ngok
Marshall, R. L.
Moore, Gerald H.
Williams, Roger A.
dis-establishment of 168, 169, 171
and distance learning 141–142, 144, 145–149, 154, 157, 160–162
Distance Learning Unit 145–149, 160–161
early development 55–67
enrolment statistics 71, 74, 88, 89, 90, 104, 109, 110, 123, 126, 128, 129, 134, 139, 151, 152, 157, 241, 254–256, 304 (n110)

equipment 83
establishment of 3, 28, 29, 37, 39, 44, 46–54
evening courses 71
examinations 74, 121
expansion of activities, rapid 139
external degree courses 27, 112–117, 140, 141, 145–146, 150–158, 159, 160
external examiners 121
external examining bodies 42, 46, 73, 77, 104, 112, 129, 141, 151, 156
external studies 140, 145–146
External Studies Unit 145–149, 158, 159
Extra-Mural Law Centre 105, 114, 261, 300 (n17)
and Extra-Mural Studies Fund (HKU) 83, 89, 97, 140, 257–260, 314 (n25)
fees 41, 43, 51, 61, 83–84, 97, 98, 139, 154, 156, 257–260, 285 (n64), 293 (n164)
field trips 85, 124, 154
financial difficulties 3, 54, 55, 87
funding of 3, 41–42, 51, 55, 57, 58, 64, 65–67, 68, 82–85, 87, 88–89, 95, 97–99, 105–106, 107, 114, 154, 257–260, 300 (n14)
governance structure 53, 58, 100, 137, 140, 145, 157–158, 165, 169
government schools 65
government subventions 57, 65–67, 68, 95, 97–99, 114
and Hong Kong community 107, 111
and human resource development 140
identity, sense of 140
institutions 140, 142, 144, 153
international collaboration 27, 67–70, 86, 90, 140, 149, 150–158, 202, 294 (n21)
language problems 77–78
leadership role among Hong Kong institutions 140, 142, 144, 153
liberal courses 51, 71, 72–74, 75, 83, 84, 86, 92, 102, 103, 110, 135, 241–242, 297 (n95)
library facilities (photo 12), 61, 81, 83, 85, 92, 105, 114
and lifelong learning 110, 122, 127, 159, 242
marginalisation within HKU 85–86
and mass media 76
medium of instruction 52
morale of 98
name change (1992) 4, 137, 158
neglect of by HKU 36, 61, 82–83
non-vocational courses 51, 86
number of courses 71–72, 74, 86, 89, 90, 105, 110, 128, 241
number of students 58, 71, 74, 86, 88, 89, 90, 104, 110, 123, 126, 128, 129–130, 134, 139, 151, 157, 241, 304 (n110)
and open education 141–142, 160–162
and Open Learning Institute 142–149, 159, 169
overseas study tours (photos 4 & 5), 77, 86, 208, 294 (n20)
part-time degrees 94, 113
part-time tutors 90, 101, 114
planning 89, 91
postgraduate degrees 150
professional courses 86, 87, 94, 101–104, 110, 117, 126, 135
and profit-generation 52, 83–84, 169, 259–260
public lectures 75, 76, 90
quadrennial plan (1970–74) 89, 97, 102
quality of programmes 69, 88
rationale for 37–40, 62–64, 72–74, 102, 139, 159, 212
recognition of 55, 57–61, 68, 86, 91, 100, 118, 139, 159, 162
refresher courses 73, 77, 78, 84, 105, 119, 126, 127, 129
research 63, 101, 119, 139, 159
resident tutors 63–64, 67
residential courses 76, 86, 118
restructuring (1991–92) 137, 140–141, 158–168, 169, 171
retrenchment 66, 87–91, 110, 208
review of 137–141, 158, 160–168

self-financing policy 83, 85, 98, 147, 242, 243
service to community 54, 86, 107
Six Year Plan (1988–94) 145–146, 158
specialist staff tutors 99
staff duties 63, 88, 90–91, 99, 104
staff morale 98
staff salaries 41, 64, 83
staff-student relations 76, 80, 134
staff tutors 63–64, 67, 88, 90, 99, 100, 101, 104, 109, 114, 121, 123, 128, 138, 147, 148, 150, 289 (n71)
staff workloads 90, 293 (n3)
staffing 3, 54, 58, 61–67, 72, 77, 86, 87, 88–89, 99, 156
status within HKU 55, 57–61, 68, 85–86, 91, 99–101, 139, 162, 242
student rallies 66, 67, 68, 80, 86, 90
students 73–74, 77–80, 105–107, 128–136
characteristics of 73–74, 77–78, 92, 105, 119, 129–130, 133, 136, 292 (n138 & 139)
facilities for 106–107
financial needs of 107
number of 58, 71, 74, 86, 88, 89, 90, 104, 110, 123, 126, 128, 129–130, 134, 139, 151, 157, 241, 304 (n110)
perceived inferiority of 60, 61,
strengths of 132, 136
success of 86, 136, 169
weaknesses of 130, 303–303 (n63)
study leave 85
summer schools 34, 37, 50, 51, 90, 294 (n21)
support from HKU 80, 83, 87
teaching materials 147–148, 151, 160
teaching methods 74–75, 141, 150, 154, 162–163
teaching quality 121, 134
teaching role 99–101, 139
Ten Year Plan (1988) 158–161, 162
town centres 3, (photos 8, 11, 12, 13, 14 & 15), 81–82, 87, 94, 104–110, 112, 137, 261, 298 (n106)
'town and gown' 86, 112, 136, 245, 247
triennial plan (1967–70) 89, 97
triennial plan (1972–75) 106
triennial plan (1978–81) 98
tutors' conferences 80
University attitude to 57–61, 85–86, 91, 99–101, 139, 162, 242
and University Grants Council 87, 88–89, 91–101, 103, 106
visitors 68, 69, 93, 96, 120, 160, 290 (n83)
vocational courses 72–74, 75, 78, 84, 86, 92, 94, 96, 101–104, 110, 111, 123, 126, 128, 131, 135, 242
workload of staff 90
See also School of Professional and Continuing Education

F

Fairleigh Dickinson University 269
Fan, S. C. 307 (n42)
Far East Bank 305 (n111)
Federation for Continuing Education (in Tertiary Institutions) 172, 202, 218, 312 (n4)
fine art courses (photo 13), 41, 45, 50, 72, 99, 126, 135, 198, 207
First World War 14
Fisher, Michael 151, 152
Florida Presbyterian College 294 (n21)
Fok Po-choi, Michael 133, 134
Forster, Prof Lancelot 21–22, 24, 28
Fortress Tower 205, 262
Forward company (Shanghai) 210, 211
French language courses 43
Fu Jen Literary Society 10
Fudan University 208, 210, 265, 268
Fung Ping-fan 19, 283 (n33), 289 (n61)
Fung Ping-shan 16
Fung Ping-wah 16, 19
Fung Tung 134
further education 5, 30

G

Garden Road guard house 114
general studies courses 218

geography courses 72, 152
Gibson, Prof J. B. 93–95, 98, 101, 102, 103, 251, 295 (n37)
Glasgow University 89, 294 (n13)
Global College (Suzhou) (photo 27), 211, 217, 232–233, 265, 329 (n101 & 102)
Global EduTech Management Group 232
Gold Coast (Africa) 35
Goodstadt, Leo 132
Gosling, Rosie (photos 16 & 18), 152
Government House conference (1961) 65
government policy
    See Hong Kong Government
Government Vernacular Middle School 15–16
Gower, L. C. B. 115, 116, 301 (n27)
Gransden, J. H. 47, 285 (n79)
Grantham, Sir Alexander (photo 2), 36, 45
Grantham Training College 31, 81
Great Britain
    See United Kingdom
Great Depression 17
Greenwich University 203, 266
Gregory, Prof W. G. 134
Guangzhou 241, 265

H

Hangzhou 210, 241, 265
Harris, Prof P. B. 252
Harrison, Prof Brian 285 (n77)
Hawaii University 125, 269
Hawkridge, Prof David 160, 162
Hawkridge Report (1989) 160–162, 310 (n112)
Herklots, Prof Geoffrey A. C. 18
Herries, M. A. R. 92, 95–96, 97–98, 100, 103
Hewlett Packard 201
higher diplomas 213, 219, 226, 235, 245
Hill, R. Ashton 18
Hilton Hotel 114
Hiscock, Mary 115
history courses 72, 76
HKU SPACE
    See School of Professional and Continuing Education
HKU SPACE Community College 198, 212, 213–239, 245
    Academic Board 219
    academic quality 215, 218, 219–220, 221, 226–227, 228, 236
    Academic Secretary 216
    accommodation 223–225, 234
    achievements of 217, 220, 223, 228–229, 236, 238–239
    administrative structure 216–217
    Admiralty Learning Centre 223–224, 236
    Advisory Council 216, 220, 221–222
    Alumni Association 223
    articulation to degree programmes 226–229, 230–231, 236, 242, 328 (n68 & 85)
    associate degrees 11, 213, 215–216, 217–218, 219, 224, 226–227, 230, 233, 235, 237, 245
    awards and qualifications 215–216, 226, 230, 236, 242
        Advanced Certificate in General Studies 215–217
        Associate of Applied Science in IT 218
        Associate of Applied Science in Life Sciences 218
        Associate of Applied Science in Physical Science 218
        Associate of Arts 218, 230
        Associate of Arts in Legal Studies 218, 229
        Associate of Business Administration 218, 231
        associate degrees 215–216, 217–218, 226–227
        Certificate in General Studies 215, 217
        higher diplomas 213, 219, 224, 226, 230, 235, 245
        pre-associate degrees 217
    campuses 223–225, 231, 236, 237
    Career Development Programmes 219
    China projects 213, 223, 229, 231–234, 239, 329 (n93)

College Council 216, 220, 221–222, 326 (n22)
and community college concept 214–215, 217, 227, 229
community engagement 216
competition from other providers 217, 219
courses and programmes 215–216, 217–220, 236
accountancy 218, 219
architecture 219
business administration 218
Chinese 218
English 218, 221–222
general studies 216
information technology 218, 219
insurance 218
interior design 213
law 218, 228
librarianship 219
media and cultural studies 230
phonetics 221
Putonghua 218
sales, marketing and advertising 219
science 218
translation 221
enrolment statistics 216, 218, 228, 231, 236, 238–239, 242
entry requirements 215–216, 219, 220–221, 226, 230, 236, 326 (n34)
establishment of 214–215
external assessors 220
fees 214, 233
funding 215, 223, 225, 235
governance structure 216–217, 326 (n22)
government loans for 225, 235
higher diplomas 213, 219, 224, 226, 230, 235, 245
and HKU SPACE Global College (Suzhou) 217, 232–233, 329 (n101 & 102)
Island East campus 223, 224, 225
Kowloon East campus 223, 224, 225
language problems 221
leadership role in Hong Kong 217, 226
library 224, 225
and lifelong learning 213, 221
Management Committee 216
mission 213, 214
Multimedia English Learning Centre 221–222, 224
and Po Leung Kuk Community College 217, 229, 234–236, 239, 264, 330 (n125)
principal 196, 216, 220
and Project Springboard 218
public response to 217, 223, 226–227, 231, 235
quality assurance 215, 217, 219–220, 226–227, 236
recognition of 223, 226–229, 232, 236, 238, 242, 325 (n13), 228 (n83)
relationship with HKU SPACE and HKU 219
scholarships and prizes 222
as a 'second chance' at education 11, 215, 220–221, 226, 237, 238, 245, 326 (n34)
self-funding policy 225, 242
staff-student consultative committees 220
staffing 216
students (photo 26), 213, 220–223, 224, 225, 233
Students Union 223
sub-degree programmes 213, 217–220, 226, 236
success of 217, 223, 226, 228–229, 232, 236, 237–238
teaching methods 216, 220, 221–222, 224–225, 237
top-up degrees 213, 227–228, 229, 230–231, 236, 329 (n90)
United Centre Learning Centre (Admiralty) 223, 231
and vocational training 218, 219
Wanchai Learning Centre 221, 225, 237
HKU SPACE Global College (Suzhou) (photo 27), 211, 217, 232–233, 329 (n101 & 102)

HKU SPACE Po Leung Kuk Community College 234–236
Ho Wing-chiu, Stephen 122, 303 (n71)
Hodgkiss, John 307 (n42)
Holford, John 244, 313 (n18)
Hong Kong
adult education in 20, 26, 27–28, 30–32, 63–64, 66, 73, 85, 87, 110, 243
cost of 32, 37, 41–42
demand for 32, 38, 39–40, 45, 50, 90, 92, 102, 142, 150, 155
inadequacies of 142–143
merger of institutions 95–97
numbers enrolled in 32
standard of 32, 42, 142
types of 32
and 'brain drain' problem 150
business community in 156
Chinese community in 39
as a 'cultural backwater' 40
economic development 2, 10, 30, 31, 73, 75, 102, 111, 113, 118, 119, 123, 242
economic recession in 144
education system 10, 28, 29–30, 50, 222
as education hub 40
graduates, under-supply of 140
Handover (1997) 150, 208–209, 214
higher education in 36, 65, 173
industry in 31, 103, 119, 120, 243
Japanese occupation of 20, 22, 29
knowledge-based economy 140, 190, 243
legal profession 112–113, 117
Legislative Council 37, 42, 103, 114, 181, 289 (n61), 300 (n17)
new towns 75
population growth 30, 85
professions in 14, 73, 76, 87, 103, 111, 112, 123, 150, 174, 209
riots (1967) 105
secondary education in 222
and Sino-British talks 144
social problems 126
Hong Kong Archaeological Society 305 (n111)
Hong Kong Arts Development Council 122
Hong Kong Association of Career Masters 305 (n111)
Hong Kong Baptist University 125
Hong Kong College of Medicine (for Chinese) 10
Hong Kong Common Professional Examination Certificate 174
Hong Kong Electric Company 305 (n111)
Hong Kong Federation of Youth Groups 76
Hong Kong Government
and adult education
low priority of 10, 20, 24–25, 26, 30, 40, 63, 88, 97, 98
provision of 66, 85, 110, 137, 142, 243
subventions for 4, 37, 41–42, 56–57, 65–66, 68, 82, 84–85, 88–89, 95, 97–99, 101, 112, 114, 115, 181, 25, 243, 300 (n14)
Adult Education Division 65
Attorney General 114
Chief Executive 190, 199, 215
civil service 122
Colonial Secretary 65, 113
Committee on Higher Education (1951–52) 36–40
and democracy, suppression of 86, 180
Director of Education 10, 31, 53, 65, 118
Education Commission 138, 141, 142–143, 144, 148, 150, 190, 213, 214–215
Education Department 22, 31, 56, 65, 125, 305 (n111)
Education and Manpower Branch 144, 218
education policy 2, 5, 10, 20, 63, 85, 93–96, 101–102, 214, 243
Evening Institute 31, 39
Evening School of Higher Chinese Studies (photos 1 & 2), 31–32, 37, 42, 43, 45, 47, 49–50, 51–52
extra-mural studies policy 65, 85, 93–96, 101, 137–138, 142
higher education, expansion of 138, 142, 214–215, 226, 228

higher education, neglect of 28, 65, 101
higher education policy 101, 102, 137–138, 142, 173, 190, 214–215, 228
Housing Authority 133, 134, 305 (n111 & 113)
housing management courses, support of 132, 134
and immigration control 234
Immigration Department 305 (n111)
judiciary 115
Labour Department 305 (n111)
Legal Department 114
and legal studies, support of 112, 115, 116
libraries 122, 124, 125
lifelong learning policy 190–191, 197, 243
and low priority of adult education 10, 20, 24–25, 26, 30, 40, 63, 88, 97, 98
niggardliness of 65–66
and overseas educational qualifications, regulation of 187
and post-secondary education 31, 50, 85, 101–102, 138, 228, 243
Prisons Department 305 (n111)
Recreation and Sports Service 305 (n111)
Resettlement Department 133–134
and sub-degree programmes 213, 214–215, 217, 225, 226
subventions for adult and extra-mural education 4, 37, 41–42, 56–57, 65–66, 68, 82, 84–85, 88–89, 95, 97–99, 101, 112, 114, 115
technical and vocational education 85, 86, 138
tight-fistedness of 28, 65–66, 85, 98, 110, 181, 225
university autonomy, interference in 97, 101
and the University of Hong Kong 55–57, 62, 76
Urban Renewal Authority 134
Urban Services Department 132, 133, 134, 305 (n111)
Working Party on Chinese Medicine 199
Hong Kong Housing Authority 133–134, 305 (n113)
Hong Kong Housing Society 133
Hong Kong Institute of Education 187
Hong Kong Island 64, 68, 92, 129, 299 (n117)
Hong Kong Jockey Club 82
Hong Kong Law Journal 116
Hong Kong Library Association 76, 104, 123, 124–125, 305 (n111)
Hong Kong people, characteristics of 74, 78–79
Hong Kong Philosophy Society 152
Hong Kong Police Force 73, 76, 90, 305 (n111)
Hong Kong Polytechnic 103, 296 (n67)
Hong Kong Putonghua Education and Assessment Centre 197
Hong Kong Rotary Club (photo 9), 66
Hong Kong Teachers' Association 36
Hong Kong Technical College 31, 41, 49, 57, 117, 118
Hong Kong University
See University of Hong Kong
Hornell, Sir William 18
Hotung, Edward 14, 19
Hotung, Grace 19
Hotung, Sir Robert 14
Housing Authority 133–134, 305 (n113)
housing management courses 111, 131–135, 174, 198
Howarth, William (Bill) (photo 23), 151, 164, 185–186, 251, 252
HSBC 131, 305 (n111)
Huang, Prof C. T. 251
Hubei College of Traditional Chinese Medicine 268
Huddersfield University 269
Hughes, Ieuan 3, (photos 3, 6 & 7), 3, 55, 62–64, 65–66, 67, 70, 72, 74, 76, 77, 78–79, 82, 84–85, 86, 87, 88–90, 93, 99, 100, 102, 135, 244, 251
Hui Wai-haan 19
Hull University 68, 267

I
IBM 201, 305 (n111)
immigration from China 38
India 69
Indonesia 69
industrial management courses 119, 120
industrial relations courses 119
information technology courses 201, 207, 218, 219
INSEAD 119
Institute of Adult Education in South East Asia 70
Institute of Bankers 131
Institute of Housing Managers (HK) 133
Institute of Housing Managers (UK) 133
insurance courses 218
intellectual snobbery 35
Inter-University Council for Higher Education in the Colonies 36, 44–45, 115
interdisciplinary studies 120
interior design courses 213
international affairs courses 72
International English Language Testing System (IELTS) 221–222
International Institute of Technology and Business Management 208
international studies courses 72
internment (by Japanese) 23–24
Iowa State University of Science and Technology 269
Island East Campus 207, 224, 264
ISO 9000 202

J
Jakarta 69
James, Prof D. G. 44–45
Jao, Y. C. (photo 6), 67, 76, 290 (n75)
Japan 128
Japanese language courses 128, 130
Jardines 36
Jennings, Sir Ivor 45–46
Jennings-Logan Report (1954) 45–46, 49
Jinan University 208, 209
Jockey Club (HK) 82
Joint Board of Extra-Mural Studies 92–93
Joint Committee on Extra-Mural Studies 93–94, 96, 98, 103, 106, 143, 295 (n32 & 44), 296 (n55)
Jones, Mouat 36, 45
journalism 32, 41
June Fourth Incident (1989) 150

K
Kan Lai-bing 124, 125
Kansas University 269
Keeton, George W. 112, 114
Kennedy, Peter 244
Keswick Committee 33–42, 86, 101, 283 (n33)
Keswick, John 36
Keswick Report (1952) 3, 29, 31–32, 32–33, 33–42, 43, 49, 51, 57, 72, 86, 101, 112
King, Prof S. Y. 251
Kingston University 266, 269
Kirby, Prof E. S. 43, 44
Knowles Building 206
Kowloon 64, 68, 81, 82, 92, 109, 129, 205, 299 (n117)
Kowloon Bay 207, 225
Kowloon East Campus 207, 223, 264
Kwok Chan 53
Kwok, Ina 67, 290 (n75)

L
La Trobe University 270
Lai, T. C. (photos 5 & 7), 61, 62, 67, 76, 88, 91, 92, 96, 251, 293 (n3), 294 (n20), 295 (n32)
Lam, Agnes 244
Lam Chi-fung 283 (n33)
Lam, P. B. L. 178–179
language courses 27, 50, 72, 74, 78, 92, 111, 128–131, 198
language education 43, 50, 72, 74, 128–131
Lantau Island 76
Large, C. G. 109
law courses 71, 72, 74, 105, 111, 112–117, 126, 127, 132, 133, 135, 145, 173–174, 198, 209, 218, 228, 299 (n4)
Law Society of England and Wales 113, 115
Law Society of Hong Kong 113

Lee Chak-fan (photo 29), 232, 244, 252
Lee King-chi, Joseph 133, 134
Lee Ngok (photos 16, 18 & 22), 137, 139–140, 144–145, 153–154, 155, 156–157, 162, 165, 172, 176, 179, 180, 182, 185, 202, 206, 208, 243, 244, 251, 252, 306 (n7), 307 (n42), 311 (n133), 315 (n57)
Lee, Peter C. Y. (photo 30), 222, 247–250, 297 (n79)
Lee, Richard Charles 82, 283 (n33)
Lee Shiu 221, 225
Leeds University 182
legal education 112–117
  See also law courses
Legislative Council 37, 42, 103, 114, 181, 289 (n61), 300 (n17)
Leicester University 266, 269
Leong, Prof W. S. 138
Leung, C. K. (photo 7), 232, 245, 290 (n76)
Leverhulme Conference (1964) (photo 6), 69–70
Leverhulme Trust 69, 85
Li Choh-ming 96
Li, Ellen 53
Li, Simon 132, 134
liberal education 86
liberal studies courses 39, 41, 43, 51, 72, 73, 241–242
librarianship courses 74, 104, 111, 123–125, 219
Library Association (HK) 76, 104, 123, 124–125, 305 (n111)
Library Association (UK) 124
lifelong learning 1, 5, 64, 110, 122, 127, 189–191, 197, 221, 242, 243
  definition 189–190, 191
  in Hong Kong 190, 197, 242
lifewide learning 191
Limerick Institute of Technology 152
Linton, M. D. 311 (n133)
Lions International (photo 9)
Liu, James J. Y. 71
Liu Ming 135
Liu, Y. W. 148
Liveright, A. A. 93–94
Liveright Report (1967) 94
Liverpool University 269
Llewellyn, Sir John 142
Llewellyn Report (1982) 138, 142–243
Logan, D. W. 45–46
London Institute 216
London School of Economics (photo 16), 119, 152, 230
London Society for the Extension of University Teaching 9
London University
  See University of London
Lugard, Sir Frederick (later Lord Lugard) 2, 7, 8–9, 10–11, 209
Lugard Hall 15
Luk, Michael 3, 187, 194, 208, 248, 249, 252
Lupton, Prof Tom 120

M

Macau Ferry pier 108
Macintosh, Duncan 128, 130, 164, 244, 251, 252, 309–10 (n93)
Mackenzie, Norman 23
Makerere University College 60, 62
Malaya 10, 35, 77
Malaya (Carr-Saunders) Commission 35–36
Malaya, University of 35, 37
Malaysia 69, 70
Malpas, Prof John G. 192
Malpas Report (2002) 192–194
management studies courses 99, 111, 117–123, 127, 135, 155–156, 208, 302–303 (n63)
Management Studies, Diploma in (photo 9), 117–123
Manchester Business School 120, 121
Manchester Metropolitan University 151, 266, 269
Manchester University 62
Mandarin language 77, 131
Mark, Priscilla
  See Tso Mark, Priscilla
marketing courses 120, 154, 219
Marshall, R. L. 47, 251
Martin, Michael R. 307 (n42)
mass education 53, 86
mass media 76, 94, 138, 141

Mass Transit Railway 108, 207, 225
mathematics courses 50, 72, 152
Mathews, Jeremy Fell 134
McGill University 270
McIntyre, Prof A. J. 118
McLellan, David 283 (n33)
McMaster University 270
media and cultural studies courses 230
medical profession in Hong Kong 18, 22
medicine courses (photo 21), 22, 72, 73, 97, 126, 145, 173
Melbourne University 115, 270
Mellor, Bernard 37, 40, 42–43, 44–45, 52, 59–60, 93, 283 (n33), 285 (n79)
Michigan University (Dearborn) 268
Microsoft 201
Middlesex University 230–231, 266, 269
migration from China 30
Mok Yiu-kwong 133, 135
Monash University 175, 176, 267
Montana State University 269
Moore, Prof F. C. T. (Tim) 307 (n42)
Moore, Gerald H. 3, 47–48, 54, 55, 56, 57–60, 62, 66, 67, 68, 71, 72–73, 75, 78, 82, 84, 86, 102, 135, 251, 286 (n85)
Morgan, Leonard Geoffrey 283 (n33)
Morrison Hall 12
Morton, Prof Brian S. 252, 306 (n6)
Murdoch University 270
music courses 41, 45, 50, 72

N
Nanyang Commercial Bank Building 107
Napier University 122, 266, 269
New England, University of 26, 142, 267, 268, 270
New Territories 64, 68–69, 75, 91, 235
New Zealand 69, 153
Newcastle University (UK) 267
Ng, Jennifer 152, 216
Ng, Prof K. W. 217
Ng Yip-lap, Frederick 125
North Point Learning Centre 205, 207, 262
North Point Teaching Centre 177–178, 262, 314 (n31)
Northcote, Sir Geoffry 21
Northcote Training College 31
Northumbria University 269
Nossiter, Prof Tom (photo 18), 152
Nottingham University 267, 269, 324 (n235)
nuclear physics courses 50
nursing courses 174

O
open education 5, 137, 139, 140, 141–143, 150, 155, 160
Open Learning Institute 97, 142–149, 159, 169, 308 (n65)
Open University (HK) 142
Open University (UK) 142, 148, 160, 167
Oracle 201
oriental languages courses 131, 304 (n110)
oriental studies courses 72, 78
Osaka University of Foreign Studies 268
Otago, University of 157, 268
Oxford Brookes University 269
Oxford University 9, 112

P
Pang, Laurence C. T. 290 (n76)
Pannam, Clifford 115, 300 (n21), 301 (n24)
PCCW 201
Perry, Rose 19
personnel management courses 118
Peterson, Carole 151
pharmacy courses 18, 157
Philippines 69, 70
philosophy courses 72, 152
phonetics courses 73, 221
planning courses 99, 118, 158–159
Po Leung Kuk 234–235, 264
Po Leung Kuk Community College 234–236, 330 (n125)
Pokfulam 200, 206, 234
police 73, 76, 90
politics courses 133
Polytechnic University of Hong Kong 103, 296 (n67)
polytechnical courses 45
polytechnical institutions 5, 40–41, 50, 97, 103

Portuguese language courses 41, 50
Prescott, John 99
Priestley, Prof Kenneth Ewart 47, 53, 283 (n33)
prisoners of war 23
professional and continuing education 1, 5, 21, 40, 86, 101–104, 111, 126, 135, 139, 140, 166, 180, 190, 243, 244
Professional Certificate in Law (PCLL) 116, 151
professional studies 3, 10, 101–104, 111, 218, 297 (n86)
Project Springboard 218
psychology courses 72, 127
public housing estates 132
Putonghua language 130, 197
Putonghu language courses (photo 14), 128, 130–131, 221

Q
quality assurance 4, 14
Quarry Bay Learning Centre 263
Queen Mary Hospital (photo 21)
Queen's College 10
Queensland, University of 26
Queensland University of Technology 270

R
radio 94, 138, 141
Radio Hong Kong 76, 131
Radio Television Hong Kong (RTHK) 305 (n111)
Rear, John 115
recurrent education 190
Redding, Prof S. Gordon 99, 119, 123, 138, 155, 157, 175–176, 245
Rediffusion 76
refresher courses 22, 34, 43, 73, 77, 78, 84, 105, 119, 126, 127, 129
refugees from China 38, 40, 126, 135
research 63, 159, 167, 244–245
Resettlement Department 133–134, 305 (n113 & 115)
resident tutors 63–64, 67
residential courses 76, 118
Ride, Sir Lindsay (photo 6), 28, 43, 44–45, 47, 52, 53, 54, 59, 65, 66, 69, 80, 82, 93
Rigby, Sir Ivo 115, 301 (n27)
Robertson, Prof J. M. 134
Robinson, Prof K. E. 95, 97, 101
Rochdale 'Economic Class' 9, 62
role education 127
Rotary Club (HK) (photo 9), 66
Rowell, T. R. 31
Royal Hong Kong Police Force 73, 76, 90, 305 (n111)
Rural Training College 31
Ruttonjee, Parrin 19

S
Saigon 32, 69, 77
St Andrews University 269
St John's Hall/College 12, 80, 206
Sales, Arnaldo 283 (n33)
sales, marketing and advertising courses 120, 219
Sanchez, Teresa 15
School of Professional and Continuing Education (HKU)
  Academic Advisory Committees 174
  Academic Committees 167, 174, 204
  academic development 198–201
  academic standards 174, 175, 179, 193, 198, 202–203, 212
  academic status of 167, 171, 175, 176, 184, 189, 193, 196, 202
  accommodation (photo 24), 205–207, 223–225, 261–264
  Accumulated Fund 183
  achievements 184, 193, 204, 212, 241–246
  administrative functions 174, 186
  administrative structure 167, 176, 186–187, 192, 277, 317 (n79)
  Advisory Board 122
  Alumni Association 6, (photo 30), 241, 245, 248
  autonomy within HKU 172, 181, 186–187, 193, 194
  awards and qualifications 194, 195, 325 (n13)

Bachelor of Arts in Media and Cultural Studies 230
Bachelor of Business (photo 19)
Bachelor of Pharmacy in Chinese Medicine 200
Bachelor of Science in Business 230
Bachelor of Science in Nursing Studies 174
Certificate in Traditional Chinese Medicine 198
Diploma in Traditional Chinese Medicine 199
Diploma in Tui-na 200
Executive Certificate in Anti-Corruption Studies 209
International Master of Business Administration 209–210
Master of Business in Accounting 175–176
Master of Housing Management (photo 20), 174, 175
Master of Traditional Chinese Medicine 200
Postgraduate Certificate in Laws 173–174
Postgraduate Diploma in Information Technology 201
Technical Certificate in Medical Laboratory Science 173
Board of Directors 216–217
Board of Studies 166–167, 173, 174, 182, 185, 202, 313 (n7)
'buffer system' of funding 177–178, 179, 314 (n25 & 29)
capital projects 177–178, 179, 205–207, 211, 223–225, 232, 323 (n206)
Centre for Executive Development 209
China activities 4, 171, 198, 208–211, 231–234, 241, 244, 248
Chinese medicine 198–200, 207, 208, 209, 320 (n163)
Chinese medicine clinics 200, 207
Chinese Medicine Division 200
Collaborations Approvals Panel 204
Committee on Quality Assurance (1996) 203
Community College 198, 212, 213–239, 245
See also HKU SPACE Community College
and community engagement 189, 194, 195
as company limited by guarantee 188
competition with HKU departments 175, 176, 192, 193
competition with other providers 243
Continuing Education Division (proposed) 167, 312 (n142)
and continuing and professional education 176, 185, 198
co-operation with HKU departments 171, 172, 173–174, 184–185, 187, 189, 191–192, 197, 245
courses and programmes 167, 171, 172, 219, 242, 279 (n3), 312 (n5)
accountancy (photo 23), 208, 209
art and design 207
business management 198
business studies 208, 209
fine arts 198
housing management 174, 198
information technology 207
languages 198
law 173–174, 198, 209
medical laboratory science (photo 21), 173
nursing 174
science 198
social studies 208
sports education 209
cross-subsidisation of courses 180
Cyberport Institute 197, 198, 200–201
as 'degree broker' 176
degree programmes 176, 184
deputy director 186, 187, 193, 248
director 167, 187, 182, 185–186, 195–196, 208, 217, 243, 244, 251
Distance Learning Unit 167
early years 172–176
enrolment statistics 172, 197, 200, 201, 211, 212, 238–239, 241, 254–256, 315 (n45), 324 (n249)

equality with HKU 167, 175
establishment 158, 168, 169, 172
exchange students 206
external advisors 182, 202, 203
External Studies Division (proposed) 162–163, 167, 312 (n142)
facilities 189
and faculties at HKU 193–194, 195, 196
fees 172, 192, 257–260
field trips (photo 20)
financial autonomy of 171, 172, 177–182, 187, 188
financial contributions to HKU 177, 178–179, 180–181, 183, 243, 259–260, 314 (n26 & 33)
financial management 173, 188
funding 171, 177–182, 183, 192, 257–260
golden jubilee celebrations 6, 241, 245, 248–249
governance structure 53, 166, 172, 173, 184, 192–193
and HKU faculties and departments 167
and Hong Kong community 176, 187, 188, 189, 194, 241, 244, 245, 248
identity of 171, 172, 185, 188–189, 194
incorporation 187–188, 193, 317 (n88)
integration with HKU 184, 192, 195, 244
Internal Validation Panels 204, 219–220
international collaboration 171, 172, 175–176, 184, 209, 241, 244
internship and placement 201
joint consultative committees 195, 196–197
joint programmes 174, 197, 209, 210
leadership role in Hong Kong 212, 244
learning centres 171, 205–207
Admiralty Learning Centre (photo 25), 200, 207, 223, 262–263
Austin Tower 200
Island East Campus 207, 224, 264
Kowloon East Campus (photo 28), 207, 223, 264
North Point Learning Centre 177–178, 205–206, 262
Shanghai Learning Centre 210, 211
Town Centre 177, 205, 206, 207, 261
United Centre 231
Wanchai Learning Centre 221
liberal courses 241–242
and lifelong learning 1, 189–191, 193, 195, 197, 211–212, 242–243, 318 (n99)
as a limited company 167, 171, 187
logo 172, 194
Management Board 166–167, 173, 177, 179, 185, 186, 187, 188, 191
market orientation of 172, 173, 208, 243
mission 5–6, 172, 184, 190–191, 192, 208, 212, 214, 244, 271–272
naming of 164, 165–166, 188, 194, 311 (n139), 313 (n1), 317 (n88)
perceived inferiority of 175, 185, 193, 198
planning 158–168, 172, 184, 186–187, 189, 194–195
postgraduate programmes 173–174, 198, 200, 201, 209
professional training 200
profit generation 177–178, 180–181, 192, 243
quality assurance 4, 14, 187, 189, 192, 197, 198, 202–205, 212, 219–220, 322 (n195)
Quality Assurance Committee (1999) 189, 203–204, 205, 219
Quality Assurance Manual 203–204, 322 (n195)
recognition 204, 242
registration of programmes 181
research 167, 175, 187, 201, 244–245, 313 (n18)
reviews 182–186, 188, 192–194, 202
School Advisory Board 189
school secretary 181, 186
self-funding policy 177, 178, 180, 181, 187, 192, 242, 243
service to the community 6, 176, 195
SPACE Fund 177–180, 183
SPACE Online Universal Learning System (SOUL) 216

staff 167, 172, 173, 175, 180, 182, 185, 187, 200, 212, 241, 317 (n82)
status within HKU 171, 175, 176, 242
strategic planning 158–168, 172, 184, 186–187, 189, 194–195
students 5, 180, 205, 206, 212, 324 (n250)
and sub-degrees 214
subventions from HKU eliminated 177–182
success of 184, 193, 204, 211–212, 241–246
Suzhou Global College (photo 27), 211, 217, 232–233, 265, 329 (n101 & 102)
T. T. Tsui Building (photo 24), 195, 206
teaching facilities 179, 201, 205–207, 210, 212
Teaching and Research Unit (proposed) 167
Ten Year Strategy (1993) 198, 202, 318 (n99)
Town Centre 177, 205, 206, 207, 261
Traditional Chinese Medicine, Centre for 199
Undergraduate programmes 174, 176, 199–201, 209
University (HKU) attitude to 171–172, 174–175, 176, 180, 182, 184, 189–190, 192, 195, 196, 242, 244, 325 (n13)
and vocational training 242
See also Extra-Mural Studies, Department of
science courses 14, 15, 17, 72, 126, 198, 218
Scott, Dorothea 53
Second World War 16, 20, 22–24, 36
secretarial practice courses 43–44, 46, 50, 71
Shakespeare courses 71
Shamshuipo Prisoner of War Camp 23
Shanghai 40, 210, 211, 231, 265
Shanghai University of Traditional Chinese Medicine 199, 208
Sheffield Hallam University 266
Shek Kip Mei Regional Centre 205, 262
Shen, S. M. 187, 203, 252
Shenzen 210, 233
Shenzen Research and Development Centre 210
Shepherd, Vincent 115
Sherlock, Philip 67
Sherrin, Prof Chris 151, 152
Shortridge, Prof Ken 138
Shun Tak Centre (photo 15), 108–109, 112, 137, 153, 205, 207, 261, 314 (n25)
Simon Fraser University 270
Simpson, Prof R. K. M. 18
Singapore (photo 20), 35, 37, 69, 70, 77, 283 (n31)
Sino-British talks (1984) 144
Siu, Perry (photos 6 & 7), 67, 290 (n75), 295 (n32)
Sloss, Duncan J. 21, 23, 28
Smith, James Middleton 15, 19
social sciences courses 14, 145, 148
social services courses 133
social studies courses 208
social work courses 25, 94, 104, 111, 126–128, 133
sociology courses 72, 127, 152
South China Morning Post 67
Southampton University 269
Southeast Asia 69, 70
Southern Queensland University 182, 270
SPACE
See School of Professional and Continuing Education
SPACE Community College
See HKU SPACE Community College
Spanish language courses 43
sports education courses 209
staff tutors 63–64, 67, 88, 90, 99, 100, 101, 104, 109, 114, 121, 123, 128, 138, 147, 148, 150, 289 (n71)
Standing Committee on Youth Organizations (HK) 76
Stanley Civilian Internment Camp 22–24, 25, 28
State University of New York at Buffalo 269
statistics courses 119, 152
Straits Settlements 10
Strathclyde University 266, 269

Styler, W. E. (photo 6), 68–69, 70, 71, 88, 91, 290 (n84)
Styler Report (1962) 68–69, 71, 76, 77, 81, 84, 91–92
sub-degree programmes 213, 226, 231
summer schools 34, 37, 50, 51, 90, 294 (n21)
Sun Yat-sen University (Guangzhou) 265
Sunderland University 267, 269
Supreme Court Library 114
Surrey University 267, 269
Sutherland Report (2002) 195
Sutherland, Prof S. (photo 18)
Suzhou 211, 217, 232, 241, 265
Suzhou Global College (photo 27), 211, 217, 232–233, 265, 329 (n101 & 102)
Suzhou Industrial Park 232–233
Suzhou University of Science and Technology 232
Swatow 32
Sydney 67, 70
Sydney University 268
Szczepanik, E. F. 56

T

T. T. Tsui Building (photo 24), 195, 206
Tang Chi-ngong School of Chinese 32
Tang Ping-yuan 103
Tawney, R. H. 9, 62
Taylor, Prof Richard 182–183, 202, 316 (n61)
teacher training courses 14, 27, 73, 92
teachers 73
Teaching and Learning Quality Process Review (TLQPR) 204, 220, 227, 321 (n184)
Technical College (HK) 31, 41, 49, 57, 117, 118, 282 (n9)
technical education 5, 10, 40, 66, 103
Technical Institute (HK) 10
technical training 4, 10
technology and education 141–142, 146, 147, 160, 200
Telegraph Bay 200
television 94, 141
Ten Year Building Scheme 135
Thailand 69, 70, 77
'Third Generation' education 248
Thomas, William 112
Thomson, W. K. 113
Ting, Robert 75
Topley Committee and Report (1981) 138
Toronto University 270
town centres (for teaching) 81–82, 94, 104–110
trade unionism courses 43
translation courses 145, 221
Trench, Sir David 70
Tricker, Prof R. I. 156–157, 184, 202, 311 (n133), 316 (n61)
Tricker Review and Report (1995) 184–186, 193, 194, 202–203
Tsang, Currie 216, 217
Tsang, Mrs Selina (photo 30)
Tsao, Nana (photo 7)
Tsim Sha Tsui 109, 200, 207
Tsim Sha Tsui Learning Centre 200, 263, 264
Tsinghua University 209, 210, 265, 268
Tso Mark, Priscilla (photos 4 & 7), 64, 67, 77, 151, 251, 289 (n53), 290 (n72), 294 (n20)
Tsuen Wan 75
Tsui Lap-chee 252
Tung Chee-hwa 190, 201, 215
tutorial classes 5, 9–10, 50, 62, 73, 75, 79
tutors 63–64, 67, 68
Tyler, Prof E. L. G. 311 (n133)

U

UCLA 269
UGC (HK) 3, 87, 88–89, 91–101, 103, 106, 142, 143–144, 180, 182, 184, 204, 227, 228, 243, 245, 296 (n67)
Ulster University 266, 269
undergraduate education 4
social divisiveness of 34–35
UNESCO 69, 70
United Centre (Admiralty) 223, 231, 262, 263
United Christian Hospital 305 (n111)
United College (CUHK) 91
United Dockyards 305 (n111)
United Kingdom 69, 241

adult education 2, 9–10, 11, 26, 28, 29, 54, 61, 62–64, 102
Adult Education Committee 189
Board of Education 28
colonial education policy 33–36, 38, 41, 54, 62, 73
Colonial Office 24, 33–34, 36, 115
colonial universities 33–36
Commission on Higher Education in the Colonies 25, 33–35
correspondence courses 33
Education Act (1870) 10
Education Ministry 51
education policy 54, 61, 62–64, 83, 86, 102
Education and Science, Department of 118
extra-mural studies 26, 51, 54, 58, 59, 60, 62–64, 72, 81, 83, 84, 86, 99, 101, 241
funding of adult education 28, 51, 61, 62, 83, 84
higher education policy 54, 59, 61, 102
imperial obligations 25, 29, 33–34, 38
Inter-University Council for Higher Education in the Colonies 36, 44–45
Reconstruction, Ministry of 189
self-government of former colonies 25
United States of America 69, 101, 214, 241, 297 (n86)
United States Information Service 106
Universal House 105, 107, 112, 261
Universities' Joint Board of Extra-Mural Studies (HK) 92–93
University (1937) Report 8, 18, 20–21, 22
University of Adelaide 270
University of Bath 265
University of Birmingham 26, 222, 238, 269
University of Bristol 26, 186
University of California 268
University of Cambridge 9
University College Ibadan (British West Africa) 47
University College London 114
University College of Wales 62, 89
University College of the West Indies 67
University of Chicago 214, 325 (n5)
University Development Committee (1939) 18, 20, 21–22
University of Essex 269
University of Glasgow 89–90, 294 (n13)
University Grants Committee (HK) 3, 87, 88–89, 91–101, 103, 106, 142, 143–144, 180, 182, 184, 204, 227, 228, 243, 245, 296 (n67)
University of Greenwich 203, 266
University of Hawaii 125, 269
University of Hong Kong
1937 Report 8, 18, 20–21, 22
and 3+3+4 reform 197, 228, 238
Academic Development Committee 164, 168, 194, 195
administrative obstinacy of 59
academic staff 99
academic standards of 37
Administration and Management, Centre for Studies in 120
and adult education 20, 22, 28, 83, 241
adult education, early neglect of 22, 28, 39, 42, 44
Architecture, Department of 134
Architecture, Faculty of 273
Arts, Faculty of 8, 11, 12, 13–15, 16–19, 26, 27, 30, 43, 44, 48, 126, 139, 144, 158, 167, 229, 232
Business and Economics, Faculty of 273
Business School 175–176, 184, 210
Calendar 11, 15, 16, 19
Capital Building Programme 106
Centre for Media Resources 146, 148
and China 8, 21, 22, 244
China Affairs Office 234
Chinese, Department of 71
Chinese Studies, School of 20, 32
Commerce, Department of 18
community service 38, 39
company secretarial practice courses 43–44
competition with CUHK 143
Continuing Education Department (proposed) 158–160

Continuing Education Division (proposed) 162–163, 167, 318 (n99)
continuing and professional education 20, 141, 145, 176, 195, 241, 244
  funding 177–182, 315 (n53)
  policies 173, 182, 188, 193, 195
  support for 171–172, 177, 188
Continuing and Professional Education and Lifelong Learning, Board for 188–189, 193, 194, 203, 216, 219–220, 236, 275–276
Convocation 106–107, 143, 307 (n31)
Convocation Room (photo 18)
Council 45, 46, 47, 52, 56, 58, 64, 69, 108–109, 114, 115, 119, 144, 149, 159, 164, 167, 168, 173, 177, 178, 179, 180, 181, 184, 187–188, 194, 195–106
courses and programmes
  accountancy 43–44, 50
  Bachelor of Arts 14
  business management studies 119
  Chinese language 50
  Chinese Studies 15–16, 38
  commerce 14, 15, 17–18
  Commercial Certificate 14
  education 50
  Education, Diploma in 32
  engineering 16, 73, 120
  English language 17
  Experimental Science 14, 15, 17
  industrial management studies 119, 120
  languages 27, 50
  law 112, 113, 115
  Letters and Philosophy 14, 15, 17
  management studies 119, 120, 155–156
  MBA 157
  medical refresher courses 22
  medicine 73
  pharmacy 18
  social sciences 14
  social work 25
  teacher training 14, 27, 73, 92
Court 47, 52, 53, 119, 168
CUPEM 174, 305 (n126)
Davies Working Party and Report (1991) 158, 164–168, 169
Development and General Purposes Committee 60, 89, 138, 164
and distance learning 144, 145, 148–149, 160–162
Economics, Department of 43, 148
Economics and Political Science, Department of 50, 71
and Education Commission 143–144
Education, Faculty of 146, 273
Eliot Hall 48, 54, 80
elitism of 9, 20, 27, 30–31, 37, 38, 61
Endowment Fund 108, 206
Engineering Alumni Association 305 (n111)
Engineering, Faculty of 8, 12, 15, 16, 18, 20, 21, 26, 30, 173, 273
English, Department of 15, 48, 222
evening classes, lack of 25
evening courses 43, 44, 50
Extension Studies, Committee on (proposed) 160
Extension Studies, School of (proposed) 158–160, 162–163
extension work 22, 23–24, 186, 190
external degrees 143–144, 158, 167, 307 (n31)
external students
  academic status of 2, 3, 7, 8, 12, 13, 14, 20, 26, 27, 54, 242
  careers of 19
  demographic details of 15, 16–17
  fees 20, 24, 27
  high attrition of 12, 15, 16, 26
  language concerns about 27
  legacy of 54, 86
  marginalisation of 3, 12, 13, 14, 20, 26, 27, 28, 242
  number of 11–12, 15, 16–17, 24, 26, 27
  perceived inferiority of 2, 7, 8, 54, 61, 242
  progression to undergraduate studies 13, 14, 16

quality concerns 13, 14, 16, 27
regulation of 15, 20, 27
used as cash cow 13, 21, 24, 28
external studies 2, 4, 7–28, 54, 140, 143–144, 145–149, 157, 167
External Studies Committee 168
External Studies Department (proposed) 158–160
External Studies Division (proposed) 162–163, 167
Extra-Mural Law Centre 105
extra-mural studies (pre-1957) 2, 3, 19, 21, 25
Committee on (1954–55) 47, 48, 50
governance of 53, 58
number of students 44
policy on 36, 37, 29, 42, 45–46, 48–52, 54
poorly funded at HKU 52
as a profit-generating activity 52, 83
and public relations 53
resistance to 42, 46, 55
Working Party (1954) 46–47
extra-mural studies (post-1957) 55–86
conferences 69, 244
educational policy gives way to financial imperatives 85, 98
inferior status of 58–61, 99–101
lack of commitment to 61, 82–83, 88–89, 98
policy on 57–61, 62–64, 69, 83–85, 91, 100, 137, 155–157, 160–162, 164–165
subventions for 83, 88–89, 177–182, 257–260
support for 80, 83, 87, 101, 137, 177
See also Extra-Mural Studies, Department of
Extra-Mural Studies, Board of (1957–67) 49, 52, 53, 58–59, 60–61, 74, 82, 86, 100
development plans 82
and extra-mural policy 56, 60–61, 64, 74
functions and powers 52, 60–61, 86
meetings 56, 74
membership 53, 59, 61, 251
supervision of courses 71
terms of reference 61
See also Extra-Mural Studies, Committee on (1967–91)
Extra-Mural Studies, Committee on (1954–55) 47, 48, 50
Extra-Mural Studies, Committee on (1967–91) 100, 107, 108, 118, 138, 144, 146, 155–156, 154–165
abolition of 166
and course approval 118, 121, 155
and development policy 107, 144, 158, 159–160, 164
meetings 146, 155
membership 100, 138, 251, 297 (n79)
powers and duties 100, 145, 162, 166
and quality assurance 202
reform of 140, 160, 166
terms of reference 100
and the University subvention 100
Extra-Mural Studies, Department of
See main entry for Extra-Mural Studies, Department of
Extra-Mural Studies Fund 83, 89, 97, 140, 257–260, 298 (n106), 314 (n25)
See also SPACE Fund
fee income 3, 11, 13, 20, 24, 28
Finance Committee 108–109, 167, 179, 180, 181, 314 (n25)
Finance, Director of 178–179
Finance Office 178–179
financial problems 19–20, 21, 30, 36, 45–46
Fit For Purpose review (2002) 195–196
four-year undergraduate curriculum 197, 228, 238
General Purposes Committee 164–165, 168, 194, 311 (n129)
Geography, Department of 158
halls of residence 12
History, Department of 139, 158, 187, 249

and Hong Kong community 1–2, 6, 22–23, 28, 38, 48, 53, 54, 76, 80, 86, 107, 178, 241
Hong Kong University Press 146, 249
Interim Committee (1945–48) 24–25
Joint Establishments Committee 47
Joint Working Party (1989–90) 158, 162–165
Jubilee celebrations (1961–62) 80
Jubilee Radio Committee 76
and the Keswick Report (1952) 42–46
Knowles Building 206
language policy 31
language problems of students 77–78
Language School 27, 125
Law, Department of 106, 115, 116
Law, Faculty of 113–114, 115, 174, 273
Library 11, 45, 61, 81, 92, 125, 175, 224, 314 (n33)
Library Fund 61, 83
and lifelong learning 1, 189–191, 193, 195, 197, 242, 244, 318 (n110)
Loke Yew Hall (photos 1 & 2), 80, 216, 248
Lugard Hall 15
Main Building (photo 10), 36, 48, 81, 104
Malpas Report (2002) 192–194
Management Studies, Department of 119, 120, 121, 123, 147, 155–157, 175–176
matriculated students 8, 12, 15, 20, 26, 27, 54, 58, 60, 215, 242
matriculation 2, 4, 7, 10, 11, 13, 57, 60, 215, 220, 242
matriculation classes 13
Matriculation Examination 11, 13, 16, 23
Medical Research Building 48
Medicine, Faculty of 8, 12, 16, 18, 26, 30, 113, 173, 174, 198–199, 273–274
mission of 1, 5, 8, 21, 27, 28, 86, 99, 136, 184, 191, 209, 244
Modern Languages, Department of 47
number of students 71
'one-line budget' 180, 181
and open education 141–142, 145, 160
Open Education, Committee on 145, 146–147, 148, 159–160, 165, 166
and Open Learning Institute 142–149
outside practice 149
part-time students 27, 31, 143
pedestrian soullessness of 22
penny-pinching policies of 178
Philosophy, Department of 152
Physics, Department of 186
Political Sciences, Department of 148
Poon Kam Kai Institute of Management 135
Postgraduate Certificate in Laws 173–174
postgraduate programmes 143, 173–174, 245
post-War development problems 44–45
post-War reconstruction 24–25, 29–30, 36
professional studies 3, 31, 49, 73, 166
professorial status 58, 64
Provisional Powers Committee (1946–48) 25
Psychology, Department of 147
quadrennial plan (1970–74) 89, 97, 102
quality assurance 204, 219
re-establishment in 1948 36
refresher courses 22
Registrar 13, 14, 52, 93
as a research-led institution 172, 175, 244
residential basis of undergraduate education 8–9, 11, 12, 38
St John's Hall/College 80
School of Traditional Chinese Medicine 199
Science, Faculty of 17, 22, 26, 30, 144, 146–147, 186, 216
Senate 16, 20, 23, 24, 27, 43, 45, 47, 48, 49, 52–53, 56, 58, 59–61, 64, 68–69, 71, 73, 85, 89, 99, 100, 106, 113, 119, 121, 137–138, 144, 145, 148, 155–156, 157, 159, 162, 164–165, 168, 173, 176, 180, 181, 184, 185, 191, 193, 194, 195, 202, 219

Senior Management Team 195, 196, 319 (n136)
Seven Year Plan (1959–66) 64, 65
Social Medicine, Department of 48
Social Sciences, Faculty of 119, 120, 144, 147, 174, 175, 187, 274
Social Work, Department of 128, 134
Sociology, Department of 148
SPACE Fund 177–180, 257–260
space problems 45
sports fields 80
staff teaching at SPACE 173
staffing 47
Statutes 58, 101, 139, 194, 195, 242
strategic development 194–195
students 8, 12, 25, 36, 54, 71, 79, 180, 299 (n130)
Students Union 80
summer courses 22, 25, 50
suspicions regarding SPACE 175
Tang Chi-ngong School of Chinese 32
'Teacher' status 58–60, 85, 99, 101, 139, 140, 242
'Teaching Department' status 58–60, 86, 91, 99, 242
teaching/research policy 21, 28, 175, 245
Tricker Review (1995) 184–186
triennial plan (1967–70) 89, 97
triennial plan (1978–81) 98
triennial plan (1991–94) 159
and UGC 91–101, 103
undergraduate education 8–9, 20, 28, 30, 79, 110, 126, 197, 245
University (1937) Report 18, 20–21, 22
University Development Committee (1939) 18, 20, 21–22
University Development Report (1939) 20, 22
University Gazette 62
University Ordinance (1958) 58, 60
University Reopening Committee 24–25
Urban Planning and Environmental Management, Centre of 174, 305 (n126)
Vice-Chancellor 82, 100, 119, 182, 187, 188, 195, 199, 216
See also Cheng, Patrick Y. C.
Hornell, Sir William
Ride, Sir Lindsay
Robinson, K. E.
Sloss, Duncan J.
Tsui Lap-chee
Wang Gungwu
Vice-Chancellor's Advisory Group 195–196, 319 (n136)
visiting students 4
vocational programmes 13–14, 21, 73–74, 242
University of Huddersfield 269
University of Hull 68, 267
University of Illinois at Chicago 269
University of Kansas 269
University of Leeds 182
University of Leicester 265, 269
University of Liverpool 269
University of London 25, 26, 43, 47, 82, 89, 112, 114, 115, 116, 152, 230, 266, 269
external degrees 9, 112, 116, 151–153, 230
External Division 152
external law degree 82, 85, 105, 111, 112–117, 150, 151, 266, 292 (n106), 301 (n27), 301–302 (n35 & 39)
graduates (photo 18), 112, 139
open days 152
University of Malaya 35
University of Manchester 62
University of Melbourne 115, 270
University of Michigan 268, 269
University of New England (Australia) 26, 142, 267, 268, 270
University of New South Wales 267
University of Newcastle upon Tyne 267
University of Nottingham 267, 269, 324 (n235)
University of Otago 157, 268
University and Polytechnic Grants Committee
See University Grants Committee
University of Queensland 26
University of St Andrews 269
University of South Australia 270

University of Southampton 269
University of Southern Queensland 182, 270
University of Strathclyde 266, 269
University of Sunderland 267, 269
University of Surrey 267, 269
University of Sydney 268
University of Technology Sydney 270
University of Toronto 270
University of Ulster 266, 269
University of Victoria (Canada) 270
University of Wales 267
University of Western Australia 148, 70
University of Western Ontario 118
University of Wollongong 268, 270
University of York (UK) 269
Urban Council 124, 247
Urban Renewal Authority 134
Urban Services Department 132, 133, 134, 305 (n113)
URBTIX 122

V
Vernacular Middle School 15–16
Victoria University (Canada) 270
Victoria University of Technology 267
Vietnam 69, 70
Vine, Peter A. L. 113
vocational courses 72–74, 75, 78, 84, 101–104, 128, 131, 242
vocational training 4, 10, 31, 38, 49, 66, 72–74, 86, 101–104, 111, 123, 126, 135, 143, 218, 219, 242, 297 (n86)

W
Wanchai 107, 221, 224
Wanchai Learning Centre 221, 224, 264
Wang Gungwu (photo 18), 165, 184, 206, 307 (n42)
Weatherhead, Prof Brian 252, 307 (n42), 311 (n133)
West Indies 35
West Indies, University College of 67
Western Australia, University of 148
Western Ontario, University of 118
Williams, Roger A. (photo 9), 87, 89–90, 93, 95–96, 100–101, 102, 105, 106, 109, 110, 119, 137, 138, 139, 182, 208, 251, 294 (n13 & 20), 306 (n7)
Wing On Centre (town centre) (photos 11, 12, 13 & 14), 107, 108, 109, 112, 261
Wise, Prof M. J. 89
Wollongong University 268, 270
women 8, 15, 16–17, 39
 distracting influence on male students 8
 and gender balance in student body 16–17
Wong, Florence 19
Wong Lung-tak, Patrick 117, 302 (n400)
Wong, Nana 67
Wong, Prof S. L. 186, 252, 253, 316 (n74)
Wong, Prof Y. C. 297 (n79)
worker education 9, 53, 73, 84, 190
Workers' Educational Association 9, 28
working class 9, 53, 73, 84, 190
World Trade Organization 232
World War I 14
World War II 16, 20, 22–24, 36

X
Xinhua News Agency 208

Y
Yang Fujia 210, 324 (n235)
Yim Chi-keung, Kenneth 130
York University (UK) 269
Young, Prof Enoch C. M. (photos 27 & 30), 186–188, 189, 190–191, 195–196, 203, 208, 243, 248, 249, 252
Young, Prof Rosie T. T. (photo 16), 145, 252, 311 (n133)
Yu Shuk-siu, Patrick 112

Z
Zhang, W. Y. 245
Zhejiang University 265
Zhuhai 210, 231–232, 265